Map of Manhattan, 1865.

I never look at an old building or an ancient room or gaze at an old looking glass, but I think of their former owners and the faces that have gazed in it.

James Edward Kelly

Abraham Lincoln's suit and hat.

# Tell Me of Lincoln

## Memories of
## Abraham Lincoln,
## The Civil War
## &
## Life in Old New York

By
James Edward Kelly (1855-1933)
Edited by William B. Styple

Belle Grove Publishing Company
2009

© 2009 by Belle Grove Publishing Co.

**Library of Congress Cataloging-in-Publication Data**

Kelly, James Edward, 1855-1933.
  Tell me of Lincoln : memories of Abraham Lincoln, the Civil War, and life in
old New York / by James Edward Kelly ; edited by William B. Styple. -- 1st ed.
     p. cm.
  Includes index.
  ISBN 978-1-883926-23-6 (alk. paper)
  1. Lincoln, Abraham, 1809-1865--Anecdotes. 2.  Lincoln, Abraham,
1809-1865--Friends and associates--Anecdotes. 3.  Presidents--United
States--Biography--Anecdotes. 4.  New York (N.Y.)--History--Civil War,
1861-1865--Sources. 5.  United States--History--Civil War, 1861-1865--Sources.
6.  Kelly, James Edward, 1855-1933. 7.  Sculptors--United States--Biography. 8.
Artists--United States--Biography.  I. Styple, William B. II. Title.
  E457.15.K43 2009
  973.7092--dc22

                                                           2009017771


Belle Grove Publishing Co.
P. O. Box 483
Kearny, N. J. 07032
Website: bellegrovepublishing.com

Printed in the United States of America

ISBN: 978-1-883926-23-6

First Edition

# Table of Contents

## Public Sculpture by James Edward Kelly

Monmouth Battle Monument, Freehold, N. J.

The Call to Arms Monument, Troy, N. Y.

Saratoga Monument Panels, Schuylerville, N. Y.

Sixth New York Cavalry Monument, Gettysburg, PA.

Clarence Wheeler Memorial, Woodlawn Cemetery, the Bronx, N. Y.

Gen. John Buford Memorial, Gettysburg, PA.

Battle of Harlem Heights, Columbia University, New York City.

Father George Deshon Relief; Father Augustine Hewitt Bust,
St. Paul the Apostle Church, N. Y. C.

Gen. Horatio Wright Memorial, Arlington National Cemetery

Gen. David S. Stanley Panel, Cullum Hall, West Point, N. Y.

Gen. William F. Smith Panel, Cullum Hall, West Point, N. Y.

Gen. William F. Smith Panel, State House Montpelier, VT.

Gen. Ely Parker Bust, Rochester Museum, Rochester, N. Y.

Gen. James R. O'Beirne Panel, Fordham University, N. Y.

Gen. Fitz John Porter Statue, Portsmouth, N. H.

Washington at Prayer, Federal Hall, New York City

Gen. James H. Wilson Bust, West Point, N. Y.

Gen. Thomas Sweeny Bust, Green-Wood Cemetery, Brooklyn, N. Y.

Gen. John M. Schofield Panel, Schofield Barracks, Hawaii.

Gen. O. O. Howard Bust, Howard University, Washington, D. C.

The Defenders Monument, New Haven, CT.

Barbara Fritchie Memorial, Mt. Olivet Cemetery, Frederick, MD.

Rochambeau Monument, Southington, CT.

World War Memorial, Kingston, N. Y.

McKinley Memorial, Wilmington, DE.

Caesar Rodney Monument, Wilmington, DE.

# JAMES EDWARD KELLY
## 1855 – 1933
## A SCULPTOR OF AMERICAN HISTORY

### By WILLIAM B. STYPLE

The old sculptor whose heroic bronze statues memorialized the gallant figures of American History had quietly passed away. His body was lowered into the grave. Prayers were spoken, dirt was thrown and the few mourners and diggers went away. No one bothered to mark the spot, and in a short time grass grew and the artist was forgotten, and soon those who knew him were gone and forgotten too. Nearly three quarters of a century passed until I stood on that empty spot and made a promise to this sculptor of American heroes. I felt that I had to do something for the memory of James Edward Kelly.

Throughout his life, James Kelly had three passions: Art, American History and New York City. He was born on July 30, 1855, in what he called, "the old Manhattan of blooming gardens, fragrant orchards and well-cultivated fields; a city surrounded by gleaming waterways and sunlit woodlands that soon deepened into almost primitive forests." Over time, he saw those farms and rural villages of the island disappear, cut up into city blocks and filled in with shops, brownstones and more elegant homes, only to be torn down and replaced with bigger stores, tenements and gaudy mansions, which were also torn down and rebuilt higher until they scraped the sky.

He grew up during the violent tumult of the Civil War—in a city as divided as the nation itself—and from his bedroom window the boy watched as blue-clad patriots marched off to answer President Lincoln's call to preserve the Union, while the Copperheads at home rioted in the streets and swore death to the President; each side claimed to be fighting the second American Revolution in order to be free from bondage, whether it be held by master or government.

His immigrant father, Patrick Paul Kelly, was born in Glasgow and came to America in 1851, settling in New York City with his bride Julia Finley—both fleeing British oppression for new-found freedom in America. The young couple became fervent American patriots, filled with hopes and new promise in their adopted land. During the Civil War, the Kelly family were staunch supporters of Abraham Lincoln and the Union—an unpopular position, as most of their neighbors were Irish immigrants with Democratic sympathies. Years later James Kelly wrote, "My father was continually having rows and cutting the acquaintance of old friends. All praise Lincoln now, but it took nerve to stand up for him in certain sections at that time."

Each morning at the Kelly breakfast table, father and mother read aloud the newspaper dispatches from the battlefield and their son listened intently and gazed at the fanciful woodcut illustrations of the commanding generals on horseback. These stories with pictures fired the youth's imagination, but also distracted him from his schoolwork; he later admitted that his days at school were more spent drawing Lincoln and his generals on his slate than numbers. This worship of military heroes filled young Kelly's thoughts and daydreams, and the boy announced to his mother that one day Grant, Sherman, and Sheridan would come and visit him, and he would draw their pictures—a childhood prophesy that came true decades later.

On a typical Sunday afternoon, the elder Kelly took his son on a street-by-street tour of old New York, visiting historic buildings, witnessing military processions, identifying eminent soldiers and sailors, watching the newly innovated ironclads from the old Battery, and traipsing the battlegrounds of Revolutionary New York. These father and son walks formulated a life-long interest in history for James Kelly, both of the United States and New York City.

At the same time, Mrs. Kelly seemed to have a keen, spontaneous insight into her son's artistic capabilities. She encouraged his drawing, especially with American history themes, and enrolled him in painting classes in the Academy of Design. She also tried her best to discourage her son's rough and tumble boyhood adventures such as rafting on the Hudson and brawling with the neighborhood youths, but to no avail—for boys growing up in New York City (then and now), arguments are usually settled with violence.

After four bloody years, the Civil War finally came to a close in Virginia with the surrender of the Confederate Army under Gen. Robert E. Lee on Palm Sunday, April 9, 1865. The nation and the Kelly family celebrated the triumph for nearly a week when at dawn on Saturday, April 15th, the elder Kelly came home clutching the morning newspaper. Nine-year-old James Kelly never forgot the sight of his father: "His face was colorless, his eyes were full of tears and in a dazed manner he said, 'President Lincoln has been shot.'"

The Kelly family sat overcome with sorrow, and after the death of the President was announced, mother took crepe and hung it from the front window. Young Kelly stepped outside and looking down Eighth Avenue saw that his family's black streamer was the only evidence of mourning in sight. "How long after, I do not recall," Kelly wrote, "but long enough to impress me with the delay and make my mother's very conspicuous, and later some of our neighbors began to drape their windows."

President Lincoln's body was brought to New York City and lay in state in the City Hall on April 25th, where an estimated half a million citizens passed solemnly beside the open coffin. Patrick Kelly went to view Lincoln's remains, but his son did not. Why he was not taken to view Lincoln was never clear in James Kelly's mind, but this lost opportunity had a beneficial effect: Kelly became increasingly desirous to seek out and question those who had witnessed other important events in American History, such as the firing on Fort Sumter, the speech at Gettysburg, the tragedy at Wounded Knee, the charge at San Juan Hill, and above all, the assassination of Abraham Lincoln.

By the time Kelly reached age eighteen, his artistic skills qualified him to be apprenticed with Harper's Publications—whose *Harper's Illustrated Weekly* was considered the most powerful political newspaper in the country. During his apprenticeship, Kelly made the acquaintance of several eminent "Special Artists," such as Alfred R. Waud, Theodore R. Davis, Thomas Nast and most notably Winslow Homer, who took an interest in the young artist and gave him both encouragement and artistic advice. As an artist for Harper's, Kelly was trained to approach a subject with a focused eye and a fine memory for details—nothing was to be left to the imagination—every detail was to be carefully depicted. This unwavering attention to accuracy, especially in his historical pictures, became the prominent feature in James Edward Kelly's art.

On assignment from his publishers, Kelly had the opportunity to meet and sketch many of the commanding generals of the Civil War, including his boyhood heroes—Generals Grant, Sherman, and Sheridan. Along with sketching their portraits, Kelly interviewed his subjects about their wartime experiences and carefully preserved those interviews in notebooks. He had always felt a great lack in history of personal details, and wanted to ask from those officers every question that he would have asked Washington and his generals had they posed for him. These Union commanders freely discussed their wartime experiences with Kelly, often telling him the stories they left out of their memoirs—including their private thoughts of rival generals or of President Lincoln. Fortunately for historians today, Kelly spent more time interviewing than sketching.

In the fall of 1876, the twenty-one-year-old artist started a series of illustrations for *Scribner's Monthly*, which, when published, caused a sensation. Kelly's "open air" drawings were internationally recognized for their originality, vigorous action, strong accents, and powerful contrasts—artwork that defied the conventions of the time and sparked an illustrative revolution. One critic observed that Kelly's pictures were: "so characteristic that an interested reader would know them by the style without looking for a signature, which was sometimes frequently omitted."

Kelly was credited as founder of a new and daring style of illustrating dubbed "The New School of Wood-engraving." On January 6, 1881, the eminent art critic Richard Watson Gilder took special notice of this craze and in his article, "Art in its Present Development," wrote at length of the sudden departure from the centuries-old method of wood-engraving. He called Kelly an "impressionist," an artistic term not commonly used at that time in the United States.

Gilder wrote:

> Those who watched the progress made in illustrative art in our day, as seen in the pages of Harper's and Scribner's magazines, must have been struck with the great advance made in wood engraving.
>
> J. E. Kelly, a mere boy in years, was one of the earliest workers in the new departure. He was directed by Mr. Alexander Drake, Art Superintendent of Scribner's, to make sketches of the "Horse-Hotel," that is the stables of the Third Avenue Railroad ... to draw as the subject "impressed" him. The drawings were fine and free and dashy, and the young artist submitted them to Mr. Drake, who appreciated their spirit...

Gilder continued with his lengthy review by mentioning several other contemporary artists, and in summarizing, returned to Kelly:

> But Kelly, one of the early "impressionists," fell back a bit in the race. Whether he was elated at his success, or, perhaps, which was more likely, he did not think it necessary to study up, certain it is that some of the later youngsters seem, perhaps but for the moment, to have outstripped him.

What Gilder didn't know at the time was that the artist had switched mediums; Kelly had given up illustrating magazines and began sculpting monuments. He ambitiously designed five bronze bas relief panels—thirty feet long, six feet high—depicting scenes from the 1778 Battle of Monmouth, New Jersey, and when they were completed, Kelly garnered additional fame and was internationally recognized not only as a great illustrator but also as a distinguished sculptor.

Gilder explained in another review, published in 1891, Kelly's absence from the magazine pages:

> The course of my metropolitan meanderings once took me to a stockyard, at a very busy season. Great droves of bullocks were awaiting sacrifice upon the ravenous altar of the big city. Among the pens and sheds a young man went about, making sketches on a pad. He was a slender young fellow, with a finely chiseled face and a pair of eyes that somehow made me sure he would do the scenes he was noting justice. And he did. They were signed simply, "Kelly."
>
> I saw a great many more cuts with the signature, in later years, always full of spirit and thoroughly original in style. Then they suddenly ceased. I thought—and regretfully, though I did not know him—that the artist was dead; but he had only laid one tool by to take up another. My draughtsman of the stockyards had become a sculptor.
>
> The first of his works that I saw were the panels for the Monmouth battle monument. In these bronzes, modeled in an almost defiant boldness and contempt for the conventions, the same original and

intrepid spirit showed as in the artist's sketches and drawings. They were the product of no school, the result of no methodical teachings. They spoke for their author as a man following his own bent and supported by his own natural gifts.

As in all of Mr. Kelly's sculptures, the details are valuably accurate. The artist, it is but fair to state, is in him not merely the man of instinct and sentiment. In spite of his fine, nervous constitution, he is also a student of the minutest facts, and in the execution of this and other works of a cognate character has become in a manner a historian as well as a sculptor. A monograph on the researches and discoveries he made for his Monmouth panels, for instance, would prove a valuable volume to the collector of Americana.

Kelly's artistic success lasted for another four decades with nearly eighty public and private bronzes (including fifty military portraits of generals and admirals) placed throughout the United States, from New York City to Arlington National Cemetery to the Gettysburg Battlefield.

In 1919, Kelly met with an old New Haven gentleman, Henry C. Blake, who had heard Abraham Lincoln speak during his 1860 lecture tour of New York and New England. Blake told Kelly that he remembered Lincoln as a strong and vigorous leader of men and not at all slack-looking, downcast or meditative—as he was usually depicted by other sculptors. After describing Lincoln in detail to Kelly, Blake looked earnestly at the sculptor and said, "I have often wondered if *you* could make him."

Inspired both artistically and historically, Kelly declared, "From that very moment, I became desirous of gathering material to justify me in making him an active, vigorous leader. My ambition was to model President Abraham Lincoln in bronze—the embodiment of the spirit of the time as well as the men whom he led in triumph. From that very moment, I began to actively seek out any living witness who could tell me of Lincoln."

With his usual enthusiasm, Kelly developed his artistic conception of Abraham Lincoln—tentatively titled *Right Shall Be Might*—by searching out and conducting a series of interviews and correspondence with well-known figures who personally knew Lincoln, veteran soldiers who had briefly met or had heard the President speak, and even common folk who simply caught a fleeting glimpse or passed alongside his casket.

Over a period of several years, Kelly diligently recorded over sixty eyewitness accounts which he carefully preserved in his extensive notebooks—hundreds of pages of highly significant oral history—detailing Lincoln's physical appearance, personality, and qualities as a statesman. This testimony confirmed Kelly's mental picture and his belief that the real Lincoln was seldom depicted correctly in art. "Make him living!" wrote Lincoln's Secretary William Stoddard, "for he was one of the most 'all alive' of men."

However, a series of unfortunate circumstances left Kelly's vision of Lincoln in bronze unfulfilled. Bankruptcy and illness ended his career as an artist and he spent his last years in poverty writing his memoirs with the hope of publishing his conversations with Lincoln's contemporaries. Sadly, Kelly died without realizing his dream, and his treasured notes were boxed up and stored away for decades.

I first encountered the Kelly Papers in early 2003, at the New-York Historical Society, and after sorting through and reading thousands of pages of handwritten notes and interviews, I felt as if I was sitting in the same room with the venerable figures of our nation's past or exploring with Kelly the cobblestone streets of 19th Century Manhattan. I immediately realized their importance to students of American history, and I resolved to rescue James Edward Kelly from obscurity and gain him the recognition he deserved.

My mission started with the 2005 release of my book, *Generals in Bronze, Interviewing the Commanders of the Civil War.* In the final paragraphs of the book, I wrote of discovering Kelly's unmarked grave and of my vow, and not long after publication, I began to receive unsolicited donations from Kelly admirers across the country—all wanting to assist in marking the grave of a man who had dedicated his life to memorializing the American Hero. Over $8,000 was raised, and a black granite marker was purchased. My thoughts then turned to an epitaph. I recalled reading an 1896 magazine review of Kelly's sculpture describing the artist and his American themes:

> We have been sometimes asked, why is James E. Kelly called the American sculptor?
> He is the American sculptor, for he has made historical events of this country his chief aim, an American genius, and as a genius has conquered. He partakes of the soil he was born on, who, by strong individuality, hard study, and unceasing labor, accomplishes his purpose, creating ideals of his works full of original thought and action. He has fought the fight, and is there.

The title of the article was:

*James Edward Kelly—A Sculptor of American History*

It seemed to me a fitting epitaph.

The purpose of this volume is to present Kelly's research regarding his proposed statue of Abraham Lincoln, along with his memories of New York City during the Civil War. Over a thirty year period, Kelly wrote several variations of his memoirs—all in an attempt to attract different publishers. One version can be considered a walking tour of old Manhattan; a second version gives considerable attention to his artistic career; a third version focuses more on his friendship with the great military figures of the Civil War, and finally another version prominently features his material on Lincoln, of which Kelly said: "Some of these notes on 'Our Abraham' may seem unimportant and trivial, but as even a glimpse of one you love may give pleasure, I include them all."

To create this volume, I use passages from each version of Kelly's memoirs—a few of which appear in *Generals in Bronze*—and chronologically organize Kelly's life into five chapters. The first chapter consists of his early years. The second chapter describes his training as an art apprentice. The third chapter tells of his successes in art and his encounters with the great men of the age. The fourth chapter contains Kelly's detailed interviews and correspondence regarding Abraham Lincoln. The fifth chapter depicts Kelly's final years. My explanatory comments appear throughout the book in italics. Some disturbing 19th Century racial descriptions and offensive terminology have been left intact to preserve their historical integrity. For editing purposes, I have used brackets to identify persons, regiments, events, locations and dates; parentheses are original to Kelly.

Unfortunately, we do not have the artist's vision of Lincoln in bronze, but very fortunately for us, and for future generations of Americans, we do have his diligent research. Through these preserved writings, Kelly's passion for history will stand forever as a tribute to Abraham Lincoln and the men whom he led in triumph.

**Sources:**

Bruce, Robert, "The Art and Sculpture of James E. Kelly," Privately printed. 1934.

Gilder, Richard, "Art in its Present Development," Newark Daily Advertiser, Jan. 6, 1881.

Gilder, Richard, "James E. Kelly, Sculptor," The Collector, Feb. 15, 1891.

"James E. Kelly—Sculptor of American History," Decorator and Furnisher, Nov. 1897.

Leach, Anna, "James Edward Kelly," Outlook Magazine, 1896.

National Cyclopedia of American Biography, 1935.

Roof, Ann, "A Historian in Bronze," The Outlook, 1905.

It is with great pleasure that I mention all those who have assisted me in the preparation of this volume.

My sincere thanks to my friends: Sonia Krutzke, Kathi Pehlman, Henry D. Ryder, Ed Bearss, John Valori, Jim Nevins, Jack Fitzpatrick, Bernadette Loeffel Atkins, Cricket Bauer, Clark "Bud" Hall, Rick Uhler, Jeff Kowalis, Chuck Laverty, J. D. Petruzzi, Jim Madden, Mark Knowles, Ed Wenzel, John DePue, Gerald McMahon, Patricia Beekman, Kathryn Spetz, Patricia Bollander, Seth Weine, Marilyn Westenborg, James Lighthizer, Norman Tomlinson, Patrick Falci and Mike Kraus.

Also special thanks to: Ted O'Reilly—at the New-York Historical Society and the Librarians at the Art Institute of the Smithsonian Institution. Nancy Carmer—the City Historian of Portsmouth, N. H.; the Librarians at Howard University; Pastor Robert O'Donnell at St. Paul the Apostle Church; Kathy Kersey at Cullum Hall, West Point; Doug Litts at the Smithsonian Art Museum, Patrice Kane at Fordham University Library; Karen Fix of the Conservation Artisans Group; Kathryn Murano at the Rochester Museum and Science Center, Sheila McCreven at the Pejepscot Historical Society, Gloria Swift at Ford's Theatre, Susan Sarna at the Sagamore Hill National Historic Site, David Schutz at the Montpelier State House, and the librarians at the New York Public Library.

I proclaim here eternal love and gratitude to my devoted family: my dear wife, Nancy, and my wonderful children, Kim and Brad—who patiently listened to me telling (and re-telling) Kelly stories and following me throughout Manhattan in search of the artists' former haunts. Kelly seems now, like a long-lost uncle—a beloved member of our family.

Lastly, in remembrance of several friends who have passed away while preparing this volume, I owe an eternal debt of gratitude.

Brian C. Pohanka died on June 15, 2005, just as *Generals in Bronze* was being published. Although desperately ill, Brian spent his final months reading Kelly's writings and stressed their importance to me and urged me to complete this second volume and carry on with honoring the memory of those who gave all for their country.

John Henry Kurtz not only offered me his talent and skill as a great Civil War historian, but also shared a thorough knowledge of 19th Century New York City.

Debra Fitts was another kind and supportive friend, and a dedicated battlefield preservation activist. Her enthusiasm for my work and her encouragement is greatly missed and will be never forgotten.

The same spark that burned inside James Kelly—a genuine love of American history—also kindled inside my companions. I don't think I have ever met more dedicated persons to the preservation of the American Hero. They were patriotic, but I don't think they ever considered themselves patriots to be championed. The ranks are thinning.

William B. Styple
March 20, 2009

# Chapter One
# Boyhood in Old New York
# 1855-1870

I remember when New York bloomed with vast estates, bowered streets, fragrant gardens, lovely houses, great men and women—this is the city that is still vivid in my memory. The city and its history, has been described so often that it would be hopeless for me to attempt to do more. I will merely try to people the streets with the great men and women and historic events that have come under my observation.—James Edward Kelly

## My Beginnings

My mother tells me I was born in New York City on July 30, 1855, but about my first recollection of things is in our little cottage at Keyport, New Jersey, where we had moved on account of my delicate health. It was here my brother was born, and not long after died. It was here that I first remember my mother's face as I sat on her lap on a winter's night in 1857 as she screamed at the face of my father who appeared at the window covered with snow and wrapped in white flannel which he had placed around his head to protect him in the long walk across the bay on the ice from the boat which was blocked. Danger thickened as he neared the shore, as he had to jump from one cake of ice to another, but the light at the little window which was placed by mother had guided him safely, and brought us together again.

My father, Patrick Paul Kelly was born in Glasgow, Scotland, on October 10, 1825, and was an optician and jeweler by trade; my mother, Julia Francis (Finley-Golden) was born in Jamestown, Ireland, on September 10, 1832; they married in 1850 and came to the United States the following year, settling in New York City in 30th Street near Eighth Avenue. I was baptized by Father Michael McAleer at St. Columbia church in 25th Street.

According to my mother, I seemed destined to be an artist. While just a child in skirts, mother was called from the room; and to keep me from mischief for a few minutes, she placed me in the center of the dining room table. In some way I found a piece of chalk and began copying one of my little wooden toys, probably a horse and cart. As my mother returned and caught a glimpse of a scrawl on the table, she gave an exclamation of impatience. Then, stepping forward and examining the drawing more closely, she clasped her baby in her arms and kissed me effusively. Turning to my father, she called out, "Come and see what Jimmie has done!" Thus my first sketch is remembered by my mother's joy and encouragement, which continued through all the remaining years of her life.

My mother always took an interest in art. There was a youngster in the village who used to attempt to draw. He used to come to my mother for sympathy and encouragement, which she always gave, along with a few cents. He never amounted to anything, except that he was the first I had ever seen do any drawing. Once my mother took me to a Daguerreotype gallery to be photographed and I felt the importance of artwork, and appreciated the directions of the operator so well, that I posed like a rock. So well, in fact, that in spite of my toe head, freckled face, and mouth like a young catfish, he was so delighted with the result that he insisted on taking one for himself.

## The Wide-Awakes of 1860

Abraham Lincoln was nominated in [May] 1860, and one of the most picturesque organizations that rallied to his support was the "Wide-Awakes," originally organized in Hartford, Connecticut. I remember them as they paraded through at night. They wore glazed French fatigue caps, and short black glazed capes, which I suppose was to preserve their uniforms from the dripping of their torches.

The torches were made of tin, shaped like a flask, swung from a half-circle of tin attached to the end of the staff; from the spongy wicks flared a long red flame with a reeking black trail. The officers carried colored lanterns, and all wore garlands of bright flowers hung over their shoulders. In memory of Lincoln's rail-splitting days, they carried numbers of fence rails borne on the shoulders of two men at the ends.

The nights of their parades were glorious in my sight. I can recall my mother placing candles in little clamps in each of the window panes of our small cottage, so as to illuminate in honor of the event. As they marched through the streets to the rugged rhythm of bugles, fifes and drums, the blaze of their torches and transparencies lit up their joyous faces, bright uniforms, their garlands of flowers, flags and campaign emblems, the men carrying rails, the various badges, etc. The applauding crowd cheered them from the sidewalks, gateways and vine-clad porches. What a thrill it gave me! How the memory has endured!

We children also had our "Wide-awake" parades, decked with garlands our mothers had made for us and each one in turn, straddling a pole carried on our shoulders. From my experience in riding it, I seriously thought that rail-splitter meant the boy that straddled the rail.

Lincoln's election made no impression on me, nor did "Old Abe," as he was universally called, in affection or derision. My mother never spoke of him otherwise than "Mr. Lincoln," and my father followed suit. My mother was a valiant partisan for him, and my father equally so. I recall the hideous caricatures of Lincoln in the papers at the time, also lithographs of him without a beard in the store windows.

My mother bought me a medal with a beardless portrait of Lincoln, and pinned it over my heart, where it dangled from its red, white and blue ribbon during the war. The rest has grown vague. It was New York in 1860 that decided Lincoln's election. He is described as sitting up listening for the returns until he heard that New York gave him 362,646 votes and 50,000 majority; followed by cheers for the Empire State—*New York Made Lincoln President!*

## Boyhood Memories of the Civil War 1861-1865

In 1861, I was six years old when we moved from Keyport to Brooklyn. Some old friends of my mother coming from Ireland induced us to move with them into a two-story house on Bedford Avenue, between Gates and Quincy—second door from Quincy. I was then sent to the school in Bedford Avenue and the first day I went, the teacher was crying and speaking to the class of the death of a boy by the name of Charlie Ring—poor little fellow, I wonder if anyone but myself remembers his name now. As I did not know my way home, they put me on the teacher's table and had the school assembled and asked if any of the children knew where I lived or lived near me. One little girl offered to see me home and I being ashamed made her walk ahead. She took lunch at our home and I repaid her kindness by throwing stones at her whenever I saw her.

My first recollection of the war was a servant girl of our friend, who sometimes worked for us, telling me that if I was not good, the Rebels would ketch me. I did not know what a rebel was, but it struck terror in my heart, and I was subdued accordingly. Then all of a sudden it seemed that every young man was wearing a colorful uniform. The first soldier I knew was my uncle Morris Golden—the adopted brother of my mother who told me on the back stoop of our house that he "had listed." I did not know what that was, but my interest was aroused by him appearing in uniform of red cap, short blue jacket, and full red pants, like the French troops.

Another friend in the same house named Mack McKenna joined the Duryea Zouaves [5th New York Infantry]. This bright costume to my eye was even more attractive—red fez with yellow tassel, white turban, short roundabout jacket with red braid embroidery, red vest and sash, red baggy trousers gathered at the knee, leather greaves and white canvas leggings. His mother criticized his wide pantaloons and wanted to cut them down to fit him. "Oh, no Mother, that would never do as I carry my rations in them," he told her.

The Zouaves or Zu-zu's as many called them, effected the fashion of cropping their hair to the skull which was called: "getting the hair filed," or a "Dead Rabbit Cut," along with a mustache and imperial. Their officers wore a French cap or McDowell cap with the low front pulled over the nose or turned up and cocked to one side of the head.

The small boys quickly caught the war fever and they thronged to the soldiers in gaudy costume. My mother was all enthusiasm. She made me a replica Zouave uniform, also a red-white-and blue rosette to pin on my jacket. Rosettes were worn by everybody, man, woman and child, and of course my mother's busy fingers were kept at work making them for my little friends. After a while, ribbon grew scarce with her so she knitted them with colored material which quieted my clamor.

My mother was Union from the word go. She used to say that when she saw a soldier, she felt as though she could hug him. She got me all the illustrated papers, and on special occasions she would lend me the box of watercolors she brought from Ireland. I would cut the figures out and put blocks behind them so they would stand up. She bought me some little figures of soldiers in papermache of the Seventh Regiment; they were quite expensive and beautifully made, but she was always ready to make a sacrifice for me. Swords and guns, and in fact anything I wanted, she would save for and get. We would go often to Fort Schuyler to see the troops in camp there. On our way, the proudest event in my life happened. A Zouave in the car, evidently attracted by my costume, took me on his knee, while we rode to the fort. I have never felt so important since.

The first time the blight of war was brought home to me, was when a young friend of my father, Alfred B. Clark, from Fishkill, N. Y., who had also enlisted in the Duryea Zouaves, stopped at our house with his wife and baby the night before he started to the front. His radiant uniform as he sat with his baby in his arms and his young wife beside him, made a lovely group, while she sang that charming old love song, *Ever of Thee I'm Fondly Dreaming*. It was a happy evening in spite of its undercurrent of sadness. I slept in my little trundle bed in the same room with them that night; and in the morning I snuggled at his feet, as he sat on the bedside buttoning his leggings and lacing his leather greaves, and answering in a kind, tolerant voice my searching childish questions of what they meant. I began to rummage through his traps; the haversack of white canvas covered with pitch which was flaking off with wear.

My mother gave Clark an introduction to our neighbor Mack McKenna, who was a bugler in the same regiment; and later, Mack wrote to mother saying that they had breakfast together, advanced to the front, and poor Clark was killed at the first volley at the battle of Second Bull Run.

Later an article appeared in the papers from a clergyman who said his son had been wounded in the fight and as he lay there, he saw one of the enemy take a photograph from the body of a dead Zouave—he asked him for it—he handed it over—he sent it to his father, it proved to be Jeanie and her little child—the portrait the clergyman forwarded to the poor widowed Jeanie.

In the summer of 1862, we had moved to 105 Nassau Street, to a little old time Dutch house made of brick. The 139th Regiment, under Col. Anthony Conk, camped in Brooklyn City Hall Park, and one of our friends named [Patrick Henry] O'Beirne was Quartermaster.

I had been greatly taken with the other uniforms, but with O'Beirne's, I was completely bewitched. He was a tall, thin, stealthy, bumptious Irishman with flaxen hair, and a long, very long, fiery red beard which almost covered his jutting chest, while his cap rested on the bridge of his nose. His uniform was the shiniest blue broadcloth, against which his bright gilt buttons and shoulder straps seemed to reflect the blazing glory of his beard like a splendid sunset; but he had one alloy to his glory—that was ME—I used to lay in wait for him and follow with my eyes riveted in admiration. He could not shake me. He would say, "Run away home, Jimmie; that's a good boy." Then, Jimmie would stop, and then trot after him like a young pup. When he halted to talk to a friend, I would sit on the curb with my feet in the gutter and wait till he went on. Meanwhile, to make people aware that I knew this vision of a soldier, I would call after him, "Mr. O'Beirne, when are you coming around to the house." He would try to shoo me or coax me to go away, but no, Jimmie wouldn't be "shook." I followed him till his regiment went to the front. I wonder why he did not spank the devotion out of me.

This hero worship has never left me. The sight of a soldier has always made me glow. I felt that if one of them brushed against me in the street, I had touched something sacred. I can recall seeing in a barber shop a young cavalryman with his brass shoulder scales. I thought they were epaulets whose gold fringe had been shot off in battle. I followed him and studied him in awe so that he seems as vivid to me now, as he was in those early wartime days.

The first historic event I saw was the reception of Colonel Michael Corcoran [on August 22, 1862] as he was escorted up Broadway on his release from a southern prison. He had been captured at the Battle of Bull Run, July 21, 1861, with the remnant of the 69th Regiment, which had formed a hollow square. Col. Corcoran became famous on account of having been held as a hostage. When our Government threatened to hang some southern prisoners, he wrote to the Government not to compromise their dignity by treating with the Rebels—but to hang the Rebel prisoners if they thought better of it; later he was exchanged. The enthusiasm and cheers were unbounded when he arrived in New York. My mother took me to Broadway, opposite Barnum's Museum. I have an indistinct recollection of a procession—a carriage—a figure standing in the rear right hand side of the carriage. I stood atop a store door—my mother supporting me as the carriage passed with applause and shouts—"There he is!" and then the rush of the crowd as they swarmed after the carriage.

I do remember clearly seeing the volunteer soldiers as they came from the front, sunburnt and dusty—it was peculiarly picturesque as they filed up Fulton Street. The flags tattered, their McClellan [McDowell] caps jammed over the noses, the blue of their coats turned brown or yellow while the light blue pants became a yellowish green. One had a kitten perched on his blanket roll above the knapsack. They seemed to have a slight stoop—a long swinging gate and their hair burned at the tips with the sun, but their arms glittering and grim—it was the only highlight about them.

I distinctly remember the day that my uncle Morris came home from the war, having served his three year enlistment. He was weather-beaten to the color of mahogany. We had a joyous greeting. He gave me his haversack, and I sat down to rummage at once. In the bottom I found among the crumbs, a jack-knife and other service tools. We then sat down to dinner. He afterwards gave me his service cap, which I wore with the pride of a Crown Prince. I never heard him describe any of his adventures except the march of the Sixth Corps to Gettysburg, thirty miles from where they started. On arriving at Gettysburg he was barefooted, his contract shoes having gone to pieces on the rocky roads. He said that when they reached the field the Rebels were charging Little Round Top thinking it was defended by State Militia, "Gen. [John] Sedgwick ordered a countercharge," he laughingly added, "and when they saw our brown faces instead of the pale ones of the militia, they called out , 'It's the Sixth Corps!' and broke."

# Copperheads

During the war, writing paper and envelopes were decorated with patriotic pictures and emblems, as well as portraits of the commanders. I remember showing one of Washington on horseback, to a neighbor, and in doing so said, with great fervor, "George Washington, the Father of his Country." She repeated after me mockingly, "George Washington, the Daddy of his Country." It gave me a terrible shock. It seemed blasphemous to me. I took a violent dislike to her, which I never outgrew, even after the cause of it was forgotten.

President Lincoln and the loyal men of the North had to fight enemies in the rear as well as in the front. The Germans—the "stay-at-home"—as well as those at the front, were Republicans. Many of those "stay-at-home" Germans married Irish girls, evidently agreeing with humorist Artemus Ward, who wrote: "This ungodly Rebellion must be crushed, even if it takes all my wife's relatives."

The sympathizers with the South were called "Copperheads," after the snake of that name. And some seemed to glory in it, by filing the head of a copper cent, and wearing it as a badge. From what I heard, the prejudice against Lincoln was intense on all sides, even by many loyal men.

Once, I was playing with a boy in his mother's kitchen. She was an American. She was washing dishes and discussing the war with a neighbor. She took up the carving knife from the hot water, with the steam ascending from the hot blade, and shrieked out, "I'd like to stick this into that old Abe Lincoln." I don't know why this incident should have impressed me so, as that sort of talk was very familiar. My father was continually having rows and cutting the acquaintance of old friends. All praise Lincoln now, but it took nerve to stand up for him in certain sections at that time.

One day, returning with my father from visiting the camp of Colonel Conk's regiment in City Hall Park, as we walked up Nassau Street past a corner gin mill, a young soldier boy came out, under the influence of liquor.

A burly, bloated-faced policeman, evidently a copperhead, collared him. I could not make out for what cause.

Instead of taking him over to the camp, he threw up his club and started to beat him. My father, holding me by the hand, worked himself forward, and as the policeman threw his club back, my father grabbed it in his iron grip. That's all I saw. The crowd closed in. My father holding on to the club with one hand

and me in the other; I was crowded, crushed and almost smothered—my nose and eyes being almost ground off in the melee. Evidently the policeman got the worst of it, as when things settled down, my father strolled leisurely up Nassau Street, still holding me by the hand. And I do not recall his ever referring to the incident. But the policeman must have had to nurse a twisted wrist.

In the spring of 1863 we moved to Park Avenue near Cumberland Street, and then Draft Riots came on [in July 1863] and there was great excitement in the darkey colony, which were separated from our house by an alley. Most of my chums were darkies except Jakey Hunter and a little boy grandson of the man who owned the large house on the corner; the boy died while we lived there; he was a fine little fellow and his last "Hullo Jim" from across the street as he was going home where he was to die of fever, still rings fresh and clear.

Here I formed a friendship with Ed and Sam Sparks, and Mr. Gray's children—three girls. One day we had a little fire in the yard. All at once, the middle girl said: "My dress is on fire! My dress is on fire!" The flames ran up its front. I tried to put it out, but it gained on me, so I grabbed the waistband and busted it letting the flaming dress drop to her feet, which so scared me that I rushed off and climbed over a fence and did not put in an appearance for several days. Her mother, who I believe saw it, used to have fun with me asking why I had not been round, while I was puzzled how to explain my absence.

I then went to No. 1 School and my teacher, Miss Emmanuel, seemed to take no interest in me and my drawings which consisted of soldiers. She used to ask me to sit down at the blackboard and draw pictures while she read aloud to the class.

There was a lean, freckle-faced youngster, somewhat older than myself who took a fancy to me; he lived round the corner and used to waylay me, and gave me a thrashing whenever he could. I used to come home and complain. My mother told me never to fight and with that peculiar love for her, I never thought to disobey, and would take a licking although in my heart, I never felt fear. At last my father said to me that I must take care of myself, and I determined to do so.

I was standing on the corner of Park Avenue and Cumberland St. and my man came along. My two friends, Ed and Sam Sparks and five little fellows stood by. He started in as usual and I pitched into him. He laughingly beat down my guard and battered my face pretty badly. More with rage than pain, I began to blubber and snatching a shinny [stick] from Ed's hands, started for him and brought it down on his head—I did not see him for months.

Having tasted blood, I seemed to enjoy it and was always ready to pick a fight, but always tried to make my opponent strike first. I was cured of that by a young, red-cheeked Englishman who during noon recess, as we had a quarrel, responded to my invitation to hit me be planting one on my left cheek, which then swelled up like an apple. After this my method was attack, regardless of consequences.

# Our Block, 1864—The Earth was New to Me

May, 1864. The sun was in full blast, but it was not quite noon. And as our block faced the west, the sidewalk was in shadow. Everything else stood out in intensity of glittering high light and sharp clear cut shadows, and impressed itself indelibly upon me, a boy not yet nine-years-old who stood in the doorway surveying the surroundings of our new home. We had moved from a pretty, little cottage in Brooklyn to the middle building of a block of brick tenements on the East side of Eighth Avenue between 57th and 58th Streets.

The first thing that struck me as strange was a large pine box opposite our door placed by the City to receive the ashes and garbage of the neighboring houses until the street cleaners saw fit to empty it. Meanwhile it was filled to overflowing, and pails, barrels, soap-boxes, in like condition, lined the bank of the gutters. Goats were running around pretty lively. One was standing on his hind legs and nibbling the poster, advertising a picnic, off the side of a garbage box. Another one was nibbling the label off a tomato can. This habit of the goats gave rise to the story that they lived off tomato cans.

The street cars were two-horse affairs with a plain arched roof. There were also a few one-horse cars built like stages with the driver seated aloft and the entrance behind. These cars only ran as far as 59th Street. A large, three-story wooden house painted white stood on the southwest corner of 58th Street with "M. Duhme, Grocer" over the door. Next to it was a small two-story wooden building, the lower floor divided in the centre; the south side a butcher-shop, the northern half a lager beer saloon with the sign "Reisenweiber" over the door. An immense mound of beer kegs were in front of the saloon.

The rest of the block, running back a hundred feet was a vacant lot or cow pasture. It was enclosed by a board fence with here and there one pulled out as an entrance for small boys, whose frequent visits polished the edges of the lower one. The weather beaten fence was covered with painted signs principally: "S.T. 1860X Plantation Bitters," "Walker's Bitters," "Kelly's Old Cabin Bitters," in fact everybody must have needed bitters judging from the signs.

The raw brick buildings, the cold blue flag-stones, the littered streets, intensified the mellow beauty of the scene beyond. Stately horse chestnut trees were adorned with clustering blossoms whose pearly whiteness was intensified by the deep green of their broad leaved foliage. The vine-clad grape arbor was in the rear of the saloon. Back of that facing 58th Street was a large brown stone house and cupola. This building was surrounded by grounds with greenhouses which flashed back the rays of the cheerful sun. Its peach orchard was in full blossom and in the pasture on the 57th Street side a cow grazed, followed by a calf. South of 57th Street, and over the rolling ground to the west, were truck gardens laid out in patches whose different colored greens from the brilliance of the lettuce to the deep tones of the radishes gave a crisp freshness to the scene. Between the undulations of the land could be seen the deep green ridges of the palisades which banked the Hudson on the Jersey shore. All was bright. All was sunshine. All was bloom.

# The Boy

As I stood gaping around a singular, indoor-looking boy came up. He was a head taller than I. His hat was made of black silk and quilted by a circular seam that started from the crown spirally to the outer edge. It was somewhat small for him and perched on his high bulging forehead. His dark hair was oiled and brushed in long, slick soap locks in front of his ears and curled up around his blue veined temples. He had a short, cock-nose with a few decided freckles—like fly specks; a long flexible upper lip, which vainly tried to conceal a large buck tooth, the other not quite grown; an upper lip, quite flat and firm. He also wore a shiny paper collar and neat black tie called a butterfly, and rather shabby, but well brushed shoes, a little too large for him.

"Good morning," he said with precise emphasis, "I see you are a stranger." I told him I was.

"My name is Harland Hitchcock. We have not lived here long and we expect to move soon. We are a very respectable family, and I am not allowed to associate with the boys around here, but (eyeing me with his pale blue, weak lidded eyes,) I think my sisters would not object to my talking to you. The children are all at school. I do not go to school as we expect to move soon. I have always lived in very respectable neighborhoods. We are at present reduced."

I looked him over, but could not quite comprehend what he said, so I asked him if his father was in the war.

"No," he said, "is yours?"

"No," I hesitated to admit, "but my brother is."

I had no brother, but I felt I must have some claims to his admiration.

"Was he ever wounded?"

"Lots of times."

Just then a fat fellow came up to the garbage box and began to root with an iron hook. He had a tin kettle on his head like a helmet with the handles drawn under his chin like a strap; a blue jean shirt ragged and patched; his fat, red arms stuck far beyond his sleeves and his wrist looked as if he had a string tied around—like a fat baby; large baggy pantaloons and an old pair of army shoes. A two-wheeled hand cart was beside him to which a couple of large, fat dogs were harnessed. He gathered the various things that struck his fancy and taking up the cross bar of the cart he and his dogs tugged it over the cobbles diagonally across the street to where the empty beer kegs were piled in front of Reisenwebers.

"That is Schwietzer," said the boy, "he lives over on the rocks in 55th Street. He sleeps in a barrel and eats dogs. He has a lot of dogs."

Then old Schwietzer began to drain beer kegs in a pail and put it in his cart. As he was at work, the grocer boy fired a tomato at him which spattered over him; Schwietzer grinned, picked up the tomato and trundled his cart off toward the rocks.

"Will you walk to the corner of 57<sup>th</sup> Street with me?" said the boy. "I have some letters to post for my sister. I am your neighbor; I live next door." He pointed over the drug store. In front of it was a little hunch-backed German astride a chair with his elbows on the back on which a little raccoon rested while it played with his long black goatee. He looked up at us smiling; his crisp brightness was carried out by his sparkling black eyes; his oily hair combed behind his ears.

"That's Dr. Coolis," said the boy. "He has lots of pets. He has rabbits, guinea pigs and more birds."

I looked in the store. It was as bright as he was. On the counter was a large aquarium against whose green water plants the goldfish glowed. Bright flowers and bird cages were arranged where they would not interfere with the business, and a couple of white poodles, clipped like lions, pattered in and out.

We walked down the block. Next to the drug store was a grocery store with a wooden awning extending to the gutter; a coal box at the curb. A placid, kindly looking woman was standing in the doorway with a beautiful little child in her arms. The boy said, "That's Mrs. Darragh, her husband keeps a stone yard near 57<sup>th</sup> Street dock.

Next to this was a cigar store with a tall, wooden Turk in front of the door. The next store was a forlorn little candy shop; the window was sparsely covered with a few tin pans of taffy and a few glass jars containing lemon sticks. The boy said, "Frankenstine, the artist lives in there and he paints." In the back there were a few paintings of landscapes, most of them views around Niagara, all unframed. As I looked in the open door there was a short counter to the right on which there were a few more jars of candy, but the rest of the store was hung around with unframed studies of landscapes. At the left of the door was a tall, handsome looking man with long dark hair and beard in a flowered dressing gown and slippers, painting an enormous view of Niagara as big as a horse blanket. It glowed with purples and reds, such colors as I had not been used to; the sky, the water, and the foliage sparkled with all the colors of the prism. I could not resist going in, and fumbling a large copper in my pocket, I entered timidly with my friend at my heels. I being the capitalist, the artist paid no attention to me, but went on with his work. I looked in the back room and there was a pretty youngish woman cooking. She came out and waited on me. I bought a square of taffy with my big copper cent, and watched with awe the artist putting in his bold strokes. At last the utter silence forced me out, and my friend's voice gradually asserted itself, and I divided my taffy with him.

Sitting outside on a barrel nearby was a man whittling a chain from a broomstick. His arms were large, muscular, freckled, redskinned and redhaired.

"That's Jim McCormick. He is assistant foreman of Black Joke," said the boy.

"What is 'Black Joke?'" I asked.

"The Fire Engine '33'," he said, pointing to the figures 33 smeared with tar on the side of a telegraph pole, whittled on a door and chalked in enormous figures on the sidewalk, and I had before noticed it on the garbage box. "There's the Engine House," pointing up the street a little over from Broadway on the north side.

It was a two story brick building. It had a small, old fashioned hand engine, painted black mounted on the roof. A beautiful silver maple tree grew in front at the curb and in front of it was a large wooden fire hydrant. Ledges of rock cropped up from the lot between the Engine House and Broadway. On the corner of the engine house roof was a rack and wheel with a rope running down to the yard so that the alarm could be given by anyone from the street.

"Black Joke Fire Company was named after a Hudson River privateer that distinguished itself in the War of 1812," said the boy in the tone of an official guide, "it was commanded by Captain Brown, armed with one long Tom [cannon], two smaller guns and a crew of sixty men."

North of the engine house was a hotel on the corner with a balcony running around the floor above the saloon where a crowd of sporty looking fellows tilted back in their chairs with their feet on the railing with the boot soles leveled at the public like the guns of a battery. I think this habit was caused by wearing tight boots and they did this to ease their feet. They were all smoking and flashily dressed.

One stood a little aside from the rest, looking into space.

"That's Pete Masterson the Alderman," said the boy. Pete was very compactly built. Plug hat cocked a little over the eyes with hooded lids; a thick hooked nose, large black dyed moustache, hair well oiled, parted down the back, and brought well forward over the ears. A straight thick red neck with deep seams at the side; turned down collar; low cut vest showing lots of shirt front; big cluster diamond pin with a heavy watch chain which dangled a locket; hands jammed in the pockets of his pants, the thumbs sticking outside tattooed near the wrists; the pants were broadcloth peg-top pattern gathered close around a pair of neat square toed highly polished boots. He had a cigar in his mouth which he would roll occasionally with his lower jaw, his only sign of life.

The others seemed to imitate him as much as possible but were coarse copies. Occasionally one would dance a jig, varied by a double shuffle. This and squirting tobacco juice seemed to be their only occupation.

Suddenly Pete's eyes showed a look of interest; then the crowd took it up: a loud bang of a distant bell, then the responsive clang of Black Joke's bell. Away went Pete, darting up the street. "Fire, Fire, Fire," yelled the crowd as they rushed after him. From all sides the crowd poured. The red headed man on the corner sprang, tilting over his chair joined the rest. They had hardly reached the engine house when out came Pete in fire hat, shirt-sleeves, swinging his trumpet, started towards us. The gang rushed the engine out of the door. It was a glittering steamer and it gave a heavy lurch as the men at the tongue swung in the direction of Pete. Volunteers came from every direction, jumping out of the cars and howling as they tugged at the ropes. The engine lurched and swayed down the unpaved street. As they swung down Eighth Avenue, the black smoke began to curl out of the funnel and the wheels began to rumble over the cobblestones.

At last she was under way; the ropes were fully manned. Red shirts and firehats were in the majority, but citizens of all conditions and ranks were mixed among them while belated ones came speeding from hallways everyone yelling at the top of their lungs.  It was perfect Bedlam.  The engine left a trail of burning embers which made the barefoot boys skip as they followed adding their shrill voices to the deep bay of the men.  I stood transfixed a moment.  I said, "Come on!"  My friend hesitated, at last gave way and off we went.  As I slipped and stumbled over the stones I saw nothing but the glittering engine through the black trail of smoke.  It swung down 53rd Street towards Ninth Avenue.  My friend halted on the northeast corner.  "Come," I said.  "No."  "Why?"  He drew himself up and said primly, "I am not afraid of getting mashed, but I hate the smell of smoke."  I looked on him bewildered, but was too shy to go alone.  Down the street I could see clouds of smoke above the surging swelling crowd.  "Look-out! Look-out!" and with mad bellows and yells another crowd swept down Eighth Avenue dragging an old time hand engine with "36" on her.  They went headlong through the crowd which closed rapidly behind.  Shortly, after we caught a glimpse of the men working at the levers and the water began squirting on the flames.

The fire was finally subdued, and from where we stood we could see the funnel of Black Joke and its glittering boiler swaying through the crowd like an armored elephant as it made its way up the street.

At last Pete Masterson appeared, looking as cool and impassive as usual, with a cigar in his mouth and trumpet tucked under his arm.  Jim McCormack walked behind him, his helmet in his hand and looking as though he had been boiled.  The line of men at the ropes came tramping along with a crowd of men and boys shuffling around and behind.  As they neared our block, at the sight of the head of the column, their relatives as well as passers-by swung themselves along the curb and gave the firemen a greeting such as they would victorious troops.

One little child ran out to get its father, who slacked the rope to within the youngster's reach, letting him take hold and march ahead.  This little act received a laughing applause.  The accompanying boys started to chant with their shrill voices:

"Say don't you hear the fire bells a-ringing?
Say don't you hear the fire engines rolling?
Say don't you hear Pete Masterson calling?
Pull on, pull on, my jolly Joker boys!"

# Evenings on our Block

After I had my strawberries and cream, with my Mother's arms around me, I leaned out of the low sill of our window and watched our new neighbors.

It was a glorious sunset which left its blazing trail over sky and land and lit up the cloudbanks as it descended behind the wooded crests of the purple, shadowy Jersey palisades.

Our block seemed like a village in itself. Men swung off the horse cars in front of their homes; others came from different directions on foot, but all had that bounding step that indicated they were on the homestretch. Children would rush and greet some by gripping their legs, which would almost trip them up as they sought with uplifted eyes and smiles the responsive ones of wife or children of the upper windows. Stone cutters, carpenters and policemen—clad in their garb of grey, like Confederate Generals, all with their bright tin dinner pails, all clean and neat, with a manly independent bearing. Their clothes were neatly patched—people were not ashamed of patched clothes in those days—but all were neat, well washed and thrifty looking.

Competing with the horse cars on Eighth Avenue were the stone trucks and dump-carts drawn by their plodding horses—the slack drivers sucking their short, black clay pipes. Brewery wagons drawn by gigantic Flemish horses with their glittering brass mounted harness made them look like horses that should bear some armored knight, rather than pounding their way along the prosaic cobble stones while their soggy drivers sound asleep wobbling like a huge mound of jelly against the pile of beer kegs behind him, trusting to the huge bulk of his team to force a passage through the lighter vehicles to his brewery.

After the slight lull of supper time, children began to appear; the larger boys running over to Slattery's lot and their echoing cries proclaimed a ball game. The little girls formed in groups, one mustering a few little tots on a door-step with a short stick and a book, and started to play school, and the way she stamped and scolded enabled one to judge the style of her teacher. Others formed rings and began to sing *London Bridge* and *Little Sally Waters*. A couple of boys strode through on their tall stilts, and then with howls a string of boys holding a clothes line attached to a soap box came dashing down yelling, "Fire! Fire!" —upsetting several youngsters as they tore by. An Italian with a hurdy-gurdy music box came by with a knowing-looking monkey attached to a string which allowed the monkey to scale the fronts of the houses where the women and children threw coppers in his little cap. After the men in their shirt sleeves with their pipes began to cluster in the doorways or lounge against the awning posts or coal box at Darrah's the Grocer. In a short time their voices began to get higher and above the voices of the children. We could hear the expressions: "Little Mac," "Old Abe," "Great General," "If he'd had a chance," "Napoleon," "baboon," etc.

A wounded soldier hobbled by on crutches and Granny O'Rourke, over one hundred-years-old, came by with a pail of coal on her hooded head which she just purchased from Darrah's. Children ran after her playfully, which pleased the old woman, who stopped with her doting smile and with her hands on her hips danced a little jig balancing the pail of coal.  She died at 105, but the undertaker said, "People do not live to be one hundred."  And so he engraved 99 on the coffin plate.

Then a lamp lighter came along, clapped his short ladder against the iron post, pushed up the glass bottom of the four-sided lamp, lit the gas with a sulpher match, shouldered his ladder and disappeared.

The mothers and older girls, having disposed of their dishes, appeared with babies in their arms and nursed or coddled them as they sat on the doorsteps, or some standing in groups swaying their infants and all wagging their heads over local gossip, at the same time unconsciously stroking some whimpering youngster tugging at their skirts.

The little German druggist, "Coolis," brought out some chairs in front of his store, and straddling one with arms folded over the back, lit his cigar and he soon had a circle around to whom he expounded.

Lights began to flash from "Reisenwebers," and people began dropping in. Then a big, flossy-bearded German with his child in his arms turned from "Coolis's" group, and with big soft slippered feet carefully picked his way across the street, his broad wife with a baby on her breast and child by the hand smilingly followed.

Shortly after this, their voices could be heard mingling with the loud talk, singing and laughter in Reisenwebers, while in contrast to this, a lean, pallid Irishman was to be seen coming from the direction of the shanties on 58th Street. His woebegone wife following and evidently pleading with him; he with curses ordered the poor thing back and disappeared behind the flapping doors of Hughy Tiernan's saloon.

Horse cars came laden front and rear and roof with German merry makers, heading from the picnic ground of Elm Park and Lion Brewery, singing their native song and chorus and managed by swaying in time to keep the car tethering fore and aft.

Just then, a cry came from the corner and there was a general rush. Hughy Tiernan is fighting drunk; he has thrown a man out of his saloon, knocked him down and in his rage, is kneeling on his chest and is beating his head against the sidewalk.  The men were dumb and hesitating; the women pleading and hysterical.  No one dared to interfere at these times; Hughy is a maniac.

A buxom, red-cheeked young woman pushed her way through the crowd, "Oh, you murderous villain!" she shouts at the same time smashing Hughy a blow under the ear and collaring him, pulling him to his feet.  Hughy stands swaying, white as tallow, his jaw slack, and his eyes half closed; she had struck the forerunner a knockout blow and with another jerk she swung him around and bundled him in the back door.  All is now congratulations, such as, "It takes Mrs. Tiernan to settle it."

The victim staggered to the horse trough and knelt by it, sousing his bloody head, while the gossip policies and songs of the children were renewed. Our blinds were drawn, my mother, lighting the kerosene lamp, brings out her sewing, while I lay on the floor with my toys, my father reading Dickens' scenes aloud, while my mother must have been wondering to what new scenes my father's gypsy instinct for moving would lead her.

# 53rd Street School

My mother, thinking it was time for me to go to school, took me down to a little building on 53rd Street, between Seventh and Eighth Avenues, north side. The school consisted of two small dwelling houses, three stories high. The two buildings were connected by an extension where the side yard had been; it was called the "Large Room." At the farthest end of the room was a platform, on which the principal, Miss McKenna, sat. On her right was a piano, on her left a large globe. A reading desk with a Bible was in the center. The small, low benches for the scholars extended across the room, with aisles on each side.

My mother turned me over to a pretty, little Jewess named Miss Blun, who registered and examined me, according to the regulations of that time. She took me to the principal and I remember her saying, "He reads beautifully, but he knows nothing about arithmetic." As this was the standard of grading, I was placed in the lowest class.

I had a general knowledge above my companions and above most children of my age. The surroundings made me indifferent, giving me a self-confidence that prevented me applying myself, and from that I lost all habits of study. My first teacher, Miss Redding, was a pretty, refined girl, who won my heart at once. She was kind to me, but only stayed a short time, then left to get married, and I was quite mournful for a long time. Miss Carroll succeeded her. She also treated me well. I remember being late, which called for a whipping, but she hustled me through the crowd without giving me any punishment. As I took my seat in the classroom, I found myself impressed with my pretty teacher.

The walls of the classroom were smeared and cracked, and in the long, dull, drowsy days that followed, the stains and cracks were a great source of interest to me. I saw in them my heroes, my castles, and I dreamed my dreams. A blackboard was on the wall behind the teacher, and running round the wall were hooks for hats and coats. The clothes of the majority of the boys showed evidences of the war. They were dressed in cut down uniforms—dark blue blouses and light blue pants—which were turned up, with patches of various colors at the knees, elbows, and seats. Soldier caps hung on the hooks beside caps and straw hats of the less fortunate ones like myself who did not have a soldier for a father.

A characteristic of the schoolboy was the inside of the cuff of his jacket which was generally worn away from pulling it down to polish off his slate on which he spit to wipe off the figures. As we went down into the yard, which extended as far as 54th Street, for a short recess, the boys began pushing, pulling and kicking each other amid wild yells. I soon found, as a new boy and better dressed, I was getting more than my share, so I started in with the pushing, pulling and kicking, and was left alone for the time being.

I developed a considerable skill in drawing profiles of Lincoln and Grant, which caught the fancy of the boys, and I found them a sort of ready money for anything I desired—soldier's buttons, brass company letters, or corps badges were readily exchanged for three Lincolns or three Grants, as the case might be. In fact, I could tempt almost any boy to exchange his treasures for them. Sometimes I would draw a "Zu-zu"—as we called the Zouaves, and later added a fireman to my stock in trade. This soon took a high place in their favor, and there was a big run on them. But the proudest boy in the class was the one who told us that his mother was thirty-three-years-old. How I envied him, as mine was only thirty-two.

Shortly after, a batch of us were promoted to the front room, and I found myself in the class of Miss Bell, and here my school life began to take on a character. As for our teacher, the boys worshiped her. She was a large, young girl; well formed, with a long, humorous Scotch face with yellow hair, bright blue eyes, and a happy smile. She received us in a white dress with blue butterflies thickly fluttering over it—short puffed sleeves, a little below the shoulder, showing firm white dimpled arms. In her pretty white hand she carried a hickory pointer. Her large hoops (the fashion of the time) puffed out her full skirts, so that she seemed to float around like a cloud over which her butterflies fluttered. As we shuffled and stumbled to our seats, like a lot of stupid sheep, she called us to order—which of course had no effect, at which she swooped down upon us like a thunder cloud this time. Whether by favor or accident, I, being on the end of the seat, she put her arm around my head, as a rest, and beat those around her with the stick. It flew and broke in half and grabbing the stump, she finished the job. But it was done in such a wholesome way and with such vigor, like a big sister, that the boys, while whining and parrying the blows, responded with admiring sniggers. Returning to her desk, she frowned fiercely at us, then her mouth twitched, and her eyes danced with a merry laugh, which the boys joined to the echo. In this way she captured them with a swoop.

The boys were then sorted according to size, and I found myself in next to the last row to where the taller boys sat. I learned the boys had proclaimed my powers as a "drawer," and pitted me against the champion "drawer" of the class—a tall, dark haired boy. He challenged me to draw a "Zu-zu," which we did while we should have been doing our sums. The boys passed them along the line, and mine was declared the winner. Even my competitor acknowledged it, but that did not satisfy me. At recess, I told him I could lick him, at which he smiled good naturedly. I, not to be balked, charged him. He received my face in the flat of his hand, and down I sat. I charged again. He laughed, stepped back, and down I went as before. He would not fight me, but upset me half a dozen times before I stopped. After that, I grew very fond of him, and he was very kind to me.

One day, Miss Bell, in her impulsive way, kept a little fellow in at noon hour. After a while, she began to pity his lonely, forlorn face, so she called another boy and sent him out for cakes, which she gave to the little fellow, so instead of punishment he had a treat. Her desk used to be covered with flowers which the boys had stolen from Central Park the night before, and quite often a tomato can with some gold fishes which they had caught in a neighboring pond.

She used to ask me for sketches. So we all gave tribute in some manner to her cheery, inspiring personality. We all loved our little teacher, Miss Bell.

We were then promoted to the class of a lady, Miss Mary Carroll, with the eye and profile of an ideal Duchess, full-throated, full-chested, with power and dignity in every line and movement; a full, rich mellow voice, everything expressing unconscious authority. Our classroom had two rows of seats running around the three sides. Her table and chair were in the center of the amphitheatre.

One day, she was pacing the room in her usual stately manner, when suddenly, a squeal and she jumped up on her chair (one might just as well expect a Cathedral to stand up on one corner), but there she was—pale, with eyes bulging, pointing with trembling finger to a small, bewildered mouse huddled in the center of the room.

With a roar, every boy was on his feet, those in the front seats rushed at it; tearing round the room they bumped over the table, then in a heap they fell in a tangle of whirling legs, howling and laughing, while those in the back row pelted the whirling mass with every book they could lay their hands on. Then one youngster struggled to his feet and held before her startled face a little, flat, gray thing by the tail as he would an autumn leaf by the stem. Miss Carroll descended from her perch, looked at the litter of books, then at us, and burst into a hearty laugh in which we joined. She seemed nearer to us after that.

One day, Miss Carroll pinned a silver medal on my coat, for what I do not remember; I think it was for good conduct. It was to be worn for a month. I ran home and showed it to my mother, and after that my troubles began—how to keep it out of sight of the other boys. I pinned it on the inside of my jacket. Every morning Miss Carroll would call me up and pin it on the outside of my jacket, and as soon as I left school back it would go. This continued for a month, then with a sigh of relief, I saw her hand it over to another boy. Although I may have deserved it, she never offered it to me again. Later, when she became a friend of my mother, she told her that medals were wasted on me.

## The Union Home and School for Soldiers' Children

On the Northwest corner of Eighth Avenue and between 57th and 58th Streets, there was an old, noble, colonial mansion built in 1817, the former homestead of Frederick Christian Havemeyer.

It was a stately white building facing east. The piazza, supported by heavy pillars, ran the length of the house. The top of the piazza had a railing around it, as did the flattened top of the gabled roof. On the gable end facing 57th Street was painted in black letters, "Union Home and School for Soldiers' Children." Above the crest of the roof from a staff, a flag was flying for which the children's fathers died.

The children both boys and girls, seemed to be allowed a great deal of liberty. They wore blue jean smocks or shirts, which made them conspicuous as they ran and frisked barefooted through Slattery's lot, or over the rocks of Havemeyer Hill. Some of the larger ones attended our school. Everyone I saw brought me a fresh sorrow, for I felt they had no father. This was mingled with a sense of envy that their father had been a soldier. Still sorrow was the dominant feeling, and my poor little heart almost wept for the little orphan boys when I saw them. In spite of the fact, they were a healthy, tousled, cheery little lot.

While walking up the road alongside the orphanage, a stone flew by and kicked up the dust at my feet. Then a perfect volley banged all around me. I looked up. A group of orphans stood breast high above the fence of the Union Home. They gave me another volley which I was too bewildered to acknowledge, but stood and admired the way they lined up and delivered their shots at me. I had never been in a rock fight before and afterwards learned that it was an understanding between the orphans and neighboring boys to pelt each other on sight if they had their blouses on, but at other times, the larger ones who went to our school were never interfered with. In fact the fighting was purely a friendly affair. A passing boy was looked on as a target, not an enemy.

Boys were primitive in those days, and to my mind it was a good thing for them. They were like the old time warring clans. Every avenue was arrayed against the other, and almost every street and colony of shanties. A boy felt if he was on an errand in a strange neighborhood, he must fight his way there and fight his way back. Even to Sunday school I have had to fight my way, and for that reason most boys went in crowds—for mutual protection. But as I could not expect my friends to be devoted, I had to fall back on my fancies for a body guard and defense.

As I had seen pictures of Admiral David Porter's Fleet running the batteries at Vicksburg, I imagined myself an ironclad; so I would turn up my collar, pull my cap down over my eyes, and start on a jog trot up the south side of 57th Street. This of course attracted the attention of the orphans and the fellows in the group of shanties which ran through 57th and 58th Street.

As soon as I got within range, a volley of rocks would begin showering all around me, splintering on the narrow strip of flagging, or denting, and bounding back from the fence. This would continue until I swung round into Ninth Avenue, across and behind the bluff.

Strange to say I never was hit but once, although I scorned to dodge, as ironclads never dodged. Of course I could have gone with perfect safety through 54th Street, as there was nothing but vacant lots, but I had started going through 57th Street and nothing could turn me. One day they formed a line across the street and headed me off. I kept right ahead to ram them, so they collared me. A big fellow, their leader, asked me where I was going. I told him. He hesitated, and seemed not to know what to do with me, and I seemed indifferent to the threats of the others. So he said, "Give us a chew of tobacco." I said I had none. "Go on then," he said with a grin. They never fired at me again. So my romantic raids were spoiled.

# Blind Maggie and the Shantyites

My mother had a school-mate named Maggie who had been stricken blind, and was sent to the Blind Asylum at 34th Street and Ninth Avenue. When she called on my mother she was led by a little moon faced Dutch girl, who could just see well enough not to run into things. After a while she confided to my mother that she was in love with a blind broom-peddler named Malloy. She showed my mother his tintype and asked her to describe him. It appears it was the custom for blind sweethearts to exhibit each other's portraits to their friends, and depend on their descriptions for a knowledge of their charms.

Finally Maggie brought him to the house. He was a tall, gaunt, young Irishman with a long nose, and a black ruffle of beard round his jaws—like Lincoln. His was almost blue with powder marks. He had been blown up in a powder blast, losing both eyes, which were concealed with green goggles.

My mother was enthusiastic over this love ideal, and persuaded her musical friends to give a concert, and her financial friends to patronize it—in St. Martin's Hall, at the junction of Seventh Avenue, Broadway and 47th Street. The result of Maggie's concert was two hundred dollars.

On the strength of this they got married, and it was decided they should build a shanty and go housekeeping. My mother selected a spot between 56th and 57th Streets on a rock about 100 feet back from Ninth Avenue.

This was a great experience for me, as I used to go every day and watch the construction of the shanty. The fresh earth with its spring-time odor, and the saw-dust from the hemlock planks was a great joy to me. Of course there was great interest shown in the blind couple by the neighboring shantyites, and this gave me an opportunity to know them in their home life.

The shanty being finished, it was decided that it would not be necessary to paint it, as the Malloy's being blind could not see it. The simple furniture bought, and a big stove mounted, which Maggie polished till it became the most conspicuous object in the room.

I used to go every afternoon to see Malloy on his return from his day's work with what brooms, brushes and dusters he had not disposed of. I used to guide him up the hill, which was entirely unnecessary, but I felt he could not get along without me.

Putting down his brooms in the corner, he would sit down on the door-step and empty his pockets of the various things that had been given him during the day. One of the principal things that used to amuse him was the quantities of religious tracts which he would get me to read aloud. When he heard them, he would respond with loud roars of laughter, which I could not see the force of at the time, but I suppose they warned him against sins he could not possibly commit such as riotous living, etc.

Back of Maggie's shanty in a hollow of the rocks, was a shanty of different type—low, dirty, with the original white-wash worn off by storms—cobbled with old painted and unpainted boards with a section of rusty tin roofing on top, which caused such a style to be called ironclads, and a rusty stove pipe cocked to one side, was sticking through the roof. Cleats were nailed on the slanting chimney, leading up to the stove pipe, so that one could climb up to fix it in case it got storm wrenched.

The woman was tall, gaunt, ragged and bare-footed. Her children equally ragged and bare-footed—full of fight—and pelted all strangers who came within their range. But the oldest sister, a rosy, buxom girl, worked for my mother, and they made me welcome. Oh! how I envied them their savage freedom: their collection of mongrel dogs of all sizes and their ducks, their geese, their bantam chickens, and their two goats—which most of the shantyites kept to supply their milk. The bantam roosters used to interest me, especially when I used to shy a piece of rock at them; they would charge it and give it a clip with their spurs as they jumped over it.

The shanty inside carried out the suggestion of the exterior. It consisted of two rooms, a rusty old stove, a wobbly old table, cleats nailed against a post to ascend to the loft. Some sticks nailed across the far bins or bunks near them in which the children slept. In my fancy it had all the charm of a cabin on a Desert Island as described in *Robinson Crusoe*.

After I had become acquainted with the inhabitants of the neighborhood, including the goats, I met one huge Billy Goat that the boys rode whenever they caught him. He had no horns—long lap ears—red eyes, and a red goatee. His hair was worn off at all his projections showing his tough, leathery hide. He could have posed for the original scapegoat, for his bleared eyes made him look like a hardened old sinner. He generally hung round the gin mill corners and had the reputation of being a hard drinker of whiskey.

This reputation was encouraged by the bartenders, furnishing him with whiskey on bets, with the other bums. And as the Billy would drink all they would give him, it all went for the good of the house. The secret of Billy's strong head for whiskey was that he belonged to an old fellow who ran an illicit still in a shanty among the rocks near Seventh Avenue and 57th Street, and Billy used to feed on the whiskey mash.

There was a story current of the old fellow that when his copper tubing had burned out, he hid them in the cranny of the rocks at some distance from the place, then called at the Revenue Headquarters and reported that he had discovered an illicit still. It was investigated and seized by the officers, and the old fellow received the customary reward as an informer. With the proceeds of this reward he started business afresh with brand new coppers, and supplied his customers with their illicit potato whiskey.

One day I heard a band playing, and saw a funeral procession lined up in front of the shanties on 57th Street. Then a coffin draped with Old Glory borne on the shoulders of some veterans as they marched through the alleyways between the shanties. Placing it in the hearse, then with colors flying, the band playing, they filed down the narrow wagon track that ran through 57th Street.

I heard afterwards that the veterans had gone to the widow and said, "It will cost for a band, but you are so poor we thought we had better offer you the money instead." She said, "No, poor Larry didn't have much pleasure when he was alive, and I want him to have a good time now that he is dead."

Toward sunset one beautiful summer evening, I heard an unusually loud explosion; all day long they were blasting rocks above 57th Street, but this crash was louder than the others. Then I saw men running towards the rocks. With other evidences of excitement, there came a thick ever increasing crowd, of women coming across the lots, anxious and wild eyed, as they heard that someone had been killed. As many had husbands and sons who were rock men, each feared the blight had fallen on her. Then the word went out Patsy Flemming's father had been blown up. Then came a party of men carrying their wounded comrade to his shanty home, while one comrade ran to the Paulist Church, another ran in the opposite direction for Doctor Clow. Soon the Priest and the doctor came hurrying along, and disappeared in the vine-clad doorway. The Priest reappeared, and the wail that came out as he opened the door, we knew the man was dead.

"Was he prepared?" an old woman asked. The Priest nodded. The men uncovered their heads; the women blessed themselves, and muttered a prayer. And as other excited women came hurrying over the lots they received the same answer: "He was prepared."

I ran home through the twilight and told my father that Patsy Flemming's father was dead. He expressed regret for the poor fellow. I said, "But, he was prepared." My father answered, "That's all very well—but..." I was very much surprised he did not receive my statement with the resignation of the dead man's comrades and their wives when they said, "He was prepared."

## Dutch Groceries

The groceries, whether kept by Hollanders or Germans, were called Dutch groceries. They were generally on the corner, and were sheltered in front and sides by large wooden awnings, which were supported on posts planted at the curb, and against one of these posts, rested on end, a pile of wooden shutters to put over the windows at night; they were clamped into position with a long iron bar.

A low wooden stoop ran around the sides of the store, with two flat doors to go down to the cellar. On the stoop was a great display of vegetables and fruit of all kinds, which, with their picturesque arrangement and contrast of color, lit up the cool shadows cast by the awning.

At the doorpost, dangled a big dried codfish, and beside it a keg of salt mackerel. On the other side of the doorway, hung a bundle of brooms, and beneath it, a barrel of soft soap. Around the corner, on the side street, was a coal box—divided in the center—one for charcoal, and one for hard coal. These were sold by the pail to the poor or the shiftless. Charcoal was used by housewives in summer to cook with. Instead of stoves, they used a small furnace made of baked clay, about the size of a pail, and bound with iron hoops; they used to place them in the yard to boil water for washing.

The charcoal was also peddled around in immense wagons with an overhead wooden cover, like a prairie schooner. It was very long, quite high, and painted black, with "Charcoal," in white letters on the side. It was generally drawn by two mules, and driven by a Negro.

Inside the grocery, the floor was sprinkled with white sand which was worked into various patterns by dragging a broom over the surface. The store was rich with the odor of spices and fruit, but the predominating and most stimulating flavor of all, came from a barrel of rich black molasses, which was enough to make any boy hungry. Behind the counter were some quaintly pictured tea boxes, and at the end of the counter, was a rack for pies, and a pile of all kinds of bread.

A barricade of soap and cracker boxes partly concealed a small bar which dealt out whiskey and cigars; lager beer, at the time, was only being sold at the saloons devoted to it. Whiskey sold at three cents a glass, and cigars at three cents also. I have heard my father say that behind the barricade used to be a resort for old time policemen. They wore a copper star, and were called "Stars" or "Coppers," which developed into "Cop." In case of a row, if they felt like it, they would cover it up, or stay behind one of these barricades, so as not to bother their friends. There was quite a row among them when uniformed police were proposed.

Back of the bar, through an open door, lit up by the sun streaming in the back windows, could be seen the fair haired, rosy cheeked wife, knitting beside a cradle, with her golden haired children grouped around her; as for the grocer himself, men called him Hammond—his last name being Kracke. He was a great big blue-eyed, pink-cheeked, curly haired man with a large, flowing, brown beard, and with a soft, rich, kind voice. He spoke broken English, while his clerks (which he had to change often, as they generally went into business as soon as they learned English, which was in a very short time, and without any accent), all looked alike—blonde hair, china-blue eyes, small regular features, square forehead, pink cheeks, slightly olive skin—head inclined to be slightly flat in the back. Here their delicacy ended; their hands were large, red and purple looking, no veins visible in many cases. They shuffled about in carpet slippers, and blue yarn stockings.

But each of these corner groceries had an offset to the cleanliness and content of the Dutchman. The shelter of the awning, the coal box with its flap top, and the barrels, were an inviting shelter and lounging place for what was known as "gangs," or "corner loafers." Here the unemployed crowded round during the day; and after working-hours, the crowd swarmed, and from that time, till far into the night, they "hung" around, practicing negro steps on the cellar door, littering the sidewalks with tobacco juice; and, by their hoarse voices or arguments, and sometimes quarrels, disturbed peaceful citizens far into the night, being a public nuisance. Nothing would scatter them but the grocer forcing his way to get the coal, or the alarm of fire. Then they would break and head for the engine house, with wild howls, and catching the rope, would tear, yelling like fiends, to the fire.

## Postage Stamps for Cash
## Drawing Profiles of Lincoln for a Penny

Change was short during the War and postage stamps were legal tender. Men were paid with sheets of them. In the stores, old women would bring them out of their bosom and find them stuck together, and then with the oath, "Bad luck to you, Abe Lincoln!" they would start to soak or lick them apart.

Others carried them in little books, arranged in different amounts, and they had little trouble, but for busy people and children, as well as irresponsible persons, they must have been a great loss on account of them sticking together, and through clumsiness or haste many of them were destroyed. Then Fractional Currency [paper money], as they called it, was introduced [in 1862], or by some people called: "shinplasters."

The idea of postage stamps then in use inspired designers, so they imitated stamps on their currency. The earliest I recall was a five cent stamp printed in brown ink on buff paper, two by three inches. Then they would engrave two—five cent stamps for a ten cent currency printed in green ink. And so on, till a row of five cent stamps meant a quarter, etc.

As I look back, I seemed to push everything to the limit. So it was with my coin collecting. I had a knack of drawing heads of Lincoln or Grant for the boys in school, so I could draw their portraits like a check to pay my way. Whenever I ran out of money, I would draw a Lincoln head, and, as a rule, the buyer would hand over a coin in exchange.

I used to go into the stores where I was acquainted and give the regulation money for all sorts of old coins the storekeeper might have in his till. They did not know the value of them, nor did I. But the fact that a coin was strange was enough for me to collect and the storekeeper to get rid of.

One young storekeeper, with whom I became very friendly, kept a grocery store in the building where I formerly lived. I used to go around after school and spend my time with him. He would go through his till and fish out all kinds of coins. It was a perfect mine for me. He was a lusty, fair-haired young fellow, and used to lie full-length on the counter, resting on his elbows, rummaging through the till, which he had pulled out and placed before me. He had a dried up little father with a grim, wrinkled face and a stubby gray tuft on his chin. He traveled round in his shirtsleeves, and his straw hat pulled down on his ears.

One afternoon, I went round after school and found the store closed. I could not understand it. I found out later the grocery store was only a blind. My amiable friend was a counterfeiter, and his old father was caught at work in the back room. This proves the worst have a kind streak in them.

# The Russian Fleet

Starting with my parents from the foot of Murray Street on the 3 o'clock boat *Matawan*, Captain T. V. Arrowsmith, on a trip to Keyport, New Jersey, where I had lived for five years as a child, the little steamer passed a fleet of warships anchored in a long line down the Hudson River. They were the old-time windjammer type—high black hulls, with broad white stripes from stem to stern, marked with black port holes from which grim guns projected; sky-scraping masts, Old Glory fluttering from the fore and the Russian flag at the gaff. My father told me they were the Russian fleet that had been anchored there for some time, and it was generally understood that they had been sent over by the Czar of Russia to assist the United States should England join the South in war on the Union.

The papers announced that Admiral David Farragut and the Russian Admiral were stopping in the Astor House at the same time, which seemed significant. Passing down the harbor we approached old Fort Lafayette. The dark, time-stained red brick walls shone out in bright relief, the blue uniforms of the sentries at their posts. Then at the port-holes appeared heads and smiling faces, and waving straw hats and felt hats in greeting. I could see the gray sleeves and shoulders of their uniforms.

"Those are Rebel prisoners," said my father, smiling. The passengers responded by waving their hats and calling in friendly recognition; it was quite a cheerful scene, and did not suggest war-time. Reaching Keyport, we stopped with our old friend, Capt. Barnes. I used to trail after his big boy Billy, who would sit on the sunny side of the barn whittling, and sing endlessly a song with the chorus:

> Hiptie—doodle-doo.
> Jeff Davis, how are you?
> The Monitor licked your Merrimack.
> Quite handy—O!

Poor Billy Barnes, whose father was in the oyster business; he started in an oyster smack down the coast to gather seed oysters. He was captured by the enemy, and died from hardships while in prison.

# Grammar School Number 17 on 47th Street

In 1864, I was promoted to the grammar department of P. S. 17, between Eighth and Ninth Avenues.

It was a thrilling day for me as I started down Eighth Avenue. The block below 48th Street was very attractive to me. There was a great variety of houses; one a high brownstone around the corner occupied by Angevine's tea store, and a druggist. Then, as I passed several low, narrow brick and wooden houses, I was brought to a standstill by a very fine earnest looking wooden Indian standing in front of a cigar store. The noble Indian was full of individuality and expression and it was always a pleasure to study it. The cigar store itself was another great attraction. The window was well stocked with cigar boxes, pipes and tobacco bags, and also with strings of Beadle's salmon colored dime novels. Inside the little shop the shelves were banked high with them. What a wealth of romance they represented to me then! Each cover was illustrated by George White, showing dashing scenes of plumed Indians and fur-capped frontiersmen—as a rule in a death grapple.

These novels were outlawed by the parents and confiscated by the teachers, but as they were so small and flexible, the boys used to hold them within the leaves of their books and read them when they were supposed to be studying. A boy's wealth was standardized by the number he had on hand.

I never saw any harm in them. In fact they inspired boys with a sort of chivalry. In my case they did good. One called, *The Yankee Champion*, by Sylvanus Cobb, Jr., helped to fill the Revolutionary days with romance, and to be like the hero was one of my ambitions.

On the 47th Street corner was a three-story peaked wooden house with dormer windows. It was occupied by a large grocery store and had a large, wooden awning, under the cool shadow of which there were baskets of richly colored fruit—the whiff from the bins of fresh flavored garden truck was very invigorating as we passed under the awning after our dead heat around the avenue to get to school on time.

Turning into 47th Street toward Ninth Avenue, I passed some bright little cottages well shaded with fine trees, and little front dooryards aglow as usual with flowers, but their fragrance was almost dispelled by the overpowering of malt— rich heavy and steaming. It came from Rottman's and Eckhoff's breweries where men were loading the hot grain into carts to feed cattle. I understand that it was claimed it made the cattle boozy.

On the opposite side of the street was the house of "Hudson Fire Engine No. 1" foreman, John Hamill. It was an old time piano pattern, so called. Some firemen were lounging under the shade of the trees, others burnishing up the bright work of the machine, or flushing the floor and sidewalk.

Passing the brewery, I came to a little candy shop such as always hugged the lee of a school; its little bell on a string over the door was kept on a continual jingle by children going in and out. Behind its small window pane were displayed small jars of peppermint and pans of taffy, popcorn balls, and other bait to catch the children's coppers.

The candy shop was kept by an angular lady with a most discouraged air. I never saw her smile, but the place was very clean and the knick-knacks were very bright, and the sweets, crisp and fragrant. The molasses taffy was baked in pans and marked out in blocks of generous size; it was as black and sticky as tar. After finishing the candy, we generally carried the paper on the palm of our hand till we met an unsuspecting friend, and slapped the molasses side on his cheek. That gave us as much fun as eating its sticky sweetness.

Next door was my school, Grammar School No. 17, a large prim, building whose plain brick walls looked dingy and time-stained. A fat policeman stood at the girls' gate and a tall, lean one at the boys' gate on the west side. A clanging of a bell from the cupola gave final warning to laggards who came tearing from east and west.

Entering, we were ordered to our room. Our class was the east one on the north end of the Assembly Room and separated from it by glass folding doors; these were pushed back when the school assembled. Our seats were arranged on steps, and the other classes were in regular rooms from where they marched into the Assembly Room to the music of the piano.

Going to school one bright day in the spring, I passed a boy lying in the grass on the causeway of Eighth Avenue near 57th Street. In front of him several geese were grazing. I asked him if he were going to school. "Na," he grunted—"fever 'n ague!" Oh, how I envied him, and in fact envied any boy who could get fever and ague. I used to fish on the ponds covered with green scum, and did everything I could to bring it on, but never had the good fortune to develop it, so my school days are regular.

## Miss Egbert

Next promotion landed me in Miss Henrietta Egbert's class. She was a handsome blond with bright, red cheeks and very regular features. I recall her with very large hoops, and a bright, silk, pea-green gored skirt, which fitted over the hoops without a fold, like the cover of a balloon—as was the latest fashion. She had a stately, reserved manner and a quiet dignity. My first day in class found me on the end of the seat to the right. My mother, proud of my promotion, had dressed me in my best—much to my disgust. The boy on my left was a mouse-colored, squared-face little German tough. He eyed me from the corner of his little blue eyes, evidently not approving of my appearance. He whispered from the side of his mouth, "I'm going to lick you as soon as we get out." Taken by surprise, I timidly looked him over. Then the thought of the licking began to hang over me. I got very nervous and began to sweat and rub my hands together between my knees in a shifty way. I counted the minutes until recess.

We used to have many fights when the teacher was called away, and, as I had already won my spurs, I was inclined to use them at the slightest provocation. The fight was arranged behind one of the sheds. A line of boys on each side, leaving a space about ten feet long, and three feet wide; in this they put us, and at it we rushed. It was dead silence, so as not to attract the teacher's attention. We would rush in, punch, till one went down. The other boy seemed to be stronger or heavier. In any case, I found myself down, and down again. My chum, named McGuire, would pick me up by the collar and whisper in my ear, "Keep it up," and throw me in. The boys, leaning over and crowding, nearly smothered me, panting, bleeding, and badly battered. Still I had no thought of giving up. At last the bell sounded. We rushed for the pump. The German got there first. They were pumping on him to wash off the blood. "Give it to him," said McGuire. I rushed at him, and threw him aside; then I put my head under the spout. The boys pumped on me while the others washed off the blood. The other boy seemed to have lost all heart, and stood by till I was finished. By this act, though beaten the worse, I was proclaimed the victor.

## Sunday School

In 1864, I went to the Sunday school of the Paulist Fathers. The old yellow church with its two towers was a landmark for the whole section. You could see it from Third Avenue. You could see it from the river, and you could see it from our school in 53rd Street. It was a small church then in length—the towers being the center of the building. The church was about fifty feet long; the other half devoted to the residence for the priests; it was afterwards extended another fifty feet as the congregation grew, and it seemed one of the largest buildings in the world to me the day it was finished.

It was on a terrace about six or seven feet above the level of the streets which had been cut through. It took in the block between 59th and 60th Streets, and extended half the block down toward the river. The plot was in a high state of cultivation and the carriage drive, whose entrance was on Ninth Avenue and 59th Street, wound in a graceful curve through banks of flowers and shrubs. The neighborhood consisted of bleak rocks crested with shanties and here and there a place blasted out in which was erected a brownstone house. The level places and hollows were generally occupied by Dutchmen with market gardens, so the beautiful flowers and vines around the ochre colored church shone out very brightly amid the grim surroundings.

Of course Central Park in the neighborhood was somewhat of a rival in our eyes, but the scraggy saplings and rather veneered look of the landscape could not compete with the high state of cultivation to which the Paulists had developed their place.

Father Isaac Hecker, the head of the Order, was of course an object of great veneration in our eyes. He was thin, close on six feet tall, sturdy, erect; his every movement full of force and vitality. He had dark brown hair and kindly but keen blue eyes which would beam or glint through his gold spectacles; he had a strong full Roman nose and a clean shaven upper lip and a short reddish beard. His complexion was rather weather beaten. This is as I recall him as he jumped off a car, bag in hand, evidently returning from some mission.

As he made his way through a group of us who were playing marbles on the corner, he returned our salute with a cheery, "How do you do, boys," and made his way up the garden path toward the church. My mother used to go to him in her troubles and he is the only one who seemed to have any influence on my father.

Although many of his Irish parishioners looked askance on the Paulist, referring to them as Protestant priests, still he seemed to know how to handle them. In one case, a man was living in one of the shanties with a woman unmarried, and Father Hecker called one day and said that he wanted that scandal stopped. The man resented his interference. Father Hecker said, "I am a bigger man than you are, and I don't intend to leave this house until you marry the woman." When he did leave, he had accomplished his object.

Being too young, I never got to know him intimately before he lost his health. His interest in me and my work was shown by the message he sent me through my father: "Tell Jimmie to always feel when he is at work that Father Hecker is looking over his shoulder and praying for him."

Father Augustine Hewitt's face always had a great fascination for me—its wonderful purity and beauty of outline. There was a stateliness about him that seemed to overawe me as a child. I would fix my eyes on him and watch his every motion. One day in Sunday school when I had been put out in the aisle for bad behavior, he came along, gave me a light tap on the ear and told me to go to my seat. The mechanical way in which he did it inspired no resentment on my part. My attention being more occupied studying his features than paying attention to what he did.

Father George Deshon had a great attraction for me for an entirely different cause, namely, on account of being an Army man, West Point Class of 1843. He was the direct opposite in personal appearance to Father Hewitt—a square, erect military figure. He used to raise chickens, and the boys used to get in and steal the eggs, and one day he caught a boy with a hat full of eggs coming out, and he stopped him and gave him a lecture on stealing.

The serving girl who was watching from the kitchen window called to him and said, "Father, so you caught the boy?"

"Yes, and I gave him a good lecture."

"But did you take the eggs from him, Father?"

"Well, there, I declare I forgot it."

# Central Park

Central Park was the playground of my boyhood, and the study of my youth. I recall being taken there in the early '60's by my mother and her friends to hear Harvey Dodsworth's band in their rather primitive music stand on the Mall. There were some fine trees of the natural growth, but most of them had been set out and were little more than saplings, where they had been placed under the direction of the landscape designers, Frederick Law Olmsted and Calvin Vaux.

Col. John Y. Culyer, who was Olmsted's assistant at the beginning, afterward did fine service in the Civil War, and later laid out Prospect Park, Brooklyn. He told me that to avoid mechanical planting, Olmsted would take a handful of white gravel and throw it broadcast—and then ordered the trees to be planted where they fell. At that time, the walls of the Park were not yet finished—nor the other stone work, such as the bridge, Casino and the Terrace;

yet were available to the public.  It was a great treat for me to watch with wonder the carvers at work on the rough-hewn panels on the walls and pediments of the Terrace, and to see a nugget of stone hewn into a life-like bird, or bloom into a graceful flower.

It is remarkable that I never saw any evidence of vandalism, as is now shown in the mutilation of these interesting carvings; it took representation of Continental "culture" to introduce that.

There was one temptation that was irresistible: we would go up on spring evenings at lilac time, and fill the breasts of our jackets until we bulged like frogs, then prepare to run the gauntlet of the policeman at the Park gate.  As we approached we would give wild yells, fan out and rush down and past him, while he stood helplessly, holding up his club defiantly in the air.  But I have reason to suspect that he was only acting his part, and enjoyed the distraction.  On the following day, our teachers profited from these forays by having their desks almost buried in mounds of lilacs, and the air of the musty school-rooms was stimulated by their fragrance.

## Barber Shops

It being warm weather, my father sent me down to "get my head filed," as the soldiers used to call it—meaning clipped to the skull.  Our barber shop was characteristic, being kept by a German as most of them were.  It was an old fashioned store with double doors in the center with a stone step worn to a deep gully from passing feet; large windows with small panes.

Entering, the barber was seen forcibly stirring a lather in the cup with all the earnestness of a chemical experiment.  He was tall and gaunt; light grayish blond hair, brushed back like a mane; great hollow eyes—a grim set to his face, like the portraits of [Field Marshal Gebhard L. Von] Blücher.  His appearance illustrated his name, which was really: Mr. Grim.  He wore a yellow linen coat and trousers and carpet slippers which flapped on the white sanded floor.  Portraits of Lincoln, Grant and [Franz] Sigel decorated the loudly-papered walls, along with some posters announcing a chowder excursion, the Scottish Games, the Caladonian Club.  A big Newfoundland Dog panted by the cold stove.

A young German boy, an ex-schoolmate, grinned recognition and took possession of me and started to cut my hair.  I began to study the rows of shaving mugs in the pigeon holes against the wall.  Some had sentimental matters, some merely names, one a bull's head, another a horseshoe, and another a hearse which belonged to the undertaker.  One had a horse car and I asked the boy if they indicated the trade of the owners.  "Yes," he said, "and I broke the mug of the horse car driver and he made me get a new one and just as I got it, he lost his job and don't come here anymore.

The man in the chair next to me was about half finished.  His hair had been dyed black and heavily oiled, parted evenly down the back and brushed briskly to each side till it looked like a split mackerel.  The sides were brought well forward over each ear in soap locks—like a horse's blinder. He breathed heavily through his broken nose and he tried to follow the motions of the barber as he put the finishing touches on his moustache. It was black as well—so black as any "b'hoy" (as they used to call the Bowery Boys) could wish. Old Grim with his head cocked to one side like an artist putting the finishing touches on his masterpiece, the man then got up and gave his place to a friend who just came in with a black eye to which Grim applied a leech which he fished out of a bottle. He then started to lather him, while the leech got in his work, when "boom, boom" rang the Black Joke's bell. "Bang," went the sitters heel as he bounded to his feet, snatching the towel, he swiped off both leech and lather, grabbed his hat and bolted for the door while Grim, razor in hand, rushed to the door stamping with rage while I wistfully watched the "Black Jokes" disappear down Eighth Avenue in a trail of black smoke—I always did hate having my hair cut! Getting back in my chair, the boy went at me again.

There was another barber shop on Ninth Avenue and 48th Street. His windows were a great attraction for the boys; it was festooned with strings of teeth as a sign he pulled and bled, in addition to this, he stuffed birds. I spoke of him to my barber friend. "Oh," he sniffed patronizingly, "he is one dose old fashioned Sherman barbers."

An old Hebrew came in wearing a velvet skull cap with long white hair and beard, silver spectacles, a huge shiny nose and a pair of lips that sucked complacently the stem of a long porcelain pipe. His flat carpet slippers shuffled with great deliberation across the sanded floor, muttering something in German at which the barber turned on him sharply. Another low voice unctuous remark and the barber seemed to bristle up and with frantic gestures replied in a rattling volley of German. The old man raised his eyebrows archly, muttered another muffled remark, put his pipe in his mouth and shuffled out in the sunshine. The barber's hand trembled so that it looked dangerous for his sitter as he screamed out, "I hate dat man! He makes me so mad! He contradicts me, everything I say, and de vorst of it, he is always right, the thackass!"

# Tobacco

My father told me that on his arrival from Scotland, he went into an eating house to get an American breakfast. A young man was eating something he had never seen before so he told the waiter to give him some of that (pointing). It proved to be buckwheat cakes and sausages. He said he had never enjoyed a better breakfast.

This made him desire to see more of the American institutions, so he went into a court room. As the Attorney was summing up a case, he took out a tobacco box and put a fresh quid in his cheek. As he did so, the Judge made a sign; the Attorney passed the box to the Judge who, helping himself to a quid, returned the box. The Attorney put the box in his pocket, and resumed his address.

Tobacco was considered common property. Any one would ask for or give a chew to a stranger, as in old times they did with snuff.

The origin of tinfoil on tobacco is said to have come from Gen. Winfield Scott going into Anderson's, Broadway and Duane Street, where Mary Rogers was employed, and whose [1841] murder Edgar Allan Poe has immortalized.

Gen. Scott told [John] Anderson he wished there was some method of keeping tobacco from drying up during his campaigns in Mexico.

Anderson did up some in tinfoil, and Scott taking a chew with gusto said, "Ah, is not this a solace." At which Anderson gave the tobacco the name of "Solace."

Tobacco stores were a great attraction for boys. Their windows were perfect picture galleries—with their tobacco bags and picture labels with the Chief—showing Washington on horseback, Colonel Ellsworth, Gen. Sigel, Little Mac, Garibaldi in his red shirt, Gen. Grant. Most boys' ambition was to keep a cigar store, so that they could read all the dime novels, look at the picture papers, and smoke all the cigars they wanted.

For one who considered himself a gentleman in those days, it was the custom when he met a lady while he had a cigar in his mouth, to ostentatiously remove it and throw it into the street, as a sort of burnt offering.

Quite a contrast to the present day young men who will talk to a lady, and at the same time suck a flabby cigarette, and blow the smoke through the nose into her face.

My experience as a smoker was confined to umbrella frames, which we would pick up on the dump. The frames of umbrellas were made of rattan at that period, and we would cut them up into the length of a cigar and smoke them. One day as a lot of us were lying on the roof of a shed in the sunshine, a fellow came along and seeing what we were doing, called up, "You shouldn't smoke that rattan—it will give you yaller jaundice." I don't know what "yaller jaundice" was, but there was something terrifying in it, so I threw my butt away, and have never smoked rattan or tobacco since.

# Fourth of July 1864

"Fourth of July," was my first thought as I was awakened at daybreak by a roar and crash, and clouds of thunder smoke that poured into our open window. Its stimulating odor quickened my breathing and thrilled like a bugle call. I can understand and sympathize with the old soldier who had a habit of firing off a pistol and sniffing the barrel, instead of taking snuff.

I rushed to the window and looked upon a sight new to me. The sidewalk was full of men with guns and pistols, boys with pistols, firecrackers and small brass or iron cannon. Girls were also busy with firecrackers and torpedoes. Everybody was blazing and backing on his own hook. The men would ram down a charge full to the muzzle of their pistols, line up on the gutter, aim in the air, turn their faces aside and fire away amid showers of wadding descending from the heavy clouds of smoke.

Stout Germans sat at their windows in their shirt sleeves, with long porcelain pipes in their mouths, gravely and industriously loading and firing their muskets. The very air was blue with smoke slowly soaring skyward, and bystanders were in constant danger from the kick of toy cannon mounted on blocks. A boy would load one to the muzzle with powder and wadding, then ram down the charge with a large nail for a ram-rod, and hammer it with a stone. As a rule they kicked on being fired, whizzed through the air, and would occasionally burst.

Chasers sputtered and whizzed across the sidewalk, causing passing girls to grab their skirts and skip aside with little screams of mock terror. Pinwheels hissed and spun on the trunks of trees and awning posts, and a frantic yelping dog tore along with an old kettle primed with firecrackers tied to its tail. The mounds of ashes piled along the gutters were mined by enterprising boys, then blown up amid showers of cinders.

Oh, what a ripping, joyous racket it was! There was not a goat in sight, they had all scampered to the highest peak, and the ganders in quaking frenzy, with craned necks, spread wings, skimmed and tip-toed across lots as they sped with their waddling family for refuge into the middle of the nearby ponds.

General Charles W. Sandford did not take his usual ride in the park as he was busy mustering the militia downtown. A roar of cheers greeted a neighboring butcher, in his gray uniform with his long side whiskers streaming over his shoulders as he mounted his gray cart horse and galloped down the avenue to join his troop, the Washington Grays. All these sights put me in a wild state of excitement and taking my wooden pistol and a pack of firecrackers, I started out in search of adventure. I drifted among the crowd till I met some of my chums and made our way among the rocks near the Engine House. One of the fellers took a powder flask and ran a trail of powder along the rock while we knelt along in a row to watch the effect as the boy touched it off—a flare! We looked at each other in amusement as all our eyebrows and eyelashes were singed yellow—laughing at the effect, not realizing the danger of blindness we had escaped. We then joined the crowd that swarmed in every direction.

Germans and their families crowded the horse cars (many men and boys perched on the roof), heading for the uptown picnic grounds at Elm Park, 94th Street or Lion Brewery, 110th Street, some firing pistols from the car windows, or chorusing the native folk songs, in which women and children joined. They were a jolly, joyous, boisterous and happy crowd.

As evening came on, the usual heavy shower spoiled the display of fireworks at the junction of Broadway and 59th Street, but rockets were sent up on every side, empty barrels were blown apart by packs of firecrackers going off inside and the howling child who had blown off his fingers, was led off to the Doctor in Upham's Drug Store. Engines tore down to the usual Fourth of July fires, their flames reflected in the low-hung clouds that were driven by the arching rockets.

A young Englishman, tall, amiable, blond-bearded, kind-eyed and soft voiced, with his little rosy wife, kept a small candy and toy store in the neighborhood. Carried away with the spirit of the occasion, toward evening he took a hand full of rockets, went out on the sidewalk, and before a crowd of small patriots, prepared to set them off. While clearing a circle, he absentmindedly put the lighted punk into the same hand with the rockets, setting one afire.

It began to flare and sputter, sending a flame down his bare arm and starting the rest. He set his teeth and held the rockets aloft, enduring the fiery torture until one after another of them shot skyward. Next day my mother met him with his poor arm swathed in cotton and oil; she expressed her sympathy and added, "I wonder you did not drop them." "How could I?" he answered with a quiet smile, "they might have hurt some of the children."

Two days later, while at breakfast, my father read aloud the news of the destruction of the *C. S. S. Alabama* under [Raphael] Semmes, by the *U. S. S. Kearsarge* under [Capt. John A.] Winslow [off Cherbourg, France on June 19, 1864]. I can only remember the remark about Semmes dropping his sword overboard so as not to surrender it, as custom and honor demand. But he was saved from surrender by the British yacht, *Deerhound*, rescuing him and taking him to England.

## Eighth Avenue to City Hall

It was a bright Saturday morning, and taking what money I had saved, I started downtown with my father on the Eighth Avenue horse car for City Hall Park where they had old coins for sale.

The cars had room for twenty-six passengers, thirteen on each side, with seats running lengthwise, seven windows on each side. The seats were covered with plush carpet. A small kerosene lamp at either end of the car gave dim light at night. The conductors and drivers did not wear uniforms, nor was there any method of checking fares; it was left to honor.

The cars had no signs on them except one which said: "Passengers 5 cts., Children under the age of 12, 3 cts. No child allowed to keep a seat while grown people are standing without paying full fare."

While that rule was enforced no one ever saw feeble old men or tired women standing while fond mothers allowed their dear children to sprawl over the seats. My mother used to carry the principle further by making me give my seat to any little girl who came aboard—oh, how I hated those girls!

The cars on Fourth Avenue were more expensive; they charged six cents fare, all others were five. The effect on the Fourth Avenue passengers was remarkable. They had a most important air—it was aristocracy for a cent! The women would sail in and spread their broad hoop-skirts as though entering a Victoria carriage. Other cars held thirteen passengers on a side; not so the Fourth Avenue. It depended on the whim of the ladies how much they would consider each other.  They would puff out like angry hens and maybe get eight passengers on a side, and no man would dare break through their bristling stares to take a seat.  In fact, they made the cars look like they were made for ladies only; or, for hoop-skirts only, for the lady played a very small part in the spread. Like a mast on a yacht under full sail.  The conductors were cowed, and stepped gingerly between the clouds of skirts and took the six cent fare humbly from the inflated ladies.

As we rode on, my father started reading his "Times."  The *New York Times* was my father's favorite newspaper.  He said he had taken it since the first copy was pushed under his door to advertise it in 1851.  My father lost no time mornings in hurrying out to get the newspaper and started reading the latest news from the war front, until he struck the Indian names of the gunboats, or of the southern rivers.  These were, as a rule, too much for his Scotch tongue, and he found them unpronounceable; then he would pass the paper over to my mother to finish the account.

I went outside and stood by the driver as Eighth Avenue became less familiar and more interesting, amusing myself by looking at the different emblems of trade.  Passing an oyster cellar, there was over it a large ball swinging from the end of a pole.  It was made of wooden hoops covered with canvas painted red, like a Chinese lantern.  It was lit up at night by a candle inside. Sometimes the boys used to have fun pegging stones at it, which would upset the candle and set it on fire.  Bake shops were indicated by a sheaf of wheat carved in wood and gilded, which swung over the door.  The butcher shops had a large gilt bull's head.  The barbers of course, had their striped poles.  The druggist had a gilt mortar and pestle.  The pawn shops had the three balls.  A large wooden boot with a red top indicated a shoe shop, while wooden Indians, sailors, Highlanders, and Turks were ranged on each side of the avenue, like a picket line, in front of their respective tobacco shops.

Between 52nd and 51st Streets, on each side of the way, were two old time cottages.  Their yards were protected by wooden railings, and contained many fine chestnut trees; their flower beds bordered with a box were ablaze with brilliant flowers.  The sidewalks were skirted with lofty trees: silver maple, chestnut and weeping willows which almost met across Eighth Avenue.

At 51st Street, southwest corner, sat a rheumatic old man with a very red and bulbous nose, under a tree on an old blasting powder keg; he hobbled out and gave a shift to the switch with his iron tipped rod, while our car bumped and jingled along to the depot at 49th Street.  There we changed conductors and drivers.  Horses were uncoupled from the car with a long iron hook with a tee handle.  All drivers carried them until a driver killed a passenger by hitting him over the head with one.  They used chains after that.  Passing a large vacant lot on 49th Street and reaching 46th Street on the west side, were low sheds or shanties, with Jewish clothiers and other small dealers.  The same was at 45th and 46th Street.  Behind them ran market gardens down to Ninth Avenue on the east side. Old houses mixed up with modern ones now filled up the avenue.  I then went and sat beside my father.  As we reached 33rd Street my father pointed out on the east side of the avenue, a house in the middle of the block, "There's where your mother and I loved when we were first maddied." At 30th Street he pointed out a large brick house five doors from the northeast corner: "There's where you were born." In old times, a wandering lane ran through 30th Street from Eighth Avenue to Broadway and a high crest of rock ran down as far as 23rd Street; it was called "Strawberry" or "Stony Hill." Reaching 23rd on the northwest corner was the Knickerbocker stables.

Many of the stores had swinging signs. The "Gen. Grant" on the northwest corner of 27th Street had General Grant mounted on a horse and was kept by John Grant whose son Hugh, became known as our honest Mayor.

In front of every beer saloon a pile of empty beer kegs lined along the gutter. It seemed the ambition of every beer man on Monday morning to display the highest pile in front of his place to indicate the extent of his business the Sunday before.

A one armed soldier got into the car with a haversack full of papers called *The Soldier's Friend*, and sold them to the passengers. There is a story told of the soldier handing a copy to General Grant, not recognizing him, and Grant put a Five Dollar bill in his hand and ordered him to say nothing.

At 20th Street, my father pointed out a large wooden building, southwest corner, "There's where I kept a jewelry store when I first came to this country. And on that top floor was your grandmother's room. One day a priest came and placed some jewelry on the counter. I asked him what it meant, he said, 'Please don't ask any questions,' and went out. I suppose someone had stolen it, but I never missed it."

My father also told of a boy who had worked for him, who stole some jewels, and instead of punishing him, gave him a kindly talk and sent him back to work. Years after, he became a prominent man, and did me a great service.

# Greenwich Village

Greenwich Avenue and 14th Street, coming together at this point marks the northern boundary of Greenwich Village in the angle formed by Eighth Avenue crossing them with Jackson Square. Facing on the Horatio Street side was the old Caledonian Club house with its golden lion in front; then we passed into Hudson Street and Abingdon Square where was a small park which was surrounded by a high railing fence and under the thick foliage of the surrounding trees the horses were watered, and, if necessary, changed for fresh ones which were lined up along the curb. North of this oasis were pretty houses with verandahs of iron framework, vines and flowers growing over them in whose shadow ladies sat reading and sewing.

On the corner of Bank Street facing Abingdon Square was the Village House—a large, white peak roofed building. Sitting on the verandah were old-time sports with white high hats and linen dusters. On the southeast corner of Bank and Bleeker Streets were the Barracks—the upper floors used as a prison for the captured British sailors from the *HMS Peacock* in the War of 1812. Looking down Hudson Street, it seemed a perfect arbor with trees on each side and fine old-fashioned brick houses with slant roofs and dormer windows lined behind them.

In some of the stores were large framed lithographs of a rather handsome man with a small curled mustache, entitled, "Bill Poole." He was a butcher and had a stand in Washington Market. He was a leader among the "Know-nothings," a sort of forerunner of the Ku Klux Klan, only they were not afraid to show their faces and fight by daylight—man to man. He was also a local Bowery "b-hoy," a rough and a gouger. He gained great notoriety by beating John Morrissey in a bare-knuckle boxing match on Christopher Street dock [on July 26, 1854]. Poole was shot [mortally wounded] in a barroom brawl in February 1855. His death caused great excitement. His last words were claimed to be, "Wrap me up in the American Flag. I die a true American!" One of his old time admirers told me that he had a funeral [on March 11] such as New York had never seen, except Lincoln's.

## Hudson Street

Hitching posts were planted along the curb and horse blocks made of marble or brownstone were in front of many of them. Their stoops were made of marble or brownstone with wrought iron posts, white doorways with glistening knobs, knockers, and door-plates. On each side of the door were long panel lights and above fan-shaped windows were arched and beautifully carved. In many cases the first floor or parlor windows were cut low with iron scroll work; the open green shutters disclosed lace curtains and through the airy railings or basement windows could be seen canaries in bright cages or aquariums, or regulation white poodles barked out from their surroundings of potted plants. Over the front of a great many of the houses grew wisteria vines, which added a regal splendor to the scene. Even the policemen with their Panama hats, their blouses, and rattan canes seemed more shapely and refined. The large cobblestones were well sprinkled and well swept. No hoop skirts or garbage littered the street. The sprinkling wagon was driven by a barefoot boy. The car had two wheels on which was mounted a large wooden cask on its side. From its rear end a piece of leather hose led to a perforated tin sprinkler.

Trees of Washington Square could be seen looming over the low buildings. From there on, were brick houses of a more ancient style than those in Greenwich Village. Some of them were called, "swell fronts" on account of convex walls. They looked forlorn and desolate, and it seemed as though it were wash day in all the houses, with the clothes dangling out of the windows, and the slack, tired-looking women lolling, and gazing vacantly out. Occasionally, a man who looked like a mechanic, out of work, lounged at the window, reading. Some of the houses had pigeon coops on the roofs, around which the birds fluttered.

As we went on, the street began to lose character. Signs with a big word, "EXCHANGE" appeared on the screens in the shop windows. It was another name for Policy Shop—a cheap form of lottery. These were generally surrounded by sporty darkies, men and women, although many whites, including half grown boys and girls, indulged in this petty gambling. Still the contrabands, as many called them, were the principal customers. The mystic numbers 4-11-44 played a part in the game, which I did not understand. A negro would occasionally ask what you dreamed about, and on the strength of your answer would be influenced in selecting the number to play. But it was all a mystery to me.

Foreign signs with gaudy coats of arms, foreign flags, as well as mounds of beer kegs, indicated Continental invasion. Derelict old carts with their metal work red with rust, were almost buried to the hub in ashes and garbage, which a few stray decrepit old men laborers made a show of removing with the stub of their stable brooms, while rug and cinder pickers, rummaging among the ash barrels along the gutter, scattered more ashes over the road than the old men were supposed to have cleaned. Beer saloons were quite close together, and in the basements, Germans could be seen sitting, eating and drinking around the tables, while stout, rosy, smiling girls waited on them.

Theatrical bill-boards were nailed against the trees, while many other trees were nearly gnawed through by the horses that were hitched to them. Several stray dogs roamed around, or buried their muzzles in buckets.

At last, our car swerved round the corner east into Canal Street. To the right I saw a small, bare-footed boy on a very large horse coming down a canal in the center of the rail road track, waving a dirty red flannel flag. Behind him puffed a dummy engine, hauling very slowly a long train of freight cars from the depot at 30th Street and Tenth Avenue down to Chambers Street depot.

There were very few trees in the street, and they looked rather unwholesome in comparison with those in Hudson Street.

After we had gone east for a couple of blocks, I noticed running along the sidewalk a large pink dog, a little further a purple one, and then a bright saffron one. I could hardly believe my eyes until it was explained as I saw them galloping along together and dash into a dyer's shop with the name of Moneypenny over the door.

## West Broadway

Our car turned into West Broadway, and through Little York Street, I could see the rear of old St. John's Chapel, which abutted on St. John's Place and faced on Varick Street. Opposite was the beautiful St. John's Park. The churchyard trees could be seen overtopping the low neighboring houses as the car jogged along.

At Franklin Street stood a tall liberty pole, its base was encircled by boards, shaped like a cone, and running to the height of six feet. Outside this, was a circle of short posts connected with a chain. The pole was about 165 feet high with cross trees with a weather vane and a liberty cap at the peak. The pole was painted white with figures running all the way up.

My father told me it was here the firemen used to meet to test their muscles and the power of their engines, by squirting water up the pole. The pole was erected by Tom Riley who kept the Fifth Ward Museum Hotel, and on Thanksgiving Day, the firemen used to meet and have tournaments to see which machine could squirt the highest.

The judges sat on the roof or in the cupola of the hotel. The winners used to mount a broom on their machine as the sign of victory. This was another survival of the old Dutch days, when Admiral Cornelis Van Tromp went up the Thames after defeating the British fleet. He mounted a broom at his masthead to show he swept the seas.

The hotel had another distinction—its museum. Inside was a headless statue of [William] Pitt, Earl of Chatham, which had been erected by the grateful citizens, on the corner of Wall and William Streets, for his services in repealing the Stamp Act, February 1776—it represented him in a Roman toga. During the Revolution, the British soldiers pulled it from its pedestal, knocked off the head and arms, and after years of shifting it finally reached Riley's Museum. I have a vague recollection of going inside with my father and seeing the historic portraits, relics and curiosities in glass cases.

Approaching Chambers Street, the track became a single one. Reaching Barclay Street where West Broadway began, there was a row of peak roofed houses running across the lower side. The single track passed under an old fashioned, slant roofed house. The lower floor of which, had been the parlor, had been knocked away, so the car shot through where had once been the parlor windows. The stairs had been left intact so that the occupants could ascend to their apartments above. The car ran through these echoing archways and turned up Vesey Street. Our car swung to the left, up to St. Paul's Churchyard and the large elm where Washington used to tie his horse while attending services. I loved to peer through the high iron railings and study the quaint epitaphs on the headstones. As we neared Broadway we heard that ceaseless "rumble and roar" which is peculiar to this thoroughfare—a sound which they said exiled New Yorkers missed like sailors who longed for the boom of the sea.

Reaching Broadway, which was the end of the route, the horses were unhitched and coupled to the other end of the car, and the uptown passengers entered.

## Broadway to City Hall

Broadway was a perfect jam of wagons, carts, trucks and stages swaying and bumping like ice floes in a spring freshet. My father grabbed my hand and coolly worked his way under the horses' heads and landed me safe on the lower point of City Hall Park. I noticed the paving stones were large blocks of granite; they had a deep gash on them like a cross to give a grip for the horses' hoofs.

A bunco steerer was once asked how he could tell a New Yorker from an out-of-towner. He replied: "I never tackles a man who crosses Broadway with his hands in his pockets."

As I looked north, the view was very effective in its sweep. North of Vesey Street was the Astor House with its stately rugged dark gray granite walls where, from the balcony over the doorway, Lincoln had addressed the people when he was on his way to be inaugurated in February, 1861.

City Hall Park contained many large, wholesome trees, some weeping willows, and a large fountain which threw the water to a great height. Above the rich verdure of the trees, the sunlit spray of the fountain with its miniature rainbows, towered John McCoomb's masterpiece—our City Hall. At that time the Park was surrounded by a high iron railing, with still higher ornamental double gates. On each side of the supporting piers, were small single ones. On the four granite piers were large granite balls from the walls of Troy, which had been presented by Captain John B. Nicholson U. S. N., May 8, 1827.

Some bootblacks were skylarking around; some bareheaded, some with old soldiers cap—all barefooted. Most of them wore clothes cut down from their fathers; the blue Army pants were cut down and rolled up at the bottom, showing they had a patriotic pedigree. A box with a single foot rest was slung over their shoulders, with the number of their favorite fire engine whittled on it or worked on it with brass-headed nails. No matter what game attracted them, they seemed to have an eye for business, for when they saw a man hailing for a shine, they would run for him like a pack of wolves, shy their boxes at him, and the one he put his foot on got the job.

Outside the railing peddlers had planted their stands. On the east side of the gate, was an old woman who sold ballads for a cent; they were printed on a sheet about twelve inches long and they had a wood-cut on top—some with a fancy border which had no relation to the subject of the song. They were strung on lines and fastened with clothes pins. To a prospective customer, the old woman would sing in a sweet, but well-worn voice the tune that accompanied the words. At another stand, a Chinaman sold little wedges from a large pink glazed lump of candy. He also sold long, slim, straight cigars. Then came an Irish woman on whose stand were apples, oranges, sliced pineapple, and large, flat molasses cakes.

On the west side of the gates, was my personal favorite—an old coin man. He wore a high, bell-crowned, greasy looking silk hat with the napp worn off at the crown; it was pulled down till he looked lop-eared. Narrow, overhanging brows with weedy eyebrows; sharp little eyes; steel spectacles which kept sliding down his long narrow hooked nose—so large that it seemed perspiring from the strain of holding itself on to his hard little face. He had shrunken, mumbling lips and a wisp of grizzled beard growing round his lower jaw. His throat was always muffled. He wore a long, weather-beaten, greenish black coat, and kept constantly shifting from one foot to the other.

His stand consisted of a couple of shelves attached to the railing, while braced against the iron bars, were several boards on which were nailed sets of large, old fashioned cents and half cents, foreign coins—ancient and modern. On the shelves were several albums of postage stamps. There were also trays of loose coins. The fascination of rummaging through them and polishing with my thumb or coat sleeve to bring out the date, still lingers. I can recall on one occasion, as my father left me in the park, I reserved three cents for carfare and spent the rest for coins, but in order to secure a fine copper cent of 1819, I had to walk all the way to our home on 58th Street.

## Broadway from Battery Park

My father and I stood at Battery Park, facing the stiff breezes which swept across the glistening waters of our Bay. Some foreign warships were coming in and we watched with interest the saluting guns from Castle Williams.

The Battery showed the reddish sandstone of which it is constructed; it then stood on a small island a short distance from the shore, and was connected with the mainland by a narrow wooden bridge. A low railing ran along the edge of the Park; a few feet below it ran a narrow beach of rock and sand, where some boys of about my own age were down by the water line, gathering flints and striking them together to flash fire.

At the time I first saw the Battery it was used as an immigrant station. Immigrants lounged about in the sun, or sat on the rough, whittled benches in their strange, foreign garb, the women and children in gaudy-colored dresses. Others leaned on the posts or railing at the parapet; their wistful faces and yearning eyes gazing seaward stirred my pity, and I instinctively grasped my father's hand with a throb of joy to be with him.

As we strolled slowly up the west side of Broadway, it was interesting to study the scenery around me. Crowded omnibuses filled the way; five opposition lines worked down to Whitehall Ferry Terminal and as they turned up town, branched out in different routes. The coaches were painted brightly with distinctive colors, yet with good taste. Brilliant letters stated their route, some with fire picture panels on the side, or pictures of Washington, Lady Washington, Lafayette, or Andrew Jackson. Others had illustrations of American history; they were evidently painted by good artists, and were spirited and effective.

The stages were tugged over the rough pavements by wiry, powerful horses. Although officially called "omnibuses," they were popularly known as "stages." They were constructed like an old time stage-coach, entered from the rear by two steps. The door was controlled by a strap which ran overhead and through a hole to the drivers' foot, by which he could slack up or close it. The New York City stage-drivers were a different type from the English stage-drivers I have read about; they had that lean, tense look of skippers on a small craft, as they munched their quids as they guided their horses over the slippery cobblestones, through the counter currents of horses and trucks, stages and bewildered countrymen.

Their lean, leather-jawed faces were blistered by the sun and as a rule bearded, but shaved on the upper lip. The beard, they claimed, helped to protect them against the bitter gales and storms that swept down Broadway and the cross streets, and round their lofty perches called "the box." Masters of their Art, some of them claimed they could put their wheels over a three cent piece. The stage-drivers must have had great strength to bring up their team on the slippery pavement, while scooping up passengers as well as answering their foolish questions, but as a rule they were not talkative as the English drivers are said to be, rather taciturn, except to one who knew how to win their hearts like Walt Whitman.

One idler asked a driver, "Do you know me?" "I'd know your hide in a tan-yard!" he answered and closed the conversation.

When a passenger pulled the strap, the driver played out on it and the door swung open. When the passenger alighted, the driver brought it up with a bang and whipped up. The fare was ten cents, which was passed up through a hole in the front. The drivers worked a zigzag course to each side of the street to pick up passengers. They would draw close up to the curb to save a lady from walking through the slippery scum of mud with which Broadway always seemed coated, but the men had to run for it and jump aboard as the driver merely slackened up.

I usually rode beside the driver, but when that seat was occupied, I would go inside and study with profit the interesting and artistic little panels of landscape scenes which were placed like a frieze above the stage windows. They were well colored and composed, and must have been above the average to have made such an impression on me. On account of the size of their hoop skirts, it was no easy undertaking for a woman to enter the stage and take a seat. I can remember as a small boy being almost extinguished by the billowing skirts of the lady passengers.

On one occasion, there was a small girl with a couple of ladies, and as there was no seat for her, I had to stand up, according to the training of my mother. She had little hoop skirts, like an inverted champagne glass, below which dangled a pair of stiff, scalloped pantelettes, the bottoms of which were all punctured with eyelets. When a woman sat down, nothing could be seen of her but a little moon face under a shell-like straw hat and long fluffy curls. It was the custom of gentlemen to hand up a lady's fare and return the change; everything was sociable and friendly—no such thing as "class."

From the top of the stage looking down Broadway, it seemed white with the roofs of stages blistering in the sun. A stately lady entered, handed up her fare and took a seat, a fire laddie handing her the change. She said, "I gave the driver fifty cents; he gave me change for a quarter." The "b-hoy," as they called the Bowery boys, gave her message through the little hole, but the driver insisted that it was a quarter. "Please tell him he is mistaken," the lady calmly replied—at which the "b-hoy," jerked the strap and bellowed through the hole, "This lady says you're a damned liar, and if you don't fork over that change, I'll come up and haul you off the box!"

"Joyous Broadway" was to be seen just after the first snowfall. The snow seemed to start everyone a-tingling. Stage sleighs were brought out, drawn by four horses, all a tinkling with bells; these were quickly filled with passengers on business or pleasure, well wrapped and with feet buried in piles of straw. The passengers all talked, joked and occasionally joined in song, while snowballs from small boys only added to their merriment.

The stage sleighs were generally yellow, with bodies ten or twelve feet long; a high seat for the driver, while the passengers sat face to face, with a trampled mound of straw between them. The fare was 10 cents. Many private sleighs with be-furred drivers, brought prominent business men, wrapped in buffalo robes, to their offices. Heavy tub sleighs laden with freight, and carts with emergency runners attached to their wheels, passed up and down, and the stages moved swiftly in their smooth ruts. Old and young men, boys and occasionally girls with stumps of brooms or shovels, cleared the crosswalks for what they could make from passers-by.

The big policemen in rubber boots helped the pretty women, and supported the old and feeble between a double line of frothing, steaming horses' heads brought to a halt by his signal. The snow had hushed all noise of rumbling and tumult; the boom of Broadway was temporarily silenced, while all mingled in joyous chaff and laughter amid the tinkle and jingle of the bells.

I remember hearing a story about one hideous night in winter, the sleet and storm was terrible. A stage lumbered into the old Knickerbocker Stables, the steaming horses halted, the starter called to the driver, he sat stark and dead—frozen at his post, but still gripping the reins.

## Barnum's Museum

Sometimes my mother and father would take me to P. T. Barnum's Museum—on the corner of Broadway and Ann Street. This was the "Land of Promise" for all good boys and girls. As I remember, it was a large, light colored building, five stories high. It had a balcony over the first floor, and facing Broadway was an expansive banner on which was painted the latest wonder of the world, and behind it a band was constantly playing. Between the windows was a large oval painting of some beast, bird, or creeping thing. Flags were displayed at almost every point, and here I found the people of my fancy realized: giants, in the person of Miss [Anna Haining Bates] Swan, eight feet [seven feet five inches] high, and dwarfs, such as Commodore [George Washington Morrison] Nutt. "What Is It?" was what Barnum called one of his curious creatures which many said was an idiot Negro boy. Here I also saw Barnum's white whale, and Ned the trained seal, who had an almost uncanny intelligence.

There was a little theatre called the "Lecture Room," out of consideration for the Deacons who could visit it with their families without scandal, and see the most blood-curdling plays with an easy conscience. The country people, so as to get all they could for their money, used to bring their lunches and stay all day, thus filling up the building. Barnum got the best of this game by putting a sign over one of the doors in flaring letters—"To the Egress." The rurals taking this for some rare specimen of a wild animal would crowd through the door—and land in the street without a return ticket.

There was a portrait of Amerigo Vespucci—the sight of it and its association with the injustice to Christopher Columbus, developed my spirit of "first aid" to the historically injured; oh, how I hated that picture.

My parents usually took me to Barnum's, but one time I went with my friend Charlie Curtis. In the scuffle to get into the Lecture Room, I found myself smothered—my face jammed in the long light blue tails of a soldier's overcoat. I put my arms around him, and, like the wren borne on the back of the eagle aloft to the sun, I found myself carried to my goal—the front row in the balcony.

Then came the delicious moments of suspense, while the audience waited for wonders that were behind the curtain, and such a curtain! It was painted with large cards scattered in every direction and overlapping one another, on which were written all sorts of advertisements. This was the only literary flavor to be found there. All the while, fiddlers were kept tuning up long enough to enable every one to read over all the cards till they got them by heart.

Then the lecture consisted of the freaks being lined up and the lecturer would question them as to their height (or lack of it), weight, etc., and they would file off. Then with a crash from the band, the curtain rolled up and we soon got goose flesh over the blood-curdling play, unsurpassed by any in the Old Bowery Theatre.

## The Bowery and the Old Bowery Theatre

One day, a boyhood friend asked me to go with him to collect a bill for his mother. We started—I knew not where. We finally reached some shipyards on the East River. I can remember the long stretch of yard, the frames of partly finished vessels, and the little crib of an office. Nothing else seemed to be in sight, except heaps of yellow pine along the shore.

Receiving his money we started back. On our way up one of the side streets, we were halted by a gang of youngsters of about our age, the leader with a table knife in his hand. They did not pay any attention to me, but began to close around my friend. He looked scared, and backing against an iron railing, took out a roll of bills saying, "Jim, here you take care of this."

The toughs immediately turned on me. The young man with the knife yelled, "Give me the money!" At which I put the money into my pocket. He again ordered to give it up, and I began to whimper as though thoroughly frightened. This threw him off his guard, and lowering his knife, he, in a contemptuous manner, started to cuff me. I let out and smashed him in his unguarded face. He gave a yowl and started for an ash barrel for ammunition.

I bolted off and around various streets, heading west till at last I found myself badly blown, under the cool shade of Anderson's Carpet Warerooms on the Bowery. Anderson used to advertise by hanging strips of carpet on the inside of his awning, and extending down to the sidewalk, forming a cooling arbor. The sidewalk was also covered with carpets, and with huge embankments of roll carpets on each side.

My friend soon trailed after looking rather sheepishly and I gave him his money. Feeling safe, we began to look around. The "Old Bowery Theatre" was opposite on the block below, so we wandered down, while I told him I had been in there many times with my father and mother; I had seen George L. Fox, in the pantomime of *Jack and the Bean Stalk*. We peeked into the Atlantic Garden next door, and amused ourselves watching the fat Dutchman, as they sat round the tables drinking. They were Germans of course, but Dutch to us.

Entering the Old Bowery Theatre, there were steps leading down into what was called the "Pit." This was the last theatre to retain it. Right and left, the stairs led up to the Dress Circle. Then came another balcony. The "B'hoys" and their "G'hals" of all ages, took possession of the front rows, and became dictators to the policy of the house. While they dictated to the house, there was one man who dictated to them. He stood there in grim majesty, in his shirt sleeves, with a long cane. He was called "Johnny the Post." He had several bruisers as assistants, and when the "B'hoys" became too uproarious, a sharp rap of his cane on the back of his seat, called them to order, and if not responded to, they were jerked from the rest and thrown out of the theatre. The first thing they did on taking their seats was to peel off their coats roll up their sleeves of their red shirts, shy their old quids into the "Pit" on some friends below, and load up with a fresh one, fold their tattooed arms, and settle down to criticize the play. They all seemed to have an ambition to look alike, by trying to stick out their lower jaw after the fashion of some under-shot. They talked out of the side of their mouths, and many of the older ones had a tuft of hair on their chin, with long soap locks pulled down over the ears. Even the small boys affected it, and tried to talk as husky as possible.

The "Pit" contained the same sort of specimens, only it seemed to me there were more newsboys and bootblacks there, and the chaff that took place between the acts, showed them to have friendly relations.

The galleries were filled with a better class of people, who came to see the one good play that took place during the evening. There was generally a tragedy, then some blood and thunder business, and followed by a comedy which lasted till one o'clock in the morning.

After the theatre, a good many of the patrons would line up in front of the nearby Oyster Stands. These were a sort of shanty built against a corner dead wall. A flat door swinging from above admitted the light, and framed a sort of shelter to the little counter, which supported the plates of the customers, also a bottle of catsup, pepper, salt, and lemons.

The Oyster Man generally had a nautical flavor about him. His hair bobbed in the back; a string of hair running around his throat; a square bushy tuft on the end of his chin, and the usual bulge in the cheek indicating a quid. They were generally a very serious set of men. I never saw an oyster man smile.

He had his oyster block on a little shelf inside, with his baskets underneath. On the other side of him was a small stove on which he cooked his stews and fries. Everything around him was compact and shining as a ship's galley, from which he had probably graduated; although his customers generally addressed him as "Captain." The rest of the little cabin was pretty well crowded with a couple of tables for ladies and "gents" who chose to sit down. While the walls were decorated with advertisements of the coming local excursion, lithographs of the yacht *America* winning the Queen's Cup, or the fight between the *Monitor* and *Merrimac*, or the [John] Hennan and [Thomas] Sayers Fight, but the fries that I have eaten here, are the only ones over which my memory lingers.

But, back to earth—Steve and I crossed the street from the Old Bowery Theatre to look in the window of a hair restorer, or wig maker, who had a wax head in the window with a clock-work arrangement that lifted the hair up and down, showing the head almost bald or with a luxurious growth. The dentist next door had upright showcases with gold leaf hung in festoons, and some especially vicious looking teeth dangled from strings, and about a bushel of ordinary teeth in the bottom of the case.

We stopped to browse in the window of Simpson's famous pawn shop, with its fascinating collection of old swords, medals, tools and trinkets; then past the clothing stores where we amused ourselves by sassing the "pullers in"—the Jewish shopkeepers that stood outside their stores. The way they would appeal or scuffle with anyone they thought fair game, would beat any Eighth Avenue merchant. There was a vicious roughness about these Bowery "pullers in," that they did not have on Eighth Avenue.

The composer Stephen Foster, in his last days stopped at a lodging house in No. 15 and died on January 13, 1864 at Bellevue Hospital, registered as a laborer. I can recall the time when his songs were sung on every side; they could open floodgates of the Nation's tears, but not the steel nippers of its wallets.

A Fife and Drum Corps came along heading a parade. The procession consisted of some bowed old men, who, to our eyes, seemed somewhat grotesque with their white beards running around their lower jaws which hung slack with age, and would only come together to shift their quids of tobacco. They wore high collars and leather neck-stocks. The collars of their coat came way up to their ears, and their blue coats, which hung loosely over their shrunken shoulders, were short in the waist, and meant to be tight in the sleeves; long swallow tails extended below the calf of the leg. They wore old fashioned hats, with a tall red, white and blue plume upon the side. I did not thoroughly appreciate that these shuffling old fashioned men were Veterans of the War of 1812.

Freight cars came along, drawn by six horses. They were bringing them from the freight depot on White and Center Streets, up to 27th Street where the passenger depot then was. On the couplings and on the top of the cars, clustered like flies, stealing a ride, were men and boys.

The old milestone which faced Rivington Street, attracted our attention, and we crossed over to examine it. It was inscribed, "One mile from City Hall," and sat over three feet above the sidewalk. It was made of white marble, but it showed signs of age; as to color, it was badly battered by trucks passing, while the top had a high polish from its years of use as a perch for idle men and boys. We paid the usual compliment by leaping over it.

Continuing our journey, passing 5th Street, where at No. 5, my mother lived when she first came to this country from Ireland. Next door, Singer lived while he was perfecting the sewing machine in the 1850's. His daughter used to take my mother in and show her the machine on which her father was working. Singer was very poor at the time, and his wife and daughter used to sing in some of the minor theatres to help support him.

Across the way at the junction of 6th Street and Bowery, Third and Fourth Avenues began. North of this was Cooper Union. Sometime before, my father had taken me to see the remains of the Stuyvesant pear tree, so I took Steve up to look at it again. It was planted by Peter Stuyvesant himself 200 years before. It was old and scraggy, and had a high iron railing around it to protect it, but in 1867, a baker's wagon ran into it, and knocked it down. Later, a small shoot started from the roots, like a bean pole.

Our legs gave out about this time, and we took the Third Avenue cars to 59th Street, and went home.


## East Side—Canal Street

From the time I was about nine years old, I used to take trips to the house of an old friend of my mother's, at 203 Henry Street, to play with the children, who were about my own age. I rode down in the Eighth Avenue horse car, which had a branch line running over to Canal Street and Broadway, and would then walk east through Canal Street, which seemed to have an unusual number of lager beer saloons in both the stores and cellars. There also were a great many oyster saloons, or "Oyster Bays," as they dignified some of them, which were distinguished by a red canvas transparency in the shape of a ball painted red, in which a candle was lit at night.

Finally reaching where Canal Street starts from East Broadway, I crossed the angle and noticed a most marked change in the character of the street and buildings, which were high, broad, dignified and characteristic—originally built by old-time merchants, when they thought that the tide of society was drifting in that direction.

The block of Henry between Clinton and Jefferson Streets, was built of fine brick, with white or brownstone moldings and trimmings; they were about five stories high, and had stoops with iron railings and balconies. Doors were ornamented with arched fan-lights and graceful moldings; roofs crowned with wooden balustrades and, in many cases, they had cupolas. Probably the original owners may have been shipping merchants, who made use of them from which to scan with their telescopes our glittering bay for a sight of their incoming argosies. Number 195 Henry was the house in which Edgar Allen Poe boarded at the time he edited the *Broadway Journal*, with its offices in Clinton Hall.

Turning into Clinton Street, to Henry, at No. 203, I reached the home of my friend. Like most of the streets of the time, it was paved with large cobblestones, and each side was bordered with lofty trees. Many of the houses had tree-boxes, a carriage block and hitching post in front. The house I visited was a very good specimen—a scraper on the stoop for muddy feet, and a highly polished brass knocker and knob on the white doorway. The halls were broad and the stairs had heavy mahogany balustrades, with a nitch for a statue at the top of the stairway. Doors were of mahogany, with glass knobs, and occasionally ornamental moldings and cornices. From the center hung a heavy, gilded chandelier, from which dangled cut-glass prisms or clusters, while the mantels were either marble or of wood, elaborately carved by some neighboring ship carver. Huge conch shells were at each side of the grate, before which was a heavy rug and glowing Brussels carpet. Some of the houses, which were still occupied by the original owners, were furnished in a sumptuous, yet cozy manner.

Lace curtains backed with red silk damask were a characteristic. Fine mahogany was the heritage of many families, but some of the more up-to-date had more spindley furniture covered with haircloth. Between the windows was the usual large mirror, with a small table on which rested an enormous family bible and two or three small gift books. On the marble center table were several daguerreotypes, one representing father and mother sitting side by side very primly, with his arm around her waist.

But what appealed to me most were the paintings of father and mother in those homes, as they were apt to be good ones—for they were painted in the days of Thomas Sully, Henry Inman and Samuel F. B. Morse. Sometimes father was represented as sitting in an easy chair, and beside him a table on which was a map, telescope or a captain's trumpet—and out of a window in the background could be seen a vessel under full sail. In other homes the father might be represented with a white-fronted fireman's helmet on the table and beside it his trumpet as foreman. Mother was shown demure and sweet, with a small, white ruffled cap which most women assumed at marriage.

Most homes had portraits of George and Martha Washington, and many of the more pretentious had large engravings of Cole's *Voyage of Life*. In one home was a small mahogany piano almost black with age, whose keys, instead of the conventional ivory, were made of mother-of-pearl. On the wall was also a framed lithograph of Col. Elmer E. Ellsworth, of the famous First Regiment of Zouaves; conspicuous in the music was the score of *The Vacant Chair*. A what-not stood in the corner, each shelf full of curios and knick-knacks.

Small, glass-enclosed extensions were added to many of the houses, in which the family used to dine in summer; they looked out on yards with grape arbors and healthy looking vines, well stocked flower beds, and fences overgrown with mock-orange vines intermingled with morning glories. One day while playing with the children, I looked out over the yard, and next door saw in one corner a sort of rustic summer house, or cabin, on the flat roof of which were vines, vegetables and fruits. Asking what it meant, I was told that they commemorated the Jewish festival of Succoth. I saw two or three others indicated over the tops of neighboring fences—the first evidence I saw of the Jewish emigration and influence which was finally to take possession of that whole section.

There were a good many Quakers in that neighborhood, and quite a number of the young men belonged to the Volunteer Fire Department. It was much to the credit of the neighboring fire companies that, although it was the custom to fight for the right of way to a fire, they respected the principles of the members of this company, and never fought with the Quakers.

## Fulton Ferry

Standing on the curb at South Street, I faced Fulton Ferry—the old one. A loud bump, a clatter of ratchet wheels, and clank of chains, indicated a boat had made fast in the slip. The gates were thrown open. The passengers rushed off, intermingling with those rushing on, like shuttles interweaving their lines of fate.

A Brooklyn crowd seemed to be a class different from New Yorkers, looking crisper, newer, with indications of a keener thrift. Not so many extremes; small tradesmen, clerks, none common or poor; a pleasant, cheerful, almost suburban crowd. The men looked as though they were going home to rest. The women and children looked happy, as though returning from a day's pleasure, and were still full of it.

I joined them, and was pushed and jammed by those rushing for New York. There were no gates at that time to control the traffic, so it was a free for all to get either way. At last I boarded the boat. With a toot, a snort, a groan, a wheeze, the swashing paddle wheels sent us heaving out of the slip, where we swung with the strong current. Getting her grip, the sturdy boat shouldered its way against the tide.

The Fulton Ferry always had pleasant associations for me as a child, when I lived in Brooklyn, during the early Civil War days when everything was a thrill. And when I grew older and learned its history, it was intensified. It was the first ferry in New York, and the first steam ferry to Brooklyn. It was designed by Robert Fulton in 1812, on the same lines as the present vessels. The floating bridge, which rose and sank with the tide, helped by counterbalancing weights, was also his design.

Fulton's design became the model for all ferry boats and when Fort Sumter was fired on, the Government bought many of them. Their light draft, strong construction and broad beam, made them fine gun platforms for the shallow rivers of the South. One ferry, called the *Southfield*, was commanded by Lieutenant [Charles W.] Flusser, and was attacked by the Rebel ram, *Albemarle* [on April 19, 1864]. The *Southfield* was sunk, and its young commander killed. He was a close friend of Lieutenant [William B.] Cushing, and he determined to avenge his death. With this seething in his heart, he perfected his plans, and by his brilliant valor, sank the *Albemarle* [on October 27, 1864] and won added glory for our Navy.

As our boat neared the dock, there being no gates, the passengers vied with one another in jumping ashore before she struck. It was a source of pride how wide a space one could clear. So many accidents happened here, that they eventually had to put up gates.

# Fulton Market

Dodging under horses' heads, or wagon poles, between the trucks and carts, and entering Fulton Market from the crisp cool air, was a most stimulating experience. On the street side were principally oyster or eating stands. They did most of their cooking on the counters which faced the passing crowd, where their bright coffee urns steamed under full headway.

The first thing that impressed me on entering was the savor of rich coffee, fried oysters, butter cakes, fruits and spices. But mingled with all, was the balsam odor of fresh pine saw dust, which always suggested cheer, probably from its association with the old time circus. But the combination of odors gave a bouquet peculiar to that place alone. I know not what to call it, except the fragrance of Fulton Market.

The Market was a one story building occupying the entire block, with wooden awnings overhanging the sidewalks, and connecting a row of stalls or little cabins which ran along and over the gutters and out into the street for about fifteen feet. The stalls ran round the entire building.

Inside were more pretentious markets. The most celebrated was Dorlan's Oyster Market and Saloon—famous throughout the land; it was the place for Society to have oyster suppers when seeing the Town.

Through all the gangways thronged a bustling, good natured crowd. The big rosy-cheeked butchers, distinctly American, with their shiny high silk hats tilted slightly over the back of their heads, greeted their customers over their big diamond breast pins which flamed above the bibs of their crisp flowing linen aprons. The butter men's faces, as they beamed over their golden bulwarks, seemed to reflect the rosy glow of the fruit stands opposite. A prominent one was presided over by an old Irish woman, Mrs. C., whose face had a patrician outline; I never saw a finer head, or knew a kinder heart.

Gangways were banked high with huge crates of wild pigeons. At that time they sold for about ten cents each. I hear now that one thousand dollars is offered for a live one, as they are supposed to be extinct. Back on the counters, from the hook racks hung game both furred and feathered. Rows of rabbits, among them a coon, or ratty looking possum dangled. An enormous black bear hung head down; also a couple of bucks.

The birds were of such a variety, it would take a naturalist to name them. In my boyish vernacular, they were turkeys, ducks and geese. The plumage was rich in coloring, and the sheen on their throats took on an additional brilliancy by reflecting the gas lights in the gangways, although it was still daylight outside. Yet, dead birds were flabby looking, and never inspired me. They suggested the work of sordid pet hunters. But a deer, dead or alive, from the curved prongs of his antlers to the tip of his dainty sinewy legs, was a graceful sight, while a dead bear suggested the skill and pluck of the man in buckskin who brought him down.

Being a hearty boy, I was distracted from what might have been a mental feast for an epicure, to a more immediate appeal. The aroma of coffee and the appetizing whiff from buttered griddle cakes, was too much for me, so I entered one of the little cabin-like cozys. The coffee came steaming. The cakes came steaming. And a bulky nugget of golden butter in the center of the table, rounded out my happiness.

While I was disposing of them, a tall young gentlemanly looking man came in. He looked like an Englishman just landed. He wore a shiny high hat well burnished. He had a fresh, sunburned complexion; a reddish-blond beard which was bleached at the ends by the sun. His coat was overbrushed till it had suffered—its shoulders also showed the effects of the sun and it also was a little short in the sleeves—no cuffs. His hands were shapely, but overwashed and red looking. He stepped over to the man in charge. I gathered he was pricing things. He went out and came back shortly, with a pretty little brown-haired, brown-eyed, girlish woman, whose hat and clothes also suggested England.

They sat at a table near me. He ordered a stew for each. Then as they started to eat they got their heads together, and talked very earnestly. After finishing the stew, they asked for coffee. She took out her handkerchief, and from a knot in the corner took out some change. As she did so, I saw a little white streak running the fourth finger of her pretty little sunburned hand, which was stenciled and showed where the absent wedding ring had been. After handing him the change, she hid her bare little hand under the table. A few days after, I saw him at a hack stand—Park entrance, Fifth Avenue. He had evidently gotten a job. I have heard my mother say that when a young Englishman or Irish gentleman could find nothing else, he could drive a horse, and she had seen friends of hers driving carriages here whose fathers had coachmen of their own back home.

## Chatham Street and the Five Points

The pictorial part of Chatham Street ran through from City Hall to Chatham Square. It was finally written up—or written down—so much, either by those of excessive imagination, or excessive ambition to be considered realistic, that the honored name of Chatham was changed to the nondescript one of Park Row.

Chatham Street buildings were, as a rule, low, narrow and stale looking; usually two or three stories high, nearly all with awnings in front to protect their goods from the weather. They extended out to the curb, some made of wood all the way, while others were on canvas rollers and could be drawn back. From their beams dangled lines and lines of coats and pants that seemed to caper in the brisk breezes.  Before each of the doorways were one or more sturdy, thickset young Jews, called "pullers-in."

They were popularly supposed to collar and pull in any unwary passerby, clap a suit of clothes on him and take his money, but I never saw anything to justify this reputation, for which I think Jewish comedians and impersonators in the variety shows were mainly responsible.  Of course they would call your attention to their goods, and would try to make a sale by wheedling, but the rough-house stories of the pullers-in were on a par with the stories of the Scotchmen's farthing pinching.  Through the small window panes could be seen more suits of clothes decked out with cards across them calling attention to their merits, such as: "OUR OWN TASTE," "THIS IS A CHANCE," "EDWIN FORREST STYLE," "DON'T MISS THIS GAY AND DASHING," and the like. Expansive plaids, broad stripes and loud colors seemed to be "our style" in Chatham Street.

Of course some of the pullers-in were tough customers, but look at the neighbors and passerby they had to handle!  And the tales of adventure or terror the rural visitors brought back from "York!"  They were suspicious of everything. I saw one gangly gawk pick up a roll of bills right in front of me.  He turned it over, and looked around with a "can't fool me" expression and a knowing grin, threw it on the sidewalk, where it was snatched up by a newsboy who scooted with it.  The fellow was afraid of what he knew not.  Of course smarties in search of adventure got as good as they sent, while long experience made them experts in giving "back lip."  Whenever I had reason to speak to any of the pullers-in, I always found them civil and obliging.

Turning onto Baxter Street, I struck one of the rays from the celebrated Five Points.  Here we began to get the effect from the City's ulcer—Pearl, Baxter, Park, Worth and Chatham Streets meeting in this hot-bed of inequity.  Chatham was bad, but Baxter was worse.  What a pity it was that such a street should be associated with the name of the young hero, Col. Charles Baxter who died in the Mexican War.

I suppose it was so full of "Land Sharks" or "Land Pirates" who formed a haven of refuge here to dispose of their plunder.  These little dens or shops were almost hidden by dangling second hand clothes which hung in festoons almost as high as the second story windows.  Strings of shoes dangled in front of the dens and junk of all kinds filled boxes—in fact anything that could be begged, borrowed or stolen.  And yet these rascals were a superstitious lot, and were played upon by the interested ones going on a Monday morning feeling sure that they could get anything for what they offered, as these sharks would not let their first customer go without purchasing, for fear it might bring them bad luck.

I walked past rows of old buildings with jagged roof lines, cobbled with misfit planks and sheets of rusty tin roofing.  It was hard to discover the original color of the paint on buildings, many of which were survivals of old New York village days.  This area was a great resort for the Fenian brotherhood, and around its portals were groups of tall, sad-eyed enthusiasts in slouch hats with long flowing moustaches, like their own ancient galloglasses, and among them were mingled ferret-eyed professional patriots in shiny double breasted broad cloth coats.    Beneath these layers in the cellars were dance halls; the entrance decorated with signs showing flags and coat of arms of foreign nations as a bait for "Jack Ashore."

The big boot in Chatham Street was one of the most noted signs in the city, and became part of the local vernacular.  It was a huge model of a red-topped, peg-soled, square-toed boot, such as were commonly worn by boys and workmen.  It was about eight feet high, and built in proportion, and painted realistically with a red front at the top.  It stood at the entrance to Schuster's Boot and Shoe Emporium on the east side of Park Row between Mulberry and Mott Streets.  It seemed to strike the fancy of everyone, and was known to everybody in the city, as well as to many in the country, and became quite a conspicuous feature when mounted on a wagon in a parade.  In fact it became such a feature that a popular oath by many when they declared themselves was "By the Big Boot in Chatham Street."

Scattered among the Jew Clothiers were open fronted stores, no awnings, each bore the sign of the "Original Cheap John" and each one claiming to be it—they auctioned everything from plug hats, a suit of clothes, a chair, or a watch. They were part-showman, part-salesman, and part-auctioneer of inferior goods. Our family doctor got a very valuable watch in one of these places by bidding it and by snapping it from the Original John's hand before he had time to flim-flam it to a cheap one.  My father was with him.  I noticed in all my father's tales about Dr. Clow, he never mentioned his own part in them.  These Cheap Johns blackguarded each other, wheedled the clueless passersby and entertained the knowing ones.

The Five Points received its name from the crossing of Baxter, Worth and Park Streets.  The old weather-beaten houses seemed to lean and sag against each other like the boozing gang that lined in front of the gin-mills or squatted on the kegs and barrels or lounged against the fire plugs or lying in the gutter where the curb was buried under piles of ashes.

"Five Points!"  What tales of terror that name recalls, and what a blight it has left upon that section!  I often wonder how much Dickens gave rein to his fancy and if he transferred some of his recollections of London crime and squalor in his description of this locality in his *American Notes*.

With these ideas, and my usual desire for exploring, I started out to see for myself, and must say that in my trip I saw evidence of squalid poverty and dissipation, but of crime, nothing.  Junk shops were in great numbers, but gin mills led with at least one on each block, on either side of the way.  Some of the buildings which had been substantial in times past were made of brick with their gable ends to the street, the small oval windows near the peak, Dutch fashion. Like many of the older buildings, their roofs were blanketed with old tin roofing; their chimneys were jagged or rounded at their tops, the bricks said to have been wrenched off in bygone riots, to be fired at the police and other objectionable intruders on the privacy of the "Points."

Many windows were broken, those that were not, being so grimy that the inmates had to open them to look out; whether it was the fondness for the view, or to escape the fumes inside, they spent most of their time lolling out on the window sills. Broad or narrow alleys ran along the sides of the houses to some battered crib in the rear. A few were made of brick, others were like pigeon houses or dog houses knocked together by some small boy. In the rear of these houses were yards, many with fences gone but a post or two still standing; these spaces were clustered with old wagons or carts, trucks and hand carts, some of which had stood so long exposed to rain and sunshine that their wheels were sprung, their loosened tires lying on the ground, and so thick with rust that they seemed to blaze in the sunshine. Those wagons made a fine lounging place for the local sports afflicted with the "day-after fever" to store up energy for their night-to-come revels.

Hearing yells up an alley on the other side of the street, I went over and up; it was so packed and crowded that I could only get glimpses of two fellows battering each other. No one seemed excited or to notice me. Children sprawled or played on the mounds of ashes, and one group was busily engaged sailing an old shoe in a puddle; tomato cans and old hoop skirt frames were scattered thickly over the street, and wolfish dogs foraged among the litter, which in most cases was up level with the curb. A wooden pump was at the corner where a couple of boys were at work by taking turns pumping water over the bare feet of their chums. A solitary young policeman was talking to a couple of toughs, and they were smiling at a scuffle going on among a group of boys. Up above a cellar entrance, an old woman popped her head, a cut bleeding over her gray hair; she mumbled in a dazed way, but no one seemed to notice her.

It is recorded by the Secretary of the Five Points Mission that in 1860, a tall, remarkable looking man entered the Sunday School. He watched the proceedings with interest, and being asked to say something to the children, he responded in strikingly beautiful language, and tones musical with intense feeling. The little faces would droop in sad conviction as he uttered sentences of warning, and brighten into sunshine as he spoke cheerful words of promise. As the visitor was leaving the room, the Secretary asked his name; the stranger courteously replied, "I am Abraham Lincoln, of Illinois."

## Lincoln's Second Election

The Presidential Campaign of 1864 impressed me vividly. My father, having a physical disability which prevented him from enlisting, let off his patriotism by having rows with the Copperhead neighbors, and celebrated his thirty-ninth birthday by taking out his [citizenship] paper, dated October 15, 1864, so that he might cast his vote for Lincoln.

The Campaign [Abraham Lincoln vs. George B. McClellan] was very bitter on both sides in our neighborhood, except in our own house and a few others.

"Little Mac" was the watch-word. To the "stay-at-home" Irishmen, he stood for peace. The loyal ones, when not encumbered, were all at the front on the line of fire. Both priests and ministers were conspicuously patriotic. The

Irish "wimen," in many cases, thought if McClellan were elected on "The War is a Failure" platform, their husbands would come back from the front.

The streets were overhung with banners, decorated (or defaced) with so called portraits of Lincoln and [Andrew] Johnson and McClellan and [George H.] Pendleton. There were the usual torchlight parades, and the air echoed with glorification of "Little Mac," and abuse of "Old Abe." The very curbstones were covered with election posters called "gutter snipes."

On the morning of Election Day, I looked out of the window and saw the polling for the first time.

The day was raw, cold and rainy. Boxes of rough pine boards were arranged along the curb with their back to the gutter in front of our house. They were about seven feet high and built like a sentry box. The roof was flat and beveled slightly to the rear. They were covered with posters and portraits, as well as the names of the candidates.

A man sat inside, with a shelf or board in front of him, from which he handed out ballots, held together with a rubber band, but he did not have much to do; for, at the sight of a voter, there was a rush of electioneering politicians who crowded around, and filled him up with election ballots. They then escorted him to the polls, one hundred feet away, in Hammond's grocery store.

I peeped in the doorway. Along the counter were some large glass globes resembling those used for goldfish, only they were closed on the top, and had supports on each corner like an hourglass. There was a slit in the top, through which was dropped the folded ballot. It could be seen as it fell into the globe. The room was filled with tobacco smoke, though I could dimly make out the glint of a policeman's buttons.

Before I could see more, I was hustled aside by a crowd of drunken roughs, who joggled the undisciplined voters swarming in and out at will. I saw a crowd on the corner starting to rush through 57th Street. I followed them to near Sixth Avenue, where they ran into another crowd, and began to pelt one another with stones.

As neither party seemed inclined to give way, they came to close quarters—so close that they threw the stones in the air so as to land on their opponents' heads. The air seemed full of them, like a flock of swallows. As they flew around me, I crouched behind an ash barrel, near the northwest corner, to dodge them.

Then a shot snapped out. The crowd ceased fighting. A fellow broke through and started to run up the half finished embankment which connected Fifth and Sixth Avenues.

The crowd started to follow but seemed to hesitate about closing in, and began pelting him with stones; at which he coolly stopped and pelted back at them, then ran along the embankment to Fifth Avenue and disappeared.

I returned to the south east corner. The man who had been shot was half lying, resting on his right arm, with his left hand on the wound in his breast, groaning heavily. He was a fine, handsome-looking workman, with black curly hair and beard. His blue shirt was dabbled with blood. I watched him long enough to impress the scene vividly upon me; when, hustled aside by the crowd, I trotted homeward, joining the other boys collecting ballots which were scattered thickly upon the sidewalks and along the gutters. In my ignorance I tried to find a ballot with the name of Lincoln on it, so I did not save what I found.

The short November day began to darken. According to the English custom, a voice rang out, "Hear ye! Hear ye! The polls are closed!" The crowd made a charge for the election boxes, carting them off to be used for the fires later in the evening.

The man in charge of the box opposite our door was an old, active politician. He was ninety, and disabled with rheumatism, which caused him to go on crutches. He had been sitting at his work in the election box, and was now so stiff he could not get out, so they had to pull the pine boards apart and peel him as they would a banana, while he was grumbling and beating off the surrounding boys with a crutch.

He was a conspicuous character around the neighborhood. He would come along on his crutches till he reached the corner, then turn around with a grim grin and say, "Which of yez bys kin help me across?" And we would rush to give him a boost. But if we ever presumed on this and bid him "Good morning," he would turn round and say, "I don't know ye." He only knew us at the crossings.

Night came on, cold, bleak, and drizzly. A bonfire was started before our door; the low-hanging clouds reflecting the other fires in every direction. The boys who had been stealing barrels for a month or so, now rolled them out of their cellars, or carried them on their heads in triumph. They built them into mounds before touching them off. The hollow booming of drygoods boxes, as they were rolled down the sidewalk, announced another kind of fuel for the flames.

With yells of a gang of large boys, the grocer's wagon was hauled along and run into the flames, but was rescued by the frantic German. Boys danced around and jumped through the flames, till at last, they were hauled off by the ear or the neck by their enraged mothers who had been hunting for them. Finally, the rain scattered the rest, and the embers died down under its dreary beat.

Next morning, my father was up bright and early, and called to us, "President Lincoln re-elected." Then we sat down to a joyous breakfast, while he read aloud the details of the victory.

# Winter

Winter's approach always oppressed me, and when at school I would see the first snowflakes, they seemed black and silhouetted against the leaden sky. It suggested suffering and cold and my heart would sink, but on school being dismissed the first tingling shock of a snowball, and the exultation of a well delivered one in return, drove quickly away my melancholy and the joys of winter were on.

I had been a weak little youngster and the doctor told me to take a rub down with salt water every morning, so I would take a basin of water and rock salt, but for good measure, I made it so strong it would hardly dissolve, and in the morning it would be partly frozen with the salt-like gravel. With this mean I would take a rub down, but in spite of it all it would leave me as gritty as sand paper. I believe one could have scratched matches on me. Then I would take a round out of the dumb bells which my mother had given me as a bribe to let her sew up my trouser pockets, so as to keep my hands from nesting there. I would then dress in a pair of soldier's pants cut down from my uncle's, which I imagined were warmer than any other, for in my fancy I thought the grateful Republic would give the very warmest stuff to the soldiers.

At that time I had not heard of the speculating Congressmen who starved our half-clad troops at Valley Forge, and that their financial successors had followed their methods in our Civil War. Nor did I know of shoddy contractors. So, it was the warmth of my imagination that made these soldier pants feel warm. I pulled on a fine pair of Napoleon boots with flaps above the knees, and after breakfast of buckwheat cakes, black molasses, sausages and hot coffee, I would put on my Scotch cap well down over my tow head, grab my shinny [hockey stick] and skates and start out for the day.

The first thing I would do was to go over to the sunken lot in 57th Street, pull off my boots and stockings, put my stockings in my pocket, rub my feet with snow and pull on my boots. I had heard that if one did not wear stockings, it would do no harm if they got their feet wet.

I would then screw on my skates and strapping them as tight as I could, and would put wedges of wood between the straps and the boot to make them tighter. By this time my feet were perfectly numb, and I would start off whether on the ice or on the street—the skates were on for the day.

When we got through skating on 56th Street pond, we would go over to 58th Street and cluster on the rocks and there wait till the strings of ashmen with their carts loaded with barrels of ashes slowly trailed up Broadway toward the shanties. We would pelt them with snowballs, and they would stand up in their carts and pelt back with volleys of cinders. Tired of this, we then started back to the ice.

Some of the boys had skates that their parents must have brought from Holland. I have seen the same kind in Dutch pictures. The runner projected very much beyond the foot and curled back over the toes with a brass knob on the end like on cow's horns. There were others of the same type but in a modified form.

One little girl, with sparkling black eyes and red cheeks, who seemed always busy munching a red apple, and wore a red cloak and hood, was an exact reproduction of Red Riding Hood with brown curls peeping out each side of her round face. We all rushed to put on her skates and she bullied us. She would then sit down on a rock and let one boy buckle each skate. She would then turn to us as she started off, throw her little snub nose in the air and say, "You, Jim and Pete, if these skates come loose, I'll settle your hash."

Some of the boys, too poor to buy skates, started to slide; others, after a while, would take off their skates and lend them to a chum, or in case of two, lend one each.  By this time we would get out our darts, which were made of a horseshoe nail stuck through a cork, with a couple of feathers at the butt.  With this attached to a string, we became very expert hitting things.  We would go round to Hammond's the Dutch grocer at 57$^{th}$ Street, and harpoon the potatoes from his baskets, then run for the lots.  The grocer would make a great show of chasing us, but as our mothers dealt with him I suppose he would put the potatoes down to profit and loss.  Going back to the lot we gathered wood and made a fire under some mound of rock, and marked our potatoes by small sticks which we drove in one, two, or three according to the numbers of boys.  When they were cooked and raked out of the embers we counted the number of holes and recognized our own.  Nothing tasted sweeter than these stolen potatoes with their quarter of an inch jacket of black cinders around them.

This, being wartime, many people were poor, very poor, though we did not know it.  I remember one long haired youngster running outdoors with a thin jacket and barefooted, watching our fun and dancing in the snow to keep his feet warm.  And when he could stand it no longer, he ran back into the house.  By this time we had taken off our skates and warmed our stiffened feet, then began to get restless for something to do.  It was suggested that we build a fort.  So we started to work piling up chunks of rock, some of them so large it took three or four boys to lift.  Another boy and I got a piece of old carpet to carry our rock between us.  This caught the eye of a larger boy named O'Rourke, but on account of his yellow complexion, we called him "Pine."

"Might being right," in his eyes he started to take it away.  I objected.  He knocked me down; I up and at him.  Down I went again; I got up and he was on me—flinging me on my back—cracking my head against a piece of rock.  I was just beginning to get warmed up.  I looked around to see if my mother was looking from the window, as I had promised her never to fight, and feeling more afraid of her reproachful eyes than his wary fists.  Then I was at it again.  Down again I went.  I felt no pain, but I was simply overpowered.  As my heroes never gave up, why should I?  Pine became careless and contemptuous.  As he lit out, I ducked and planted him in the left eye with my hard capped fist, giving a screw twist.  Down he went howling.  His friends helped him up and sat him on a large round stone.  They said, "Rourkie, don't give up."  "I am not giving up," he howled nursing his swollen eye, sniffing and crying and drooling like a sick pup, while I stood licking the salty sweat and blood from my lips—panting and peering at him through my swollen eyelids with a warm, tingling joy.

I never let up on myself—I always worked myself to the limit.  The fort remained many years and became quite a suggestive little ruin, and I shouldn't wonder, if the ground had not been built over, that some "Pick Wickian" scientists would by this time have written a dissertation on it as a pre-Adamite relic....or of the Stone Age.

# A Boyhood Reformation

Lying abed one morning when I was about nine or ten years old, I got to thinking of my past life, and came to the conclusion that I was a very idle and no good sort of boy, as I had been doing nothing but play and fight, and did little or no drawing.  So I made a resolution that I would change all that; so I got up and started at once to reform.  After school, instead of going out, I stayed in drawing soldiers, battle pieces, etc., which I kept up day after day.  My mother noticed the change and sent me out on various excuses, until she weaned me of my morbid condition.

When my mother used to read about the heroes of the war—Grant, Sherman, and especially Sheridan—I would say, "When I get to be a man, I am going to know all the Generals, and they are coming to see me." "When you get to be a man," my mother would say smiling.

In my fancy, I pictured a fine, white colonial mansion, like the Havemeyer homestead, set in a thick grove of lofty trees, with Sheridan and others in uniform walking around.  In after years, walking past my old home and looking up at the window where I used to sit with my mother and tell her my daydreams, the little prophesy came back.

# Triumph in New York

President Lincoln's second Inauguration and consequently the assured triumph of the Union Cause, stirred all patriotic citizens in New York to a most fervid state of enthusiasm, and on March 6, 1865, a most transcendent parade was organized as a public expression of their loyalty.  My mother in company with some friends took me down and watched the parade from the curb.

The contemporary accounts describe in detail of which I, as a child, received only detached impressions.

General Charles W. Sandford headed the parade in commanding thousands of veteran militia who marched behind their shot-torn flags to the heart-stirring war songs, *Rally Round the Flag, Boys* [*The Battle Cry of Freedom*], *Tramp, Tramp, Tramp, When Johnny Comes Marching Home.*

Dr. Valentine Mott rode at the head of the carriages containing invalid soldiers, which was an expression of his kind thought as well as generosity, as he paid the expenses himself.

There were many floats—those representing the Navy, with the *Hartford* and *Monitor* and other vessels; another with a derrick representing the striking of oil; others contained groups of all sorts of manufacturers.

But what most impressed my boyish vision were the Volunteer Firemen as they appeared that day.

The red shirts of the firemen in the strong sunlight looked like a river of flame above which the bright eagle crests on their helmets sparkled like golden spray.  The firemen marched with their joyous, jaunty swagger of young fellows feeling that the hearts of all were with them, and went through various evolutions. They marched in line inside the ropes forming a hollow square, the front line extending entirely across Broadway and then along the curbs to the tongue of the engine. Others would march grasping the rope with their left hand, with the right extended on the shoulder of a comrade.

They smilingly responded to the cheers and joyous greetings as they passed relatives and friends who attracted their attention in the crowd.

The engines' metal work was burnished to the highest state of perfection and decorated with their artistically painted panels, as well as with flags, flowers, and red-white-and blue streamers. While the delighted spectators from curb, window and house top, waved individual flags in rippling salute.

And extending across the entire course of the parade was a perfect arbor of flags as well as banners containing patriotic mottos. All seemed to flame the sunburst at: *The Dawn of Peace.*


## Richmond Captured! April 3, 1865

In school my teacher, Miss Egbert, left the room. Returning shortly, flushed and joyous, she called through the doorway, "Boys, Richmond's captured!"

There were short exclamations of pleasure, hitching in the seats, giggles and smiles, among the boys. We were too young for a demonstration before our teacher. She told us to go home at once and tell our mothers. That was an end to discipline. We rushed out with joyous shouts, yelling, "Richmond's captured!" And running to my mother, I told her the glorious news.

Soon there was the greatest excitement in the streets. "Extras" were bellowed by hoarse-voiced fellows, as well as shrilly calls by the boys. Flags were run up or out from the windows, also festoons of red, white and blue. The streets fairly flamed like a glorious sunrise saluting the stars. Flags of all sizes were on everything, as well as on men and horses. It was "a perfect jubilee of flags!" My mother made a red, white and blue rosette to pin on my breast beside my Lincoln badge, which I generally wore. In the evening the windows were illuminated with candles stuck with tin nippers to the sash.

Next day, on returning to school, all was a joyful bustle. The teachers and the larger boys were at work hanging and draping the Colors. As for the boys themselves, they looked like Field Marshals with medals and decorations. The pillars of the assembly room were swathed in bunting. Miss Bell's brother, a fine looking fellow, with a skill for decorating, ornamented the blackboards with patriotic emblems in colored chalks. What a wonder he seemed to me!

Saturday, April 15th, I was sitting with my mother at breakfast, when my father came in with a paper. His face was colorless and his eyes were full of tears. In a dazed manner and husky voice he said, "President Lincoln has been shot."

My mother began to sob, while I sat overcome with their sorrow, with my heart like a stone.  But while there was life, there was hope; and all that tense, hideous day we waited—waited for the news.

Boys shrieked out the latest "Extras," and a fresh horror to it, was the hollow bellowing of the men with bundles of "Extras" over their shoulders, with black borders, telling in advance the blow which the Nation had received.

My mother got some crepe and hung it on the window.  She then put some crepe over the red, white and blue ribbon which hung from my little medal.  I went into the street and looked down the Avenue, and my mother's black streamer was the only "mourning" in sight.

How long after, I do not recall, but long enough to impress me with the delay and make my mother's very conspicuous, and later some of our neighbors began to drape their windows.  And people twined crepe over their flags, as they hung them at half staff.  Next day it became universal, and people tried to outdo one another with pictorial evidence of their grief.  Black-bordered pictures of Lincoln appeared in the windows.

The Germans made the greatest display.  One lager beer saloon near 34th Street had a large, white "Temple of Liberty" built on the curb, its thirteen pillars draped in crepe, a bust of Lincoln inside of it, lighted with candles.  The crowd surged round it with admiration.  One girl in the crowd expressed her approval in these words, "Its de finest show in de hull Ate Avnye."

On Monday [April 17] when we assembled in school, the boys had black crepe tied over their Union rosettes.  In the Assembly Room, the pillars had stripes of black over the Union colors which were wound around them, and black was mingled with the flags of rejoicing.

All the old rancor against Lincoln was forgotten.  The name of Lincoln stood for Union.  Now it seemed to unite all—at least on the surface.  There was no more "Old Abe"; it was now "Father Abraham."

My father told us he saw a crowd beating a man.  A policeman came up and asked what was the matter.  "He said he was glad Lincoln was killed!" was the reply.  "Give it to the ————," said the policeman, and walked away.

Another case, when a man on the Brooklyn Ferry said he was glad Lincoln was killed, they threw him overboard, and he was drowned.

Lincoln lay in state in the City Hall [on April 25].  Why I was not taken to see him I cannot understand.  I know my father went, but my mother did not.  Nor did I see the funeral, which passed through 34th Street.  Things are hazy about that period; possibly I was sick, which would account for it.  The memory of this loss has had its effect on me, for I have always given a child a chance to see historic events.  As in parades, I put them in front of me, as I did a small boy, when the Seventh Regiment marched to the front on the way to France in 1917.

# The Carpet Beaters

With a couple of chums I started down 58th Street in the direction of Ninth Avenue. It was just a wagon track and curved a little way up on the south side. On the north side, was a rickety barn and a straggly fence for about a hundred feet or so, back of this was a market garden which reached through 59th Street; a break in the fence led to another barn then the ground rose gradually till it nearly reached Ninth Avenue. As it neared Ninth, there was a ledge of rocks and on its crest, a weather-beaten old farm house and out buildings, overhung by immense knarled willow trees. There was a row of large, old cherry trees running south toward the Havemeyer Homestead, or as we called it, the White House.

Here 58th Street ended with a sort of a little pond at the foot of an abrupt cliff of rocks about twenty feet high. Climbing these we found a party of negro carpet beaters who as a rule located there, having brought their carpets from the city by an old ramshackle wagon drawn by an aged, ewe-necked, sway-backed, spavined, gray nag with long shaggy fetlocks. It was a perfect comedy nag, but seemed too good to be true.

The negros used to spread out their carpets in the sunshine, and beat them with long, flexible wooden rods held in each hand. We used to think it great fun to help them sweep the carpets, and felt we were amply repaid by keeping all the pins we found. The front of our jackets used to bristle with them.

As we neared the cloud of dust which hung over the carpet beaters, one big sullen negro stood up and growled, "Be you Irish?"

"No," I answered, "My father's Scotch."

"Is your father a Democrat?"

"No. He's a Republican."

"Then he's not glad Mars Linkum's dead?"

"No."

At this, an aged white-headed negro who was kneeling at this work, looked up with his eyes full of tears, then bowed his head, murmured, "Poor Mars Linkum—dead." Wiping his eyes with the back of his wrist, he went on with his work.

The pins we found were later used as fishing tackle, the points of which were heated with a match to take out the temper; we then bent it into a hook, and it was not long before we could pull out catfish, sunfish and goldfish out of the pond near Central Park. The fine needle, making no serious wound in the fish, enabled many boys to make considerable pocket money, as goldfish sold for twenty-five cents apiece.

On our return we heard cheering over on 57th Street, the other side of Slattery's lot, and saw "our fellers" in a stone fight with the White House orphans. We ran over. I picked up an armful of stones and started up the hill. I had only thrown a few when I saw a long, black splinter whirling up in the air; before I had time to dodge, I received a staggering blow just above my hatband. I paid no attention to it, but later becoming hot with exertion, I pushed back my hat and found my hand smeared with blood.

That took all of the fight out of me, as I did not know how to explain the hole in my hat and the wound to my mother. I slunk home and told some rambling story about hitting it against a cart. As to the White House boys, there was no enmity between us, but there seemed to be an understanding, when we had nothing else to do, we would peg rocks at each other. Yet at other times, they would wander around among us in their blue-striped blouses, and I never knew anyone to hit them; it was only when they were behind their wooded breastworks that we attacked them.

## Eighth Avenue—Saturday Night

My mother had a great fancy for what was called "high, square bread," and a baker named Bell at 40th Street, made the best. So on Saturday night, we started down the avenue to lay in a supply for Sunday. Passing the car stables, reaching 47th Street, the crowd began to thicken. At 46th Street, the outskirts of the Jewish section began and extended for two blocks, comprising low two-story buildings, which I studied with great interest, as many of them were homes of schoolmates and friends who came to my house. When I passed, they saluted with grins.

The elder Jews seemed to look and act alike—the way they smiled, talked, gestured, crossed their arms, planted their feet and shrugged their shoulders. In fact, none of them seemed at that time to have acquired any American ways, and except for the distinctly aged ones, they could hardly be told apart. Yet many bright, pretty children played among them, and occasionally there were girls with a peculiar oriental beauty and charm of manner, which was emphasized by the pitiless downtrodden, hopeless looking elder people who still bore the effects of foreign persecution.

Weekday nights the aged men and women drew up their chairs along the curb facing the sidewalks. There they would sit with their arms folded, watching the active members of their families doing business.

On Saturday night all this was changed. The peddlers took possession, and the old people huddled around the entrances of the stores. Boisterous, howling peddlers lined along the curb, while the younger Jews, active and with suave eagerness, passed up and down in front of their shops. There was none of the reported frantic ruffianism of the Chatham Square type, as the two surging streams of Eighth Avenuites greeted each other—laughing, joking, guying, chaffing or flirting as they swept along.

In every wagon were a couple of torches, which their owners had probably carried in the last election parade; they were filled with camphene, a big spongy wick, reeking, fuming and casting a lurid light on fruit, chickens and fish, as well as on passers-by. The lop-eared, slack-necked and spavined horses stood listless and drooling; or occasionally they woke up enough to nibble at some green from a neighboring cart. Peddlers stood at the tail-boards of their carts, with the heel of their fists against their grizzly jaws, and the sinews and veins standing out on their knarled necks, brayed their wares, while another hoarse-voiced peddler, with his thumb in the gills of a big fish, swung it above his head.

Rosy, plump, keen-eyed women, all smiles—evidently prosperous boarding house keepers—were purchasing judiciously; they mingled with the lean, haggard, worn women with their children hanging on their skirts, dickering with the husky peddlers of the Sunday supplies.

On almost every corner was a crippled soldier or sailor grinding an organ with a small flag stuck in one of its corners, and his framed "discharge" on the top. In one case a soldier and sailor combined; the soldier one-legged, sat on a small bench and ground the organ, and beside him the sailor, a fine, handsome young fellow with his right arm gone at the shoulder holding out his cap in his left hand. They were both in uniform, with a good-sized flag in each corner of the organ, on which the soldier played a loud patriotic tune that set the heart thumping and started the coppers and shinplasters speeding their way.

The best types of these men soon disappeared after the War; Capt. Johnson told me that the Grand Army men stopped it. The last one I saw was a little, one-legged darkey veteran—very weazened, with a large top head and a knotty white beard. He was viciously drunk, supported by two huge policemen, each with a broad grin; one was carrying his crutches, while he was rolling his big alley eyes at them, frantically trying to fight them both.

We finally reached 42nd Street; the whole section was aflare with torches, and overhung with a haze of black smoke, through which the discordant yells of the peddlers seemed very appropriate. There the crowd seethed like a whirlpool, but all were good natured. We worked our way through the current, passing the line of cart-tails and torches, while a mass of carts disappeared in perspective as they melted into a cloud of dark smoke toward Ninth Avenue.

As I piped in my childish voice, my mother silenced me, saying, "Hush! Blind Peter!" Yes, there was Blind Peter sawing away on his fiddle, with a tin cup dangling from its neck. Peter was another friend who used to call on my mother and tell her his troubles. He was stone blind; peddled brooms in the daytime, and fiddled for parties at night, except on Saturdays. When he called on my mother, she would go over him, patch his rents in his clothes or sew on buttons.

Peter had a remarkably sharp ear, and would always stop my mother when he heard her light footfall in the street; if it were very quiet, and she in a hurry, she walked on her toes to pass him. But in this case the noise of the crowd and the rasp of his fiddle made that unnecessary. Peter varied his musical activities by blowing the organ in Dr. Ewer's church. He was something of a philosopher, and said one day:

"I didn't believe it when I heard the world turned round at night, but now I do, because when I go to sleep on my right side, I always wake on my left." This was Peter's original contribution to science. In his old age he had a most satisfactory death, passing away, so Randolph Ewer told me, at the lever as he pumped the organ during the services of the Church of St. Ignatius.

My mother having finished her purchases, we slipped into the current of paraders drifting uptown. In spite of a certain good-natured hustle, it had its charm. Everyone knew everyone else, at least by sight, and most of them had gone to the same school at various periods. In the sparsely settled districts, many had come a long distance.

Reaching 43rd Street, I saw in the toy store window a beautiful little figure of a toy cuirassier mounted, made of some composition and painted in natural color. I was fascinated with its dainty charm, and although it was expensive, my mother bought the toy. In great terror I made my way through the crowd, fearing it would be broken.

Hearing a loud intoning above the laughter and noise of the strollers, we knew that Crazy Jimmie was busy. Jimmie was the local idiot, the protégé of Father McCarthy of 42nd Street church. His face had a peculiar childlike innocence. He had taken his stand, as usual, in front of one of the Jewish clothing stores, with his arms extending, blessing the crowd. The storekeepers never bothered him for obstructing the traffic, and Jimmie wandered at will, in and out of any open doorway—be it public building or store with all the freedom of a favorite cat. He nursed the babies for the neighbors, and never seemed so proud as when relieving a mother by carrying one.

He was generally followed by a crowd of youngsters asking him to give the baby to them. His importance with his charge seemed to have no bounds, and there was no danger of stubbing his toes while carrying the baby as he raised his feet at least six inches at every step.

Reaching home, I took my treasured statuette to my little room, where my other military toys were arranged on the table. Leaning my chin in my hand, I gazed and gazed at my treasure until at last the character of the little cuirassier assumed in turn the personality of General Sheridan, then General Sherman, then General Grant, and then—I was roused with my mother's arm around me saying it was bed time.

# The Volunteer Fireman

Chivalry and romance in New York seemed to have died with the old Volunteer Fire Department—the link that bound old New York together and inspired young and old men, women and young girls.

There, every man met on the same footing. It was then that the primitive idea of the strong heart, strong nerve and strong arm asserted itself. It is a customary reflection on them as disorderly and turbulent, but one must remember that their rank and file were in their early twenties, and that their conduct compares favorably with college fraternities and that their rows or "musses" were no more serious than class rows or rushes.

The character of the men was influenced by their neighborhoods, and such men as Charles H. Haswell, the distinguished engineer and historian; Fletcher Harper, the publisher; Daniel F. Tieman, Mayor and later State Senator;

Laurence Ternure, the prominent shipping merchant; and William H. Webb, the world-famous ship builder, bespeak the types of men who were their leaders or active members. As to their patriotism, in '61 they rallied to the call of Colonel Ellsworth and, after his death, served with Colonel Noah Farnham who was mortally wounded at Bull Run; and during the War they volunteered to the number of several thousand, and served till Appomattox.

The rules of the Volunteer Fireman were: A fireman must be twenty-one, and a citizen of the U. S. The engine companies were limited to sixty men; hose carriages, forty; trucks or hook and ladders, sixty. The men fairly made a fetish of their machines, and took great pains in polishing them up. Sometimes the iron work was plated with gold or silver, and the brass work was kept in a high state of polish. The woodwork was always kept freshly painted—the Company paying all the expenses, because when delivered to them they were painted a dull gray. The back boards were, in many cases painted by the leading artists, such as Henry Inman, Joseph H. Johnson, who was assistant foreman of No. 6, also his more famous brother David, who also painted *The Burning of Harper's Publishing House*. The hose carriages were as light as racing sulkies—with their four wheels and a reel of hose in the center. They were generally painted a bright color; their metal work plated with gold and silver, as well as the four lanterns and bells mounted on springs, and tinkled merrily as they sped bounding over the cobblestones. They were very proud of their engine number, which many of their members, as well as small boy admirers, had tattooed on their arm.

All sorts of tributes were presented to the Company, such as an ornamental drag rope, pictures, carpets, flags, clocks. Many musical pieces were written in their honor. There was a song we used to sing in school, called, *The Fireman's Child*.

My father told me that when he arrived from Scotland, he took lodging with Mrs. Hayden. Her son-in-law, Uriah Haff, was connected with the "30 Hose Company," at that time called "The Edwin Forrest." My father was awakened in the middle of the night by a fellow opening the unlocked hall door, and bellowing upstairs through his trumpet, "Uriah! Uriah! Turn out! Turn out! Fire! Fire! Fire!" Jumping up, he looked out and saw that some half dozen fellows had run the carriage to the middle of the street, but were stuck in the deep snow. Dressing, he bolted out and joined them to the fire.

The regular members, so as to have no delay, stuck their pants in their boots when they went to bed, and wore their red flannel shirts, so in case of alarm they could dress in two motions, snatch their helmet off the bedpost, and be off.

It seems incredible that men of wealth and position should gladly undergo such hardships, risks and exposure through mere sentiment. The regular members generally slept at their homes, while a lot of unattached followers slept in the Engine House and helped to get the engine in shape and manned the ropes.

The first member to arrive at the fire plug, took the nozzle of the hose and attached it to the hydrant. The hydrants were about three feet high and encased in an octagon wooden sheath; the hinged top was secured with a padlock of which each fireman carried a key.

Sometime rival companies arrived together, then "plug musses" were apt to begin till one side would give way. Then the victors would turn on their hose and get busy. Another source was when there was no water near, then the other engines would string out their hose as far as it would reach, attaching the end to an engine in the rear. All of the other engines would do the same, and the last of the line would lower their sucker into the river. The suckers were long leather tubes with perforated brass ends called baskets. These were carried on each side of the engine. The foreman would give the order through his trumpet, and all hands would man the brakes, and if the man in the forward engine could not pump it out as fast as it was pumped in, her box would overflow, and she then had the ignominy of being washed, which stuck to her until she was able to return the compliment.

The foreman must indeed be a foreman, who never failed to beat his way with his trumpet when fighting for right of way with a rival engine through a narrow street. While all prepared for it, only a few made a practice of fighting, and their universal chivalry was shown by no foreman ever picking a fight with a member of the Henry Street Co. They were Quakers and did not fight, and all the other firemen respected the principles of "Peace."

A silver or ornamented trumpet was considered an appropriate gift for the most distinguished hero of the company.

They constantly polished their engines and slushed the floors till they looked and emitted that fresh piney odor like the deck of a man-of-war.

The neighboring boys caught the spirit of their elders, and hung round the doorway, and they gazed on their special heroes the same as they do now on baseball champions.

As I recall them, they were an unusually fine lot of men. Their activities kept them in perfect physical condition—lean and sinewy. I can recall only one fat man among them, and he was of German descent. Their Adam's apples were a distinctive feature—hard to find after lager beer became popular. Their spirit of emulation may have made many of them turbulent, but when their humanity was appealed to, they would face any danger no matter how appalling, as the roll of martyred firemen shows.

Drinking or card playing was not allowed in the Engine Houses. The principal use they made of whiskey was to pour a glass in their boots in winter to keep from being chilled. As for facing danger, I saw a fireman's hat in Barnum's Museum that its owner had worn at his post, till it was puckered by the heat and looked like an old prune.

July 13, 1865, was a bright sunny day and the rumor had come uptown that Barnum's Museum was on fire and that the Hook and Ladder Engines had all gone downtown, when later in the afternoon the alarm of fire brought the neighboring engines down to 44th Street near Eighth Avenue—no trucks appeared on the scene.

Following the "Black Joke" through 45th Street, I watched the runners break through the fence and run her over the cabbage and radish patches of the market gardens which ran on the rear of the house which was on fire on 44th Street.

"36 Engine" shortly followed Black Joke through the break in the fence and was hauled over the patches close up to the building and their streams were turned on. Black Joke was sending up clouds of black smoke, while 36 whooped it up and worked with vigor their old hand engine. A full breeze blew the fire towards Eighth Avenue and house after house began to wither in the flames. People in the adjoining houses began to throw their belongings out of the windows down on the beds of vegetables, they then disappeared—I suppose by going out at the 44th Street entrance, but one woman appeared on the top floor of a building next to the fire and she began to throw out her furniture. First came the straw bed then the flat irons and chairs, various knick-knacks, and finally an old fashioned clock was tossed down. She ignored the yells of the firemen to come down, but kept on throwing things out the window. Then the fire reached her house and the floors beneath her were lapped with flames and filling her room with smoke and a cry of horror from all as she appeared through this with a little girl in her arms, about four years old, and started to throw her out. A frantic yell from the firemen seemed to stop her. The next moment, the fire lit up the room behind her. She then climbed out onto the window sill with the little girl in her arms and dangled her bare feet over the edge. No ladders at hand—all seemed hopeless.

The firemen meanwhile kept a steady stream splashing around her. At last an inspiration seemed to strike someone and a man ran and put his back against the building and clasped his hands; another man stepped into the clasped hands then onto the first man's shoulders which enabled him to reach the first floor window sill. He climbed up and straddled it and another man repeated the action, swinging up alongside of him, and stood up on the next window sill while his comrade clasped his legs. This action was repeated by another man and shortly, another man was straddling the window above and steadying another. A fireman climbed up this human ladder and swinging himself beside the woman on the upper sill; then taking the child from her, took a twist on her skirts and lowered her down to his comrade on the floor below. Thus they passed the child from hand to hand until the bottom floor was reached. Bringing down the mother was a little more difficult, but the men received her on their shoulders and swung her from hand to hand until she too was landed on the ground. The man with the nozzle of the hose worked close up to the building with his fire hat reversed to protect his eyes from the shower of spray which splashed back from the stream which he kept up until his comrades had descended to a place of safety.

It was sunset by the time the fire was subdued; it had destroyed about half the block. Some pretty girls came out of the little white cottage and passed water to the exhausted men who manned the engine. The firemen swaggered slowly up Eighth Avenue. They all walked alike, with a peculiar roll of the shoulders and sway of the head and surely they, if any body of men should be proud of the spontaneous tribute which they received on all sides from men, women and children.

## Stories of the Draft Riots

*The Black Joke Fire Company was also known for their involvement in the Draft Riots of July, 1863. In March of that year, Congress passed a national conscription law, which was greatly disliked by the working classes, as the rich were exempt from the draft upon paying a $300 fee.*

*On Saturday, July 11th, a draft lottery was begun and several members of Black Joke were drafted, although it was argued that firemen should be exempt since they were protecting the city from fire. On Monday morning, July 13th, the members marched to the draft office at Third Avenue and 47th Street, broke up the lottery, and set the building on fire. When the smoke of the fire was seen by the rest of the city, riots broke out and lasted for several days. Casualties were estimated at over one hundred and twenty persons killed and about two thousand wounded.*

*While the Black Joke only destroyed the draft office, it was the Copperheads and lower-classes that let loose and attacked the houses of the wealthy or any Negroes they found on the street; many were murdered by these mobs.*

*In the decades that followed, Kelly interviewed several eyewitnesses.*

Dr. John Burke was a very popular physician in those days; his house was at No. 30 East Broadway. I have heard them tell that during the riot days, a friend who had taken an interest in a young negro, was assaulted by the rioters, and fled with him to Dr. Burke for protection, thinking the doctor's popularity would save him, but some of the rioters, enraged at being balked, threatened to set the house on fire. Mrs. Burke immediately prepared for a siege.

She had all the marble tops taken from the tables, as well as water pitchers and anything else heavy, that could be used as a missile, and carried them to the front top room; she also had the water pitchers filled to give them additional weight. All these she proposed to drop on the heads of the rioters if they should attempt to enter the house. The family mounted guard all day until darkness came, watching the distant fires; at last the mob could be seen breaking into and looting the stores on the opposite side of the street.

Then they heard a voice call out, "Let's go over to Burke's," and over they came with their booty, gathering under the lamp-post, they began to sort their loot, and in their arguments and excitement, for each one to get his share, they forgot their interest as to Burke's. A day or so later, as the priest of St. Mary's Church went in to say Mass, he found all sorts of clothing, hats, boots, and various other articles scattered over the floor. They had been thrown in through the open windows by those of his parishioners whose conscience had reasserted itself and shifted their burdens on the priest, who had to call in the neighboring storekeepers to identify their goods.

## Interview with Mrs. Miller about the Riots

Years after, I interviewed a friend and neighbor, Mrs. Louise C. Miller, and speaking of the Draft Riots, she said:

Mrs. M—My two sons had gone to the war, and my husband [John Miller] was a leading Republican. He was appointed as an officer to carry out the Draft. The Democrats were so angry that they threatened to burn our house. My friends advised me to leave, but I said, "If I don't stay where I belong, where shall I stay?"

Towards the afternoon, I wrapped up little Emma in an American flag as she lay asleep, and put her behind the door, and then went over to see my friend who lived near the corner of 61st Street.

We were sitting on her front porch as we saw the rioters coming up Ninth Avenue. Danny McMahon, who was standing near, ran into the Paulist Church and told Father George Deshon, who came out and stood in the middle of the Avenue.

As the rioters came up, Father Deshon raised his hand and called "Halt!" They came to a stand. I ran over to him. He said to them, "Where are you going?" They pointed to me and said, "There is that black Republican woman. She should be killed, and have her house burned." Father Deshon talked to them. They made no attempt to go further, but went back. I started to thank Father Deshon for what he had done, but he took me by the arm and told me to go on home.

They were great hairy men like animals. They did not belong round here.

K—I wonder how he was able to stop them?

Mrs. M—They were strangers, and did not know who the man next to them might be, and I suppose he had the Holy Cross on, and they were afraid. The rioters afterwards got hold of McMahon and beat him so, that he was in bed for two months.

Father Hewitt was beaten and dangerously wounded when he tried to stop the rioters, in 54th Street and Tenth Avenue. He was brought home in a carriage—I remember it! Of course Father Deshon would take nothing for what he had done, but when they were taking up a collection for a new organ, I sent him One Hundred Dollars.

## Speaking of the Riots with
## George Galvin, Lyman Starret, Tom Egan and John E. Kelly

In after years, I became friends with Mr. George Galvin who had been foreman of Washington Hose, No. 12 at 380 West 43rd Street during the Civil War and in his later years Secretary of the Exempt Fireman's Association at Jefferson Market.

He showed me a battered brass trumpet that belonged to his old friend, Lawrence Austin, saying, "Poor Larry. He gave me his old trumpet saying, 'I want you to have this.'"

I asked him how it had so many dents.

"Oh, some times I dropped it," he said.

"On some fellow's head," I inquired.

He flushed, grinned, but did not answer.

Galvin commanded his company during the riots, and stationed his men at the Fifth Avenue Stage Stables at 43rd Street. He described the destruction of the Colored Orphan Asylum, and how most of the children had been saved by [Charles H.] Allerton, a Scotchman, who kept the Pigs Head Hotel at 41st Street and Eleventh Avenue.

Galvin said, "The night before, he had come and taken the children away and over to Weehawken in rowboats. Next day they burned his hotel."

"Did you come in contact with the Rioters," I asked.

"Yes," he answered, "I was going through 35th Street, when they tried to stop me. I said to them, 'GO ON!' and they went on."

"Were you alone?" I asked.

"No," he said, "I had the machine with me."

I can imagine that was the time the trumpet got some of its dents.

He added, "I never did anything heroic. I never rescued anyone. The nearest I came to it was when I went into the cellar of a house on fire, and found a dog there with some pups. I was going to bring her out, but she rushed at me so fierce, that I was afraid to touch her, so I grabbed one of the pups and ran out. I took it to the Engine House, and we raised her. She used to sleep in the bunk room, and at the sound of the fire bell, she would start barking, and run up and down the room and shake any fellow who didn't wake up. She always followed the machine to the fire."

In the 1890's, I also became friends with Mr. Lyman Starret, who was a member of "30 Hose," called "The Edwin Forrest," and later renamed "The George B. McClellan." He was very quiet, and had to be approached on all sides to get inside his guard. From boyhood to manhood, I have heard him say but little. A quiet, amiable smile was generally the answer to my questions, so the following is the outcome of many attempts:

S—During the Draft riots on Eleventh Avenue, near 42nd Street, when they burned down the Pigs Head Hotel and some other buildings, and started to burn down the gas house, we went to work to put them out. The rioters did not interfere with us personally, but when we got the stream going, a fellow came up with an ax, and 'Zip!'—cut the hose. They told us they would do it again if we kept it up, but after a while the fire extended to the houses in which some of them lived; then they were glad to let us go to work.

Foreman Tom Egan later told me what he witnessed during the Draft riots. He remembered seeing Colonel Henry O'Brien who had been viciously tortured and killed by the rioters as he lay in the backyard of a home where his friends had brought him.  He was still breathing as the neighboring Priest made his way through the crowd of rioters to give the Colonel the Last Sacraments.

After he had done so, he rose to his knees and then discovered someone had stolen his watch.  Later in the day a rioter was found killed on the corner of the avenue.  When they searched him to see who he was, they found the watch which he had stolen from the Priest.

A neighbor and a namesake, John E. Kelly, from upstate who had joined a band of citizens as a home guard to defend the city, had been quartered at the Armory.  He told me when the body of soldiers and citizens were marching from the Armory—the Rioters on the neighboring houses pelted them with bricks they had wrenched from the chimneys.  One fellow made himself conspicuous by standing where he considered himself safe, and with a musket kept firing down at our troops.  Then one of the so-called Invalid Corps, a wounded cavalryman, stepped from the ranks, whipped out his revolver from his holster, fired and shot the fellow dead.  He fell from the roof to the side walk.

The home guard in their excitement were about to fire a howitzer on the mob when a young officer rushed up, grabbed the muzzle of the piece and swung it one side and by his dominant personality dispersed them without loss of life.

Later they heard cries and yells as a carriage was seen to drive full speed up Seventh Avenue; the mob closing in behind pelting it.  An officer in it was seen to rise, draw a revolver and empty it into the pursuing mob.  He believed this was Colonel Thaddeus Mott who had come to take command of the Arsenal.

## Interview with Colonel Abraham Bassford about the Riots

Col. Abraham Bassford was a veteran of the Civil War and helped defend the city during the riots.  His voice was strong and full, and with the exception of a slight halt in the right leg from a war wound, he was a fine manly specimen of vigorous age.  Speaking of the Draft Riots, he said to me:

B—When the Draft Riots broke out in New York, July 11, 1863, I was Major in the 14th New York Cavalry, of which Thaddeus P. Mott, son of Dr. Valentine Mott, was Colonel.  He commanded a battery of four guns; I commanded a troop of cavalry.  We were stationed at Riker's Island, and our recruiting office was on Broome Street.  We had 300 recruits, most of whom never fired a gun; we had no horses and no sabres—only revolvers.  I reported to Gen. John E. Wool, whose headquarters were at the St. Nicholas Hotel.

I saw him—a very old man; he ordered us to rescue Gen. Charles W. Sandford, who was besieged at the armory, 36th Street and Seventh Avenue.  The rioters had threatened to burn it down.  We marched up there, Col. Mott ahead with his battery.  I had also command of two complete companies of the Seventh Regiment.  The regiment was at the front with the other militia regiments.  There were no other militia regiments in New York at that time; the men that I had were invalids, or men unable for various reasons to go to the front, but had volunteered to turn out. They had rifles while my men, as I said before, had only revolvers.

Col. Mott ordered the spectators to disperse, then he fired with blank cartridges; then you ought to see the crowd and carts go (as he said this the Colonel laughed heartedly), then he fired with grape. He did it only to scare them, no one was killed; this cleared the street, but they fired at us from the roofs of houses, and pelted us with bricks and crockery. They did not kill any of my men, but wounded a number of them. I fired on them and captured about two hundred and fifty—half of them were boys, sixteen to eighteen-years-old, dressed in women's clothing in disguise.

We rescued Gen. Sandford, took him home and placed a guard over his house. The rioters were led by Rebels who wanted to burn the city, but if the citizens had done their duty, they could have suppressed the riots in the beginning. They were a pack of damn Copperheads; the loyal men were at the front. The Copperheads wanted to have me tried for murder, Damn them, for what I did that day. Then we bivouacked at Lafayette Hall, and marched over to Gramercy Park.

The houses of these wealthy and patriotic men attracted the attention of those thieving Copperheads and their southern leaders. Ten thousand damned, cutthroat fellows from around Canal and Hudson Streets said they were going to burn down the buildings surrounding Gramercy Park. On hearing this, I started down with my men, and picketed on the north side of the iron fence, ready to mount an attack. The men with their shelter tents camped inside. The park was full of hand grenades. I had my headquarters in the hotel.

Archbishop John Hughes was head of the Catholic Church in New York at that time. He sent for the Catholic rioters to come to his house; then came out on his balcony and said, "If you men interfere with those soldiers, or the Government of the United States, I will excommunicate every one of you!" That settled it, otherwise, while we might have killed a good many, they would have cleaned us out. Archbishop Hughes saved us—God bless him!

I hate to think of the War. I felt like a murderer to shoot at my brother. But if we had not done it, they would have come north, and there is no knowing what conditions they might have placed on us. When Beauregard fired the first shot in the War at the *Star of the West* in Charleston Harbor, he united the North. People were by no means united; many wanted to let the South go to avoid war—they knew that war is terrible. There were a lot of damn fellows in the North in favor of the South, damn Copperheads; also a lot of other fellows too damn cowardly to go to the front.

*What Colonel Bassford did "that day," was that he shot and killed a man who had got into a struggle with Colonel Mott. The event still played clearly in his mind, although nearly sixty years had passed. Charges were brought against Col. Bassford at the time, but it was ruled that the killing was justified.*

# The Docks

"Down to the docks," was a familiar phrase among us boys, and in fact, was a general term for the venerable wooden wharves that jutted from the waterfront of Old New York.

They were very picturesque in their primitive weather-beaten condition. Holes were generally cobbled with planks instead of being repaired. Yet there was a charm about their rugged, storm-wrenched timbers, and a glow of color on their shivered water-logged spills, where they were braced with massive rusty spikes and chains, as well as being splotched with rich green seaweed.

The 55th Street dock was a favorite resort for us on Sundays. It was here the brick boats or schooners from up the river used to unload. All was silent on the boats, made fast or moored round the docks, and most of the hands were sprawled over the decks, sound asleep, except one big freckled fellow who was trying to pump a hymn tune from a brand new concertina.

A story is told of a fellow wandering to the end of one of the docks and falling overboard. A deck hand on a sloop pulled him out with a boat hook, and asked him, "How did you kum to do it?" "I didn't kum to do it!" gurgled the dripping fellow, "I kum to fish!"

That's what most folks came to do on Sundays.

It was a study to see them clustered round the end of the dock, and watch their methods of having a good time. No one looks so eager or so joyous as a fisher-boy—or as woe-begone and anxious as a fisherman who has a reputation to maintain. The boy who has none to lose, with whoops and wild kicks of delight, jerks his fish from the water like a rocket, and lands it flopping behind half way cross the dock. While the old men would draw in their catch with faces as blank as shingles, and no matter how large it was, would depreciate it, and tell you of a larger one they had caught in the past. The whole edge of the dock was fringed with just such characters, some with poles of various patterns, and others with drop lines.

Behind them stood a crowd of young fellows—mechanics in their Sunday clothes, ostentatiously smoking big cigars, hands in their pockets, loafing round trying to kill time; most of them gazed silently out over the river, at a few pleasure boats which were scudding over the blue waters.

Some little distance out was a small boat containing four boys, on which they had erected a homemade sail. All other water sport and traffic seemed suspended, judging from the sloops moored round the docks.

Something in the air made us look round. A black storm cloud or thunder head came glowering across the sky towards us. The wave crests began to flash like sabres against the darkening Hudson; gulls began to fly low.

There seemed to be trouble in the little boat. Its sail began to flutter excitedly, like a wounded bird, and then the boat suddenly capsized. Four black heads bobbed in the water round her, and then lined up over the keel. Then one boy scrambled up and straddled it, whipped off his jacket, he began to wave it.

All was excitement and not a boat to be had. Yet everyone began to give orders. What was to be done? Looking towards the shore, we saw a small boat drifting up; in which sat a couple of slack-jawed looking fellows, but they refused to face the squall, nor would they lend us the boat, but kept out a safe distance so we could not take it. We cussed, coaxed, and beguiled them, but with no effect. They merely gaped at the poor little fellows struggling for their lives.

"Look! There goes one!" yelled an excited youngster, as he pointed toward the 44th Street dock, from where a small boat was darting out and heading toward the wreck. How the two fellows at the oars pulled! Butting and rising over the heavy surge and chopping tide. The boy astride the boat waved his jacket frantically. The three other heads bobbed up and down. Oh, if they could hold out a little longer! At last! At last! Alongside! We saw them haul in the black-headed youngsters aboard the relief boat and let their wreck adrift, and made for the dock below, as we headed for shelter from the storm. The storm then commenced to rip, boom, and splash around as though to make up for lost time.

## My Friend Will Anderson

As we were promoted to Mr. Barrow's class, we were lined up according to size. We squared our shoulders or shrunk down, so as to appear the size of some friend we desired to sit by. I was pared off with a boy about my own age, and as our friendship had a great effect on my future life, I will describe him in detail. His name was Will Anderson. He had yellow hair, square brow, glistening blue eyes, a short hook nose, a clean cut straight mouth, square jaws; his face was tanned with the sun.

He said his people came from Nyack; his father of English ancestry, his mother of Dutch. We became friends immediately. He told me his father had been a Hudson River boatman when a boy, and a cook on a brick boat, but now he had a fine express [carriage] route on Cortlandt Street. He invited me down to his house at 416 West 48th Street—a three story brick house with a porch. A low wooden railing ran along the walk which was bordered by a bed of flowers. Behind the house was a brick stable with loft. A high arched grape arbor ran back the length of the stables (about twenty-five feet) was rich with foliage and half ripe fruit.

Mr. Anderson was the same cut as Will, only taller with sharp, hard lines. His hair was jet black, his eyes black and he wore short black whiskers, and by his clean cut, energetic personality typified the American who had built up our Nationality. He always wore a white shirt, neat turned down collar, a black broadcloth coat and neat boots. On Sunday he would take off his coat and take possession of the kitchen and cook the dinner, as was the habit of many of the old time Americans. The dinner was a masterpiece in quality and effect, heightened by the fruits and flowers with which he garnished the table. The characteristic of the men of the period was to take off their coats as a sign they were at home.

After dinner, Mr. Anderson would go out and sit on the feed box near the open door of his stable. He had a great attraction for me, and I would perch up beside him and listen.

He took great interest in my Revolutionary sketches. "How things are changed," he said, "When I was a boy we were taught to hate the Englishman as you would a snake. There was one story I used to hear when I was a boy which I don't see in print now, although it used to be in a book we had in school. It said that when Major John Andre had landed [on Sept. 20, 1780] and was making plans with Benedict Arnold for the surrender of West Point, it was arranged for an English vessel to go up the river and send a boat ashore to take him off.

"There were two fellows in the village, one a white and the other a Negro. They started up the river to get some cider—I think they were out shooting. They saw an English vessel out on the river and then they saw a boat pull off for the shore. One of them said, 'Let's go and have a shot at the Englishmen.' So they crawled up to a point of rocks near the shore, and when the Englishmen got within range they fired on them—at this the English, not knowing how many they were, pulled back to the ship and sailed down river. This is why Andre did not get back but had to go round by the way of Tarrytown and was captured, which never would have happened if it had not been for those two fellows. The old Negro lived at Nyack, and I remember seeing him when I was a boy. Our school teacher, when we read the story, pointed him out to us and told us he was the one."

On Saturday mornings I used to visit the Anderson's stable early. There was a fine old bulldog named Jack, and a beautiful carriage dog named Lady, and a nondescript half grown pup Judy to greet me. I then watched the men in the cool of the morning getting the horses ready to start. One, a fine old ex-artillery horse was called Kicker. He was a great square framed horse with U. S. branded on his shoulder. His temper had been broken by bad treatment. He would kick and bite everyone but me. Then a long-jawed, amiable fellow with fiery eyes and a long sad face, with a shambling gate, was named Dick. Then there was a vicious Roman nosed black I called Nosey, and a pretty, little golden sorrel named Dolly. I sketched them as they were being curried, as they were starting out in the bright sunlight, and as they returned reeking with sweat after a hard day's work, or wet and dripping from a storm—lit by the stable lanterns which cast weird shadows and gleaming lights on their steaming hides. The smell of the horses, the hay and the stables always seemed to hang round me and my poor mother used to say sadly, "You have been to Andersons again. What do you there? What do you expect to be, a hostler?"

I spent so much time at Anderson's stables that it seemed more like my home. One time, while sitting on the bottom of a stable pale sketching a horse, a terrible rumbling and clatter came down the street. I ran out. Down galloped a runaway horse. He was a huge fellow. He was dragging an empty coal cart and the thundering flapping of the loose trail board must have added to his terror. Indeed he was a wild-looking specimen: eyes bulging, nostrils squared, mane flapping, hoofs pounding—the empty cart jerking and swaying over the uneven cobblestones.

Anderson and an express man [driver] ran in front of him. The express man then quailed and rushed back on Anderson and upset him.

Then it was my turn. With head swaying up and down, he loomed over me and seemed to mount the very air. Springing, I grabbed the shaft with my right hand and was jerked along catching his flying rein with my left hand. I got my grip and swung like a tassel in the air, then brought my right shoulder under his lower jaw like a curb, while momentum carried us down the street. With a jerk I swung him toward a sand heap in which he plunged fetlock deep. This brought him to a standstill. Anderson said, "That was a good job!" This incident was very valuable to me, for the memory of that headlong rush of the horse has inspired many of my works.

## Hudson River

Billy Cornett used to build little center-board sailboats, catboats and rowboats, on a small sandy beach between 50th and 51st Streets, at "The River," as I have always heard it called, as if there were no other river. At the first flush of spring, after school a party of us would meet and count our pocket money. If we had thirty cents, we would start down to Billy's and hire a boat for an hour or longer if the pool permitted.

On our way down 51st Street we passed several brightly painted cottages, their little white front dooryards all aglow with the bloom of spring. Nearing the river, we passed the lumber yards, as well as the brownstone yards, of which there were many, on account of its being the brownstone age, as it was called from the number of New York houses built of that material. Crossing the railroad tracks at Eleventh Avenue, we went to the end of a stumpy little dock, and saw just starting out, a flat-bottomed skiff with home-made sail, loaded to the gunwale with a gang of shouting, yelling youngsters tussling for the oars and giving conflicting orders.

At last, when the most dominant got control, each oarsman or oar-boy started pulling away on his own hook, catching crabs and throwing showers of spray. As we knew them, we showed our friendly feeling by pelting them with pieces of brick that splashed the water over the boat and boys. We then went down to where Billy was cobbling a catboat, paid our thirty cents and started out on the end of the float where some small boats were drawn up.

Picking out one, we gave Billy's boy helper our jackets, as was the custom, to insure return of the boat. We then scrabbled aboard, and as we could all row equally well, there was no confusion. Some were in favor of going directly across to the Weehawken shore, where a large wooden sign was posted marked with large black letters on a white ground, "TELEGRAPH LANDING—DO NOT ANCHOR," as it was a good spot to dig clams.

Above this section the water fairly bristled with shad poles holding the seines, but as we had been there several times, we decided to head for Guttenburg. Oh, the delight of it—the indescribable feeling of exultation when the cool green water lapped our gunwale, and the salt spray splashed our faces! We looked at the beautiful scene through our brine-splashed lashes, and licked it off our lips as we strained at the oars, and felt the cheering, stimulating caress of the sun on our backs and bare arms. We felt like bold buccaneers.

We passed the Stryker Cove with its rocky shore, low and jagged, rich green, and heavily fringed with tangled sea weed. Behind, was a white railed fence which protected, but did not conceal, a most perfect specimen of an old time blooming garden, a white Colonial mansion surrounded by great overhanging trees—it was the home of General Stryker who served during the War of 1812, in the defenses along the upper part of Central Park. The grounds were in a high state of cultivation, as the old General was a great lover of roses. A high picket fence guarded them from vandal boys.

The grounds were entered through a high pillared gate near the homestead, at the head of what was called Stryker's Lane, which ran through the original Stryker property over to the Hopper homestead on Broadway. Pretty cottages of brick or wood with fine trees in front added to the beauty of old Stryker Lane.

On a jutting rock just above Stryker's, was the Hopper homestead. It was painted brown, and was not so impressive as the Strykers, but is to be commemorated as the home of Hopper Stryker Mott whose chronicles of Old New York makes us his debtor. The grounds ran out as far as 55th Street, where there was a brick dock, with many up river schooners made fast, and clattering with dock hands unloading bricks.

Passing 55th and 57th Street docks, we entered a little bay—between 60th and 61st Streets. It had a fine sandy beach from which bulged a big rock with some red veins in it, which gained it the name of blood rock, from which the boys were diving. As they were school mates, they yelled at us and swam out to the boat, catching on to the gunwale. They threatened to upset us but we grabbed them by the hair and shook them off. Then, getting our stroke, we headed across the river to a large white building on the Jersey shore, opposite 79th Street, called the Guttenburg brewery, which was the only building that was in sight north of the towers of the Monastery of Hoboken, except here and there one caught a glimpse of a white house through the trees of Weehawken. All else was primeval forest.

The brewery glittered pure white against the deep rich green, which crested on the dark gray battlements of the Jersey shore, then unscarred by the rock mongers. The brewery was built against the cliff, and ran a few stories above the road, which made a landmark like a chimney on a peak roof.

Passing round some shad poles, where fishermen were unloading their seines, we beached our boat. Some of the boys jumped out to swim or dig clams, while I generally remained in the boat to look back to our own island. The city seemed quite low. The conspicuous points were the church steeples with their crosses. The towers of the old Paulist Church were the most conspicuous object above the trees [on 59th Street]. It seemed to mark the limit of the city. After that there was nothing but green foliage along the river except the railroad embankment, and a passing train, tearing a vicious rent in the beauty of the scene. But nothing broke the broad buoyant sweep of the glorious river, and its beauty seemed heightened by the picturesque schooners, whose freshly painted green and black hulls were loaded down with their cargos of bright red brick.

"Time's up!" I called. All came aboard and we headed for home. The tidewater was strongly against us, and we waited for a tow. At last a swaggering little buffer of a tug boat came puffing along with a trail of canal boats. We threw a line to a good natured idler who caught it, and passed it through a ring bolt at the stern. Our boat reared on its stern post, plunging and bounding in the wake of the canal fleet. Till at last, nearing home, we would cast off and rest on our oars to let racing barges go by and watch the sinuous workings of the oarman's brown muscles, as the boat's bows cut like little shark's fins through the heaving current.

Nearing the dock, we would meet some friends in another boat and would have a race till one of us was winded. Then we would decide to catch the rollers of the *Mary Powell*, called the fastest boat on the river. About the time the setting sun made the river glow like molten bronze, the beautiful steamboat would come skimming along with the flags flying and its band playing, while her long swells, as they sped to shore, would make our little boat, as well as every boat in sight bob and curtsy to the queen of the river, and then they would roll on getting larger and larger until they broke against the rocky shore, or railroad embankment with a continuous roar, like a salvo in her honor.

Then the satisfaction of arriving home to supper, burned like sailors, as we thought, and displaying our hands with fresh blood blisters which made us feel very heroic. This was kept up during the summer till we were as tough as young goats.

But the Hudson days I loved most were the dark and stormy days of fall: To take a heavy boat, with my friend Will Anderson and push out over the grayish green waves, there to be tossed and battered about as we faced the current—then to feel the keen lash of the spray making our cheeks tingle. While our hands, now brown, tanned and calloused as bacon rind, gripped the wet handles of the heavy oars as we made our way up and across to the Jersey shore, beaten and whirled by the dangerous billows which seemed stirred to fury by the howling and the buffeting of the fierce gale. That I am here now was not through our own power, but that Power which guards, guides, and gives joy to the stormy petrel.

## Baseball

Gen. Abner Doubleday is [mistakenly] credited with having invented the game of baseball in 1839. My earliest recollection was when baseball was in the air, although looked upon somewhat askance by sedate people. There were no professional clubs that I know of, consequently no sitting like a bunch of Turks watching professionals play. Men and boys played themselves in an amateur way for the interest of it; there were no mats, mitts or breastplates, which in those days caused many accidents to the hands. Those possessing a broken nose could pass it off on baseball, while sprained knuckles and injured fingers were displayed with the same pride as German students display their scars. Young gentlemen's clubs used to take excursions to the Elysian Field, Hoboken, New Jersey to play baseball.

"What sort of a game is base ball?" asked one rosy Irish immigrant to my friend Austin Ford, for whom he worked. "Why do you ask?" inquired Ford. "Why," he replied, "I have a beautiful stepson, with beau-ti-ful teeth. He went out to play base ball, and came back with four of them in his stomach. Now what sort of game is base ball?"

I remember as a boy starting to play myself, and in the first game was hit on the end of the little finger with the ball, and suffered so badly that it cured me, and I never played again. One morning I went over to 57th Street to Slattery's lot to watch the boys play baseball, for everyone seemed to be doing it. They gave a whoop of delight on seeing me. "Ah, here's little Kelly—he'll just make the nine." When I refused to play, they looked at me with amazement, and one of them, about twice my size, gave me a swat on the side of the head.

Recalling mother's orders, I took it and stepped back; but, urged on by his companions, he did it again and again. I took it again and again, each time stepping back, and was finally backed up an incline to the fence which ran toward 57th Street. Then for good measure he took a piece of dry cow dung, threw it and struck me in the cheek. That settled it; I had objections against that sort of treatment.

With a howl of rage I rushed down the incline, made a jump at him, grabbed him by the throat and wound my legs around him, punching, scratching and tearing open his collar. He was struggling for breath, surprised and bewildered. I beat and beat him until I was out of breath, then dropped on my feet and let him go. He hung his head and started off with his friends who looked at me with real horror, as they would a mad dog. He said nothing—there was a dead silence.

He was in the center of the group, wagging his head with explanations, while I sat on the rich covered sod tingling with that particular joy after a well fought and victorious fight. But a greater thrill was in store for me. A few days later I passed a crowd of the larger boys, and one of them was telling about the fight. He did not pretend to notice me, but I heard him say with a laugh, "and little Kelly licked him!"

## Riding Horse Cars in Winter

The cold, bitter gale from across the Hudson River nearly swept me into the sunken lots, as I waited at the lower corner of 57th Street for the horse car to come down Eighth Avenue. The wail of the wind through the telegraph wires on the lofty poles gave additional dreariness. Then the sharp scrape of horses' shoes on the cobblestones seemed to add to the tingling cold.

The driver had no shelter but stood facing the gale. As usual, he wore a soldier's overcoat with the cape brought up over his head and ears, just showing the peak of his heavy woolen cap.

The conductor wore a large fur cap, with woolen comforter round his neck and ears, and a huge, seedy overcoat, ragged and patched at the pockets from being worn away by making change. His heavy knit gloves were cut off at the ends of his blue fingers.

Swinging aboard, I went inside and sat down. The car floor was covered in straw a foot deep, like a litter in a horse's stall. Working my feet in as deep as possible, and wrapping as much as I could rake in round my legs, like the rest of the passengers, I braced myself for the long cold ride to Vesey Street.

The window panes were so encrusted with ice and frost that one had to scratch it off to see the street. I began to get restless, so I went out on the front platform, where I found great pleasure in watching the straining muscles of the lean horses. The cold seemed to have no effect on me—and I never wore gloves. My father used to worry and ask me to keep inside, but as he did not make it an order, I stood beside the driver through my young years.

Reaching Vesey Street and after finishing my errand, I saw that it had clouded up, and began snowing heavily, so I made up my mind to return home.

I jumped on the rear platform of a car as it was leaving Vesey Street, and worked my way inside. It must have been very hard for the poor shop girls in their thin shoes as the snow began to deepen on the sidewalks and streets.

The only heat in the car was a smoky kerosene lamp at each end, which the conductor lighted when it began to get dark. The fumes of the kerosene mingled with those of the wet straw and damp clothes of the passengers made it hard breathing, especially as the ventilators were all closed to keep out the drifting snow; while the passengers on the front and rear platforms, men and girls some of them, without hardly a foot hold, were pelted by the heavy storm. I worked my way up and out to the front beside the driver, who by this time looked like a snowman.

Yet in spite of these apparent hardships, there was a cheerful friendliness among the passengers. They would talk and laugh with one another like villagers, and occasionally, someone would start singing, in which many would join. And the men would chaff one another, and from the laughter of the girls among themselves, it was hard to believe there was such a thing as storm or hardship.

The drivers were well known to the regular passengers, and a certain set would seek his side, as I did, and talk things over. Some of the conductors were very jolly, and the men who were generally smokers on the front platform, had a cheerful, if storm-beaten trip.

The snow becoming thicker, the car jumped the track. "All out!" was the cry. The men started out, leaving the women in the car, and lifted it back on the track. On we went. Suddenly, one of the horses stumbled and fell heavily; the front edge of the car ground harshly into the quivering quarter of the poor creature. It lay there with its long neck extended, eyes bulging, tongue lolling and frothing. Its lean flanks heaving and sighing, was the only response it gave to the beating, howling and yelling of the volunteer aides who always swarm a fallen horse, pulling and pushing in different directions. Finally all the men got out and dragged the horse across the smooth snow to the side of the track.

A team from the car following was brought forward and hitched to our car. And again we started through the blinding storm, as a snow plough, with a roar, swept down on the opposite track. It had a dozen horses or more, and came with the rush of a cyclone; the whirling sweepers throwing snow to one side, and enveloping the driver and his assistants in a cloud of mist. One of them stood at the left of the driver, with a nail keg full of stones, from which he pelted the leaders, as no lash could reach them.

Behind the snow plough came another car with four horses and an extra driver at the brake. It had started from the stables after the storm had begun. Here we began to slack up, as the horses of a heavily loaded truck in front, seemed unable to get along. Their shoes having no calks, in their efforts to tug they slipped and sprawled to no effect; then losing heart, they came to a standstill. Our passengers, after growling and swearing loudly, threatened to get off and walk, but when they did get out, they began to shove and put their shoulders to the wheels until they had worked off their bad temper, then the truck started amid the laughs and jokes of the men.

The snow seemed to make the passengers unusually sociable. The men began hobnobbing, and reminisced of snow storms they had passed—some as pioneers—some as soldiers—while the clear air rang with the girls' merry laughter, as they were bumped and jounced, which seemed to be reechoed by the joyous bells of the sleighs which began to dart along the streets.

So it went on till we reached the 49th Street stables. Here a fresh double team was attached. By this time I had as thick a blanket of snow as did the driver, but I was all aglow at the thought of our cozy fireside.

The girls and young fellows who got off the car did not excite sympathy, for their laughter came rippling back as they snowballed one another as they ran joyously over the fields of untrodden snow.

On arriving home my father gave his usual lecture about the danger from exposure to the bitter cold on the front platform.


## New Year's Day Calls

There was great preparation on all sides for calling and receiving on New Year's Day. Parties were made up and lists prepared. Those who had money hired a coach or sleigh, while others less fortunate footed it. Cards of the day were characteristic, and generally ornamented by some appropriate design of Father Time, with the Old Year going out and the New Year coming in, etc., or with some elaborate copper plate scroll of the professional penman. Girls prepared all sorts of refreshments and vied with each other with the number of their callers. The Postman and the Newsman sent broadsheets called "Carriers Addresses," which consisted of doggerel verses wishing a Happy New Year and returns. A greenback was expected in return.

Bakers sent cakes representing animal hearts, etc., decorated with caraway seeds coated with sugar, pink or white, a survival of the old Dutch customs. Small boys ran from store to store bursting in with yells, "Wish you a happy New Year, what are you going to give us?" The streets were filled with cutters and sleighs with jingle bells—it was joy inspiring.

After church, two or three of my friends would gather at my house, and well primed with cake, coffee or lemonade, we would start out for the day visiting our neighbors and gradually extending our circle. The glow and tingle of the walk was heightened by the gust of warm spice-laden air that greeted us, as our pretty little girl schoolmates received us at the doors in all their holiday finery.

We lined up on the sofa, and they overwhelmed us with the embarrassment of riches: oranges, cake, apples, lemonade, coffee, doughnuts, raisins, and spicy New Year's cake, etc.

We were ready to receive it all. Some of the little pretty girls, a little stiff in their finery, would give little giggles, and nervously try to pull the short dresses over the knees of their dangling legs, while we, equally embarrassed, after we had eaten or spilled our refreshments, would whack or punch each other on the knees, till we finally mustered up courage to bid a happy New Year and start for the next house. Sometimes a boy would flunk about calling on his girl; then we would grab him and make him walk up the stoop, and hold him there while we rang the bell.

Among the grown up people, the same eagerness to start and cover ground was shown. New Year's morning, with shutters closed, and blinds drawn down, gas lighted, the young ladies prepared to receive their guests. All seemed to reflect the glow and color of the pendant prisms on the chandeliers and candelabra.

The girls in full dress with flowers in their hair, clustered around a long table. Its glistening silver coffee urn, liquors, etc., with the usual turkey and other substantial things, which they served to the groups of merry friends who had driven up in their cutters. Among those who received special attention were some young veteran soldiers, whose empty sleeves gave the girls an excuse to hover around and serve them.

The brightness of this scene was intensified by the rich mahogany doors with their crystal or brass knockers; the crimson hangings of the windows, the deep toned walls and carpets, the heavy carved frames with their ancestral portraits by Gilbert Stuart or John Trumbull, which, in their turn, seemed to absorb as well as reflect back the rich and radiant glory of these rooms.

The beaming Negro butler smilingly welcomed and ushered in the new arrivals, who in many cases did not remove their overcoats, or in the cases of some older men who wore shawls.

Most of the guests seemed anxious to make a record for the number of calls they made—as the girls were anxious as to the number of calls they received by counting their visiting cards—but others evidently came to stay judging from the way they clustered around the beautiful young girls. One sang by request the then popular song, *Ever of Thee*, while a taller and fairer one accompanied her lightly on the harp.

## Abuses of New Year's Calls

Abuses gradually crept in from this open hearted hospitality. I remember a specimen: I called on some friends who lived in an old time frame house set back in a lot. A long grape arbor led back to the stoop. It was a bright, warm winter day. The downy snow was beginning to lose its grip on the grape arbor and gaunt vines and melt and fluff off. The wooden fence posts, as well as the clothes posts, still retained their snowy wigs.

The room exhaled the aroma of good cheer. As we were sitting there, having a jolly good time as our intimacy since children warranted, one of the girls, sitting at the window, gave a gasp of horror. A large excursion stage drew up at the gate, and down the brick walk came a gawky, swaggering, pale-haired, pale-eyed fellow, with a big accordion under his arm; his soft hat pulled over his right eye, with four dents in it, which, in the slang of the day meant, "I, AM, A, GAMBLER!" and his long purple jaws rolling a long frayed cigar in his mouth. Behind him, were twenty or more of the same toughs.

The girls looked dazed as they pounded up the stoop, and one gawk announced himself as one of the schoolmates of one of the younger boys. They pushed into the room until they packed it solid. They were a dull, fumbling lot of lumps. After the girls had wedged through them and passed around refreshments, and they had stolidly gorged themselves, they had nothing to say except when they guyed each other in their cracked voices, or gripped or crunched each other's knees for want of a better idea. I was jammed in a corner, nearly upsetting a globe of stuffed birds on a small table, as the fellow with the accordion tuned up with the songs, *The Flying Trapeze*, and *Tassels on her Boots*, in which he was joined in their rasping choruses that almost brought down the white-washed ceiling in the low parlor. After this I managed to work my way out, and the next day I read that this "Social Club" had all been arrested later in the evening going through Harlem for being drunk and disorderly.

But the charm of it all was the meeting of old and sometimes estranged friends—the welding of broken links, the hearty shouts of laughter, at the sight of some rosy, jolly old veteran insisting on his New Year's right to kiss some shrinking maiden in her seventies, who would protest, mildly with her laced-mittened hands; or in the greeting of those old gentlemen who were never allowed out except under the guidance of some lusty granddaughter.

But our joys were in the last call, prearranged, when the rush was over and the girls would spread a special feast, and we would all sit around; and while disposing of cold turkey, cakes and cranberries, as though we were just beginning the morning. We would rehearse the joys, humors and triumphs of the day. As years went on, some exclusive ones used to hang out baskets on the door knob to receive cards from the pilgrims of friendship. This sort of frigid acknowledgement soon killed the enthusiasm, and after a few seasons, the joys of New Years calling were no more.

## Tom Rushton—A Youthful Encounter

A big, strong, fine-looking Englishman, named Tom Rushton, came to board with our neighbor, Mrs. Cawley. He was at least six feet tall; soft brown hair and mustache; brown eyes and round face, with a brief, rather tip-tilted nose; red cheeks—a fresh looking fellow. Rushton had taken an interest in me, in a semi-patronizing way. I, a boy about eleven or twelve, was intensely fascinated by his manly form and general air of importance.

Rushton used to take me with him, I suppose from the constant tribute I paid to his physical strength, which he returned by criticizing everything about me, as regards my physical development. In fact, he was constantly criticizing everything in this country. He would take me to the swimming baths at 30th Street and Sixth Avenue, and while in the pool, would take great pride in displaying his figure in and out of the water, and constantly talk of his wonderful prowess as a sailor in our Navy during the war, though he was constantly running down his officers and companions. When I was about fifteen, I had grown to be about five feet seven inches, and spent most of my spare time taking exercise by boxing or wrestling.

Rushton married and called at our house with his bride, a big, flushed-face English girl, good natured and jolly. By that time I had all the grace and outline of a poker. He said, "Stand up, Jim; I want to show you how to take care of yourself among those Yankee boys you go with. You know you have no vigor—they have no figure—they are like you." I did so, and stood at attention while he gave me his lecture, as a horrible physical example to his new wife.

"Now stand up!" said Mr. Rushton. I did so. "Throw out your chest!" I did so. At the same time he struck a menacing attitude, like an old-time English boxing print. "Now I am going to strike you," and his big fist shot out at me. I ducked, crouched, countered and planted a screw twist on his little nose. The blood flowed. My mother screamed. His wife went into convulsions of laughter. He grabbed his poor little gumdrop of a nose, the blood streaming through his fingers. I gasped, thinking I had killed him.

My mother jumped up. "Jimmie!" she cried, grabbing me by the collar and shaking me until my teeth rattled, saying, "How dare you hit him?" "I didn't mean to," I whimpered, while Rushton ran to the sink with his nose grabbed between his fingers and thumb, and bled like a stuck pig. At last he stopped the flow of blood, and holding his nose, snuffed out, "Why—why, I didn't mean for you to hit me; I meant to hit you," at which his wife burst out in another roar of laughter.

## Apprenticeship 1870

My formal education ended when I turned fifteen years old, and my father decided that it was time for me to learn a trade. A friend of my father's was an enameller of jewelry, and got me an apprenticeship as a jewelry engraver for brothers Henry & Paul Siebert, at No. 1 John Street, northeast corner of Broadway.

We sat at a large table forming a half circle across from a window; the table had four small circles cut in the edge, large enough to insert our chests and rest our elbows on the projections. Jewelry of any size, or flat pieces, were rested on a round flat little cushion, stuffed with sand, but pieces such as rings or trinkets were set in a lump of very hard wax mounted on the end of a short block of wood called a stump. The stump was screwed in a small iron vice, which had a base like a cannon ball, which rested in a round cushion-like bird's nest; by that means the engraver had a firm grip on the jewelry and could turn it in any direction.

I was given a graver, and set to work cutting lines on a piece of flat brass. Boss Henry would call out, "Dig deep, Jimmie, dig deep!" As my fingers were unusually strong, I did so, and put my graver clear through the watch case, which pulled down the profit, at least on that particular job.

At noon the boss said, "Go down to the saloon and bring some beer." "No," I replied. "What?" he said in amazement, and the others stared.

"Why?" he asked, after he caught his breath. "Because," I answered, "I belong to the Good Templars Temperance Society and don't carry beer." There was a silence; when he growled out, "I was a damned fool like that myself once; I used to belong to the Good Templars." A dead silence followed; then drawing himself up, he sneered, "Would you mind going to a saloon and buying some sandwiches and pie?" "All right," I answered. He handed me the money and I went off and bought the lunch. I never saw beer while I stayed there.

It was tough work, and in a few days the ends of my fingers looked like drum sticks, with clots of burned and calloused flesh.

That was the summer of 1870, and the Franco-Prussian War was going on; Henry Siebert was pro-German, and Paul was pro-French. They would fight and abuse each other, and jump up quivering with rage as though they were going to stick each other with their gravers, but it ended there. Day by day the French defeats were proclaimed with joy in the papers, and the enthusiasm for the Germans was unbounded.

To stand up for the French was to invite abuse, and of course, I invited it by asserting my opinion in and out of season, which added to my disfavor with the boss. One day the boss began to abuse the Irish, saying that they were in the Draft Riots. I said, "The Dutch were in it, too!" Here I was wrong—the rank and file of the rioters were Irish, and "True Americans." "Oh, go to hell," said my boss. "I don't allow any man to talk to me like that," I replied and grabbing my vise, "I'm no Dutchman; I'll brain you." He blazed out, "I don't ask you to take anything from me—Get Out!" "I'm not ready to go yet," I replied, and went on with my work; I was afraid to go home, and sat it out.  He must have been afraid of me, for I stayed on, and on Saturday night demanded my wages, two dollars, which he gave me.  At this time another jeweler got him to take on his nephew, and the second Saturday night, with my two dollars, the boss gave me a note to give to my father.

On my way home, stiff and tired, I stopped in front of the *Herald* building, Broadway and Ann St., and read the posted headline: "BATTLE OF SEDAN—Fall of Napoleon III."  Heartsick at the fall of my hopes, I went home and handed the note to my father; he opened it and read:

> Dear Mr. Kelly,
>> I don't want James around any more.  I would advise you to put him at some business that requires less exertion.
>> Henry Siebert

My father looked up and said quietly, "What are you going to do now?"

"I am going down Monday morning and lick him," I replied.

"How are you going to get down?"

"Why ride down, of course."

"No, I won't give you the money; and after you walk down, you'll be so tired out when you get there, he'll lick you!"

This struck me as true; by Monday morning I had forgotten all about it, and started looking for a new trade.

My father then tried to find me a position as a wood engraver.  At that time, for artwork to appear in newspapers, artists made their drawings in full detail on wood blocks as a guide to the wood engravers.  He took me to a printer in William Street by the name of Bloom, who had worked for him as a boy.  Mr. Bloom gave me an introduction to the engravers who did his work, but as they did not need a boy, they gave me an introduction to the engraving firm of Meeder & Chubb.  They agreed to take me as an apprentice; the arrangement was nothing for the first year, two dollars a week for the second year, and so on.

On coming out, my father said in his low, confidential voice, in which he generally got very Scotch, "Jimze, (as he always called me when he felt in that mood) I noticed that the other boy in there is broad in the back and short in the legs, while you are long in the back and long in the legs.  Now when he starts in to thrash you, which he will do in a few days, don't let him get a grip on you for he'll break your back!  But run in on him, reach round, grip him by the seat of his trousers; lift him off his feet, and butt him in the face.  Now remember!"

With this final introduction from my father, delivered with a strong Scotch accent, in a tone as though he was reading a verse from the Scriptures, I entered into the Art World.

Going to work the next day as office boy, I had to sweep the floor and kindle the fire.  My employers were Mr. Philip Meeder, a dark, fine looking German, with a large hooked nose and a huge black mustache.  Mr. Fred W. Chubb was a delicate featured man of English descent with kindly blue eyes and a red mustache with side whiskers.

Meeder was self-assertive and brilliant; Chubb was retiring and gentle. The journeyman was William Myrtle, a fine big wholesome German boy, with large, soft, brown amiable eyes. Mr. Thomas D. Sugden, a veteran of the Civil War, was the head engraver, but mostly worked from home; he was very sedate, but on acquaintance, I found him very sentimental in his love for Art. We became friends at once and are friends still. The fellow my father had warned me about was the former office boy—black haired, swarthy, broad shouldered, square built, stocky; thick legs, and a jaunty swagger—Charlie Bernstein was his name.

I had been at work only a few days and was busy sweeping the floor at noon hour, when Mr. Sugden, William and Charlie came in—William smoking a big cigar, Charlie smoking a pipe. They had been out to dinner. Charlie evidently felt his oats, being out with the men. As he passed me, he rubbed his open palm over my face—my hands being engaged holding the broom. I put the broom in the corner and stepped in front of him. He looked at me with amazement, then understanding my challenge, said, "Wait 'till I hang up my coat!" Putting down his pipe, he grinned at the others, carefully tucked up his sleeves, and waddled towards me like a bear on his hind legs. I felt his grip closing round me. I slid down, according to directions, reached round, gripped him by the seat of the trousers, lifting him off his feet, and butted him—lifting him with my knee at the same time. As he fell, his shoulders struck the top of a turtle-back trunk. He fell over, and behind it, where it was never swept. He came out smeared with dust. He looked dazed. Putting his hand in his pocket, he pulled out a small, flat silver watch, saying, "If I was not afraid of breaking this, you'd have been laying on the floor!" This cleared the air, and was our last scuffle.

Our shop was somewhat commercial, and made transfers for our own engraving and for the trade. They took a print from some other book for which they wanted to make another engraving, soaked it in alcohol and potash to soften the ink, placed it face down on a boxwood block, run it through a press which transferred it to the block. The engraver then cut the wood away, except the black lines; that left the picture in relief like type, from which other prints were made. Transfers were generally engraved by boys, to practice the kind of lines that made different tints, so when they had a drawing to reproduce they knew what kind of tint was necessary to render it.

I did not show much skill in either handling the graver or judgment in rendering tints. I could not understand it at first, but when it came, it came like a flash, and not by practice.

At first I was set to work cutting facsimiles from drawings in the *London News*, and after a time I ventured to make my own drawings on wood. But I found that after I had made my drawing, the labor of cutting it made me lose interest; I could cut other people's work better.

Mr. Sugden was attracted by my drawings and we became close friends. He started in to give me the benefit of his knowledge. He had a large collection of wood cuts, principally from the *London News*. These were fine subjects for him to refer to, as they reproduced the best Masters. He was continually trying to add to his collection of wood engravings and used to sometimes take me on his haunts. At noon hour we would start out and turn through Theatre Alley, which originally led to the stage door of the Old Park Theatre. It was about fifteen feet broad, with sidewalks about two feet wide with small cobble stones, inclined to the center, which depression acted as a drain. I was told that the Alley was used as a place wherein to settle fights, "Meet me in the Alley!" was the challenge.

Old book shops were plentiful with their stalls or bins of bargains at the head of their cellar steps. We stopped at one and descended. The atmosphere of old books attracted me with that magic odor which has affected the minds of book lovers through the ages. Then came the joy of the hunt. I have never ridden to hounds, but can imagine the thrill of the "view hollow," but it cannot equal the wonderful sensation that stirs one at the sight of an old print glowing with the sunshine of the past—"the light of other days." There were never such prints before or since, as appeared in the *London News*. They alone would make England dear to me. They conquered where her armies failed, and won us with the charm of England.

One morning a new man appeared at Meeder & Chubb. He was a German of the Kaiserbrand. His name was Leonard; quite tall, round-faced, round-eyed which were whitey-blue, with a hesitating nose through which he seemed to snore being so heavily loaded with snuff; a fierce yellow moustache; a high narrowed brimmed silk hat, gray trousers cut tight to his sleek legs and took the shape of his boots; a cane with silk tassels, but all spoiled when he took out a big bandana handkerchief and blew his nose like a porpoise. He did not talk English and began to treat me as they treated all inferiors, beginning from the Kaiser down.

This I resented, so one day while I was sweeping the floor and raising a big cloud of dust—he resented it—I became indignant. He whirled on me with a mad snort, grabbed a heavy arm chair, dashed it on the floor and swung back his arm like a scythe and with chin extended and eyes bulging with rage, he rushed at me. I brought my broom to a charge bayonet caught him right under his bulging chin. This brought him to a halt at once. To my astonishment, he drew himself up, clicked his heels, threw out his chest, wheeled left and started out of the room—this way showing his contempt for me. William entering, they began talking German while William laughing heartily and looked at me. I said, "What is that Dutchman saying?" As soon as William could pull himself together he answered, "He says you were going to hit him in the snoot, and if you had he would have picked you up, carried you out in the hall and dropped you over the banisters." Here he lay back in his arm chair and laughed at my rage, till tears filled his eyes.

Mr. J. R. Pierson had a wood engraving establishment on the same floor with Meeder & Chubb. He was genial, kind and an assertive friend. After he got to know me a little, he would give me odd jobs to draw. He would walk into our office and say, "Jimmie, I have a job for you," and tell me what he wanted and walked out regardless of whether my boss liked it or not. As this was the first order of the kind I was much elated, and went around showing the sketches to the different engravers. This amused Mr. Pierson, who called out, "Jim reminds me of a young pullet going around cackling after laying her first egg."

It was good training for me, and I shall never forget Mr. Pierson as the friend of my "pullet days."

# Chapter Two
# Rise of the Young Artist
# 1871-1878

"It would not be making a just comment on Mr. Kelly or his work to fail to refer to his marvelous sympathy with and knowledge about horses. Horses from whom he has worked have actually in many cases learned to pose for him—although one not intimately acquainted with the animal might be inclined to smile at the idea."—An Art Review in Outlook Magazine.

## The Academy of Design

Spending the rest of my days engraving other artist's designs at Meeder & Chubb did not appeal to me. I grew restive, and my father called on Mr. Meeder and asked him about my getting some work at designing, as reports were against me as an engraver. In the meantime, it was decided that I would apply for admission to the Academy of Design to attend drawing classes at night.

According to the rules of the Academy, it was necessary to submit a drawing in crayon from a plaster-cast. I sent a study of the boy on the right in the *Laocoön*. On receiving word that I had passed, I rang the doorbell on the Fourth Avenue entrance, and was received by a stout, round-faced Englishman, with a big bulgy mustache, goatee and paunch; that was the janitor, Porterfield, who took my card and led me down the hall to a pair of double doors at the entrance to the Antique Room, which faced on Fourth Avenue.

I can remember standing at the top of the steps leading down to the school, with my heart in my mouth, yet thrilled with exultation that at last I was an art student. Before me extended a long, wide apartment for about 75 feet; to the right opened three alcoves, called the first, second and third. The first was for beginners, filled with classical busts, from which the students at their easels were copying with crayon.

As I stood there bewildered, young Wallace Denslow caught sight of me, and came over with congratulations, then conducted me to where Gaul was at work, and introduced us. Gaul was called "Billy" at that time, which with success became Gilbert, and we became friends for life.

From the time I entered the Academy, my whole spirit seemed transformed; all I thought of was ART, and everything was gauged by its relation to it.  Every man, woman, child or animal was an unconscious model, and every rock, field or wood, as well as every stretch of river, were foregrounds or backgrounds to my historical fancies.  At that time I used to put in a stirring day. I would start downtown on an Eighth Avenue car, and regardless of the weather, take my post beside the driver, so that I could study the horses and various incidents; work at my desk until noon, and then prowl around, sketching the shipping, or the queer streets, where I would go with impunity.

In 1872, we moved up to 875 Eighth Avenue.  It was during the Grant and Greeley Presidential Campaign which was very bitter.  One evening I was riding the Eighth Avenue horse car, I stood on the rear platform with my back to the rear window.  Reaching 46th Street, a very tall stout man jumped aboard, swung heavily against me, recovering himself, he lurched to the seat on the side on which he entered.  I at first thought he was boozy, but saw it was Horace Greeley.

He had hardly braced up when a man opposite leaned over and shook hands with him.  They exchanged a few words, then Greeley dropped his chin on his chest and went sound asleep.  It was the first and I regret to say the only time I had ever seen him.  My father had brought me up to reverence him.  He had thrown aside his eccentric dress which was identified with him and wore a black slouch hat and a black broadcloth suit which intensified his silver hair and whiskers which encircled his pink and white face with its childlike purity of expression.

I got off on 52nd Street.

Greeley's defeat in the election of November 9th seemed to shatter him physically and mentally.  He died three weeks later on November 29, 1872.  The city showed his memory every honor.  His body lay in state in the City Hall. When I saw it, the change was remarkable.  He had become thin and shrunken, and I noticed on his wan left hand what looked like a plain gold wedding ring.

# Harper's Publications 1872-1874

My father called on the Harper Brothers Publishing House and Mr. Charles Parsons, head of the Art Department, and asked them to take me on as an apprentice to draw on wood for the engravers.  He was first told that they never received apprentices, and as to my drawings—many boys had applied, some had better drawings, some worse—so he would not encourage me.  Still this did not down me.  I do not know what my father said to Mr. Parsons, but the result:  I was to go down to work and apprenticed till I was twenty-one.  I was the first apprentice that Harper ever took.

I entered the Art Department at Harper's, and met Mr. Parsons.  He looked me over, and said, "Go over there, and make a sketch of some of the gentlemen in the office," pointing to a desk in the far corner.  My first sketch I showed Mr. Parsons who nodded approval and handing me a few issues of *Harper's Weekly* said, "Now take a picture and copy it."  I took one and copied it line for line. "Very good!" was Parson's remark when I showed it to him. Taking it from me quickly, he said, "Go and draw it from memory!" I did so—line for line. Walking over, I handed it to him. He compared the drawing with the original. Looking up sharply, he said, "Kelly, you have a good memory," and handed both back. The copy was remarkably close. All this was to try me out as a Special Artist, I suppose, if I was in a position where I could not sketch, but memorize.

I took my place and looked over my surroundings. In the room was Theodore R. Davis, their Special Artist during the Civil War. He was lean of feature and form; long hair, and crisply chiseled face. When he spoke, his voice was so deep and strong that it seemed like a ventriloquist making a lion's roar come out of a delicate china vase.

One day I showed Davis a poem called, *News of Lexington*. He told me it was by Thomas Dunn English; then with a low sympathetic falsetto voice he sang, *Ben Bolt*, and told me it was by the same author. I was entranced. It was the first time I had heard it. He also sang *Sherman's March to the Sea*. It opens with the lines, "Our camp fires shown bright on the mountain." It set me off, and tended to idealize Sherman in my eyes.

Davis was full of war stories. He told of asking Sherman to sit for a sketch on horseback. "Oh, don't bother," said Sherman, "just take my photograph and put it on Washington's white horse. It will be alright. Why every General I can remember has been put on Washington's white horse."

The next stall was Edwin A. Abbey's. To describe him is difficult. He was just Abbey. There was no one like him: short, agile, joyous with light brown hair; a finely modeled brow, straight nose with sensitive nostrils; a flexible mouth with crisp glowing lips, blue-white teeth and a delightful merry laugh; a voice refined, rich in tone and winning. His hands were firm, shapely, and high bred, which showed his heritage and mental alertness.

His desk was on a line with mine, so I had a fine chance to study him under all conditions—the various expressions of his mobile face, and the dexterous, nimble aptness of his pencil stroke. At that time, Abbey was about twenty years of age.

After about a year at Harper's, I became best of friends with Abbey. Whenever he got into trouble drawing a piece of anatomy or drapery, he would come over to my table and I would help him by posing.

Charles S. Reinhart occupied the desk in the corner; he was about thirty, and seemed quite old to me. He was tall, very erect, slim and shapely in figure; features almost classic in their perfection of outline; crisp, brown, curly hair, and a very small brown mustache. Reinhart was considered the leading artist on wood of that period; he had received fine training in the German Art Schools, where he had studied for several years, although a native of Pittsburgh. He was a brilliant talker and very kind hearted, often staying in the office after the rest had gone correcting my drawings and advising me until the light failed. He was very sensitive. I have seen his eyes fill with emotion and his lip twitch at an affecting tale; he and Abbey were inseparable friends. It was a great source of instruction for me to hear them talk on their theories and the literature of art, for at that time I had looked upon drawing only as a means of expression of my ideas. I can still remember Reinhart's look of amazed amusement when asked what "technique" was.

Among the distinguished men who dropped into the Art Department was Alfred R. Waud, who had been Special Artist for *Frank Leslie's* and *Harper's Weekly* during the Civil War. He followed the Army of the Potomac and sketched some of our great battles. Waud was a fine type of Englishman, a blond with rosy cheeks, long light hair, and a full red beard. He was very humorous, but inclined to be sarcastic. He talked in a very low voice with a slight suggestion of a lisp, and as he reached the point of his story, brought it lower and lower, till the listeners were bowed in fascination before him.

His brother, Will Waud, was also distinguished for his bravery. Admiral George Dewey speaks of him in his memoirs as having been on his ship in the Battle of Manila Bay, and like Farragut, took his post in the mizzen top so that he could observe the battle.

Edwin Forbes used to come in; he had also been a Special Artist during the Civil War and has made very valuable sketches of army life. He had but one arm.

Alfred Waud said that Forbes told him he had never felt fear. "But," Waud added, "that is the difference with me. I never could get used to hearing bullets whistling round my ears, and shells bursting round my horse's croup. While it was going on, I generally felt a little nervous."

Captain Ulysses Eddy later told me he had seen Waud sitting on an earthwork sketching, while the shots were flying around him, and he would keep up a conversation and tell jokes to our soldiers behind it.

Robert Lewis had just returned from France and had the conventional artist makeup: long hair, mustache and imperial. Later, when we became acquainted, he showed me some of his life studies, which were a revelation to me. He died before he had achieved distinction.

Paul du Chaillu frequently bustled in. He had just returned from the Artic Circle and was preparing his book: *The Land of the Midnight Sun.* He brought all sorts of curiosities and relics from that region to aid the artists in illustrating his book—a low, boat-shaped sled, costumes of many kinds, and weapons used by the natives.

Du Chaillu wore a straight, flat-brimmed stove-pipe silk hat, and a long tailed frock coat. In actions he was crisp and chirpy like a bird. Who would think to look at the fellow that he had spent four years [1856-1859] in Africa where he discovered the gorilla and the almost unknown pygmies of the interior? When on his return, du Chaillu proclaimed his discoveries, and his statements were promptly challenged by the swivel-chair scientists. This reflection on his integrity so enraged the little man that he pulled the nose of a prominent know-it-all savant connected with the British Museum. Shortly after that he silenced all doubts by producing the skins and relics. In after years, I got to know him. Speaking, of someone about whom I referred to as a "nice fellow," he replied with an earnest look in his eyes, "Kelly, there are lots of nice fellows, but one has to be a nice fellow to find them."

Thomas Nast was the great feature of Harper's at that time, but he never lowered himself to come in the Art Department among the draughtsmen. When he came to town he did his business with the Harpers in their private offices. To equal, or beat Nast, was my ambition as a boy, but I always had a great desire to see him, though I never met him until a short time before his death, after he departed from Harper's.

He was undersized, with strong, bushy, iron-gray hair; a full very smooth forehead; bright, black, searching eyes; nose hooked, sharp and hard looking, suggesting a parrot's beak; a long, flowing, black moustache and long goatee; a dark olive complexion. He had a most wholesome, warm and genial manner and personality, and his rich, deep voice, and its gracious intonation, added to his attractiveness. He talked with the precision of a foreigner, although he was but a child when he came from Bavaria.

His charm was typified by his Christmas sketches; his ruthless political cartoons were prompted by the characteristics of his hawk-like beak.

Through a mutual friend, I was later invited to his home in Morristown, New Jersey. His house was lined with his cartoons, and the very stairways were full of sketches. He showed me a painting of the head of Christ, also a large painting of a girl washing a window, seen from the outside, which was quite unique; and a large, glowing, cozy painting of Santa Claus, which had been painted for the St. Nicholas Society, but they had rejected it.

I spoke of his illustrations of the novel [by George F. Harrington] called: *Inside. A Chronicle of Secession*, and told how much I admired their character. He seemed surprised and replied, "You are the first that ever spoke of them."

He showed me his original sketches during the war. He gave me an engraving with the account of his painting, *Lincoln Entering Richmond*, which he told me he had drawn from description.

In our Art Superintendent, Mr. Charles Parsons, we were all very fortunate. He showed us great consideration, and his criticisms were searching, but just. He was a handsome man, fine features, flowing hair and beard; a keen, active, rather nervous manner. He always tried to look at a piece of work from the artist's point of view, without asserting himself, but his text was refinement and delicate grays.

As a growing boy I was a combination of strength and weakness. My strength consisted of a powerful appetite, and the ability to carry an enormous lunch under my arm to sustain me during the day. When I arrived mornings, Abbey would call out, "Look out, Kelly, don't drop it on your feet!" Then Davis would pipe up with the joke which he got off regularly every morning, like the end man to the interlocutor in a minstrel show. "Abbey, did you ever hear what the Duke of Wellington said at Waterloo?" "No," Abbey would answer. Then Davis would say, "The Duke rode down the lines, and halting, called out, 'Is Private O'Kelly in the ranks?' 'He is, My Lord,' they answered. At this the Duke slapping his hand on his leg, roared out, 'Then let the battle begin!'"

I was overgrown and lanky. My strength ran up and down. I had no cross-braces. After I had worked awhile, my chest and back would ache. This, added to the quiet of the room and my isolation in the corner, used to get on my nerves.

Mr. Parsons had a habit of going up and down the room at a sharp pace, giving out blocks and looking at the work, and would often stop, look kindly down into my face, and say softly, "Kelly, you look tired. You had better go down to the docks and make some sketches." What a grateful relief it was.

I once heard him telling a friend, how as a boy he had to work very hard, and long hours, and had suffered so much, he resolved if ever he had men under him, he would treat them differently.

After this kind advice, I would joyfully start down stairs, stand on the stoop and take in my surroundings.

During this time my secret ambition was to paint a picture of "The Fight on Lake Erie," so vividly described in Commodore Oliver H. Perry's Log Book. I used to make sketches with all the spare time at the office. To obtain help for the sketch, some two or three other lads my own age were pressed into service, and a method devised for the obtaining of the "spray effects" of cannon shot hitting water. To accomplish this, we took up a load of stones and rowed out on the Hudson, steering our little boat near the 55th Street dock where some vessels freighted with bricks were unloading. We threw stones at the deck hands, and called them all the names we could think of. All of that so enraged the men that they gave us several volleys of bricks, which fell around us, some of them very close. The plunging bricks, flying spray and spice of danger, as well as the laughing and tossing of the boat, inspired me with the spirit of the scene. On my return home I made a new composition, and in other trips to the river my friends posed in the sunshine to give me the effect as they strained at the oars.

I showed the finished drawing to Mr. Parsons, who said, "Kelly, I should advise you not to waste your time on war pictures—there's no demand for them. Learn to draw ladies and gentlemen." But I would not take his well-meant advice. Some time later, Charles Dana Gibson entered the field and proved Mr. Parsons right, though I doubt my ability to have rivaled him, as he was equipped by nature in every way to illustrate such subjects, being tall, handsome, shapely and refined. He only had to look in a mirror and study his own reflection to find the ideal young American, which together with his studies of women of equal charm, have brought him fame and fortune.

## Winslow Homer

One day in the Art Department, an erect, slim, well groomed military looking gentleman walked in; dark, close cropped hair, sparkling black eyes, straight prominent nose, dark mustache brushed abruptly aside with a slight twist—like a cavalry officer, clean cut sensitive chin, a fine full throat; his hands were well bred and shapely. He had the graceful movements and bearing of a thoroughbred. He was dressed to perfection, markedly so; his black cut away coat and steel gray trousers had the set and precision of a uniform.

Mr. Parsons greeted him as "Mr. Homer." They sat down while Mr. Parsons looked over the drawings which he had brought and made some suggestions.

The man was Winslow Homer and no one could have been more kind to me when I was a boy just starting in art.

I have an impression that his drawing that day was of a group of boys climbing on the face of a cliff. Mr. Parsons was quite critical and would make suggestions while Homer would take in good part and make the corrections. He sold many sketches which are to be found in the old *Harper's Weekly*. This is the same Winslow Homer who in later years snubbed wealthy, would-be patrons after he had turned his back on the world for a quiet life among fishermen.

During his visits to Harper's, he was always civil and coolly polite to all. A short time after, Mr. Parsons called me up to his desk and said, "Would you like to meet Mr. Winslow Homer?" I said, "I would be glad to." "Then take up this block with this note," said Mr. Parsons.

I called at his 10th Street studio. To my knock the door was partly opened and Homer stood in the opening. I said, "Mr. Parsons sent these," handing him the block and note. As he opened the note, a card dropped at his feet. Picking it up, he read aloud: "Introducing James E. Kelly." Then seeming to read more he looked at me quizzically and smiling, said, "Come in." Then opening the door wide he ushered me in. I have often wondered what was written on that card.

The room had a reddish carpet; I can recall on the easel was his boys on the stern of a sailboat [*A Fair Wind (Breezing Up)*]. There were other canvases turned with their faces to the walls. Everything was in perfect order—spick and span—looking like himself. As he started to talk to me, he stopped, went over and picked up a thread of lint from the dustless carpet and threw it in the scrap basket. He then read the note and the manuscript, turning to me he said, "This is a poem calling for a young man making love to a young lady in a boat. Now I have no model for the young man, will you pose for the young man?" "Yes," I said, "glad to."

He continued, "There is a young lady coming in a little while who will also pose." Shortly after a tall, buxom young girl came in. She had a glowing complexion and a mass of golden reddish hair. He introduced her as, "Miss Clark," saying with a laugh, "Miss Clark, I am to illustrate a poem in which a beautiful young lady is having a nice young man make love to her. Now here is a nice young man who has consented to make love to you. As the beautiful young lady, will you pose?" The girl was taller and somewhat older than myself, looked down at me with a big girl manner, her lips twitched and laughingly said, "All right."

Then Homer said, "I will show you how to pose." He then grouped us. She was supposed to be sitting in the boat fishing, while I was kneeling behind leaning over holding her reel. Every little while she would start laughing, but my back had such a kink in it, that it did not seem like fun. After he finished the study, she left. He then showed me the picture on the easel. I said, "Didn't I see that in the Academy?" "Yes," he said, "that was three years ago, but I didn't know how to finish it at the time." As I was leaving, he said, "I thank you and if you ever want to know how to paint, come to me and I'll teach you."

After that, Winslow Homer always showed me marked favor. When he visited the Academy of Design, he would always stop and greet me with his genial smile and hand clasp. I was so shy I hardly talked to him. He would generally end our meeting by saying, "Come down and see me." The more I grew to admire him, the more bashful I got, which he evidently understood, and whenever he met me in the gallery he would walk over and shake hands with me, and at the same time ask how I was getting along and say, "Come down and see me."

One night in particular I recall at the Academy, I was standing with a friend, when Homer came in with a crowd of friends. I think Homer Martin was with them. At the sight of me, his eye lit up and with a smile, he came over with his hand advanced to greet me. I was so embarrassed; I would have bolted if there was a chance, but stood uncertain. He shook hands as usual and again asking me to see him. He rejoined his friends and as they left the gallery, my friend laughed heartily saying, "Oh, how funny it was to watch when you saw Homer coming over to speak to you!" laughing again, "Oh, how you did twitch!"

Another time I was going through the halls of the 10th Street Studios and met Homer. He said, "Are you coming to see me?" "No," I said, "I am going to see Billy Gaul." (As we called Gilbert Gaul when a student) "All right," said Homer, "come down anytime."

At last I did muster courage and I found myself inside Homer's studio. It had the same well-brushed, well-dusted, neat look that it had when I first saw it. He then started over to the west end of the studio pulling out some studies he had made at the front as Special Artist for *Harper's Weekly* during the Civil War. He sat on the floor while I sat beside him on his left. The picture, which has obscured the memory of the rest, was one of Lincoln holding little Tad by the hand standing beside General Grant. He told how he sketched them as they stood on the railway platform—I think he said at City Point. I asked, "Did they pose for you?" "No," he said, "I wouldn't think of asking such great men to pose for me." "Why if I was you, I would have asked them," I said, "I should think they would be glad to pose for you." To me, Homer was a bigger man than either of them and I couldn't understand his modesty.

I said to him, "I saw that painting [*The Bright Side*] of yours showing a party of darkie teamsters sleeping on the sunny side of a tent." "Yes," he said laughing, "I painted them from life just as you see them and the funny part of it is just as I had finished, that darkey poked his head out of the tent door and looked at me and I painted him just as he was."

He had a story to tell of each of his sketches. One day he said, "I was sketching, when a small boy and his little sister came up. He said, 'How much will you charge to make my picture?' I said, 'I'll make you for a cent.' So he ran home and got a cent, then came back and gave it to me. I made a sketch of him and his sister and handed it to him. Two or three days after, I met him and asked him if he still had the picture, he said, 'Yes.' I said, 'I'll give you ten cents for it.'

'All right,' he said, and brought me the sketch and I gave him the ten cents. When I came to New York, I sold it for thirty dollars."

He had painted a sketch of a zouave, which I remember vaguely. I spoke of it to him. "Yes," he said, "I got the uniform from a fellow who I saw just as he came from the front. I spoke to him and took him in a store and bought him a new suit for his old uniform."

He pointed to a pile of shoes in one corner. Picking some up he placed them on a table saying, "You should practice drawing old shoes and getting their character," and pointed out their different character and expressions in the various types of well worn shoes.

During the intervals of his talk, if anything was out of order, he would shift it in place, and a thread or a piece of paper on the floor would bring him to a stand while he would pick it up.

Homer not only gave me the full run of his studio, but instructed me in some of the essentials. He taught me all I really know, and in a most unusual way, he made me spend a winter drawing nothing but old silk hats and derbies, and finally old shoes. All my colleagues thought I was connected with a haberdashery. Homer insisted that all that could be learned about drawing could be learned by drawing but old hats and shoes. He then said, "Did you ever practice drawing high hats? You should practice drawing high hats." Taking out his own, he placed it on a table saying, "There is a great deal of drawing in a high hat—to get not only its curves, but its delicate variations in the outline which owes it style. It is not merely making a stovepipe, but to show its quality." He then placed it on its side and fore shortening to show part of the inside; he pointed out the beauty and grace of the complicated lines and the precision required to give the proper effect. He then added, "They are generally drawn badly; if you can't draw a high hat correctly, you can't draw anything."

One time I called, he was at work on his painting of *The Cottonpickers*. It represented two negro girls picking cotton; it was unfinished at the time. It showed a delicate gray sky as a background, which brought out in fine relief the brilliant bonnets, and the deep, rich, warm flesh tones of the dusky young girl with an arm extended picking the cotton bulb from the deep green cotton plant, which reached almost to her waist. No one can describe its charm or even suggest its effect, as it was a Homer masterpiece, and no one could conceive one of his pictures but himself, but on seeing—it strikes one so natural that it is a wonder that you have not painted it yourself.

One evening my father came down to Homer's studio to look for me. Homer told him I had not been there, but invited him in. My father was greatly taken with Homer and the reception he received. He showed him the *The Cottonpickers*, and explained how he had gotten his sketches for the work. He also showed some cottonballs from which he made his studies. He seems to have gotten confidential and told my father of his struggles and how he received no recognition till he was over forty. I believe my father went there at other times, as he was greatly taken with his personality.

Abbey always expressed the highest admiration of Homer and seemed elated at his visit to our studio in the University building. He was also impressed by Homer's attention to me that day.

One morning Abbey said, "Didn't Homer tell you he would teach you to paint?" "Yes," I replied. At the same time Abbey presented me a fine box of oil colors and advised me to go down immediately and remind Homer of his promise.

The next day I went down and knocked on Homer's studio door. He opened it partly, then recognizing me, smiled and said, "How do you do?" I blurted out, "Mr. Homer, you said whenever I wanted to learn to paint, I was to come to you." "Yes," he said, still smiling but continued to hold the door knob. "Well, I've come," I said. "Oh, you have," he answered in a hearty laugh, "Walk in!" Then looking me over, he asked, "When do you want to begin?" "Oh, anytime—now," I anxiously replied. "Oh, you do," he said, "well let's get to work."

Looking around, he picked out a small stretcher about eighteen inches high. Placing it on his easel, he took his clean palette and said, "This is the way to set it. You begin with white (placing a dab near his thumb hold), then with yellow ochre, then with red ochre, then with permanent blue, and then with raw sienna, then with burnt sienna."

As he finished he whirled around, leveled his black eyes upon me, and said sharply, "Will you remember that?" "Yes," I promised.

He then put some oil on the palette, and taking his brush, thinned out the sienna, saying, "You sketch it in with this," as he brushed in a small figure of a girl. Then with a light touch of a flat brush which he rested with its own weight, he drew a streak of white, yellow, red and blue to a common center with a few light flips of his brush. Homer blended them without puddling, which did not crush the minute granulations of the paint, and applied a light, deft, crisp touch to the canvas without the colors losing any of their original sparkle.

Wheeling around, he again asked, "Do you understand that?" "Yes," I answered. "Will you ever forget it?" "No." Then turning, he repeated his strokes, and after every telling one, would turn, fasten his black eyes on me and repeat, "Do you understand that?" "Yes," I would answer. "Will you ever forget it?" "No," I promised—and never have.

Then Homer added:

"If you make a mistake in laying on your color, don't try to correct it, but take it off with a palette knife and paint it on fresh. No matter how often you get it wrong, take it out with your knife and paint it in fresh." Homer finished the little figure—a brilliant one in effect; then sitting back, he finally asked, "Will you ever forget what I have told you?" "No," I repeated with emphasis. "That's right!" he answered, as he got up and I started to leave. Shaking hands, he said smilingly, "Don't forget what I have told you, and if you ever want anything more, come back and see me."

I left and went back to school with my new box of oil colors, and set up my easel and canvas and began to work on the model in class. The professor came around and seeing my layout said, "Kelly, your manner is very affected," and then walked on to the next student. After he left the room, the students started laughing and snickering. But Homer's hand with its masterly strokes, were in my mind's eye; and his words—"Do you understand?—Will you ever forget it?" were ringing in my ears. So I was deaf to their chaff.

When the teacher returned, he stopped, looked over my shoulder at my work and went away without uttering a word. Later, when the professor returned to make his rounds, he stood beside me and looked intently over my work. Then, in a voice loud enough to be heard by the whole class said, "Kelly, if any one should ever tell you to change the style of your work—*Don't do it!*" My status in the classroom was quickly changed.

One day Abbey came into our studio with a flintlock gun, which had a stock of the Revolutionary period; the hammer was gone and it was cracked at the stock. He said he had received it in a trade with Homer for a costume. As I recall the history as told by Abbey, it belonged to Homer's brother, who was in the army during the Civil War. He closed on a Rebel who, seeing no escape, dashed the butt of his gun against the ground, knocking off the hammer and cracking the stock near the pan. It looked like a treasured relic, and had initials carved on the butt. I made a trade with Abbey for it before he left for Europe. It was of great use for me later on in my work.

## Leaving Harper's

One day Abbey came to me and said he was going to leave Harper's because they would not give him $40 a week. He said he proposed to set up a studio, and asked me to go with him. I jumped at the opportunity, and was for leaving at once, without consulting anybody, but he said I must get a release from Mr. Parsons, as I had arranged to stay with him until I was 21.

I told Mr. Parsons my plan. He looked up kindly and beaming on me through his spectacles, said "Mr. Kelly, if you want to go with Abbey, you will not be happy here." He then wrote out a release which he finished with this wish, "I hope your proposed arrangements will be to your mutual advantage."

In the fall of 1874, Abbey and I left Harper and hired a studio at 35 Union Square. The building was originally the home of the Townsend Family, and bore in its construction, evidence of past dignity: a high brownstone stoop, pillared entrance, broad halls, etc. It had been turned into business offices, and the top floor was cut up into studios with skylights.

Abbey never demanded anything of me, but my affection for him made me not hesitate to do anything for him. So I arranged that as he had a reputation to keep up, and I had none to lose, I would carry out the ashes to the street, get water from the basement, and go to the publishers as though I were employed by him, while he was to sweep up, kindle the fire, etc.

He must have been under a hard strain at that time, as he had not much work, and what little money he had seemed to disappear. One day, he came all aglow and bustle, with the news that his mother, sister, and cousin were to call and see the new studio. Then we started in and made the dust fly, and got the room in ship shape; so trim that we could not think of mussing it up again by working. So we dawdled around till at last they arrived.

The first commissions I recall Abbey getting were from Charles Marvin, the Art Editor of Scribner, Armstrong Co. It was a drawing of Ichabod Crane for a school book which they were publishing. My lanky figure, long nose and sunburned face seemed to suit the part. They were also publishing Volume I of Bryant & Gay's *A Popular History of the United States*, and Abbey was commissioned by them to make a couple of large pictures: one was *Columbus Before the Council at Salamanca*, and the other *Endicott Cutting the Cross From the Kings Banner*. I posed for all the pictures, and Smithwick engraved the *Endicott*. William Cullen Bryant, the poet, and Sidney Howard Gay were the editors of the *History*. Gay had been assistant editor to Horace Greeley on the *Tribune*. The principal artists of the day, both figure and landscape, were employed on it, and the greatest engravers on wood and steel were employed to cut its illustrations, which made it a perfect treasure house of graphic art. This *History* which ran through four volumes has probably the most valuable collections of artists and engravers that have ever been gotten together in this country and it is specially valuable for the index, which gives the artist and engraver credit—this was not the custom at the time.

Later, Abbey got a commission to illustrate the early scenes of the Revolutionary history. One subject, *Mrs. Murray entertaining the British Officers*, I posed for the officers. These drawings were published in the January and February numbers of *Scribner's Monthly*.

Mr. Parsons sent Abbey a commission to illustrate Dickens' Christmas Stories for Harper's Household edition. We had great fun over it. He would read the story, and I would act out the character, and when I got a position to suit him, he would call time and make the sketch. I seldom saw him make a composition. He would say to me, "Stand this way," and I would do it. Then he would sketch the figure on paper or directly on wood. He would then sketch the companion figures, and work on the backgrounds until the composition was finished. I never could understand how he held them together. I believed I posed for all the figures, "Old Scrooge," with "Marley's Ghost."

Abbey tried in every way to get publishers to give me work, but they would not trust me, as I was so young, but he always encouraged me to keep on, especially in the historical subjects. His personality and criticisms enthused me, but a natural reserve prevented me from showing it. I don't suppose he ever knew. He finally persuaded Scribner's to give me a commission and I find the following memorandum in an old note-book:

> "July 9, 1875
> Drake gave me his first order through Abbey.
> What a brick he is.
> Love him as a brother."

Abbey came down one morning with a boy carrying a very small trunk, covered with cowhide; some relatives had given it to him. Opening it, he brought out an old leghorn coal-scuttle bonnet, and a skimpy gown of the early thirties. They inspired him. He began to work on his epoch-making painting, *The Stage Office*. It was nearly life-size, showing a young girl sitting pensively beside a high desk, with a little trunk at her feet. In profile, beside her, a tall model-face coachman, in a long buff coat and top boots, stood at attention. The bleak office, with its notices, and little character touches on the walls, all intensified the charm of that sweet young face.

I posed for the coachman and between the time, I worked on a large black and white drawing illustrating Walt Whitman's poem "The Vigil Strange," the center figure for which Abbey posed for the figure of the father, [Walton] Taber posed for the figure of the dead boy. We worked on our pictures for some time and planned to exhibit them at the upcoming reception at the Academy of Design. We delivered them ourselves, walking up Fourth Avenue to the Academy on 23rd Street through the slush and snow. Abbey struggled, as his was the largest, and his cousin Truslaw and friend Post, walked behind us at a respectable distance. The cross-sweeper looked at us and stepped aside, and Abbey looked back, then turning to me said, "You would make me carry this picture. Look, that sweep did not ask me for any money, and he's asking Truslaw."

Delivering the paintings, we waited results. Abbey went to the opening. Next day he came in, looking a little earnest said, "I have sold *The Stage Office* for $300, and Sarony wants to buy your *Vigil* for $50. You better let him have it."

He described the prominent artists whom he had met at the reception, among them Felix Darley, whom he knew, and I admired so much. But he did not seem to grasp the importance of his success. We got the morning's paper, and began to read the criticisms. All sounded his praises. This seemed to rouse him. Notice after notice was read and each proclaimed him as the success of the year. He began to laugh like a boy, the happy boy he was. He would read an article, or I would read one; he would then jump up, begin to sing and dance. The fun was in full swing, when Truslaw and Post came in with more papers. These also bore tribute to his success, and we all rejoiced in his triumph. One paper compared him to Winslow Homer, to Homer's disadvantage. At this he looked serious, then annoyed, "I don't like that, I don't like that," he said, and began to pace the room. Then putting on his hat, he started off to Homer's studio. Abbey was a great admirer of Winslow Homer and didn't want the newspaper article to end their friendship. Homer brushed off the incident, saying to Abbey, "They used to call me a rising young artist, now they call me an 'old fossil.'"

Of course things were not always at a high tension. We had lots of fun in the large studio. Abbey's cousin, Truslaw, his friends Post and Mitchell cheered things up. We used to fence a good deal and box. Post would sing and dance, and Abbey, after hours of intense application, would sing plantation songs and dance walk-arounds.

I can recall Abbey at work from a model; the pose was very difficult, and the drapery very fine. Fearing she would disarrange it before he could finish it, he got me to sit between his knees on the floor and sketch her from the waist down, while he worked on the upper part; at the same time directing me what points to emphasize. He then joined up our sketches and finished up the picture.

As his reputation advanced, and his finances improved, he was able to gratify his tastes. He bought historical costumes, and quaint bits of furniture. The bleakness of the room disappeared, and cheer and coziness took its place.

As a tribute to his historical accuracy, Augustus Saint-Gaudens, just returned from France, wished to consult Abbey on a Revolutionary costume for a proposed design for a statue of Sergeant [William] Jasper to be erected in Savannah. Abbey said to Saint-Gaudens, "Kelly is the one," so I went round to look over his model.

Saint-Gaudens was about five feet ten inches; slight build, with reddish brown hair. His forehead was low, but full over the brow. He had a large, bold but heavy nose, and an undershot jaw. He had a soft pleasant voice, at that time rather apologetic.

He showed me a tomb he was modeling for [former New York Governor] Edwin D. Morgan. The free touch with which the garlands of oak leaves were modeled was delightful. I had never seen anything modeled with the same quality. On a turn-table he had a bust of Dr. Johnson which was rather conventional. He was also at work on the sketches and studies of the Farragut Statue, for which he had just received a commission. He showed me Farragut's uniform and cap. The cap was very small. I tried it on; it sat on the top of my head. It seemed like a 6 1/2. He also showed me the design for the Sergeant Jasper Statue; it was fine and vigorous. Better than anything I had seen of his since. But [Alexander] Doyle had the usual political pull and got the contract. Saint-Gaudens had quite a modest way of speaking of himself and his work. I was filled with enthusiasm for his work, as it had a life-like and what I then considered a refined touch. Some of my friends laughed at me for my enthusiasm.

Abbey's fame brought him many commissions. He did work for various books and histories. His style seemed to change from that time. He developed those graceful idealistic subjects and treatment, which he carried to his fullest achievement in his painting. This started his pack of imitators on a new trail, but how their pot metal brightens his golden light.

His success evidently showed Harper what they had lost. They began to send him more manuscripts; among them a picture of Patrick Henry for which I posed, published in the magazine, June, 1876. Early that summer, he came to me saying, "Harper's have made me an offer to go back," and after a little hesitation, he accepted their offer. Here our ways parted, although we met often.

C. S. Reinhart took over the studio lease and asked me to remain, but Reinhart was not Abbey, while at that time I was beginning to be filled up with work from Scribner's, both in their magazine and Bryant's *History*. I thought I had better locate uptown, where I could work outdoors with my models and my horses, and so I started back to my rocks, stables and Nature to work out my career.

# Saying goodbye to Winslow Homer—1880

The corner of Fifth Avenue and 10th Street, where the Church of Ascension stands, will always be associated with my last meeting with Winslow Homer. He was coming up and I was going down the street; I can see him still as he stood in the bright sunshine of that spring day. He wore a low-crowned derby hat, his usual cutaway coat and light trousers, dressed as for parade. The fine, artistic looking church of brownstones, whose graceful outlines were adorned with ivy, was to his left, while the nearby trees arched above him and mingled with the colonnade of trees which formed a vista to the then unsullied Washington Square.

He asked, "When are you coming to see me?" I replied, "Any time—why, now if you like." "Well," he replied, "I am having my stove taken down and my room cleaned—suppose you come another time?" "Very well," I answered, "I will be down soon." Shaking hands, he left me with a smile. So I shall always remember him.

Sometime after that I heard that Homer had moved to Scarborough, Maine [in 1883], and the time to which I refer proved the last I should see of that great and noble man. By moving to the ocean, he found the destiny by which his distinctive and lasting fame was achieved. I recall a short conversation I once had with him in regards to his work. Seeing him in sketch class and going over to him, I said, "I saw your *Prisoners from the Front.*" He responded, "Oh, I am tired of hearing about that picture." He did not say this in a disagreeable way; I can understand his feeling that he had advanced.

As Homer's fame extended he was so bothered with sightseers who invaded his studios that he had to stand at bay. He would hardly open his door in response to a knock; when he did, it would be only a few inches, as he did that first time to me—and the chances are that he would make some excuse not to let the caller in. It became such a habit of turning people away that his friends got to treat it as a joke and used to vie with each other in telling how he would dodge letting them in. The desire for solitude grew upon him with advancing years, and his friends gradually became reconciled to it. Instead of resenting it, they accepted his moods and left him alone.

Many stories are told of his methods of defense. When I spoke to Gilbert Gaul about it, he said, "Yes, I remember a man coming to our studio and asking for Homer. I said, 'Go down to the end of the hall,' and he soon came back saying that he could not find it. 'Did you go down to the end of the hall?' 'Yes, but that is the coal bin.' Later I went down and saw a sign on which was painted COAL BIN hanging on Homer's door. Seeing Homer the next day I asked what it meant. 'Oh,' he said, 'my father sent word that he was coming down yesterday, and I put up that sign so that he would not find me.'"

## The Art Students League

On the evening of May 24, 1875, as the Academy of Design was about to close for the season, Professor Lemuel Wilmarth suggested that we organize a society for mutual help to one another, by forming a sketch class—collecting costumes, buying books of reference, and such material as would help us in our art studies.

He also suggested that we decide on a small sum for dues, but if any member could not pay, his dues should be overlooked. His ideas and suggestions were received with enthusiasm and various proposals were made by the students, but nothing was decided upon, as so few were present.

Professor Wilmarth proposed a committee to call an early meeting of the students, and meanwhile that society be called "The Art Students Union." Glancing over our group, he named Carl Hirschberg, Theodore Robinson, and then he hesitated, and added, Kelly. Hirschberg then invited Robinson and myself to meet at his house in a couple of days.

We called one sunny afternoon and discussed the proclamation, which Hirschberg wrote out. They hesitated about who should sign it first, so I took the pen and put down my black scrawl. Their signatures followed. We posted it on the bulletin board of the Academy, and awaited the results.

The proclamation aroused such interest among the students, that we had a large attendance the next afternoon. The name "Art Students Union" was criticized as not being individual. Several other names were proposed and rejected, when Hirschberg called out, "League—Art Students League." This was approved by all.

As I was no longer needed as "a whipper-in" for the committee, Professor Wilmarth substituted Charles Vanderhoff.

We used to hold exhibitions of the sketches and studies we had made each month. The parents of the students, as well as their friends used to visit us, and it would be hard to collect such another group of typical American characters. Friendships were made that have never been severed. Among the artists I recall were William Hart and George H. Story. They were attracted by my studies, and I recall with gratitude their encouraging words.

At first our action caused great indignation at the Academy. We were outlawed and they announced we should never get back without an ample apology. Many Academy students would not join. One, being asked, said, "I will wait until I see how you get along first." Later, joining, he became a most notable member and the League has flourished to this day.

For some reason I was elected or appointed to an office in the League. I really forget what it was. Its' duties did not weigh very heavily upon me, for one day while I was standing with a group of my friends in the portrait class, F. S. Church swaggered in with his hands in his pockets, and drawled out, "Kel-ly, you don't want that office of yours, do you?" "No," I called back. "All right," he said, rolling away, "I'll get somebody else." I was thus informally reduced to the ranks, which was fine with me as I could then concentrate more on my painting.

# Scribner's Publications 1876-1878

The publishing house of Charles Scribner's Sons consisted of J. Blair Scribner, and his younger brother Charles. They occupied the ground floor of the building at 745 Broadway; their bookstore in front and offices to the rear. The whole place had a hospitable, bookish atmosphere, and it was a delight to explore among its treasures. It suggested a gentleman's library instead of an office.

The top floor was the Art Department of *Scribner's Magazine* and *St. Nicholas Magazine*. It consisted of three rooms; in the front room a row of seats ran along the wall, and was generally crowded with bearded men who were distinguished artists and engravers, and whose names in many cases afterward became historical. I say "bearded men" because a very young man had little chance with the publishers in those days. The adjoining room belonged to the bookkeeper Babcock, the genial friend of all the artists and engravers, and who did all he could to make it pleasant.

Beyond that was the sanctum of Alexander W. Drake, the Art Editor. On my first entrance I was so overawed that I saw little except the beautiful check for $10, and overcome by the good fortune of having my drawing accepted. That dazzling good fortune blinded me for the time being to everything else, but after two or three more visits my eyes and wits became more normal, and I was able to observe. Drake, sitting in his office, would receive artists with a benevolent, toothsome smile, and the drawing being presented, he would handle it with his long, acquisitive fingers as though looking for moth holes in an old coat.

He would cock his small round head, which was as bald and shiny as a peeled onion, and on the back a tonsure of drab hair; nose high, arched and over-reaching; a long, thick, lank, drooping mustache, through which projected several long white teeth. His pendulous, retreating chin and mumbling way of talking suggested that he might have been munching corn. If he found the drawing acceptable, he would ask its price; on a just figure being given, he would begin tapping the ends of his teeth with his long, transparent fingers, and ask for a reduction in price. It then depended upon the necessities of the artist if he held out. Then Drake, softly patting his brow with his contracted fingers, and with his wistful blue eyes, would suggest a still lower figure. If the artist still held out, he would whisper in a rather injured voice for Babcock to make out a check.

Abbey loved to tell the following story of Drake's methods of purchasing drawings:

"Drake would ask, 'How much?'

'Twenty dollars, Mr. Drake.'

'Don't you think fifteen would do?' said Drake.

'Very well, fifteen, Mr. Drake.'

Then with a fleeting shadow of a smile, Drake would call out to Babcock, 'Please make out a check for ten dollars.'"

One of my first sketches for Scribner's came from a story I heard from my composition class professor in the Academy of Design: how when he was a farmer boy in Vermont he used to plow up skulls of Hessians killed in the old [August 16, 1777] battlefield of Bennington, occasionally finding one pierced by a bullet.

I represented a young farmer who has just plowed up a skull. He has halted his team, and is pointing to a bullet hole in the forehead, to a couple of boys. I made quite a feature of the horses standing in the furrows.

I took it to Mr. Drake, who accepted it and told me he would give me ten dollars for it. As my sketch was drawn hastily without models, in crayon, I said I would like to draw it over again from nature.

"All right," said Drake, "You may do so, but remember I will give you no more for it."

I started to draw everything from nature. A friend posed for the young farmer. I drew the horses from a team of Mr. Anderson's. Another chum posed for the two boys; the stone wall and backgrounds from bits now included in Riverside Park. I then went to my friend Drier's farm in 71st Street and Broadway, and made a study of his father's plow.

After I had finished this, I reproduced my studies in an India-ink drawing, and took it down to Drake. He paid me ten dollars and I went off happy.

Some time in late June, 1876, I received a proof of it engraved by Thomas Smithwick, with the message that the horses had made such an impression on [Editor and Author] Mrs. Mary Mapes Dodge that she sent me the manuscript of an article written by Charles Barnard called "The Horse Hotel." It was a description of the then new Third Avenue Car Stables. I went over there and made careful studies of the horses and grooms. When I took in the finished drawings, Drake said nothing that I can recall, but sent me down to the Editorial Rooms of *St. Nicholas Magazine*. I had never been there before, and felt depressed; for, try as I would, I could not make my sketches look like those other artists. To me they looked queer.

I sent them in, and sat in the outer room anxiously waiting for the verdict. In a few moments a distinguished, handsome looking lady came out with my drawings in her hand. She looked round the room inquiringly evidently for an artist, but there was no one present but a sunburned boy. As I stood up she hesitated, saying, "Are you Mr. Kelly?" "Yes, Ma'm" I mumbled. She shook my hand warmly, but I was too confused to remember what she said.

On publication of the drawings, she sent me the following letter:

November 17, 1876
Mr. Kelly—
I cannot resist the temptation, now that the complete December "St. N," is before me, to send my hearty congratulations to you, on your horse-hotel picture. They are so very good, that the people will have hard work, at first, to believe that they were produced in this country.
Mary Mapes Dodge.

After Mrs. Dodge had vouched for me, Drake tried me out on some more illustrations for *St. Nicholas*, and finally felt safe in trusting me with an article for *Scribner's Monthly*, illustrating the new Aquarium, on the northwest corner of Broadway and 35th Street, the same lot where the circus people used to put up their tent.

One of my drawings showed the workmen dumping a small white whale from a crate into a tank; another drawing showed some men carrying a shark, wrapped in blankets like a mummy, from the tug boat to the crate on the wagon. I made the drawings in black and white watercolor. Yet, as before, I could not make my drawings look like those of other artists, but at last I took them to Drake who paid me what he gave Abbey—$25.00 for the page drawing and $15.00 for the half page.

In a day or so, on returning home, I found Smithwick the engraver having a merry chat with my mother. They became close friends which lasted while they lived. Smithwick called; he said to get instructions on how I wanted the drawings engraved.

I explained how I wished the brush strokes preserved with a clearness that my experience as a wood-engraver enabled me to express.

When published, the approval, as well as the abuse of the critics, gave the impression that I had done something out of the ordinary.

Smithwick cut several other drawings of mine, and then he was taken with some eye trouble which prevented him from working for some time. On his recovery he formed a partnership with Frank French, who made an individual reputation as an engraver and became quite a figure in art. Finally Smithwick became director of the engraving department at Harper Brothers. This was a great loss to wood-engraving, of which he was the most powerful representative, as an artist and a man.

Smithwick had a most striking personality; considerably over six feet high; dark hair, and a full brown beard. A broad, smooth brow; gray eyes; bold, assertive nose with a small, round scar along side the right nostril where he had been shot in the War for the Union, through which he had served in the 132nd New York Volunteers, and came out a Lieutenant.

He had a conflicting disposition: merry, joyous and generous to his friends; cantankerous and pugnacious to those who he chose to consider his enemies. Before I had the pleasure of knowing him personally, I used to hear the name, "Smithwick, Smithwick, Smithwick," used between Abbey and Reinhart in Harper's Art Department, in discussing the merits of the distinguished wood-engravers, in which they agreed in declaring him supreme.

My first glimmer of fame occurred when in August 1876, I made a drawing representing a boy carrying some dead birds over his shoulder—it was called "The Gillie Boy." When I took it to Drake, he gave it his cautious approval and introduced me to Timothy Cole, whom he proposed to engrave it.

When the cut was finished, it met with high approval and on publication attracted a great deal of attention. Drake was especially overjoyed about it, and always referred in a complimentary way to my "Gillie Boy."

During the time I was illustrating for *Scribner's Monthly*, they had an article called "Artist's Studios," and asked me to make a sketch of mine. As my work was generally done out of doors, direct from nature, I located mine in Wright's Lumber Yard in 38th Street between Broadway and Seventh Avenue. The drawing was published with the title "An Animal Artist's Studio."

I showed myself sitting on an upturned pail sketching the rear view of a horse in action. One boy was sitting on a shed holding its chin aloft, another one sitting on the ground, holding its leg as though galloping, while another held the end of its tail, pulling it aside as shown in my model. There was a good deal of fun among us while arranging the group; after we got to work, one said, "This horse will begin to think it is his birthday from the attention he is receiving."

## The New School of Wood-engraving

The newspapers used to give me frequent notices, some with the highest praise as the founder of the "New School of Wood Engraving," and others saying that my drawings were the worst published in any magazine. I never saw the former, as I was too shy to buy the papers. When one of the notices came out my mother sent me out to buy a paper. We then were living in an old cottage on 54th Street, between Ninth and Tenth Avenues and I didn't have the nerve to go to a nearby news store, so sped on to the next one—then quailed at the door, and continued on to the next one.

This was kept up until I reached a corner newsstand at Third Avenue and 48th Street, where I finally mustered up courage to go in and buy a paper. I then slunk home and finally mustered up more courage to read it. This now seems foolish and ridiculous, but is a fact. I heard that several of our neighbors had called me a "penny artist;" later they showed me the newspaper notices, and I finally became used to them as the magazines came out every month. The *Hartford Courant*, with which Mark Twain was at that time associated, said, "The boss artist is Kelly, on *Scribner's Monthly*."

Shortly after this, I was asked by Charles Marvin to attend to some illustrations. He sent for me, and gave me some manuscript to illustrate for Volume IV of Bryant and Gay's *A Popular History of the United States*, which *Scribner's* were publishing. Marvin mentioned to me, "A man came in the other day with a battle picture which he told us he had found, and thought we might use it. It is not signed. I would like to find the artist. I thought from your experience you might recognize who made it.

I walked back with him to the office and there on the desk before me was my picture of Perry at Lake Erie, which I made in Harper's when I was about 18.

I said, "It's mine." Marvin wheeled, leveled his glasses on me, and said grimly, "This is no joke. I want to find out who made it. Do you know?" I answered, "It's no joke. It is my drawing; I lost it and I will prove it mine." So I took up a pen and wrote my name in the corner, then turning to him said, "If that's not mine, it is a forgery."

Looking at me with a grim smile, he said, "Well, I want to buy it. What will you take for it? Remember it is found money."

I gave him a fair price. Without a word he sat down, wrote out a check and handed it to me. I then told him I would have my friend, Marcus Baldwin engrave it, which he did satisfactory to me in every way.

When Marvin handed me the manuscript that I was to illustrate, I felt a new world open before me—At last! I was to do historical work! I then started in with vigor to rummage for historical material, so as to make my work true in every particular. I now felt my work was appreciated, as well as congenial; and I was stimulated to do my best.

Finally I was given credit in the newspapers and magazines as founder of the "New School of Wood Engraving." Then came an article in the *Atlantic Monthly*, by W. J. Linton, on "The New School" and he took me as the representative, and speaking in metaphor, did not leave a feather on me. It struck me as very humorous and I read it to Drake, who was stricken with a panic. He twirled his fingers and dolefully whimpered, "Don't you think you could change your style?" "Yes," I flared up, "but not for you," and started right down to see Mr. Henry M. Alden, of *Harper's Magazine*, telling him of the situation.

"Well," he said with a kind smile, "if we take your drawings, we become *Scribner's Monthly*." I replied that I was not held to one style of treatment, and showed him my sketch book. Alden at once gave me an order for three articles to be published in *Harper's Magazine*, of which I suggested that Gen. Doubleday be the author. So, unconsciously, Drake became my benefactor, but this new arrangement made no break in connection with the Scribner publishing house, and I continued to work their magazine and on Bryant's *History*.

One day when I was sitting in Drake's outer office, Dr. John G. Holland, editor-in-chief of *Scribner's Monthly* came in and sat down and started to question me, asking about books, pictures and my methods of study, as well as my ideas of how a magazine should be illustrated. As I recall the occasion, I was put through a civil service examination, and responded readily, without reserve, as he had my confidence. Finally he stood up and said, "Mr. Kelly, hereafter we shall give you no more manuscripts to illustrate. You shall originate and select the subjects and the incidents you think best to illustrate, and select the authors to write them up."

I do not recall my answer to this, as I was a gawky, overgrown boy, with a sunburned face from continual exposure to the river front and stock yards, and on close acquaintance was apt to converse in the vernacular. After that talk with Dr. Holland, I would go to him and suggest an idea, usually something out-of-doors or a figure from history or perhaps someone who was making history. I remember suggesting that I had heard of a fellow out at Menlo Park, New Jersey, who had invented a talking machine, and added, "You talk into it, turn a crank and it repeats what you have said."

He told me he had never heard of it, but after questioning me, gave me an order to go out and get an article on it. I suggested that William H. Bishop should write the article. I talked it over with Bishop, who said that he was going to Europe the following Saturday. I said, "This is Tuesday—you go over to Menlo Park and make an appointment for Thursday; we can go over, I will make the sketches, you can sail on Saturday and write the article on ship board. By that time I shall have the drawings finished, and it will be published."

## Thomas A. Edison

Thomas Edison was 31 years of age, and I 22, when we first met at Menlo Park. At that time New York was beginning to hear of him; a reporter from the *New York Herald* was detailed to report his doings and sayings. This was taken up by other papers and in a short time the entire United States, and finally Europe, fairly rang and echoed with the name and wonders of Edison's work. The editor of the *Scientific American* referred to him as "that young man in New Jersey who is making the path to the Patent Office hot with his footsteps."

When the first fierce lights of publicity were focused on him, Edison showed no sign. Praise was showered upon him that would have turned the head of anyone but a superior genius, one capable of appreciating the great work he had already accomplished in relation to the much greater work he saw before him. I had met him after one of his long, concentrated vigils; he was unshaven and worn, yet was as cheerful and joyous as was his wont. He did not feel called upon to indulge in those temperamental tantrums to prove his claim to genius.

With his staff he appeared more of a comrade than a dictator. He was always ready to listen to the suggestions of the most minor subordinates, and if they impressed him favorably and proved successful, he always gave them credit. He was never assertive or opinionated, or broke into a conversation. He was not what I would call a conversationalist, but talked in nuggets. He responded to a good joke with almost boyish glee, but never tried to go one better.

Edison was the friend and ideal of my youth, and many of the joys of those days are associated with him. Personally he always seemed to look upon me as a boy, and never allowed me to grow up and, as a tribute to my having been born in New York City, called me, "A New York cockney." When Edison would meet me, he would put on a swagger and address me in the vaudeville New York vernacular.

I first met Edison at Menlo Park on May 16, 1878. Arriving at his laboratory, I stood in a hallway and saw Edison sitting at the head of a long table in the front room, at which were gathered a group of men of marked power and distinction; but, by contrast, his personality dominated them all. Bowed in reflection over some document, the structure of his head and the cast of his features took on beauty—and I might say, grandeur—which suggested a highly idealized Napoleon.

As the boy handed him my card I passed down the hall, and as I turned he was coming out of the room. He advanced with a broad smile, swinging his arm at full length, making a circle over his head, he brought down his palm in mine with a smack and a grip, swung me to one side and asked me what he could do for me. I can never recall a meeting that he did not greet me with his boyish smile and joke.

Edison showed us his first phonograph and while roaring in the mouth piece what seemed to be his favorite poems, I made a sketch of his head and the machine, which he signed, putting on his name and my name with an ink he had invented which embossed the paper so it could be read by the blind.

Having seen a good deal of Edison and liking him more and more, as I got to know him, I took this sketch and modeled it in wax which was my first relief. Taking it out to Menlo Park, Edison and his friends approved of it, and he signed his name in the model, as well as writing a letter endorsing it.

On casting it in bronze, I gave him a copy, although he was anxious to pay for it. Taking it in his hand he held it before Charles Batchelor his confidential assistant, and in a voice that indicated both feeling and satisfaction, he said, "Batch—bronze!" Turning to me, Edison asked, "How much is it?" and told his clerk to make out a check. I said, "Hold on! This is not your business. I don't want you to pay for it." As I was leaving, he came out with me and we walked up Fifth Avenue. Crossing 14th Street, the traffic of the stages and carriages was very thick. A driver in checking his stage brought the horses on their haunches; the pole swung in the air, grazing Edison's head. He paid no attention to it, but another inch closer and it might have killed him—and then what?

I recall another day when I was walking down Broadway, near Thames Street, with a boyhood friend; we had encountered a rather dissipated fellow—actually an old friend whom we had known in his better days, but things had gone wrong with him and he showed it. When we parted, my spruce companion started to give me a lecture, saying, "You are always picking up a lot of your old-time schoolmates who are no credit to you. It is all right to be kind to them privately, but you shouldn't notice them in public."

He had hardly finished saying this when along came young Thomas Edison, looking his worst, and made more so by the sight of his companion and secretary, the immaculate and exquisite Englishman Samuel Insull. Edison wore a buff slouch hat, well-thumbed with chemicals, and a seal-colored spring overcoat, yellowish at the shoulders from the same. He looked as if he had been through one of his all-night sessions—his face was unshaven, and had a printer's pallor. The sight of me started his risibles; with a broad grin, he gripped my hand and shouldered me back on the sidewalk, at which I countered with a slight jab in the ribs.

Then, with an affected toughness and in a voice like a plumber's helper, he asked, "Hullo, Kelly! still at the same business?"

"Yes," I said, "where are you working?"

"Oh, I'm working out in Jersey," he answered with a husky drawl; then getting serious, Edison, Insull and I had a short chat. On parting, he called back, "Come and see me!"

Joining my rigid friend, I said, "Do you think he looks like his pictures?"

"Who?"

"Edison," I answered.

"Is that Edison?"

"Yes."

Then my companion looked slack-jawed, and muttered, "I didn't catch his name; if I had known, I would have shown him more attention." Walking along musingly until we neared Trinity Church, he looked at the glove with which he shook the hand of Edison and mumbled, "I suppose I'll have to save that glove!"

Edison later moved to 65 Fifth Avenue to be near the Edison Electric Light Company. It was a fine old building with a high brownstone stoop. The first or parlor floor consisted of three rooms. The first used as a reception room; the middle as an office for the President, S. B. Eaton; the rear as Edison's private office. The principal furniture there were a couple of roll top walnut desks. I called one day in 1881, but Edison was out. Samuel Insull was sitting by the front window. He was a slight English boy—a marked contrast to Edison. He was fair haired, fresh complexion, but with a bold nose. He wore the conventional English high hat and frock coat, but there was an exquisite crispness in his make up which his fresh complexion and bright smile intensified. He was much interested in the distinguished men of the country and we used to compare notes over the men we met. A messenger came in and handed him a package. It was the diploma for the Grand Medal of Honor which had been awarded to Edison at the Paris Exhibition, accompanying it was an official letter from Secretary of State Frederick T. Frelinghuysen. It had a deep black border on it because of the recent death of President Garfield [on September 19, 1881]. After he had looked it over, Insull said, "I'll take it over and show it to Mrs. Edison."

Edison lived across the avenue at No. 72. I used to see the first Mrs. Edison with her little girl and boy called "Dot" and "Dash." She was large, fair haired with a fresh complexion. On his return I asked Insull what she said about the award. He replied, "She said: 'What good is it?'"

Edison always told some good stories about his different types of visitors and the different honors received. Laughing he said, "Kelly, for unalloyed taffy, give me France." One time, taking me aside, he asked me how I was getting along. I told him. He took a pencil and drew a parallel line on a sheet of paper and said, "Kelly, that is Glory," then drawing another line below it, he said, "and that is Boodle." Painting in between the lines, he said, "You want to get right in there."

## Edison and Realism—December 9, 1885

I was down to an exhibition at the Academy of Design and was talking to a friend in the North Room when I saw Edison looking at the pictures in the southeast corner. I excused myself and started over and grabbed his left arm, "Hullo—what are you doing here? I thought you never went round."

"Oh yes, I go round a great deal," he answered.

We began to talk on the various works, when he suddenly broke out, "Oh, I saw a good subject—you paint don't you?"

"Yes."

"Yes, well you will think this a good subject—it might be called Realism. You know at my place it is all tenement houses—well this horse—dead lying in the street and a little youngster was straddling his neck, and he had a cotton string in its mouth and was licking it with a lash. Oh, I tell you he was having a hell of a time. Then there was this girl with a baby and a couple more all riding him—wouldn't that make a good subject."

Then he chuckled and grinned all over at the idea.

We then went round the south side and stood before several paintings. We then went to the northwest room and he got talking about the horse picture of Realism again. I gave him a card and he leaned on the heater and made a little sketch of the scene.

"Oh, it was a horse all swelled with her eyes bulging out..."

Here he went over his description of the youngsters again.

"I'd make a sketch of that and when the English dudes call upon you, you can have it hung up and they will think that it is your taste. You can say you ordered the subject—this was a subject of Realism."

Going out, I asked him to give me a sitting for a bust, he said he would and as he was leaving me at the door of the Academy, he came back and said earnestly, "I'll pose for you."

Another time he suggested, "Kelly, you ought make designs of a horse in every possible position and patent the designs, and when any other fellow tries to make an equestrian statue, you can stop him for infringement, and get the job."

Edison was frequently quoted as an authority by those who opposed religion or other higher ideals. When questioned by newspaper reporters, who pestered him with numberless questions—as if any one with sensibilities would open the portals of his heart to a horse-shoe of space writers who checked off his inmost thoughts that man reveals only to his loved ones and his God—to such questions he would parry with a joke or snap back, "I won't answer that question—it's too damn foolish!"

At heart he was simple and sentimental; his first words on the phonograph were, "Mary had a little lamb," which I heard him repeat, and his favorite on the phonograph was *Bingen on the Rhine*, also, *John Brown's Body*, etc. I have also heard him play old-time religious hymns on the organ. I once asked him to write in the album of a young girl, and he wrote that verse from Thomas Gray's Elegy: "The Path of Glory leads but to the Grave."

I do not pretend to represent Edison as a flawless crystal sphere, but I do truthfully feel a specimen of rich ore of priceless, incalculable quality that has been forged by Providence to be an instrument that forged what is good for mankind, both present and future generations.

## Oscar Wilde

Col. William F. Morse was to manage Oscar Wilde's first lecture tour of the United States in January 1882, and he commissioned me to make a portrait. Col. Morse asked me to take a trip with him to Boston, where he was to meet Wilde. When we arrived, we went to Young's Hotel, and then to the train to meet Oscar. He looked tired, and partly streaked, wearing a scarf of a delicate rose color. Taking Wilde to his hotel, the Colonel asked me to go to the newspaper office to announce his arrival. On my return with a reporter, Oscar had himself been busy setting the stage for his reception.

He was sitting back in the arm-chair by the table, the sun streaking its brilliant light through onto the rose-colored scarf, which he had taken off and replaced by one of bronze green. All this was apparently careless, but the effect was superb; the glow of the scarf cast a delicate reflection on his face, and gave him an unusually fine effect. The reporter seemed awed, and started to take notes, while Col. Morse and I went off and left them alone. I later made a most satisfactory sketch of Wilde that was signed by him and later used as the frontispiece in *De Profundis* in 1909.

While speaking of sculpture, Wilde said, "Remember Kelly, a piece of sculpture should always be full—there should always be no blank sonnets. Always feel when making a piece of sculpture, you are carving a jewel."

When Wilde first came to this country, he stated to Col. Morse that the two Americans he most desired to meet were Emerson and Edison. As I had occasion to see Edison, and showed him Wilde's poems which had been published in the *Sea Side Library*, and pointed to some that impressed me. Edison read them over carefully and said, "They're damn good; bring him down sometime," and repeated as I was leaving, "Bring him down." I mentioned Edison's invitation to Wilde, but circumstances prevented their meeting until Wilde returned to America the following year.

## Oscar Wilde's Play, Union Square Theatre—August 20, 1883

Roger Riordan, who at that time was doing dramatic work for the *Sun*, took me to see Oscar Wilde's first play. It was a strong dramatic play; the incidents I cannot recall.

Wilde was called before the curtain after the first public appearance on this, his second visit to the country. He was very much changed; his long curls had been cut off, and he was much stouter and pale. His actions were embarrassed and boyish; at the end of the play he came out and made some remarks. He was not his old self and I felt sorry for him. Next day the papers were unanimous in abusing the play and ridiculing Wilde's personality.

Seeing these brutal attacks, in which Riordan joined, I called on Wilde at the Brunswick Hotel, and found him at breakfast. I spoke of the play, and tried to say all I could in favor of it, but it did not cheer him; he was cut too deep. Referring to the attacks, he said, "Kelly, Kelly—MY FIRST PLAY!" Sighing, he repeated, "Kelly, Kelly, MY FIRST PLAY!" By way of distraction I spoke of his desire to meet Edison, and suggested that we go down, so we walked down to Edison's office, then at 65 Fifth Avenue.

We had hardly entered when Insull came up to receive us. As I began introducing—with only "Oscar," being said, Wilde said, "I am very happy to meet you," and started to address Insull as Edison. He had hardly done so, when, "Hullo, old B'hoy!" was roared out behind us and there stood Edison with a broad grin. He had on the old buff slouch hat, hair tosselled, and looking pretty disheveled—although I have seen him worse while inventing.

Edison said with a grin, "There's our art bum!" Oscar looked queer. Edison led the way to what was a rear back bedroom and started to look Oscar over, then said, "I've seen you before; sit down." Edison sat down on the sofa with his back to the window, Wilde on his right and Insull on his left, while I sat in the chair facing them. Edison placed his feet on the rungs of my chair, which caused me to place mine at each side of him on the sofa. They began talking about Wilde's play and after discussing it for a little, Wilde became more cheerful and said, "Dion Boucicault told me, 'Oscar, you have written a play in such a way that it would take Edwin Booth, Henry Irving, Sarah Bernhardt, and Ada Rehan to render it.' Not at all; now when I write a play, I write it in such a way that if the leading man is taken sick or in any way fails me, all I would know to do is to call up one of the ushers and if he repeats my lines, the play will be a success."

Edison laughed heartily at this and turned to me, winked with a grin, and nodding his head towards Wilde said, "He's learnin, he's learnin, he's learnin."

After lots of bright talk by Wilde, cheerful talk by Edison, and earnest remarks by Insull we parted. I cannot recall all the talk, but we had a lively, chappy time as Edison always did with me—and I gave it back with interest. Finally leaving, we went down stairs and out. I expected Wilde to say something, but not a word. He dropped into a moody silence, probably thinking over the contrast of his fortunes with those of Edison.

He said he was going to Brooklyn and as I was going to Franklin Square, we took the Third Avenue "L" at 14th Street. He was silent most of the way and I bid him goodbye at the Franklin Square station and looked round and saw him sitting back—his elbow in the window looking forward. This was my last sight of Oscar Wilde. I could not understand his silence except at the possibility of being dumbfounded when Edison said, "I am greatly disappointed in the Atlantic Ocean."

## Edison's Moving Pictures

Mrs. Charlotte Ewer was invited by Edison's representatives to bring her three little children to dance before his new moving picture camera which he was just experimenting on. Edison's laboratories had moved from Menlo Park down to Lewellyn Park [West Orange, N. J.] and as I had never been there, she asked me to accompany them. Edison was not there. He had gone away on some business, so I didn't see him. The buildings were new, principally of brick and had rather a raw factory air about them. Over a short distance in the enclosure was a curious building that looked like a magnified lobsterpot. It was about 30 feet long and about 10 feet wide on a turn table, with a sky light affair on one end and a hooded affair on the other. It was covered with tar paper, set up with big nails, about an inch in diameter. It looked like an enormous coffin for a giant.

The building could, with the sky light affair, be flooded with light while the actors got in their work, and the other end sheltered the moving picture machine.

The children danced and went through their little tricks, and the machine buzzed. A couple of prize-fighters were lounging around in their boxing togs. I was told that they had been waiting around for two days to get a bright sunlight as the skies were overclouded.

Mr. William Kennedy Dickson who was in charge had a long talk with me about Edison. He was preparing life (biography) and had been detailed by Edison to develop the moving picture machine. I was shown through the works, which had become large, commercial, without the personal touch. I did not meet Edison there. It was cold and material. I spoke to some of my old friends about Edison. They said, "Edison is not the Edison that you used to know."

I afterwards saw the result of that day, in a sort of picture, peep show, on the south west corner of 27th Street and Broadway—it was called the Kinetoscope.

## Walt Whitman

One day as I was riding down in a Fourth Avenue car, a tall man whom I recognized as Walt Whitman sat opposite me, on the west side of the car, and I had a good chance to study him. Whitman was dressed as shown in one of his latest photographs at that time, in a large light slouch hat and clothes, and carried a heavy cane. What struck me most forcibly was his excessive cleanliness and crispness.

His long white hair and beard fairly sparkled like spun-glass, as did the hairs on his breast that shone through his stiffly starched white shirt. His open, shapely hands impressed me; his only apparent defects were a certain weakness in the color and quality of the eyes and the structure of the nose. His eyes were rather peering than penetrating; his nose a little wavering in outline. They did not seem to carry out the bold, forceful hands; there seemed a lead link in him somewhere.

Why I did not speak to him I cannot imagine; it was one of my breaks and a bad one, for which I can never forgive myself. My only consolation is that I studied him intensely, and except in his photograph by R. Pearsall Smith, I have never seen his cleanly quality realized. The paintings of him make him look like a frowsy, smokey old man; and all fail as to his hands. John White Alexander's portrait, as Whitman himself says, sadly misrepresents him. He seemed interested in everything, and kept shifting around in his seat when anything attracted his attention.

As we passed 17th Street, he turned and gazed earnestly over to Sarony's gallery, on the opposite side of the Square, No. 37, where Abbey and I started. It struck me that he might be thinking of my painting illustrating his poem, *The Vigil Strange*, then on display in Sarony's window. I got out of the car shortly without speaking to him—an opportunity lost.

## Meeting P. T. Barnum

I wanted to get an opportunity to study an elephant for an article I was illustrating for Scribners, so I went down to the old Harlem Railroad Station which had been closed since the opening of the Grand Central, and turned into a place of entertainment called, "Madison Square Garden." Here the circus and athletic events took place, ring fights, etc. Here John L. Sullivan reigned. Here, [Evangelist Dwight L.] Moody and [Gospel singer Ira D.] Sankey started their great revivals. Here, [Patrick S.] Gilmore conducted his mammoth concerts with his famous band. His genius and popularity made such an impression on his time that the building was known as Gilmore's Garden.

It was here that I met P. T. Barnum. Barnum was a tall, bulky, soft faced, benevolent looking man—exactly like his portraits. Bailey, his partner, was sitting at a desk and while waiting for Barnum, I had a chance to study Bailey. He was a short, red-whiskered little Irishman, with an irritable, overworked manner. He was doing some business with a big, conventional, black mustached theatrical man. As the man was leaving, he said, "Mr. Bailey, come around to my theatre when you like—I will have seats for you!"

"No!" snapped Bailey, "I never accept seats from theatrical men, since I was once invited by a manager to go to his theatre. He said he would leave tickets for me at the box office. I went with my wife and another lady. When we got there, there was no tickets, and I had to buy tickets from a speculator at an advance price! Since then I have never accepted an invitation from a manager!" The manager took the snub and left. Just then Barnum came in. He had in his hand a small model of an elephant. Going over to Bailey he showed it to him saying, "The man who accompanied him wanted to dispose of copies as a souvenir of Jumbo,"—the great elephant he had bought from the English, which was the talk of the country and England at that time. Bailey did not seem to pay much attention to Barnum or his elephant, his own job seemed to be too heavy for him.  Barnum then turned to me, quiet, self-possessed, and courteous, but when he talked he munched his pendulant underlip as though it was a lollypop.

I explained what I wanted.  Barnum turned to Bailey and repeated what I had said.  Bailey, while hardly looking up, snapped-up: "No! I don't see that it is going to do <u>us</u> any good!" and went on with his work.  Barnum looked at me and said nothing.  I felt sorry for Barnum.

## Buffalo Bill

Buffalo Bill was to have his first show at Staten Island in 1886.  An old friend of mine had free tickets and invited me and my father to go with him and his brother.  His brother was a fine looking fellow, but my friend looked down on him because he was a conductor on the elevated train.  So my friend said, "You come with me and your father can take [the unnamed brother]."

We started, they going first.  My friend dodged them, and arriving at the show we were shown to our seats and after sitting there awhile I heard my father beckoning me.  He was in the front row center.  "How did you get there?" I said.  "I tripped and fell and they put me here," said he.

With a flourish of trumpets the procession filed out: Buffalo Bill leading the parade.  He was a handsome fellow with long black hair, mustache with imperial.  As he filed past our box he looked up and hollered, and doffing his hat swept it down to the stirrup.

The performance began and everything was announced by Nate Salsbury with a most powerful voice; everything was done in front of our box.  There was the attack on the stagecoach, all sorts of fancy shooting—a fellow rode ahead throwing up balls which Bill hit with a shot from his revolver, and he acted out his killing of Yellow Hand—in fact it was a real Wild West show—showing the life, as what we thought it was, perfectly.

Then Annie Oakley was announced.  She came out, placed her guns in row directly against our box and started in her wonderful shooting.  I looked over the edge and down the barrels of her guns.  A long fluttering piece of linen hung in front of our box which I hadn't noticed.  I read it upside down and it said, "Hon. W. F. Cody's Private box."  This was the explanation of the attention showed us, and was a tribute to my Father, whose fall was his fortune.

The show under the management of Nate Salsbury was a wonderful success and started him on the way to fame and fortune.  As we filed out, a fellow came up to Salsbury and said, "How did you do it?"  Salsbury said, "Showmanship."

## Mrs. Tom Thumb

The ideal of my childhood was Tom Thumb, but I never had the great happiness to have seen him, although I had seen Commodore Nutt and Commodore Foot. Tom and his adventures filled a great part of my day dreams. After his death [in 1883], his widow Minnie Warren married another dwarf, Count Primo Magri, and I saw them on one of my trips to Coney Island.

Mrs. Tom was standing on a little stage, while the Count sat dazedly in a little armchair. A young girl next to me said, "Countess, will you shake hands with me?" She did so and catching my eye she extended her dainty hand to me and as I took it said, "Have you any relics of the General?" Her face lit up and she said, "Please wait," and disappearing behind the scene, she returned with a small, very small chair, and said, "That belonged to the General." Then going back she brought out another relic, which I cannot recall, and another and another, till she exhausted her collection at hand. She seemed to glow at the interest. I took in this, and it gave me much joy.

She died on November 25, 1919, at the age of 79, and is buried alongside her General with a simple grave stone that reads, "His Wife."

## Robert Peterson, Veteran of the War of 1812

Robert Peterson, or "Uncle Bobby," as he was called by the Greenwich villagers, lived at 257 West 12th Street. He was a prosperous old time car man, as they were called, and used to wear high hats and long white smocks. The car men were accustomed to cluster around Greenwich Village, where the old houses show traces of them by alley ways under the oval windows, running to stables in the rear. Their carts were lined at night along the curbs, and were meeting places and roosts for the natives.

"Uncle Bobby" was a veteran of the War of 1812, and was born on February 28, 1800. He was a stout, sturdy old man of 83 when he called upon me at 79th Street. He had a bold nose, long white hair and a ruffle of beard around his jaw. I had the good fortune to know him and make a sketch of him for *Harper's Weekly*. He told me that he had been blind for several years, but his sight had been restored by the removal of a cataract, and added that his blindness had compelled him to think for amusement, and brought back all his old memories, which I took down. Some of them are as follows:

P—When I was about 10 years old, I was sent to sea for my health, going on Capt. David Porter's vessel, the *Enterprise*, as a cabin boy. David G. Farragut, who was about my own age, was a midshipman. As boys we became great friends; when we went ashore he, having money and I none, used to treat me to spruce beer and peanuts. There was an officer on the vessel who had no head for going aloft and used to shirk it. Porter got mad one day and said, "Midshipman Farragut, take [the shirking officer's] chapeau and place it on the main truck." (a small wooden cap at the top of a mast-head); then Porter turned to the officer and said, "Now go and get it, Sir!" He tried several times, but after going a certain height he would get dizzy; at last Porter relented, sending Farragut to get and return it to him; some men are born that way.

After a year or so, I left the sea, but when the War of 1812 was declared and the British advanced on Washington, I joined the Rifles. I was then only about 14, but large and strong. Our uniform was a high hat with a feather, green roundabout jacket and pants with yellow fringe. I was in the battle of Bladensburg, Md., August 24, 1814, and saw Commodore Joshua Barney come up with his sailors. They were dressed in white, and their guns were drawn by negroes with ropes like a fire engine. I saw his fight in defense of the bridge and saw him wounded. I was busy emptying my rifle at the British.

After the battle I heard that my father had been killed. At Bladensburg, I heard that the people were going within the British lines to get their relatives who had been killed or wounded. I took off my uniform, put my rifle in the brook, placed some stones over it and went into the British lines. They sent me to the tent of Gen. Robert Ross, who stood up to receive me and said kindly, "Be seated, young gentleman; what have the misfortunes of war thrown in your path? A father? A brother?

I said my father had been killed. He gave me a pass to look for my father's body, which I found with all the clothes taken off—they had been stolen by the negroes.

K—How was Gen. Ross dressed?

P—He wore a surtout [overcoat] and slippers.


He gave me the details on how the British had played hob after they had burned Washington, and how Gen. Ross had been shot by the two boys [Daniel Wells and Henry McComas] as he advanced on Baltimore, and stories of the preliminaries of the fight at Fort McHenry.

K—Were you in the fort?

P—No, my regiment was back on the hill overlooking it. We watched the firing during the night; could see the shells burst and light up the old flag—just as it is described in "The Star-Spangled Banner." The British shot down the flagstaff, but we erected another, and when the sun arose in the morning we saw that the flag was still flying.

When I was twenty-one, I had twenty slaves left me. I set them free—have never regretted it, and have been blessed. I have two sons who have never caused me a sorrow; both were in the Civil War, one of them shot in both arms at the same time. I wish I had him photographed with both in slings.

After my drawing was finished he examined it closely and said, "It looks exactly like Horace Greeley, and as they say I look like him, it must be a good likeness of me."

At the time I knew him, Mr. Peterson used to amuse himself raising canaries in a large coop in his yard. From his personality and the principles expressed, he must have been a noble, joyous old man, and I am sorry that I did not know him longer and better. Another incident comes to my mind, which I will tell as nearly as possible in his own words.

P—While the British fleet was lying off Fort McHenry, an Irish deserter came into our lines and said that he wanted to join the service, but our officers were suspicious of him. "Well," he said, "in that case put me down on one of the shore batteries." which they did. One day he went to an officer and said, "They are going to attack us tonight." "How do you know?" asked the officer. "I can tell by the lights," he replied, but they paid no attention to him.

"Well," he said, "it would do no harm to line up the guns on the batteries." So that night he lay along the top of his gun until far into the night. All at once he jumped up and touched it off, followed by the other guns of the battery. Then came howls and yells, and the next morning they saw the beach strewn with wrecked boats where the British had tried to advance on the batteries with muffled oars.

K—Did you see this?

P—No, but it was the story of the camp. The British then drew off and started to bombard the fort, as described in "The Star-Spangled Banner."

*While working as a Special Artist for Harper's and Scribner's Publications, Kelly covered several important New York City events, such as the construction of the Brooklyn Bridge and the clearing of the dangerous rock obstructions at Hell Gate in the East River.*

# The Brooklyn Bridge

Roebling's Brooklyn Bridge was finished in May, 1883, and the opening ceremonies were headed by President Chester A. Arthur, who as a native of New York State, and a citizen of the City of New York when he became President, was the appropriate sponsor. John A. Roebling, who designed the bridge, died suddenly in 1869, while engaged in the preliminary surveys; his son, Washington A. Roebling, took the father's place beginning in January, 1870, and carried the work through to completion. From the sick room of his home on Columbia Heights, Brooklyn, he observed the progress of the work through a telescope, and with the assistance of his wife, directed it to the final triumph. After the opening ceremonies, the President and other officials called and tended their congratulations on the great and successful achievement.

I had watched the work from the time when the butts of the piers jutted above the water line until the towers were completed; then web-like wires were stretched from capstone to capstone, and other strands were strung until the desired thickness was obtained. These were then wound around with binding wire by daring fellows in boatswains' chairs until steel cables were formed. Alongside of them ran a slotted foot-bridge about three feet wide, with a slack guide rope on each side; this was used as a footway for the workmen who constructed the four mighty cables and the other intricate wiring and steelwork which supported the main weight of the bridge.

During the construction, many venturesome citizens showed their nerve or lack of it (I could never understand which) by walking from shore to capstone, and then from capstone to capstone to the other side of the river on the sagging, swaying footway. Mrs. Henry Ward Beecher is credited with having performed the feat, and several others, but the practice was finally stopped to prevent possible accidents.

It is singular how height seems to appall even the bravest. I have heard it stated that Gen. Sheridan could not cross a bridge without being uncomfortable; and have been told on good authority how Gen. Dan Butterfield and Admiral "Jack" Philip, started to cross the footway of the Brooklyn Bridge making the compact that if either became dizzy, he was not to grab the other, but take his own chances. Part-way over, Butterfield lost his nerve and grabbed Philip. "Let go!" muttered Philip, but Dan held on. "Let go!" he again repeated, but still Dan only tightened his grip. Gradually, with the help of his sea-legs and main-top training, Philip succeeded in tugging Butterfield to safety. I can understand the General's feeling; as for myself, I am apt to get dizzy if I stand on a sheet of paper.

My first crossing of the Brooklyn Bridge was when I started to meet my mother at the old St. George Hotel. Passing over another day, I met Henry Cawley, a friend of my boyhood, who during the Civil War had saved the crew of his stranded vessel by swimming ashore with the life-line. He was wearing the uniform of a bridge guard when I saw him. One bitter winter day my father met Henry at an exposed post, and asked why he didn't get transferred to a more sheltered one. He replied, "I had a sheltered post; but one of the guards, a poor fellow, is rather delicate and has a large family to support, so I exchanged with him, as mother is gone and it don't matter what becomes of me." Shortly after, Cawley was stricken with pneumonia, and died—a hero and martyr.

## Blowing up Hell Gate, East River—September 24, 1876

General John Newton announced he would use dynamite to blow up the rock obstructions in the East River at Hell Gate on September 24, 1876 and the city was agog with excitement. In spite of the assurances of Gen. Newton that there was no danger, the people took every precaution. They seemed to expect the city would be knocked end-wards—and if this did happen, I wanted to see it.

Dynamite was almost an unknown force at that time. My father told me that the first time it was brought to public notice was when a man entered a gin mill at the water front, and asked the bartender to take care of a small box. The man never returned. Meanwhile, they bar patrons used the box to black their boots on it. At last it got so greasy that the bartender took it and threw it into the street. It went off with an explosion that left a hole big enough to bury a horse. The shock must have taken every kink out of the bartender's oily hair. (All bartenders looked alike in those days, and they all had knotty, curly hair.) Nobody knew what it was. People came in crowds to gape in the hole. At last some scientist explained it.

Letters as to the possibility of destruction appeared in the newspapers and prophets for and against were allowed full swing. When the day came, many went out of town or took to their yards and the city parks, in spite of an unusually heavy rain. Some insisted that as the city was built on a rock, the whole city would quake; though they knew nothing about it, they felt thoroughly equipped to contradict Gen. Newton's authority. A great many people tried to get as far away from the explosion as possible, others seemed attracted to it like June bugs to a flame. So crowded were the cars from the downtown districts that the uptowners could not get a foot hold, so there was nothing to do but tramp through the torrents of rain. The cross streets and avenues seemed a shining mass of wet umbrellas. My friend Carroll, who was with me worked our way through the crowds, which were so thick we were delayed, and at last had to run for it.

Reaching the straggling village of Yorkville, and running at full speed to pass the last batch of little wooden houses that hid Hell Gate from our view, as we were about five feet from the end of the last house, a slight jar, and a muffled roar told us we had missed the sight by a nose.

As I swung round the corner, a seething mass of foam was settling, showing where Hell Gate had been.

When Hell Gate was blown up the idea was to excavate as much as possible, then blow up the supporting pillars of rock with dynamite, then the river bed would sink, and they could remove any obstructing debris.

## Blowing up Flood Rock, East River—October 10, 1885

Preparations were made to blow up the last obstruction in Hell Gate, called Flood Rock, on October 10, 1885. An artificial island had been formed for working parties, and over the shaft was a frame-work tower about 25 feet high; on top was a staff with a flag flying.

I had gone up with my mother and Dr. Delaney, to Gracie Bluff at the foot of 86th Street. I stood behind my mother with my hands on her shoulders. The crowd was very thick, mounted on the rocks and up the trees.

The river was full of crafts and steamers of all kinds, which, at a given signal were stopped. The tower flag was pulled down from the staff, and shortly after, the government tug left the island and headed for Astoria. Every body in the crowd became tense—an utter silence—a sudden cry. A small boy had fallen from a tree the other side of 86th Street, and the crowd began to show signs of confusion, and look over in that direction, when some genius called out, "Keep your eyes front!"

This was echoed by a muffled roar. A huge mound of water rose in the air. From the center, rose individual ones which mounted skyward, and with them, the black skeleton tower shot up, and then falling with the mass, mixed with the boiling whirl of water. Clouds of yellowish smoke which seemed to emerge from the receding water drifted and disappeared across Long Island.

The column of water had hardly subsided when I saw a small boat heading the rest, which, with flags flying and whistles blowing, started in the mad race to be the first to go through the new channel, while waves from the explosion came rushing toward us and broke over the boulders on the rocky shores where we stood.

It was 14 minutes to 11 o'clock when Gen. Newton's daughter—little Mary Newton—touched the key that put the final seal on her father's great triumph. After the explosion it was proposed to call the spot Newton Channel, but as there was no profit in it for somebody, it soon died out.

I afterwards attended a reception given to General Newton, and the speaker, addressing him, dwelt on the fact of how wonderful it had been that such a mass of dynamite had been exploded so successfully. The General replied, and as he finished said, "If, from the care taken to make the connecting wires, it had not exploded, it would have been a miracle."

In after years I got to know the General well, also his young daughter. He posed for me at the request of Father Deshon, his old friend at West Point. I made studies of his head, which he signed. After he died I called at his house to make measurements of his head for a bust. His three sons and daughter were there, and as I turned to go, my last glimpse of him was as he lay, in full uniform of a chief engineer, with his hands clasped, and on his breast a crucifix.

## The Bull's Head Horse Market

My mother had a friend who lived in 24th Street, between First and Second Avenues. It was an old fashioned brick house with gardens in front, full of bushes, vines and flowers. When we visited her I had a chance to become familiar with the Bull's Head Horse Market.

After having crossed Madison Square, it was thrilling to see a pair of beautiful horses bearing down upon me at full speed; a lean-faced man with long flowing side whiskers, held the taut reins.

Rows of one and two story stables of wood or brick, on each side of the way—most of them painted in the primary color, blue, yellow, white or red. In fact, every owner tried to strike a discordant note to his neighbor, so as to attract attention, but the very confusion formed a harmony, like an Indian in war paint.

The cobbled, straw-littered street swarmed with horses of every breed—in every conceivable action or gait—and undergoing every possible test; while the sidewalks were crowded with horsey folks, "doing and being done for." As I passed where a runway led down to a cellar, a groom came up on a rush, tugging a skittish horse which shied at sight of me. Rearing—jerking the halter loose, he turned a back somersault and rolled down into the cellar.

In front of me a horse was straining with sprawling legs, and sparks flying from his shoes as they struck the cobbles. He was hitched to a truck which he dragged slowly, as it had a piece of timber which ran between the spokes of its wheels, blocking them. On the truck were four or five heavily built fellows; one, "laying on" the whip and jerking at the reins; the others yelling and whooping it up. I learned that General McClellan had figured out that with wheels blocked in this manner, each man represented eight hundred pounds of rolling weight. This simplified the testing of the pulling power of a horse.

Lined along the curb, were a bunch of heavy swells accompanied by a bull terrier that whined and barked at an old battered "Tom" cat which bounded across the street and disappeared down a cellar. They stroked their long Dundreary whiskers, and gazed quizzically through their glasses, and indicated with their gold headed canes, the points of a fine, clean-limbed, stag-throated young horse, which with quivering ears and fluttering nostrils, tossing its head, fairly lifted the Negro who held him.

Hostlers ran up and down with horses trailing on the halters, while keen-faced dealers snapped their whips as they sped by. A frantic horse balanced on one hind leg, pawed the air, with a small boy posed gracefully in the saddle.

The groups parted to make way for long strings of horses, five abreast, their manes braided, chalk marks on their rumps; their tails done up in straw. They were muffled in this manner to prevent them from being chafed in the cars.

At the entrance to one of these stables, more seedy than the rest, a gang of peddlers were gathered round a racky looking nag. The peddler had brought a lot of expert friends to help him judge the "critter." One was examining his long molasses-colored teeth; one looked over his spungy warped hoofs and puffy pasterns; one taking a rear view; one a side view. In fact, they were a knowing lot, but seemed innocents, in contrast to the guiley looking dealer who sat on a soap box, a short distance off, carelessly whittling a stick, but whose keen little black eyes glittered like a rat's, under the rim of his plug hat which was tilted over his nose—a nose so thin and sharp, it looked as though it could cut glass. These types and incidents struck me as good material for an article, which I proposed to Scribner's, who ordered it, and C. C. Buell was detailed to write it up.

As we started for the Bull's Head and turned into 24th Street, this sight awakened all my horse love—their flashing flanks and glittering harness were intensified by the brilliant sunshine.

All this confusion was accompanied by the clatter and beat of horse shoes, the rattling of wheels, the barking of dogs, the sharp whinny of horses, and the muffled beat as they rushed the wooden runways. These were accompanied with the snarling bawl of the speeders, the snapping of whips, or the rasping calls of the dealers. But above all, rang the clear, resounding musical notes of sledges on the anvils of the horse-shoers, around whose open doorway stood the usual fascinated group of idlers, while the fumes of burning hay which the top-heavy wagons bore slowly down the street, and the horses on each side snatching wisps as it passed.

Buell and I worked our way through the shifting groups of men and horses, and finally reached the northwest corner where the Bull's Head Tavern stood. It was a large wooden building; the two upper floors painted brown; the lower story was of brick, and was used as a bar and lunch room. A wooden awning ran above it and out to the curb. Within its shade was sitting a characteristic group of men, tilted back in heavy wooden chairs smoking big cigars, chewing quids, or nibbling straws. One was whittling a basket out of peach pit; another, dreamily coiling fanciful patterns with his whip-lash, on the brick sidewalk.

Another, was a fine-featured old man gloriously bronzed; with remarkable, bold, deep blue eyes; iron-gray hair and beard. The butt of his whip was stuck in the pocket of his coat. He attracted me so, that I went up and questioned him. He responded at once to our questions with interest and intelligence. His friends also showed a kind feeling in furnishing Buell the necessary information for the article.

The old gentleman's name was George W. Bishop. He was a horse expert to whom rich men would come and explain their wants, and he would hunt up the horse with the qualities they desired. Many of our most prominent horsemen bought on his judgment. Talking about the points of a horse he said, "Judge principally by the head." And bringing out a shapely animal, he explained his method. Buell took notes while I sketched our group.

"I can't explain what a real good horse is. They are as different as men. In buying a horse, you must look first to his head and eyes for signs of intelligence, temper, courage and honesty. Unless a horse has brains you can't teach him anything, anymore than you can a half-witted child. That's an awful good mare; she's as true as the sun. You can see breadth and fullness between the ears and eyes. You couldn't hire that mare to act mean or hurt anybody. The eye should be full, and hazel is a good color. I like a small, thin ear, and want a horse to throw his ears well forward. Look out for the brute that wants to listen to all the conversation going on behind him. The horse that turns back his ears till they almost meet at the points, take my word for it, is sure to do something wrong. See that straight, elegant face. A horse with a dishing face is cowardly, and a cowardly brute is usually vicious. Then I like a square muzzle with large nostrils, to let in plenty of air to the lungs. For the under side of the head, a good horse should be well cut under the jowl, with jaw-bones broad, and wide apart under the throttle."

"So much for the head," he continued. "The next thing to consider is the build of the animal. Never buy a long-legged, stilty horse. Let him have a short, straight back and a straight rump, and you've got a gentleman's horse. The withers should be high and the shoulders well set back and broad, but don't get them too deep in the chest. The fore-leg should be short. Give me a pretty straight hind-leg with the hock low down, short pastern joints, and a round, mulish foot.

"There are all kinds of horses, but the animal that has these points is almost sure to be sightly, graceful, good-natured and serviceable. As to color, taste differs. Bays, browns and chestnuts are the best. Roans are very fashionable at present."

Our article called "At the Bull's Head" was published in *Scribner's Monthly*, January, 1879. Mr. Bishop, after that, became a warm friend as well as an adviser, in all that pertained to my horse work. He never failed me.

Once when I showed him one of my studies, he said, "It is easy to criticize your horses; if any of the points are wrong, I can see them first thing. But when other artists ask me to criticize their horses' points, I can't do it because they have no points."

Mr. Bishop was an unusual character. I remember taking him down to Harper's so that he might look over my picture of "Buying Trotters on the Androscoggin." After he approved it, the Editors sat in a group round him, while he entertained them for a long time with his horse talk.

A few months later, C. C. Buell and I visited Dick Platt's training stable to prepare another article for Scribner's about taking a raw colt and developing its higher powers. On the walls of his office, I noticed a small frame in which was mounted a piece of red flannel, inscribed below as follows: "Piece of shirt worn by Col. Ellsworth when he was shot—taken from his body by Elias H. Platt, of Ellsworth's Zouaves." I said, "Dick, who is Elias?" "That's my name," said Dick with a smile, "but everybody calls me Dick." Platt then said, "After Ellsworth was killed, his body was placed in the Engine House at Washington, and I was guard over the body."

"Different fellows had taken pieces of his uniform as relics, so I said to myself, 'I might as well take a good relic,' so I opened his coat and cut out a piece of his flannel shirt that surrounded the hole where the bullet had entered. See, that's the place," he said, pointing to the hole, "and that's his blood surrounding it. I sent it to my brother in New York and forgot all about it, but when he died a short time ago, it was sent to me."

## The Runaway on Fifth Avenue

It was a lovely Spring morning as I walked down the east side of Fifth Avenue and 32nd Street. Up the avenue came a pair of runaway horses dragging a coupe with the hind wheels and axle which had been broken off. It scudded loudly on the curve of its rear like a sleigh, and the driver seat was vacant; the reins trailed on the pavement.

People ran out from the sidewalk in the usual way, waved their arms wildly and darted back to safety. The streetsweepers waved their brooms from a safe distance. Some men grabbed at the reins but they were jerked through their hands. Watching carefully, I stepped into the street and as it neared, and grabbed the traces of the off-horse near the collar, swinging my elbow over it, I was carried on with them. With the downsweep of the reins, I grabbed him near the bit with my right hand, then with my left hand, and bringing my shoulder under the curb, bore down on his jaw and after a few bounds it came to a standstill. Its companion naturally had to halt also.

It was an old trick of mine, and was done without any effort. As I stood at the head, holding the reins with one hand and quieting them with the other, I looked into the coupe. On the right was a lovely old lady with white side curls, in a partial swoon. On her left sat a fine young girl with her hands clasped between her knees, with a blanched face, and startled eyes staring back at me.

A crowd of onlookers gathered and a large, handsome blond-bearded man stepped forward to help the old lady and young girl out. As I stood watching, I felt something warm on my hand that held the reins. Looking up, a tall whiskered policeman had grasped my hand, as well as the reins, in his large gloved hand.

I made a sketch of the incident, but put a mounted policeman catching the horse instead of myself, which was more picturesque. It was published by *Harper's Weekly* [April 9, 1881].

Another well-received horse picture I made from life, depicted a typical street scene in New York and appeared on the cover of *Harper's Bazar* [June 26, 1880]; it showed a fashionable young lady attended by her groom, when about to take a morning ride in Central Park, finds herself suddenly confronted by a train on the elevated railroad, which came dashing along just as she is passing underneath the track (at Broadway and 53rd Street).

Thanks to her admirable horsemanship, she curbed the startled steed without losing her calmness, and rode coolly on while the groom endeavored to soothe his frightened, rearing horse. A flagman in the background is frantically waving the danger signal, and a woman is rudely snatching two children out of the way.

(Above) "Jimmie" Kelly—at age eleven.
(Right) James E. Kelly, the young artist for
Harper's and Scribner's—circa 1877.
(Below) The sculptor at work in his studio
on the bust of Admiral George Dewey, 1899.

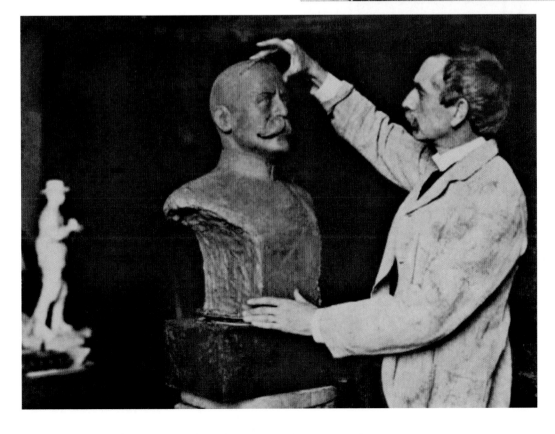

(Top) "New Year's Day," *Harper's Young People*, January, 1880.
(Bottom) "Passing the Batteries," *Harper's Young People*, March 2, 1880.

(Top) "Sailing on the Hudson," *Harper's Young People*, November, 1880.
(Bottom) "The Tournament," *Harper's Young People*, November, 1879.

(Top) "The Old One-legged Sailor," *Harper's Young People,* May 4, 1880.

(Left) "Carrying the Shark," *Scribner's Monthly,* March, 1877, for an article on the New York Aquarium.

(Below) "Jake on His Mule," *Saint Nicholas,* June, 1879.

(Top) "The Pension Office in New York," *Harper's Weekly*, November 11, 1882.
(Bottom) "Perry at Lake Erie," by Kelly for *Bryant's History of the United States*.

(Top) "At the Old Bull's Head," *Scribner's Monthly*, January, 1879.
(Bottom) "Henry Bergh (founder of the A.S.P.C.A.) on Duty," *Scribner's Monthly*, April, 1879.

(Right)
"Facing the Music,"
*Harper's Bazar*, June 26, 1880.

(Below)
"Squatter Life in New York,"
*Harper's Monthly*,
September, 1880.

THE GILLIE-BOY.

(Above) "The Gillie Boy," *Scribner's Monthly*,
August, 1877.
(Right) "A Brave Girl," *St. Nicholas*, June, 1878.
(Below) "Attention," *Harper's Weekly*,
 April 9, 1881.

ATTENTION!

(Left) "At the Old Bull's Head," *Scribner's Monthly*, January, 1879; Kelly appears at left, C. C. Buell center and George Bishop on the right.

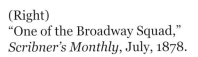

(Right) "One of the Broadway Squad," *Scribner's Monthly*, July, 1878.

(Left) "An Animal Artist's Studio," *Scribner's Monthly*, January, 1880.

(Top) Kelly's painting inspired by Walt Whitman's poem: "The Vigil Strange."
(Bottom) Kelly's painting inspired by Edmund Clarence Stedman's poem:
"Kearny at Seven Pines."

(Top) An engraving of the Molly Pitcher bas-relief on the Monmouth Battle Monument—Thomas A. Edison is depicted as a beardless artillerist "thumbing the vent." (Bottom left) Bust of Edison by Kelly, circa 1880. (Bottom right) Kelly's first sketch of Edison with his "talking machine," at Menlo Park, May 16, 1878.

(Top) "Sheridan's Ride," 1878.
(Bottom) "General William Tecumseh Sherman," 1896.

(Top) "The Crowded Hour at San Juan," 1902.
(Bottom) "Wilson at Selma," 1914.

1840    1917

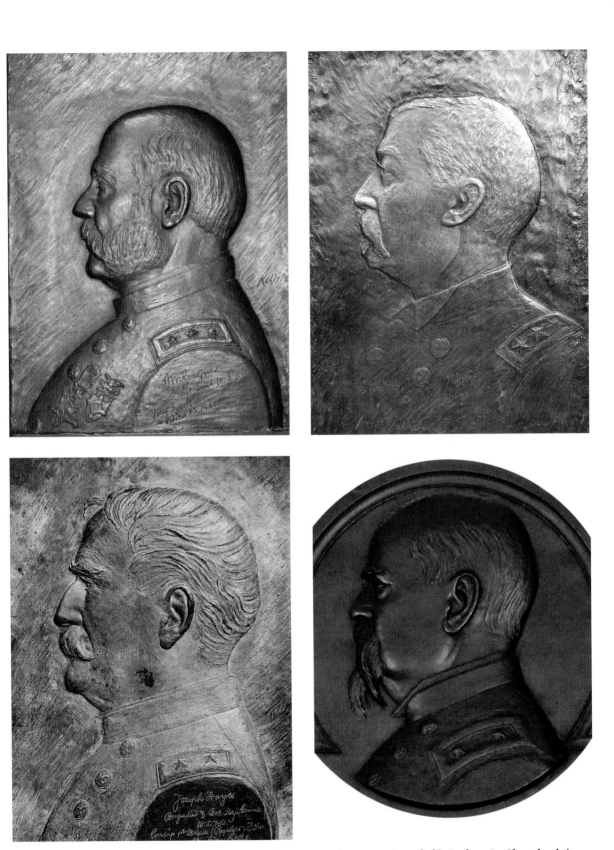

Bas relief panels by Kelly of Union Commanders. *Opposite page*: (Top left) Joshua L. Chamberlain; (Top right) David S. Stanley; (Bottom left) James R. O'Beirne; ( Bottom right) Horatio G. Wright. *This page*: (Top left) John M. Schofield;(Top right) Philip H. Sheridan; (Bottom left) Joseph Hayes; (Bottom right) William F. Smith.

(Top) Clarence Wheeler Memorial,
Woodlawn Cemetery, Bronx, N. Y.
(Bottom left) General Fitz John Porter
Monument, Portsmouth, N. H.
(Bottom right) "The Call to Arms,"
Troy, N. Y.

# SCIENTIFIC AMERICAN

(Entered at the Post Office of New York, N. Y., as Second Class Matter. Copyright, 1904, by Munn & Co.)

Vol. XCI.—No. 16.
Established 1845.

NEW YORK, OCTOBER 15, 1904.

[8 CENTS A COPY
$3.00 A YEAR.

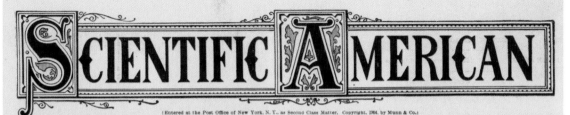

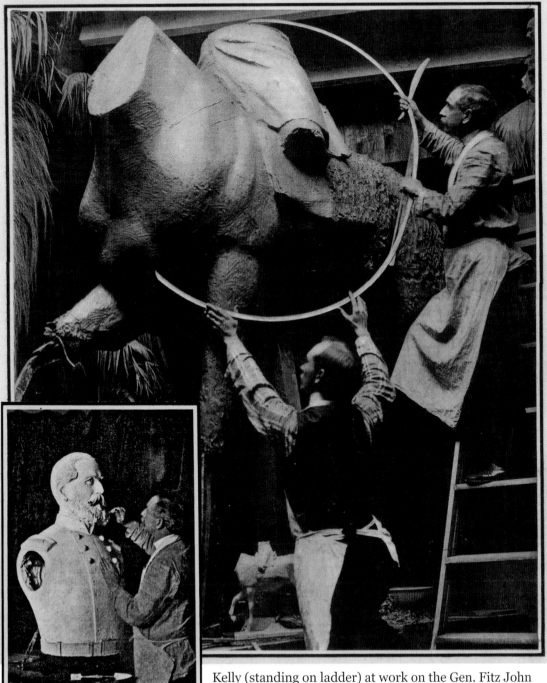

Kelly (standing on ladder) at work on the Gen. Fitz John Porter equestrian statue—illustrating a cover story on bronze casting for the October 15, 1904 issue of *Scientific American*.

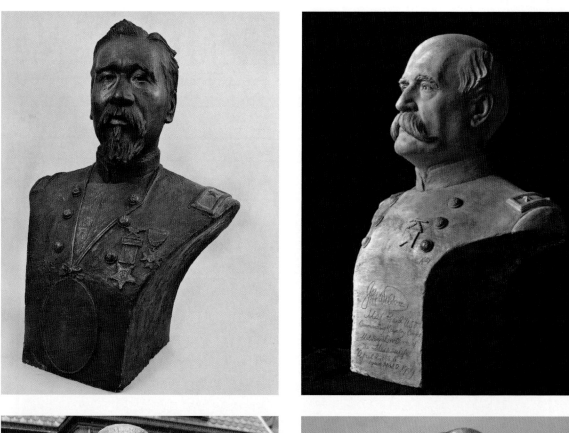

(Top left) Bust of Gen. Ely Parker; (Top right) Bust of Gen. James H. Wilson;
(Bottom left) Bust of Gen. Thomas Sweeny; (Bottom right) Gen. John Buford.

(Top left) "Washington at Prayer,"
Federal Hall, New York City.
(Top right) Detail of Washington—
"The Council of War at Hopewell."
(Bottom) Kelly's studio model of
"The Defenders of New Haven."

(Top) Caesar Rodney statue, Wilmington, Delaware.
(Bottom) Kelly with Gen. James H. Wilson, inspecting the Rodney statue.

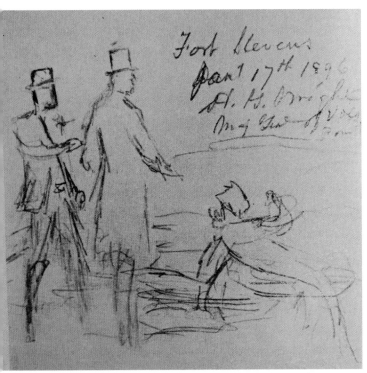

(Top left) Thumbnail sketch of Lincoln under fire at Fort Stevens, as described to Kelly by Gen. Horatio G. Wright, which was later made into a bronze bas relief (Below) to mark the spot where Lincoln stood during the battle.

(Top right) Eleven-year-old William Vallete, Company B, 20th New York Volunteers.

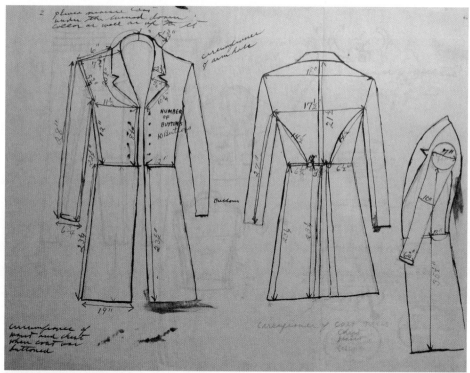

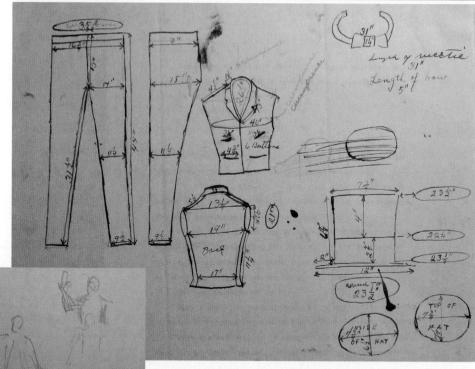

*This page*: (Above) Kelly's detailed sketches of Lincoln's coat, vest, pants, tie and hat—along with their carefully recorded measurements—to be used in a correct artistic depiction of Abraham Lincoln. (Left) Kelly's thumbnail sketch of Lincoln delivering the Gettysburg Address, as described by eyewitness Arthur Briggs Farquhar. *Opposite page*: (Top left) Thomas Proctor; (Below left) "Death of Lincoln," by Alfred Berghaus, showing Proctor standing at left; (Top right) Kelly's thumbnail sketch of the death of Lincoln; (Bottom right) Kelly's bird's-eye view of Lincoln's deathbed scene as described by James Tanner.

Thomas Proctor Present
At Lincoln's Deathbed

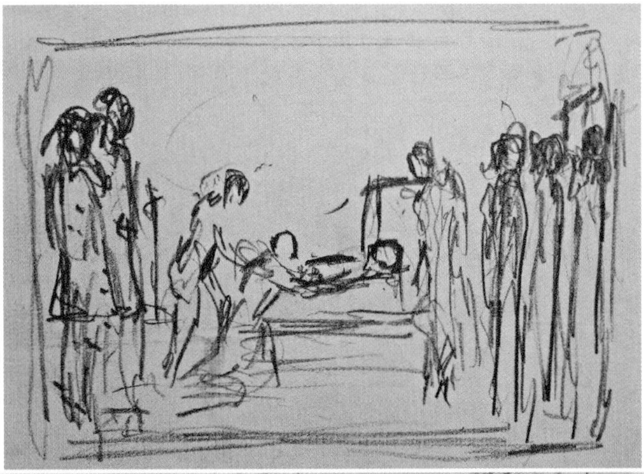

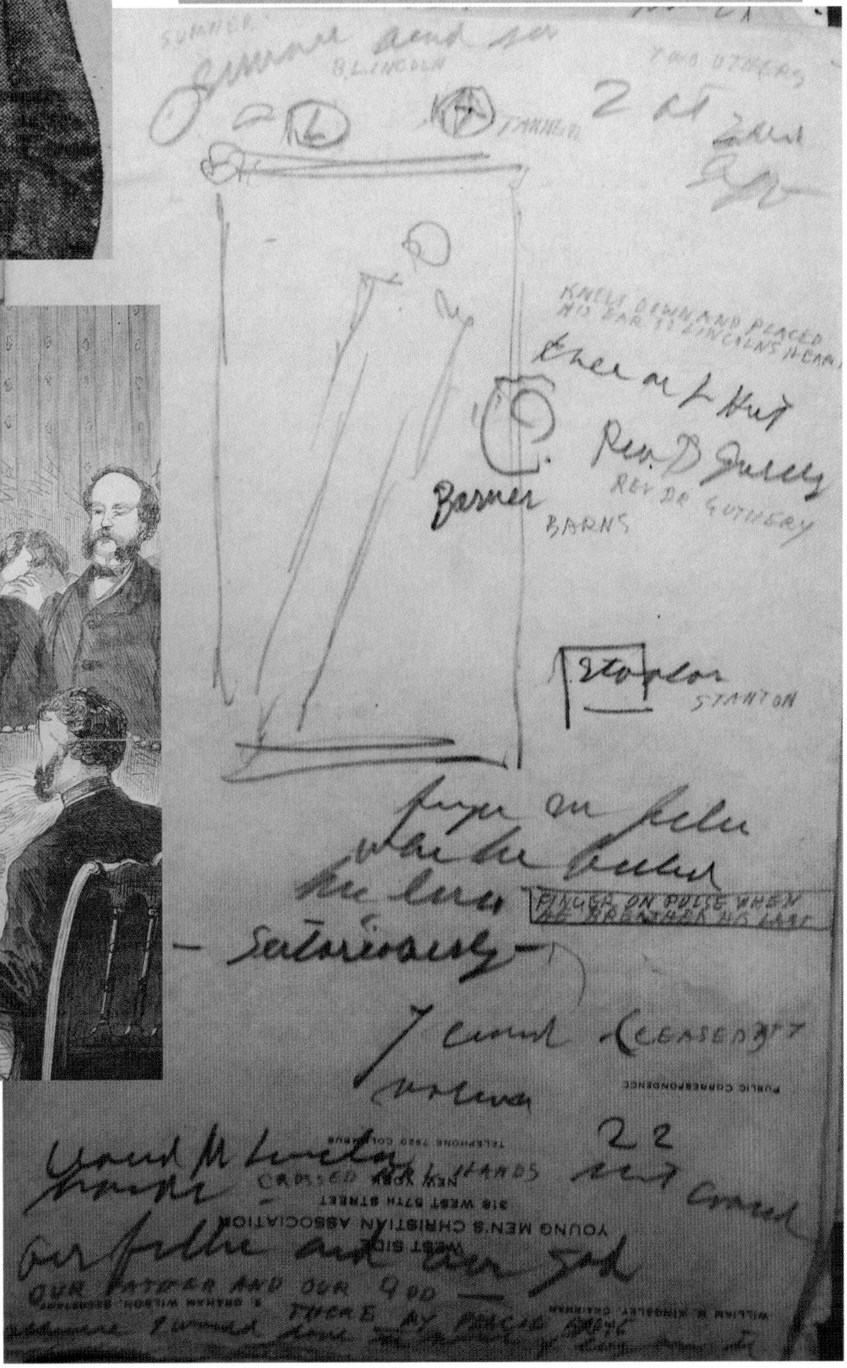
SUMNER
B. LINCOLN
TWO OTHERS
TANNER
KNELT DOWN AND PLACED HIS EAR TO LINCOLN'S HEART
REV DR GUTHERY
BARNS
STANTON
FINGER ON PULSE WHEN HE BREATHED HIS LAST
CEASED
CROSSED HIS HANDS
OUR FATHER AND OUR GOD
WEST SIDE
YOUNG MEN'S CHRISTIAN ASSOCIATION
318 WEST 57TH STREET
NEW YORK

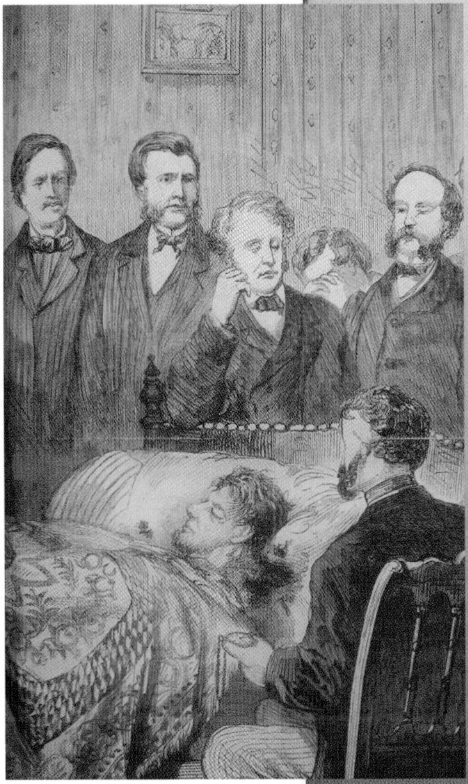

(Top) James Edward Kelly's finest hour: Kelly stands in the center of the speaker's platform at the unveiling of the General John Buford statue at Gettysburg, July 1, 1895; at his right stands, Colonels Alexander Pennington and Jerome Wheeler. Seated front row are: J. M. Buford, Generals John Tidball, David Gregg, Wesley Merritt, Theophilus Rodenbaugh, James H. Wilson, an unidentified trooper, and Colonel John Calef.

Kelly later wrote of this occasion: "General Wesley Merritt announced to the audience: 'Peace has its victories as well as War, and the victor of this occasion is James E. Kelly, Sculptor.' At which a cheer was started. Then Generals Wilson, Merritt, Gregg, and Pennington, seeing I hung back, pushed me forward and stood behind me while I received it."

(Below) The gravestone of James Edward Kelly, Saint Raymond's Cemetery, the Bronx, New York.

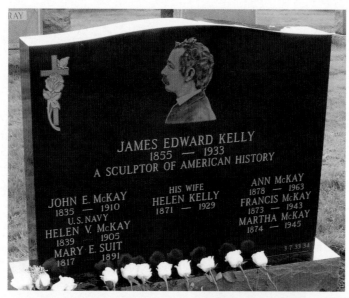

# Chapter Three
# In the Presence of the Great
# 1878-1918

I had always felt a great lack in history of certain personal details. I made up my mind to ask from the living officers every question that I would have asked Washington or his generals had they posed for me, such as: What they considered the principal incidents in their career and particulars about costumes and surroundings.—James Edward Kelly

## Sheridan's Ride

Fired by the dash and the vigor of the poem "Sheridan's Ride" written by Thomas Buchanan Reid, I made a large illustration of Gen. Phil Sheridan on his horse Rienzi in black and white, and sent it to the exhibition at the Academy of Design.

The reception was positive; Clarence Cook, critic for the *Tribune* wrote of it saying, "Kelly has shown Sheridan making that wondrous ride when he witched the world with his wondrous horsemanship, and he and glory reached the goal together."

The drawing was bought by Benjamin L. Farjen, the famous English novelist, and attracted so much attention that I determined to paint it.

My neighbor, Capt. William Alexander had served during the War in the First New York Cavalry with Gen. Phil Kearny, and also was a member of Gen. Sheridan's staff; Capt. Alexander promised me an introduction to Gen. Sheridan, the next time he visited the Fifth Avenue Hotel.

At 9:30 AM, June 15, 1878, I finally met my boyhood idol—Gen. Phil Sheridan.

Alexander and I went in by the 23rd Street entrance to Room 1, on the right. As the door was opened I saw Sheridan before he had time to look up and see me, and was instantly enthused by his bearing. He was five feet, five inches in height and stood very erect on his firm, shapely legs—every inch a soldier, cavalier, and gentleman.

Head large—both long and deep—for a man of his size, particularly when measured from tip of chin to base of skull. I never saw him with a full beard, which would tend to emphasize the length of his face, as in the familiar group photograph of Sheridan and his junior commanders during or about the time of the Shenandoah Valley campaigns.    Rather small but finely molded and expressive mouth; long, snug-fitting cheeks; a very short neck, full throat, well-shaped and rugged shoulders and chest, the whole person solid and compact.

Dark, brilliant glowing eyes, suggestive of genius, hooded by heavy, arched, flexible brows; a fairly prominent nose with high ridge, more conspicuous in profiles than from the front; sensitive nostrils and flowing black mustache, burned reddish at the up-curved ends by the sun of the South and West.  Very dark hair; cropped unusually close; delicately chiseled but firm lips, with a short tuft under the lower one; refined, sensitive chin; jaws broad at the back, strongly held and eyes of granite blue.  I noticed how his ears lay back close to the head. All features deeply bronzed by years of vigorous outdoor life, often days or weeks in the saddle.

Sheridan's hands were fine and shapely, all their movements indicating steady purpose and reserve power in close working order.  His gestures and expressions exactly suited the occasion and the subject.  The General sat well forward on the chair, heels together and chest out.  I never saw him slouch down or lower his dignity—even in the intense heat during Grant's funeral in New York, August 8, 1885, when I observed how some of the other high officers wilted.

His legs were of normal length for a man of his height, and a distinct military bearing, partly natural, but I believed acquired principally by long training and discipline, seemed to add something to his stature.  Weight, when I first saw him, a few pounds over the 115 to 120 during the last campaigns of the Civil War in Virginia, somewhat increased through the later years.

The spontaneous grasp of his chubby brown hand, and his gracious manner in greeting a young, uninvited and unannounced caller, drew me to him in a way I could never forget.  In an instant I was seated cozily beside him, feeling as if we had known each other all our lives, while Captain Alexander waited, apparently overlooked by both of us, quietly and patiently through the interview. I was too much enthralled by fully realizing my opportunity to recall afterward the exact details of our first conversation, but from that time on, always felt the warm, constant glow of his friendship.

His voice seemed to me charming and winning, choice of words and diction perfect—a magnetic personality, with unmistakable evidences of individual force and great activity in emergencies—a good sympathetic, steadfast, and loyal friend, but a very alert, resourceful, dangerous, and unrelenting enemy, as his record proves.

When I was about to leave, entirely at my own suggestion, he remarked, "My boy, you and I are likely to see a great deal of each other in the future.  Now, if I should ever happen to show any—petulance, ignore it, pay no attention to it, as I shall not mean it."

Of course I greatly appreciated that considerate attitude, but nothing of the kind took place during all of our acquaintance.  The next instance after we parted, I bounded out to the sidewalk, and started on a rush home to exclaim to my mother, "I have seen Sheridan!"

When Marvin saw my painting of "Sheridan's Ride," he bought the right to publish it in Bryant & Gay's *History*, and at my request gave John W. Evans the commission to engrave it; and when it was finished it proved to be a masterpiece. It was true—it was bold. Every stroke of Evans' burin [engraver] expressed force, in man and horse; and his rendering of the smoke of battle, as well as clouds of dust, fairly vibrates with light and motion such as I have never before reproduced on wood.

Sometime after my father said to me, "Now you have made the painting of Sheridan's Ride, and as the poem says there will be a statue, I wonder who will make it?"

"I will," I replied. He glanced at me without comment. I put aside the sketch on which I was working, and made a design of the front and two sides of the statue. I asked a friend where I could buy some modeling wax; he said he didn't know of any place that sold it, but he wrote out a recipe how to make it. I bought the materials required and brought them home to my mother, and although she was going to have a Halloween party that night, she started to work at once compounding the materials at the same time she was preparing the supper for the guests. Having finished the mixture, she gave it to me seething [boiling]. I carried the wax upstairs to my work room on the top floor front. Took a clothespin for a base and started modeling Sheridan's head regardless of the merry making of the guests below.

The fever of the modeling took possession of me, although I carried on my illustrations for *Scribner's Monthly*, *St. Nicholas*, Bryant's *History* and *Appleton's Journal*, between times working on the model.

My program was generally to work at my illustrations till about four in the afternoon, then go up to the Mall in Central Park and make character sketches, or sit on the Fifth Avenue Drive and study horses, near the spot where I had seen the original horseman galloping, from which I had caught the action for my "Sheridan's Ride" painting. Then after supper I would start my modeling, and my mother would come in about nine o'clock with tea, toast and a book, and read aloud to me till I was exhausted which generally took till about two or three in the morning. This continued for about three months, and when the model was finished and ready to send to the Academy, I remember throwing myself on the floor and going off into a sleep of exhaustion.

My friends suggested that I send the model to the spring exhibition at the Academy, but before doing so to have it photographed and copyrighted. So, as I was about starting up to Goldstein's Photograph Gallery, Father Alfred Young of the Paulists came by our house and said, "I will go round with you, as there are a couple of spring doors in Goldstein's Gallery which might injure the model."

So I started up 52nd Street to the Belt Line with the tall, stately Father Young smilingly making a pathway for me with my wax model through the crowds of clustering children. Arriving at Goldstein's he led the way upstairs opening the doors to the Gallery.

As I placed the model on a pedestal, the operator came out with a couple of plate holders in his hand. Catching sight of the model, he gazed at it intently without straightening up, then yelled, "There he goes! There he goes!" and whipping off his hat, he yelled, "Hooray! Hooray! Hooray!" While little Goldstein with dilated eyes and hands spread, who knew nothing of Sheridan, looked on in utter amazement as though the fellow had gone mad.

I went round for the print in two or three days after, and not seeing the operator, inquired for him. Goldstein shrugged his shoulders, spread his hands, arched his eyebrows and said dolefully, "Dat day he became so excited, dat he went off on a drunk and hasn't come back since."

The Academy would not exhibit a wax model without a glass cover, so I took it down to the Academy to find if it was acceptable before going to the expense of purchasing a globe. The judging administrators were busy upstairs, so J. G. Brown came down alone; I told him about my model and pointed to it on the floor. He gave a groan and squatted down on his heels. Looking earnestly, he said with a smile, "Go buy your globe" and then started upstairs—the accepting of my first model on his own responsibility and the cheerful encouraging way he did it always endured me to J. G. Brown.

After the exhibition, Charles DeKay wrote an article in the *New York Times* advising me to do more work of its kind and influenced me in taking up the career of a sculptor.

*Charles DeKay's review of* Sheridan's Ride *appeared in the* New York Times, *April 12, 1879:*

> A bold piece of work by a bold young draughtsman is J. E. Kelly's wax image of Gen. Sheridan on his famous ride from Winchester to turn defeat into victory. It is very clever, his horse going at a rattling gait, a sort of dead run, with his fore foot going forward in what seems a stiff-kneed pace, the reins loose and blown backward, and his rider's spurs sticking into him. Sheridan is turned sideways and waves his hat. Mr. Kelly has got a wonderful amount of expression into his ugly face. There is energy there and resolve, perhaps a little exasperation; he is going to put the fight through, if any man in the world can. This is, in its way, a small triumph for Mr. Kelly, and shows again the military instinct in him which is seen so often in his wood-cuts. He loves a flying horse and waving sabre. No one could appreciate a cavalryman better.
>
> We also find here the same fault of which we have before warned him to beware, viz., too much reliance on outside effects to indicate movement. The blown sleeve on Sheridan's bridle-arm, and the blown reins are case in point. They are too much in the nature of tricks, and may end by making him rely on them, instead of learning to indicate movement in subtler ways. We trust he will not stop here, but try his hand again at something in wax or clay, for which he has made as many and as thorough studies in pencil as he has of Gen. Sheridan's ride.

*Another well-known art critic, Richard Watson Gilder, wrote a glowing review of Kelly's statuette of General Sheridan:*

...Kelly's "Sheridan's Ride," which I esteem the most significant work of any American sculptor. We have more polished and dignified sculpture in the conventional sense, but never, to my thinking, any equal in fierce and vital fire to this little piece, which carries one into battle as if one were mounted on the fiery charger of its hero. Sheridan is riding down the line of battle, rallying his broken squadrons. The man is mad with the fury of his duty, crystallized into the yet uncertain alternatives of victory or death. The old horse neighs defiance to the whistle of the rifle ball and the shriek of the shell. Every drop of blood in the man's body pumps up from his heart to swell his veins, and the horse's spirit responds to his own. The raging tumult of a great fight forms itself in one's mind as a background for this superb group, which should be converted into a national monument to one of the most gallant soldiers and most estimable men who ever served a great country in pure and heroic unselfishness.

*Although some art critics, war veterans and other public persons called for Kelly's statuette of Sheridan to be made into heroic proportions, it was his rival sculptors, such as those in the National Sculpture Society—whose members included: John Quincy Adams Ward, Daniel Chester French, and Augustus Saint-Gaudens—who pressured for a competition so they could submit their designs.*

*During this period of American Commemoration (1888-1928)—when hundreds of statues of Lincoln and the Defenders of the Union were being erected on battlefields and in public squares—the competition for sculpting projects was fierce, and Kelly, the former draughtsman turned sculptor, was not exactly welcomed into the sculpting societies of the day; those members considered Kelly an interloper—a mere magazine artist.*

A few years after the death of Gen. Sheridan [in 1888] I received a call from Mr. Charles T. Yerkes, the Chicago banker and railroad man who was visiting New York and staying at the Fifth Avenue Hotel. He greeted me with a most winning manner. He was altogether a quite handsome and prepossessing man; fine, strong, straight features, dark complexion, iron-gray hair, small grizzled mustache.

He said he wanted to consult with me about putting up a statue of General Sheridan in Chicago, and Mr. Brownell of Washington, brother of the Zouave who killed Jackson for murdering Col. Ellsworth, told him I was the one to do it.

After a talk he arranged to see my statue of *Sheridan's Ride*. On his second call he agreed to pay all the expenses after the work was finished. "You prepare to go on with the work. I am going to Europe. I will send you a formal commission, arrange with the Park Board about the site."

He asked me to send on my model to the committee showing some slight changes of which he approved. Shortly after I remember the Park Board called on me, and after a humming and hawing, asked me what I was going to do with the small bronze, when I was through. Not catching the suggestion, I said, "I will keep it." That was my mistake.

When the news came out that Yerkes had commissioned me, there was a perfect clamor raised against me and my work. Several prominent sculptors became outspoken against the statuette. I was amazed at the attacks of a critic who signed a lady's name to the work. Oh, how she scolded. One manly dig might have hurt me, but her method seemed funny. She said she had not seen my work, but knew I couldn't do it.

The Park Commission demanded a competition from Yerkes, who quailed, lay down, did as he was bid, and repudiated me. He turned and welshed on his verbal contract, and announced a competition, which I refused to enter. The prize of a thousand dollars was awarded to a man name Hagner. He copied my model so closely that some of the papers came out denouncing it, saying Yerkes had stolen my brains.

The Park Board then refused a site for the statue. I heard later that the prize winner was found in his studio where he had hanged himself. Yerkes, after keeping my model for several years, at my request, returned it. I had to pay the expenses of expressage, as well as to have it repaired. My drawings were never returned. I suppose his term in prison for swindling had broken his spirit somewhat, and showed itself under this pressure.

## The Council of War at Gettysburg

While working on the fourth volume of Bryant's *History*, I realized that the Council of War at Gettysburg on July 2, 1863 held by Gen. George G. Meade and his Corps commanders, appeared to be the best subject to be researched, as it afforded me an opportunity to illustrate the principle commanders of the battle in one group. It prompted me to propose to Mr. Marvin that I make the subject. He said, "Go ahead." I started gathering facts by calling on Gen. Daniel Butterfield, Chief of Staff to Gen. Meade, at his office and he drew a plan of how the officers were grouped. I then met him at the Union Club for further details and made a sketch of him in position. I also went over to Gen. Winfield S. Hancock at Governor's Island, and he gave me further facts as well as describing his costume. Generals [Gouverneur] Warren, Newton, [Henry] Slocum, [Martin] McMahon—Chief of Staff for Gen. Sedgwick gave me their recollections; other officers out of New York—such as Generals O. O. Howard, Alfred Pleasonton, and John Gibbon, I received written replies to my inquiries. I afterwards talked over the battle with Generals Doubleday, Joshua Chamberlain, Joseph Hayes, Alexander Webb, and Horatio Wright, and Col. John Calef who fired the opening gun; they gave me a pretty clear idea of the battle.

I showed the drawing to Gen. Hancock, he said, "You have made me very conspicuous; people will think you made it for me." "Is it correct?" I asked. "Yes," he said, "and I thank you."

I spent much time on the composition, and when finished, Marvin told me that he had given it to the well-known steel engraver, William S. Marshall, to engrave and suggested that I call upon him at 711 Broadway.

He was a tall, handsome, earnest looking man, whose appearance and sincerity impressed me; he also seemed greatly interested in the subject. I was familiar with his well-known engraving of Lincoln, but never liked it, in spite of the great praise it had received. Nothing but self defense makes me add the following:

When Marvin showed me the proof, I was staggered. Marshall had altered the effects of light and shade, as well as the features of the generals, and the coarseness of his line was crude and vulgar. I flared up and denounced it as a disgrace. Marvin smiled at my fury, saying that Marshall had come in and asked for an advance payment on the cut. "I paid him," continued Marvin, "and that is what he brought me—so I had to take it." That gave me a great setback, and I have always hesitated to show the cut, which appeared in Bryant's *History*.

I tried to make the drawing as clear to facts as possible, and I hope some day to model the scene in bronze as a memorial of a great historic setting, which will last when the little wooden headquarters will have passed away.

The year 1879, was the most interesting and opportune for me to make close observations of the commanding generals of the Union Army.

Death had removed the names of [George] Thomas and Meade from the Official Register, and Grant, who relinquished the chief command for the Presidency (and not placed on the retired list as general until March, 1885), was on his trip around the World. Official Army headquarters were in Washington, but New York City was the principal meeting place of the active personnel—the senior officers generally in full vigor, though approaching the retirement age.

For several weeks in the spring the [David] Stanley-[William] Hazen Court Martial was in frequent sessions at the Army Building, southwest corner of Houston and Greene Street, with General Winfield Scott Hancock as the presiding officer. General Sherman and General Sheridan were called to testify, and remained probably for the longest time that both were ever in the city together. James A. Garfield, a former major general of Volunteers, who a little more than a year later became the Republican nominee for the Presidency, with Hancock for his Democratic opponent, was among the many other notable witnesses.

The Centenary of the Battle of Stony Point was celebrated on July 16, 1879, in the Highlands of the Hudson, reviving memories of General Mad Anthony Wayne; and on August 30th the statue of General George A. Custer was dedicated at West Point. Hancock was present on both occasions, with his official staff, and a distinct military atmosphere pervaded New York and vicinity, of course, at the Governors Island headquarters. For several months that summer I received the opportunity to meet, interview and sketch many of my boyhood heroes—the commanders that saved the glorious Union!

*News of Kelly's sketches and detailed interviews with the heroes of the Union appeared in the* New York Times, *December 1, 1889:*

### Grant and Sheridan
### An Artist's Experience in Posing the Two Great Captains

In an interview recently with Mr. James E. Kelly, an artist who made sketches of some of the great Generals of the Civil War, that gentleman spoke of his experience in posing Generals Grant and Sheridan. Of the latter he said:

"I was introduced to Gen. Sheridan by a staff officer. He had a soft, low voice, though he has too often been represented as a loud-mouthed, swaggering bully. He had a peculiar, soothing, quieting way about him, and when he finished a sentence would partly close one eye and drive his idea into one with the other. It was the only eye among all the officers [that Kelly sketched] which most seemed to comprise the whole head, the most remarkable eye known to my experience. He had very fine, expressive hands and a graceful way of using them; but toward the end these became fat and fluffy. In photographs the expression of his face always looked set, because, I suppose, the muscles of his forehead were always moving. I had to catch his expression as I might the movements of a fly on a horse's leg.

"He posed splendidly, and did exactly as he was told—a military trait. He once sent a man after me on the run, who said that Gen. Sheridan desired to see me in haste. When I entered his hands were filled with dispatches, and an orderly stood behind him. He said that in fifteen minutes he was to start South with Gen. Grant, and in that time his posing must be completed. Then he adjusted his eyeglasses, began reading his dispatches, and dictating replies. He would hold a dispatch in one hand, read it, and pass it to the orderly over his shoulder with the other. Still he managed to divide his glances with me. Strange to say, the sketch completed under these circumstances brought out a kind word from Gen. Warren, whom Sheridan relieved of his command on the field in almost the last battle of the war and within sight of Appomattox Court House. Warren said it was the 'Ideal Sheridan.' At the time, Gen. Sheridan supposed I was merely making a picture of him, and he seemed greatly pleased when Mr. Ward sent word to him 'to come to the Academy of Design and see Kelly's very meritorious statue—Sheridan's Ride.' I requested him to make suggestions for alterations before the statue was cast. He had 'nothing to criticize,' he said, and instead approved the work with his signature."

On the outside cover of Sheridan's "Memoirs" there is a reproduction of Kelly's statue in gilt. No credit whatever is given to the artist in the book and his name was cut out of the plate. Mr. Kelly says: "I demanded of Webster & Co. to know why my copyright and Gen. Sheridan's instructions to them were ignored. They replied that he had given no instructions. I then asked to see the photograph of the statuette which accompanied the manuscript. When produced, there on the back of the photograph were instructions written by the General to credit the artist. Webster's people then said if I went to law about it 'it wouldn't come out of their pocket, but Mrs. Sheridan's. I then replied that they were perfectly safe to go ahead.'

"I first met Gen. Grant at the Fifth Avenue Hotel during 1881. He agreed to give me sittings, and I began on him the following morning. I found him perfectly immovable and unresponsive. My first attempt was a failure. Tearing up the picture, I asked him to smoke. He lighted a cigar, and then seemed to unloose himself somewhat, though not enough. Suddenly I sprang to my feet to arouse him, and said I would like to make a series of sketches showing where his personality decided battles; that I desired to represent him as he appeared when he rode up to the lines at Donaldson and ordered the advance; at Belmont, where his horse was shot from under him; at Shiloh, &c. Then he completely awakened, crossed his legs, and began to detail events, holding meantime his cigar in one hand and using the other by way of gesticulatory illustration. He elaborated on many scenes in his "Memoirs," which he afterward said he had never done previously. He gave such details as he could remember of his dress, &c., referring to Major Jacob B. Rawles and Major Theodore C. Bowles of his staff, for matters in doubt. This sketch, of course, made while he was enthusiastic, was successful. So much so that he signed it on the spot, even using the title of 'General' at the bottom, although he remarked at the time, 'I have no official signature.' He was then neither President nor officer.

"Once aroused, Gen. Grant talked incessantly. During this time his little Japanese servant was bobbing all around us, greatly astonished at the posing process and its results on paper. The General was not in the least annoyed by the boy's antics and allowed him full rope. Indeed, while with him, Gen. Grant apologized at some length to a bell boy for calling him unnecessarily. The General having no horse left over from the war, it was somewhat difficult to get an animal which would answer to pose my 'Grant on Horseback,' which is nearly completed in plaster. Happily, Capt. William H. Gunther's horse 'Don,' probably the most perfect charger in the country, was available, and his action I secured on the track in Central Park. Of course, I have Grant covered in detail by numerous sketches and designs in plaster. He had two prominent profiles, one very narrow and one very long. While not in possession either of the strong characteristics of Sheridan or Sherman, his outline from the bridge of the nose up was more perfect than either. Neither had he so many individualities.   While his hands were remarkably fine and full of expression, his face depended on the circumstances of the moment."

*After the acclaim of* Sheridan's Ride*, Kelly eventually stopped illustrating for the magazines and began sculpting monuments.*

## The Monmouth Battle Monument

One evening I was visited by Judge Maurice J. Power who was proprietor of the National Fine Arts Foundry—a bronze foundry located on 25th Street, who made a cast of my *Sheridan's Ride.*  He asked me if I would make a design to compete for the Monmouth Battle Monument to be placed in Freehold, New Jersey.  I told him, "No."  He said, "If I pay you for your design, will you make it?"  "Yes," I replied.  There were to be five bronze bas relief panels to be placed around a thirty foot circular base.

I then called upon H. C. Coultaus, the artist and told him that I proposed to make designs for the Monmouth Battle Monument.  "What are you going to make?" he asked.  At this I took up some slips of paper, and placing a small cross-legged table between my knees, sketched designs for the five panels.  My first design was *Molly Pitcher*, with her dead husband at her feet, ramming the charge into the cannon; while a wounded gunner "thumbs the vent," and a soldier stands by, ball in hand.  My other designs were *Washington Rallying His Troops*, *The Council of War at Hopewell*, *Ramsey Defending His Guns*, and *Wayne's Charge*.  Coultaus liked my designs, and when I won the award, he said he was going to keep the table, and always make his designs on it for luck.

Later I learned that my designs had won over sixty competitors.  I asked the Judge who was going to model it.  He said he had not decided; then I told him I would like to get my thumb in it.  "All right," he said, and then told me that I could model the five panels in clay in five months.  As I had never modeled anything except a portrait of a young girl in clay, I took his word for it, and a contract was made out to that effect.

Power's foundry was a small, grim four-story building, evidently erected for a factory, painted a dim yellow, with raw brick walls inside and exposed beams.  The first floor front was used as an office.  The building had originally belonged to a Mr. Waite, who could not get over the idea that he no longer owned it; every day he used to come with an old friend, where he would sit and look at nothing.

One day, I don't know what prompted me to ask him if he had ever seen Andrew Jackson.  "Oh, yes," he replied, "I saw him when he came up Broadway in a procession.  He wore a white high hat with long black streamers on it for his wife, who had just died.  I remember how he would take it off in response to cheers of the people."  Mr. Waite also spoke of the big funeral for Bill Poole, to which I make reference elsewhere in this manuscript.  Next door to the foundry was a lodging house where P. T. Barnum put up his freaks; Barnum used to send around a carriage, and load it even to the top with the queer characters in costume.

As to the foundry—to be brief: the bronze was composed of 90% copper and 10% tin, with a little lead. They used crucibles, which was able to stand the intense heat required to melt the metals. The plaster models were molded in what was called French sand, as it was imported in barrels from that country. It was also capable of taking very fine impressions, like clay, and at the same time stand the intense heat without cracking, as clay would. The mould being made of it was baked until it had the consistency of bath brick and about as hard as plaster, then put into an iron frame with a vent at each end. The molten bronze was poured into one of these vents, and when the metal appeared at the vent on the other end, it was known that the casting was a success.

After cooling, the mould was chipped off and destroyed. This is what makes a bronze casting so expensive. A cast in soft metal, which is just as accurate, can be cast in metal moulds like a bullet, and reproduced over and over again. After the cast is finished, a chaser goes over it, taking off the core marks, and the bronze is then ready to convey its message down the ages.

The top floor of the foundry was my studio—a large bare room with brick walls. According to our arrangement, the contractor built a large brick drum in the center of the floor, which was balanced so as to turn on a pivot in the center; it was thirty feet in circumference, divided into five sections six inches deep. He proposed that I should fill them with clay, which would take half a ton each; on putting in my first half ton, the center pin broke, and I could not turn it from that time on.

The Judge also advised me to get an old sculptor as an assistant, and give him $30 a week; this I did, but after he had come he complained that he was sick, and sat in an arm chair looking on, letting me do the work. Not then knowing anything about clay, I filled the sections with chunks and smeared in the cracks between; as they began to dry, cracks began to appear and pieces would fall out. Thinking it all in the job, I kept on. I would reset the pieces, and fit them into place, while the old fellow said nothing.

At last his utter laziness began to depress me, and I bounced him. Power afterward told me that the fellow let me put it out of order, thinking I would become discouraged, give it up and he would get the job. But I didn't have brains enough to be discouraged. Power then said to me, "Now you've everything ready, just slap it up." At this his mask fell off. I had not until then, noticed the crafty look in his rather dull eye, and of course he read me as I read him.

After I had worked in the clay for two or three days, he came in, walked over to a chair opposite the relief, sogged back on his shoulder blades with his hands clasped across his paunch, legs extended full length and crossed at the ankles. Gazing in silence under the brim of his hat, which tilted nose-wise, he said sneeringly, "Do you expect to carry out that model the way you have started it?" "Yes," I replied. With a contemptuous squirt of spit on the floor, as was his custom, he said with another sneer, "You'll never do it! You'll never do it! Why you have violated all the rules of sculpture."

I laughed and said, "You just wait a day or so." At this, with still another contemptuous sneer, he said, "If you should succeed after the way you have started it, I shall never presume to criticize you again, but humbly bow to your superior judgment." And then, with a mocking act of deference, he left me. With this interview still ringing in my ears, I decided upon my line of action. I took three months to get the panel of *Molly Pitcher* in condition. My mother gave me the action for Molly, and actress Nell Starret posed for the details of the figure, but I put in the character from my study of Mary Anderson, in a tragic pose, for the head. Ed Bell, the artist, posed for the figure in the foreground. For the gunner, I needed a model with a clean-shaven face. My only acquaintance at that time without beard or mustache was Thomas Edison. I went to him and asked him if he would serve as a model. Mr. Edison consented, and the figure in the panel is a portrait of the inventor when he was "lean and hungry" in his search for the secrets of nature's powers.

I went down and visited the battlefield, and studied the blackberry bushes and other shrubbery on the field, as well as the low corn on June 28th, so as to correctly render them at that period and the day of the fight. I also made a study of the Tennant Church, and with all this material fresh in mind, I carried out the panel. This finished, I sent for the Committee, consisting of Theodore Morris, Gen. W. S. Stryker, Adjutant General of New Jersey, and Mr. Burke; when they called, they expressed themselves in the highest terms of approval. I then said to them: "Gentlemen, I am glad you like it, but you will not like the other panels as well." "How's that?" they inquired. "Well, I have signed to complete the models in five months, and have worked for three months on Molly Pitcher to my satisfaction. Now I have two months to finish the other four; if you insist that I shall do it, the Molly Pitcher will be my own, and the other work, which I must do in two months, will be known as yours." At this they all gave a hearty laugh, and said, "Take your time, and make the rest as good as Molly."

I had many art judges see Molly, and they all approved; but the one opinion I valued most was that of Charles Parsons, art editor of Harper's. His expressions of approval were such that I hesitate to put them down here (as I have a little modesty left); but after that, when I would take in a drawing for a picture, he would ask, "Is that as good as *Molly*?" It strikes me that he had a design in this—he kept repeating in my ears until I finally gave up drawing and turned to sculpture. Thanks for the far-seeing vision and keen judgment of Charles Parsons!

## The Council of War at Hopewell

The next panel as I recall it was *The Council of War at Hopewell*, held by Washington, to gather the opinion of his officers as to the advisability of attacking the British on their march from Philadelphia to New York.  Gen. Charles Lee did not think the Colonials capable of facing the British regulars, while [P. J. G. de M.] Lafayette, [Nathaniel] Greene, [Anthony] Wayne and [John] Paterson, and a majority of the other officers were in favor of the attack.  To the right of the panel, Lee is shown in a fit of the sulks, with his two cocker spaniels at his feet.  I had a most interesting collection of portraits and data that would make a subject by itself.  To get the nervous energy of Lafayette, I posed for it myself in front of a large looking glass.

Just as I had *The Council of War* blocked out in clay, Power came in, and in his usual depressing way, gave me to understand that I was in for it, as the Committee had placed the monument in the hands of a supervising architect, to look after their interests; and on leaving gave me to understand that he was a German—and that I was to have a hot time of it.  A day or so after, I was standing on a platform working out the perspective of a scene with a long brass rod, when a tall, erect gentleman entered.  He had a compact square face, with rosy cheeks, blond beard, and leveling a pair of sharp, keen blue eyes upon me through a pair of gold-rimmed spectacles, and in a hard, crisp voice as though expressing resentment, announced: "I am Mr. Rapt, supervising architect of the Monmouth Monument."  "Oh, Mr. Rapt," I said, jumping down, "I am right glad to see you—you are just in time.  I'm in a snarl over the perspective; will you check it?"  At the same time offering him the clay-covered rod; he bored me through with another sharp glance, and then with a nod and a smile took the rod, and without removing either his silk hat or overcoat, he went over my lines of perspective, and with two or three suggestions, passed them as O.K.

We then sat down and had a long talk—on horses, horsemen and actors; and by the time the light began to fail, I felt that I had gained a firm friend, so much so that when the warm days began to come, he would stop in the afternoon and order me to stop work.

## Ramsey Defending his Guns

While illustrating Bryant's *History*, I found a reference stating that when Dr. James McHenry, after whom Fort McHenry was named, had before his death written on the margin of his copy of John Marshall's *Life of Washington*, an account of the heroic action of Lieutenant-Colonel Nathaniel Ramsey at the Battle of Monmouth, which had come under his observation.

After Washington had ridden up—he met Gen. Lee slouching in retreat at the head of his troops—the British after him in full cry.  Reprimanding him in language which Lee would understand and ordering him to the rear, he turned to Ramsey and ordered him with two guns, to sweep the narrow causeway, cross the swamp, and keep the British in check while he formed a new line of battle. This he did until the repeated charges of the British Dragoons wore on his men; Ramsey feared they would give way. Ordering the guns to the rear, dismounted, he stepped in the narrow pass all alone, closed on the advancing horsemen, and in the melee stalled the charge long enough to save his guns. Strange to say, although over-powered, he was unwounded. He was taken before the British General Howe who was so impressed with his action that he released Ramsey and sent him back next day with a letter to Washington commending his bravery.

The Committee originally intended to have the third panel covering the period of the action, represent Washington reprimanding Lee, but I said, "I don't care to make a gibbet of the Monmouth Monument and represent the disgrace of Lee, but prefer to immortalize the glories of our arms in the person of Lt. Col. Ramsey." The suggestion was approved by the Committee, and I started to collect the material to make the panel historically correct. I found the Rev. Dr. Brand of Emorton, Maryland, had married the granddaughter of Charles Wilson Peale, the artist who had painted the most manly portrait of Washington, and also one of Ramsey in the blue and red coat facing of the Maryland Line.

Dr. Brand loaned me the original miniature of Col. Ramsey, as well as a silhouette, and gave me a photograph of the short cutlass which Ramsey had used at Monmouth. About that time a breastplate of the 17th Light Dragoons was dug up, and a picture of it taken. With this material I started work, and my friend George Edgar Biddle, the actor, gave me the action for Ramsey's figure. There were 700 negroes in the fight, so I took one as a type and represented him hauling off the gun in the background.

## The Fight on Second Avenue—July 18, 1884

After working for some time on the relief with many petty annoyances from Power, an incident happened which gave me a standing in the section and changed the atmosphere of the foundry.

Returning from lunch, riding on a Second Avenue open car with my back to the driver and horses, I saw a heavy built young fellow, with a long golden mustache, swing aboard and begin talking to the driver. He evidently was a driver on his day off, and after a while sat down on the back of my seat, lopping over my shoulder; I lurched him off. He looked down at me, and then settled back with more force. I gave him a jab with my elbow, and as I jumped up he swatted me on the jaw, and I planted him one on the throat. He reeled back and if he had not caught the side post he would have landed in the street. The driver put on his brake, the conductor shuffled along the running board, and the three began to close on me. I stood braced covering their attack, and I was in fine fettle from having punched clay for a year or so.

Just then, a long legged old man who looked like Uncle Sam stepped up beside me and shaking his fist with a yankee drawl, "Dam yeu—yeu—aught to be cut in teuu—three of yeu—on one man!" This stalled them. Turning to me he said, "What do yeu want done?" I said, "I want that fellow to come off that platform and sit here." "Come on," said the old man. The fellow who hit me sulkily came round and sat beside me; he began to growl and talk fight. I said, "I am going to 25th Street; you can then talk fight if you want to. Now shut up, I want to read."

As I got off the car at 25th Street I heard a hail, and the big fellow bore down on me with a blazing face. The car had stopped and the passengers piled out and surrounded us, joined by a crowd on the corner. The fellow was spoiling for a fight, and started to cuss me out, which I stopped with a sock on his chin, at the same time dislocating my thumb. He laughed and turned to the encircling crowd, spit on his hands, grinned and winked knowingly. They responded encouragingly to this little piece of courtesy on his part.

It was on the southwest corner of 25th Street in front of a gin mill, under an old wooden awning that covered the sidewalk. I felt quite alone. I felt a sinking of the heart with the thought—here I am, twenty-eight-years-old, have never been licked, but now at last it looks like it, as I am outmatched.

While he was posing like a serious man, I glanced over the ground and saw a place where a brick had been removed; placing my right foot in the hole, I crouched down like a cat, and watched him, my arms hanging loosely in front of me.

He looked down on me contemptuously. He was tall, heavy, built like a policeman; a German type—fair hair, blue eyes and a long flowing blond mustache; a gleaming healthy complexion—very good looking.

"How is that for a Possish!" he laughingly said, addressing the crowd and pointing at me, while they joined in his jeer.

Again spitting on the tips of his fingers, he clenched his red fists and boomed down on me.

His huge fist aimed between my eyes. I threw out my left straight as a foil, parried it, and ducked his fist plunging down my spine, bringing his exposed face about a foot from mine. Planting him a cruncher in his mouth and nose, I boosted and staggered him backwards about ten feet, but my every joint from shoulder, hip and leg, felt the jar of the impact. He pulled himself together with a bewildered smile, and wiped the blood from his lips where I had put his teeth through.

There was a dead silence in the crowd from which his bewildered eyes received no response.

Smiling again nervously, as the sunlight struck under the awning and lit him up; I felt what a pity it was to spoil such a handsome face, but down he rushed again. I parried his lunge with my right, gave him a hook with my left, but as my left did not amount to much, it merely staggered him. The round ended in a sputter of short arm jolts.

He drew back for wind, and then began sparring and dancing round, while I pivoted with my foot braced in the brick hole. Down he rushed like a furious bull; I parried his blow as before with my left; his fist grazing the back of my head and down my spine. Responding with a screw-drive in his left eye, I forcibly lifted and sent him with a lurch tottering back on his heels; his arms wavering to recover himself till losing his balance, he swirled and fell over on his right side with a heavy souse; his face striking the sidewalk.

The crowd yelled, "Bully for the Sheeny! Bully for the Sheeny!"

This explained it.

My black curly hair—

My large hook nose—

My slim figure—

My long tailed black frock coat—

He had taken me as I had been taken before, for a Jew, which seemed fair game for a sporty tough.

"A Cop—A Cop! Run! Run!" came in warning tones from the crowd. One handed me my novel, one handed me my straw hat, while the fellow scrambled to his feet and tore down Second Avenue. I turned and saw a tall Policeman with a drawn club striding cross the avenue—a lean, grim set fellow—like a country American with a chin piece died black.

I nodded sociably as he advanced which seemed to disconcert him. He lowered his club. "What's the matter?" he said in a low voice.

"It was this way," I said confidentially, "do you see that fellow running down there?"

"Yes."

"I was in a car and he insulted me. I slapped his chops. He followed me and I have just knocked him down."

The Policeman hesitated, looked embarrassed, and then in a low friendly voice said, "Go on now as I will have to arrest you."

"Thank you," I said bowing, "good day." And I started down to the foundry.

In all my experiences at unveilings, I have never received such an ovation.

Charles Dana Gibson's cartoon in *Life*, called *The Champion* gives some idea of it. The wild cheers of men and boys, the shrills of children still rings in my ears, as well as the hustle and scuffle of feet as I led the mob in triumph to the foundry where, on entering the office, they flattened their noses against the windows. Power who was sitting inside with his foreman, looked round in some alarm, gasping, "Er, what, what's the matter?" "Oh, I have just licked a fellow up on the corner."

"Licked who?" he asked.

"Oh, I don't know; one of your ward heelers, I suppose."

He glowered at me but said nothing. On going over myself, I found my right thumb worthless and a bruise on my right arm above the wrist from warding his blows. That night the doctor put my thumb in bandages, in such a way that I could use the first joint of my thumb without pain. On my way to work next morning, a big bum sitting on a beer keg in front of the saloon on the corner, came over and inquired tenderly as to the condition of my thumb. Other people in the street showed the same interest and continued to do so till the bandages were taken off and always greeted me afterwards in a respectful manner.

Judge Power was continually complaining about the lack of money; so one day I called on Mr. Rapt, told him how I was worried by Power, and asked him if he would pay in advance for the panel on which I was working. He looked me over rather swiftly, and said, "Mr. Kelly, do you know what you are asking me?" I said, "Yes, and you can have only two reasons for refusing—one is that you don't think I can do the work, and the other is that you think if you give me the money in advance, I will not finish it." He looked at me with a dry smile, and said, "Send Power to me," which was done, and Mr. Rapt paid him the money. I didn't think at the time what I was asking of him, as I might have died, or had some accident to prevent my finishing the model, and in such case he would have been personally responsible for the money.

One day returning home from modeling, I started to get off the Second Avenue streetcar as a boy jumped on the step and crashed into me; as we were both falling, his head was about to strike an elevated railroad pillar. I swung my right hand behind his head, and the left one to guard my own; at the same time my left knee struck the elevated pillar, and we both rolled on the cross walk. The doctor examined my knee and said that the muscle was almost detached; he set the knee in plaster for a month, and so I had to walk from the hip, which made my leg as stiff as a broomstick. For some time after, my shoulder suffered intense pain, and it developed that the tendon had been injured; so I had to carry my left arm in a sling for many months, while continuing to work on the panels.

Not long after this, Judge Power came to me and asked if I would be responsible for all the delays, as they would hold him accountable as the contractor, adding, "But as you are the artist, they will not be as severe on you." I said, "Go ahead and blame me;" so we went down to Mr. Rapt's office.

The Judge opened with a series of complaints about my delay, and finished up by saying that I was inclined to lounge and entertain visitors. Mr. Rapt, who had been listening with his hands clasped and leaning back, suddenly grabbed the elbows of his chair, and leaning over with his chin projecting, said, "Judge, don't tell me any of such tam nonsense. I know that boy. I have gone there and seen him at work with his hand in a splint. I have gone there and seen him with his knee in plaster; on hot days, when I would leave my office, I would get off the car, go to his studio and find him at work—and send him home. So don't tell me any such tam nonsense, that he is a loafer."

By the time the work was almost completed, several newspapers had featured stories in regards to the work. A day or two after, a venerable, white-bearded gentleman came in and told me that he had seen the article by Hosea Ballou in the *New York Tribune* on the *Council of War at Hopewell*, and then added in a refined, gentle manner, "as I was born in the house where the Council of War was held, which was owned by our family, I felt a great desire to see it, and so took this liberty of calling." I showed him the work, explained all that he desired to know; and in his cheery manner he related many interesting incidents I cannot include here.

He also said that the house where the council was held had been destroyed. "That was a fine building, and the room was paneled," he said, which I didn't know before the work was finished.  He then added, "I remember my grandmother telling me that she was a little girl at the time, and went out to pick strawberries for Washington's supper.  She said that she didn't like Gen. Lee, as he went to bed with his two dogs and his boots on."  I now regret very much that I cannot recall the old gentleman's name.

*Kelly's work on the Monmouth Battle Monument in Freehold, New Jersey, was completed by November, 1885, but his leg and shoulder injuries kept him from accepting any sculpture projects for the next two years.*

# The Golden Argosy

After finishing the Monmouth Monument, and two panels for the Saratoga Battlefield monument and several designs for panels to be worked up for the same by another sculptor [J. S. Hartly], my shoulder, which had been injured at the time I was tripped up by the young boy at 79th Street, began to grow worse instead of better.  At last the pain became almost unbearable, and the doctor told me that the tendon had been twisted; so after applying his remedies, he ordered me at once to the country.

While there, I tried to fill an order from Harper's, but was too ill to carry out the work up to the standard.  Calling at Harper's and talking it over, I was advised to take up a line of work that would not strain me, and was given an introduction to Frank Munsey, who then published a boys' magazine, called the *Golden Argosy*.

On presenting my introduction, I told him frankly how I stood; in fact I had my left arm in a sling at the time.  He gave me a manuscript at once.

The day I took in my batch of drawings, I saw Munsey talking to a thin, handsome gentleman with a professional bearing.  He introduced him as Mr. Edwin S. Ellis, the Superintendent of the Trenton High School, and author of the *Standard History of the United States*, as well as other historical works.  He said, "Are you the artist who drew the "Death of King Philip, in Bryant's History?"  I said, "Yes."

"Well, I consider that the best Indian picture I have ever seen," he added.  "I am surprised to hear that," I said, "as one critic wrote that it was one of the worst pictures ever published."  At this he set his lips, and said, "Well, I'll prove what I think."  Then turning to Munsey added, "Will you please give that last Indian story I have written to Mr. Kelly, that he may illustrate it?"

Munsey kept me steadily supplied with manuscripts until my shoulder healed sufficiently enough to resume sculpture.

## Sixth New York Cavalry Monument at Gettysburg

In 1887, I succeeded in getting the commission for the Sixth New York Cavalry Monument, to be placed on the Gettysburg Battlefield. Col. Jerome B. Wheeler was a veteran of the regiment and after the war he married the daughter of R. H. Macy the merchant. After Macy's death, Wheeler sold out his interest to the Strauses, and took an office at 54 Wall Street to devote himself to his interests in the Aspen Silver Mines of Colorado, and there planned various ideas in sculpture which added to his pleasure and my interest. In fact, during our long friendship, Col. Wheeler was a powerful as well as an active friend. He was a mild, modest man who had a fine war record in the Sixth New York Cavalry for which Gen. Sheridan became his sponsor at the Union League Club.

Col. Wheeler donated $10,000 for the Sixth New York Cavalry monument, and I made a panel for one side representing the charge under the command of Col. Charles L. Fitzhugh, then colonel of the regiment. When that was finished, they proposed to have only lettering on the back of the monument. I said that a portrait of Gen. Devin, the original colonel of the regiment should be there. That portrait I modeled from a fine photograph, as Gen. Devin had passed away, April 4, 1878.

*The following review appeared in the* New York Times *on June 20, 1889:*

The relief for Gettysburg is a bronze medallion about six feet each way, giving realistically the charge of a troop of cavalry over a Virginia rail fence. The centre is held by a likeness of Col. Fitzhugh on a horse which throws back its head as it leaps across the fallen fence. The gallant leader's sword is brandished high, while his face turns back to encourage the troop. Behind him is the color Sergeant, who has been struck by a bullet, and a trooper who seizes the flag that is falling from the Sergeant's grasp. Further to the right and rear is a cavalry officer whose face is said to be a portrait of [Col.] Wheeler. The artist has tried to indicate the rush of a body of horsemen with its cloud of dust through which the blades of sabres show. His effort has been to paint a picture in bronze. The sabre blades that are scattered over the background represent the gleams of light on steel in the dust cloud. The horses and riders are in violent action. The leader's sabre shoots one way, the falling standard the other, and the swords streak the background with lines that have no relation one to the other. Mr. J. E. Kelly made less mark as a draughtsman for the magazines, and has carried over a certain wild energy of movement from the crayon to the bronze bas-relief. How far one can interchange the method of these branches of art will always be the question; but it is certain that Mr. Kelly has not sufficiently mastered the difficulty. Bronze, even when realistically treated in bas-relief, demands either dignity or distinction, neither of which can be fairly accorded to this relief. It also calls for fine modeling, and, indeed, insists on the instant solution, with each stroke of the tool, of extremely difficult problems of modeling in perspective. A very great sculptor might well shrink from the difficulties of such a scene. Mr. Kelly made a mistake when he transferred to-day a composition that might have passed muster in an illustrated periodical for its effect of rapid movement and military "go."

## The Buford Statue at Gettysburg

Through Col. Wheeler's efforts I also secured the commission for the statue of Gen. John Buford on the Gettysburg Battlefield, erected by the Cavalry Officers' Association in 1895. There was considerable opposition from some in the Association to discredit my work after it was announced that I planned to depict Buford standing and not on horseback—my reasoning was that Gen. Buford fought his division at Gettysburg dismounted, and made his heroic stand until timely reinforcements arrived.

I interviewed and corresponded with many old cavalrymen to learn details of Buford's action at Gettysburg; one interesting story was told to me by Alfred Waud:

W—While searching for Lee's army on the way to Gettysburg, Gen. Buford rode up to a hotel and asked some southern gentlemen lounging in front of it, if they could tell him where he could get shoes for his men (thinking that where there are shoes, you will find barefoot Confederates in need of shoes). A southern gentleman responded, "We don't know, and we don't care, and if we knew we wouldn't tell you." Buford turned to his men and said, "Boys, help yourselves." And in an instant, each gentleman had a soldier sitting on his stomach and another pulling his boots off.

When Gen. Buford's statue was cast and finished at the foundry, a group of officers on the Committee assembled to inspect it. Among them I can recall Gen. John C. Tidball, Gen. A. C. M. Pennington, Gen. T. F. Rodenbough, Col. Charles McK. Leoser and Lieut. Osgood Welsh. They all seemed to like it, but some hesitated about giving a final decision. Then Gen. Tidball spoke up and said:

"I knew Buford as a cadet at West Point; I served with him in the Mexican War, and saw him the day after he is represented here at Gettysburg—AND THAT IS AS HE WAS!" Lieut. Welsh was also outspoken in its praise, but more vehement in his manner of delivery. Col. Wheeler was uneasy over the propaganda that had been worked against me, and advised me not to go down to the unveiling on the battlefield, as it might be unpleasant for me. "No!" I said, "If there is a fight on, I'm going to be in it!"

We all started by train for Gettysburg on June 30, 1895. Among the officers on that trip, I met some who afterward became my great friends, one of them being Col. John H. Calef, whose battery fired the first gun at Gettysburg. At the Pennsylvania R. R. Station, Philadelphia, I looked out of the window and got my first view of Gen. James H. Wilson, and Col. George Meade, son of Gen. Meade, who had been on his father's staff during the battle. As Gen. Wilson stood among his greeting friends in the car, I had a good chance to study him. He suggested our National eagle, as it is generally represented grasping a thunderbolt, and the personification of a thoroughbred trooper and hero.

Reaching Gettysburg, I was greeted with icy stares. We went to the Eagle Hotel where, as we stood among a group of officers on the porch, I was presented to Gen. Wilson by Gen. Pennington. Wilson wheeled toward me with his eyes like sword points, looking coldly and stiffly at me. "How do you do, Sir?" he replied and turned away, at which Gen. Pennington, slipping his arm in Gen. Wilson's led him to a light carriage, and they drove off through a pelting rain to inspect the monument.

Later we were called to the dining room, and all sat down at the tables. On my left was Col. Wheeler, and on my right a gentleman whom I had heard was Col. [Robert Bruce] Ricketts. I asked him if he were Ricketts of Ricketts' Battery. "Yes," he replied. Col. Wheeler seemed very uneasy, and the atmosphere was cold and very frigid; I felt warm enough—in fact was ablaze for a fight.

Just at that time Gen. Wilson entered the room with Gen. Pennington, took his place at the head of the table, looking more like an eagle than ever as his eyes flashed his searching glances right and left over the crowd. Spying me, he boomed out, "Mr. Kelly—I have seen your statue." There was a hush of suspense in the crowd, as he continued, "When I was in England, on the Thames embankment I saw the statue of Gen. Outram, which I consider the finest equestrian statue in the world; and in its way, I consider yours fully its equal."

Next morning a line of carriages formed, and all the guests assembled for a preliminary view of the monument. In my carriage was Captain, later Admiral, John C. Watson who informed me after a talk that he was flag lieutenant to Admiral Farragut, and had tied Farragut in the mizzen shrouds at the battle of Mobile Bay. The others were Col. Meade, and Col. Jerome B. Wheeler, who sat by me.

Reaching the monument, the carriages formed in a half circle around it. Gen. Wilson, jumping from his carriage, strided over to the monument, and flashing his cane on high as he would a sabre, turned to me, as he pointed to the statue, and roared out, "KELLY, THAT IS SUPERB!" Then we filed back to the hotel, and after lunch the formal ceremonies began. Col. Wheeler pulled the flag from the monument, and one hundred guns were fired from the batteries. Gen. Tidball placed a wreath at the foot of the statue, and Col. Calef spiked the gun at its foot. They were the guns of his battery that had opened the battle, but as he drove a file into the touch hole, he said, "I spike this gun and it will speak no more."

The smoke from the firing of the guns had a most curious effect; it rolled along the ground until, meeting the base of the statue, it whirled around, leaving the statue seeming in the air, showing Gen. Tidball with uncovered head gazing at the bronze figure of his comrade they were honoring. Speeches followed, the statue was dedicated, after which Gen. Wesley Merritt presented me, saying, "Peace has its Victories as well as War, and I now present to you the victor on this occasion."

The next day we went to take a final look at the statue, when Col. Calef described to me the placing of his battery, pointing out where Buford and Reynolds stood, giving final instructions before Calef opened his first gun at Gettysburg, as we stood on the very spot.

After the dedication of the Buford Statue, Col. Wheeler commissioned me to make forty life-size bronze portraits, in busts and bas-reliefs, from life of the distinguished officers during the Civil War as well as the Spanish War. This kept me busy for the next several years and gave me the opportunity to meet and interview many more personal heroes of my youth.

## Clarence Wheeler Memorial

Col. Wheeler had a son Clarence who died at the age of thirteen. The family had only a front view of the boy and asked me if I could make a bronze panel representing him lying full length reading a book, as it was his most characteristic pose.

From the photograph I sketched him the way I thought he would look in profile. It pleased the family, and the Colonel gave me an order to model a figure life size and to design the monument.

Dr. Roby Wood's son, who was the same age posed for the boy and young Elsie Wheeler, under my direction, modeled the rose which is lying beside the figure of her brother.

When the relief was finished and had been inspected and approved by the family, Colonel Wheeler called down with his coachman, introducing him as a close friend and companion of the boy; then left the room so that he could feel free to express his opinion of the likeness.

I can recall the tall, grim, short-whiskered Irishman in his livery, with hands crossed in front, with left foot advanced in a coachman's pose of attention, gazing with earnest eyes and pursed mouth, for what seems an interminable time; then with a sigh he said, "It is strange to see him all one color, but the longer one looks at it, the more it looks like him."

I had the bronze bolted on a rough boulder which weighed several tons. It rested on a beveled [stone base] plinth. The idea has been followed out in many graveyards, and on battlefields.

Yet I can recall the trouble I had to get this simple idea into the head of the man who represented one of the largest monumental firms in the country. I had to make a small model of the rough boulder and plinth and water color design, and they finally carried out my design which is now in Woodlawn Cemetery.

## The Call to Arms, Troy, New York

The Troy Monument Committee awarded to me the contract for my sixteen-foot-tall design *The Call to Arms*, to surmount the shaft of the Soldiers and Sailors monument in that city. I represented Columbia as a young girl aroused by the shot on Fort Sumter, which is typified by a shot partly buried in the shattered plinth; she has grasped the sheathed sword, sounded her trumpet call, and leans forward, tense and expectant, awaiting the response of The Volunteers. Instead of the conventional trappings of Columbia, I clothed her in simple, flowing drapery, girded with a garland of stars.

The next thing was to get a studio with a ceiling high enough to fit the model, and I finally found one originally occupied by Augustus Saint-Gaudens, in the Benedict Building, which had an imposing entrance on University Place. To the left of the doorway on entering had been Olin Warner's studio; mine was at the end of the ground floor, and had a private entrance facing on 4th Street. It was amusing to watch the expressions on the faces of my visitors who, having entered by the broad, elegant doorway on Washington Square, [and later] when they emerged from my private doorway on 4th Street, which was flanked on each side by second-hand shops. Above that doorway hung an old conspicuous swinging sign painted bright yellow and across it in large black letters were the words: "BLACK EYES PAINTED."

A crowd of young bootblacks used to congregate in front of my window and play craps, and would yell, cuss and argue over their games. It used to worry the janitor and various tenants; the janitor tried various ways to get rid of them, even by throwing water on them from the upper windows—but with no effect. Wanting a shine, I called for one of them to come in; he was afraid at first, but finally risked it.

While at work he told me of his troubles with the Irish boys, meaning the newsboys. "Well," I said, "my trouble with you fellows is that you are too loud; now sometimes I have ladies here, and when you swear it doesn't sound nice. I don't care how much you swear—only swear easy." He nodded quite seriously; next day I missed them, and they never returned. I found that they took new quarters on Washington Square.

It was about the close of the day, I had been busy with *The Call to Arms*, and was fatigued with heat and hard work, and had just jumped off the ladder as Mr. Mathew Brady entered looking spruce and spirited. I had told him that I would make a study of his head the next time I saw him, and this was the opportunity. Although wet and bespattered with clay, I started to work. The interest he infused into his sitters seemed to work an inspiration to me and all weariness left me. I saw only the great artist photographer who had made the invaluable picturesque record of the century—he who had the power of bringing out the best in his sitters.

Brady's National Portrait Gallery stood on the southwest corner of 10th Street, the number was 785 Broadway. There Lincoln posed for Brady the day after making his great Cooper Union speech. Brady told me that shortly after Lincoln's first inauguration, he said, "Your portrait and the Cooper Institute speech made me President."

How that portrait belies the printed reports of his appearance. In Brady's photograph, Lincoln looks the man and leader he proved to be; his clothes fitted him well, and he wore them as to the manner born. Yet the reports that Lincoln was uncouth and unkempt were repeated even by his friends, showing that many—if not most—people see with their ears.

I remember as a child in 1860 walking along Broadway and seeing a party of small, dark men in their flowing robes walking down. They had what seemed like little candy boxes balanced on their heads, but in reality held in position by ribbons tied under their chins, the length of the ribbons indicating their rank. A Japanese gentleman told me that when one of his countrymen appeared in court, he had to bow until the ends of those ribbons touched the floor—so the lower the rank the shorter the ribbons, and the lower he had to bow. They filed into Brady's gallery to be photographed. I afterward saw an engraving from the print as a frontispiece in *Harper's Weekly*.

While working on *The Call to Arms*, visitors were frequently coming into my studio requesting to see models of my previous work. Being in need of a couple of pedestals, I sent for a carpenter. He was a tall, soft featured, mellow-voiced Irishman, with curly red hair and a long fierce red mustache, which belied his large, amiable and freckled face. Looking up to the huge model of *The Call to Arms*, he said, "Paardon me, Sirr, would you moind me lookin round? I'm a shlip of an ould bachelor—or oi moight say, a bit of an ould maid—and I was always fond of knick-knacks."

Having studied my two-ton specimen of "knick-knacks," I caught sight of his Grand Army button, and said, "I see you were in the War."

"Yes."

"Infantry?"

"Nooh."

"Cavalry?"

"Nooh."

"Artillery?"

"Nooh."

"Then what were you?"

"Well, Sirr," he replied, "you see I was always a bit of a handy man, so they put me making coffins."

Some weeks later, Gen. Alexander Webb came to inspect *The Call to Arms*, and I pointed to the pedestals and asked, "General, what do they look like?"

"Army coffins on ends," was his answer.

# General Ely Parker

My mother asked me to model a bust of Gen. Ely Parker for her. Up to that time I had never modeled a bust, but told her I would. I called on the General at Police Headquarters, and told him my mother wanted him to sit for his bust. He smiled and said, "Of course I cannot refuse your mother." He later came around to my studio and I started to work and had it well under way when he was taken quite ill. As he posed for me in his invalid chair at his home, 22 West 55th Street, he told me his many experiences during the war.

Across his breast I modeled his Loyal Legion and Grand Army badges, and suspended around his neck the large, oval silver medal, 6 _ inches long, which George Washington had presented to his predecessor Red Jacket, chief of the Wolf Tribe of the Seneca. On it is engraved the design of an Indian handing the pipe of peace to Washington, and beneath is inscribed: "George Washington, President, 1792." To the right of this, Gen. Parker wrote in the clay: "Ely S. Parker, Bvt. Brig. Gen.," and to the left he wrote: "Donahogawa, Iroquois Sachem.

I was not present, when at the foundry, Felix Weil knocked the mould off the plaster cast, but Mrs. Parker told me that when the section was knocked off and disclosed merely the face, Maude—the General's little daughter, who was looking on—gave a cry of delight and said, "Oh, my darling Papa," and kissed it. The interesting friendship established during those sittings led to his proposal and my adoption as his Indian brother.

At that time the General was confined to his house with what proved to be his last illness. He gave me a letter to his brother Nicholas Parker, an important official on the Seneca Reservation at Versailles, Cattaraugus County, New York, and also placed me in the hands of Mrs. Harriet Converse, who had already been adopted for the great work she had done in the interest of the Indians.

In company with Mrs. Converse I arrived at the reservation, and became the guests of William Jones, hereditary War Chief of the Genesees. His house was like that of any other small up-State farmer, as were the homes of the neighboring Indians. His young daughter Irene, a perfect specimen of an Indian girl, kept house for him. To the right of the house was a lawn surrounded by apple trees in full blossom. An oblong enclosure about 30 x 75 feet was marked out with board seats with preparations for a wood fire in the center; this was to be the scene of the ceremonies.

After lunch the Indians began to gather from every direction—among them Nicholas Parker, whom I recognized from his resemblance to the General, and gave him my note of introduction. He was accompanied by his sister, Mrs. Mount Pleasant, a tall, handsome, statuesque young woman, with the figure and bearing of a bronze *Diana*. As master of ceremonies, Nicholas Parker took his place at the upper end of the enclosure, surrounded by the Sachems and other officials of the Seneca Nation.

The old women and braves took their seats on the planks, the other women and the children gathering behind them and finding places to stand wherever they could. Then a very aged woman stepped forward and lit the council fire. I have been told that an old woman is the most honored member of the Iroquois Indian Nations, and that to tell an Indian that he is "as wise as an old woman" is to give him what he will take as a high compliment. I will try to state briefly the ceremonies, which were elaborate, long, picturesque and impressive.

After prayers and incantations in the Seneca language, Nicholas Parker announced in English that I was formally initiated as a brother, and as I was a sculptor of military subjects, I was to be called Ganosqua, and to be formally introduced to the Nation with the war song of Black Snake. I was later informed that Ganosqua was a stone giant whom the Indians regarded with terror as well as with reverence. It was said, that when first seen by them, their arrows splintered as they struck him, and consequently he must be made of stone. Since then they have tried to placate his wrath by selecting some member of the Nation and naming him Ganosqua; this title conveys great distinction to the bearer, but no power; and no one can assume it during his lifetime.

After Nicholas Parker's announcement, a dark, feather-crested Indian came up to me, announced his name as Half Town, and taking my right hand in his left, he started the war song, accompanied with clapping of hands and stamping of feet by all present. I was then led around the entire bordered enclosure, and after other incantations, the ceremonies were closed. Then Mrs. Mount Pleasant came over and pinned an ancient silver brooch on my breast, at the same time kissing me.

Following her came Mrs. Snyder, the oldest woman in the Nation, who had kindled the council fire. She also pinned a brooch on my breast and kissed me. Meanwhile a feast had been prepared under the trees, in which all participated. My temptation is to linger over the friendliness, hospitality and courtesy of my new-found relatives, but I must keep within bounds. The most affecting incident for me was while dining, a pretty Indian woman came and showed me a saucer of plaster in which was the imprint of a tiny baby's hand, and whispered to me softly, "This is all I have of my little one."

## General William T. Sherman

"Sherman is dead," was the first thing my friend Charles L. Hildreth said to me as I entered his office on February 14, 1891. Next day, as I was riding down on the Ninth Avenue Elevated, I saw the mourning crepe fluttering from the doorway of Sherman's home, 75 West 71st Street. I afterward learned that the rock men and laborers who were at work clearing away the rocks in the vacant lots opposite his home, had voluntarily knocked off work, so as not to disturb the dying General.

I recall the funeral, which after stopping at St. Patrick's Cathedral marched down Fifth Avenue to Washington Place, through to Broadway and down to the Pennsylvania Ferry at the foot of Desbrosses Street. The casket was borne on a caisson wrapped in the Flag; I was standing near the northeast corner of Washington Place and University Place, so had a chance to observe distinctly. Some ladies a couple of doors from the rear of the New York University building, stood at the second story window making snapshots of the procession.

Gen. Dan Butterfield, in command of the troops, rode by on horseback in full dress uniform, looking handsome and important. President Benjamin Harrison, dressed in black, rode by in a carriage; it was the first time I had ever seen him, and I can only recall his full brow, drooping nose and protruding beard. Lines on lines of troops followed, but as the day was cold and dreary, I left and walked up Broadway.

Shortly after, it was announced that a statue to Gen. Sherman was to be put up in Washington, D. C., and competitive designs were called for. I decided to enter a model and depicted Sherman with the wind behind him—wrapped in his short cape as I had seen him the first day we met, riding his horse while passing melted and twisted railroad track wrapped around a stump of a telegraph pole to balance the composition. I made him taking off his hat as I had seen him do; also I worked up very carefully around the base of the monument, a belt showing various incidents in Sherman's life.

My model statuette was sent to Washington, and was rejected by the committee of John Q. A. Ward, Daniel C. French and Saint-Gaudens. Saint-Gaudens was at the time working on his own statuette design of Sherman with no cape. After the rejection, I had the statuette stored at the Smithsonian Institute and forgot all about it, until some years after when I saw Saint-Gaudens' colossal statue of Sherman, bareheaded with flowing cape, at the entrance of Central Park.

*Beginning in 1891, Kelly began to collect research material for a proposed bust of Edgar Allan Poe, but after several years of effort the project was abandoned.*

# The Edgar Allan Poe Cottage at Fordham

In 1891, my good friend, Austin Ford the Fire Commissioner, bought the old Edgar Allan Poe Cottage at Fordham. He told me if I would go up and live in the Poe cottage, he would give it to me rent free. He knew that I had always been a great admirer of Poe, but I told him I don't care to live in a show place.

I paid him a visit shortly after, and in taking a stroll passed the cottage, I found his brother-in-law, Robert Oakley, with a saw and hammer getting ready for work. I asked him what he was going to do.

He said, "Oh, I am going to put a new roof on the cottage, as it leaks, and put up a new porch, as the lower parts of the posts have rotted." He also pointed to a prostrate cherry tree, which had blown down in a recent storm. He told me it was the one planted by Poe. I suggested that he remove the trunk and cut it up for relics. He took me through the house and showed me the room in which Mrs. Poe died, and I rummaged through the house from cellar to garret, but remember principally the little cupboards at the side of the chimney-place. I then gave him a talk on preserving the building in the original state as much as possible, and not put in any new timbers; I also told him that as the paint had gone bad, he had better repaint in the same colors and keep the aspect of the original building as much as possible. Repassing the building some time after I saw him at work; he told me that he had sawed off the bottom of the posts where they had rotted, and placed a new block under each one.

Back of the house was the rock overlooking Fordham Valley from which Poe used to sit with his wife while composing; it afforded a fine view of the Catholic College where he formed congenial companionship and where he is recollected as a quiet, reserved and modest gentleman.

One winter's afternoon, I took my friend, John J. Carty, to see the house. The day was snowy and bleak. We went through the cheerless and damp place, and up to the room where Virginia had died. The snow lay on the floor where it had drifted through the broken panes. Looking out upon the lead and copper-colored sky, we talked of the sorrows, disappointments and death which had taken place under the roof. Carty said to me that he could think of nothing that suggested such misery, except to have a jumping toothache.

I became very much interested in the life of Poe and began to collect information for a planned bust. I managed to locate several people who remembered Poe when he resided in New York, including his one-time close friend Thomas Dunn English.

## Thomas Dunn English and Edgar Allan Poe

The battle poems of Thomas Dunn English had inspired me as a boy and two illustrations, *News from Lexington*, and *Back from Bennington*, were the first pictures I had exhibited at the Academy of Design. I visited the doctor at his home, 59 State Street, Newark, New Jersey and he gave me many sittings for a bronze bas relief.

As I entered, the Doctor stood up, holding out both hands—for he was then almost blind. He was full of historical reminiscences and told me many stories of his dealings with Edgar Allan Poe. One was a possible explanation of the many conflicting stories in regard to Poe's character. During one of our sittings, Dr. English told me:

E—Poe was never a drunkard, but if he did take a glass of wine it immediately went to his head and he became irresponsible from his delicate nervous organization; he could not stand it. Another childish weakening of Poe's was a desire to appear very villainous. He loved to tell of his criminal adventures, but there was not a word of truth in it. He liked to give the impression that he had affairs with women, but there was nothing in it; he was a very pure man. He even deceived his wife. I remember Mrs. Poe came to me and asked me to speak to him about some woman she thought he was intimate with. I told her not to bother as I knew him and there was nothing in it. Mrs. [Maria] Clemm came to me and had told of some adventure that Poe had told them. I told her that it was perfectly ridiculous, and to pay no attention to him, as he was a good man and devoted to his wife.

One day Poe came to me and wanted to borrow a pistol. When I asked him what for, he told me one of his terrible tales—he said a man came to him and asked him to return some of his wife's letters, and he threatened to shoot him if he did not do it.

I said to him, "You have none of his wife's letters." "Yes, I have," he said. "No," I replied, "there is not a word of truth in that." He said, "Why?" "If it was true," I said, "you would be the last one to tell it." "You are a liar," said Poe, and with that he struck me. I immediately closed with him and he being short and lightly built, I bore him down, but he kept fighting furiously. In the confusion, Nathaniel P. Willis rushed into the room and tried to separate us, but Poe, in spite of the fact that I was on top of him and in my excitement was punching him, roared out to Willis, "Get out! Leave us alone, I've got him just where I want him!" He was plucky. I was sorry afterwards to find that the seal ring, which I forgot I had on, had cut his face. Someone asked Poe afterwards where he got the cut. He said he had run into a piece of timber.

We never spoke again. No, there is nothing in these stories that you hear about Poe's drunkenness or his moral character, and I say this, although we were never friends afterwards.

## Miss Sarah F. Miller's Reminisces of Poe

Miss Sarah F. Miller, long resident of The Bronx, remembers seeing Poe frequently, as a very little girl, and tells of her reminiscences in the following words:

M—One of the most cherished memories of my earliest childhood, is the recollection of having so often seen Edgar Allan Poe. When I was a little girl, we lived in a house facing Turtle Bay, on the East River, near the present 47th Street.

Among our nearest neighbors was a charming family trio, consisting of Mr. Poe, his wife Virginia, and his mother-in-law, Mrs. Clemm. Poor Virginia Poe was very ill at the time, and I never saw her leave her home. Poe and Mrs. Clemm would very frequently call on us. He would also run over every little while to ask my father to lend him our row boat, and then how he would enjoy himself, pulling at the oars over to the little islands just south of Blackwell's Island, for his afternoon swim.

Mrs. Clemm and my mother soon became the best of friends, and she found mother a sympathetic listener to her sad tales of poverty and want. I would often see her shedding tears as they talked. As I recall her, she always seemed so wonderfully neat and orderly, and invariably wore a pure white collar around her neck.

In the midst of this friendship, they came and told us they were going to move to a distant place called Fordham, where they had rented a little cottage, feeling sure the pure country air would do Mrs. Clemm a world of good. Very soon a cordial invitation came for us all to come and take luncheon, which was very daintily served in the large room on the first floor.

As I remember, the front door led directly into this apartment. I recall very clearly their bringing me a small wooden box to sit on at the table instead of a chair. Poe was always kind and smiling, and very fond of children. Poe's handsome face and attractive appearance always impressed me. He would come up to me, and patting me on the shoulder, tell me I was "a nice little girl."

One of my most prized treasures is a Chinese puzzle of carved ivory, given to me by Poe himself, which, for a long time I have been intending to lend to the Metropolitan Museum, but, having friends in the Bronx Society of Arts and Sciences, I have just taken pleasure in presenting it to them for exhibition in the Lorillard Mansion Museum.

My brother, John Miller of Ottawa, Kansas, also remembers Poe. I will write to him and he can give you further details.

## A Letter about Poe from John LeFevre Miller

Yes, Edgar A. Poe, his wife Virginia and his mother-in-law Mrs. Clemm are indelibly photographed in my mind. I first saw them when we lived at Turtle Bay, East River, nearly opposite the southern end of Blackwell's Island, now the foot of 47th Street (streets were not opened at that time in that part of the city). They engaged rooms at our house for a short time before they moved to the cottage at Fordham.

Our house was a full two-story, basement and attic. The house was shingled both sides and ends of cedar shingles, made with hand made wrought nails, the basement of brick. Here is where I spent the first 14 years of my life, and is why I can give details correctly. Those familiar scenes of my childhood appear photographed in my brain. I saw Mrs. Poe so seldom while she was at our house, I cannot describe her so well; she remained most of her time in her room. As I remember her she had an oval face, bright and cheerful, but very pale, which formed a very striking contrast with her hair, which by the way was not bobbed, but parted in the middle and combed down smoothly as was the custom in these days; as for her dress, nothing about it attracted my attention. I never liked Mr. Poe's eyes, but Mrs. Poe had beautiful large, loving eyes. I am sorry I cannot give better help to the artist. You can imagine what would most appeal to a boy ten years old. Poe's family only remained at our house a short time.

I was too young to know anything about Mr. Poe's literary ability, or his poetic genius, as I was only about six years old. I never liked Mr. Poe. I think he didn't like little boys; he never tried to be friendly with me and I was afraid of him and kept out of his way; he liked my sisters and gave one of them (Sarah) a small Chinese puzzle of carved ivory.

It is with much pleasure I remember Mrs. Poe and her mother Mrs. Clemm for I was on friendly terms with them—always kind and pleasant. I remember the first night they were at our house. Virginia had a dreadful cough and seldom left the house; she was very quiet and always looked pleasant. Mrs. Clemm was tall and dignified, always cheerful except when got talking to my mother (who was always a sympathetic listener) of her troubles. She did not approve of the way "Eddie" acted, and I heard her tell my mother how Eddie let his wife go home from a literary meeting alone while he escorted a married lady [Frances Sargent Osgood] home as he said to Virginia it was necessary to show the woman courtesy on account of her standing in literary society, and Virginia, the timid child, would go several blocks, crying and trembling with fear all the way.

When I knew Mr. Poe, he was very intemperate. He caused much excitement one afternoon; while intoxicated, took my father's row boat as was his custom to use it at his pleasure, went to a favorite place to swim, pretended to be drowning and called for help, two fishermen near by went to his rescue. Mr. Poe resented their assistance, and became very angry and used very abusive language and told them that if he only had a "screw auger" he would dive under their craft and sink them. They, the Poe family, soon afterward moved to Fordham where I once went with my sisters to visit them. Mrs. Poe died soon after [on January 30, 1847].

## Interview with Mrs. J. R. O'Beirne about Poe

Miss Martha S. Brennan of Fordham, married Major James R. O'Beirne in 1863, while he was recovering from his wound received at Chancellorsville. In after years, I became close friends with them and learned that Mrs. O'Beirne knew Edgar Allan Poe when she was a child. She told me the following:

Mrs. O'Beirne—I remember Poe, about 1844 or 5. He boarded with my mother. I remember him very well. His wife was very delicate. He was one of the most devoted husbands. He used to carry her up and down stairs. I never saw him drunk; maybe he went on sprees. He may have taken a glass of whiskey, but I never saw him. I was a child and he thought a good deal of me and when he would come from the city, he would bring me candy. He would say, "Come, Martha," and take me upstairs and give it to me.

I remember he would go off into the woods to write. He used to write upon wrapping paper, or, you know, that tea-paper, in pencil, and as he would write a sheet, he would put them in long rows till he had written what he wanted. He seemed to be able to judge by the length of them, like a painter would his space. Then he would take them up and number them and read them to us. He stayed with us three summers and once nearly into the winter. Mrs. Poe was very delicate. Poe was slight—black curly hair, black eyes, very high forehead and dark mustache.

K—Was his nose hooked?

O'B—Yes.

K—Did it come down?

O'B—No, not really.

K—Was it like mine?

O'B—Yes, something like that. Black eyes.

K—I want to model a bust of him. Do you think you could remember him well enough to criticize it?

O'B—Yes. The way he came to us was this: Poe kept a place across the road. There was a brook running long side of it—a sort of creek. There was a rock near us where you could get a good view of the Hudson. One day Poe, his wife and Mrs. Clemm came up and sat there to get the view and Poe came in and asked my mother for some water. She asked him to have some milk. He took it and when he returned the pitcher, he said that Mrs. Poe was so taken with the place that they would like to know if she could accommodate them with board. She told them no, that she had no room. He said they would only want two rooms—a room and a sitting room, and they finally arranged it.

Poe looked very like [John] Wilkes Booth, in a general way; of course maybe not when you saw them together, but the impression was the same.

## Virginia Poe's Bones

Edgar Allan Poe's biographer, William Fearing Gill, on visiting my studio, told me the following:

G—In 1883, a few years after I had written the life of Poe, my friend Dr. Thatcher said, "You had better come up with me [to Fordham] and visit the tomb of Virginia Poe. We drove up there, and, most remarkable to relate, it seemed like a stage setting, etc.

We found the sexton who had buried Mrs. Poe, a Mr. [Dennis] Valentine. As I entered the cemetery from the right, coming towards me from the left, was Mr. Valentine, with the bones of Mrs. Poe on a shovel. His men may have left them.

K—Was the skull there?

G—Yes, part of it. Mr. Valentine said, "Why don't you take care of it?" (I suppose Dr. Thatcher had told him who I was). "I buried Mrs. Poe, and they are taking down this cemetery and commencing to make some improvements." "Why don't you write to the family?" I said. He said, "I have written to Mr. [Peter] Poe in Baltimore, but he has never replied, so I think it is right you should take them and look after them." Then I took them. Mr. Valentine put them in a paste-board box, such as they put floral pieces in—you know, wreath and anchors—and I took them home.

Some time after, one of the papers published an article in which it said, "Mr. Fearing Gill is such a Poe enthusiast that he sleeps with the bones of Mrs. Poe under his bed," which was almost literally true.

Some time after this, an event happened which I can hardly tell anybody."

As Gill said this, he stopped—hesitated—and though awhile in a serious, over-wrought manner—then pulling himself together, he continued:

G—One morning about six o'clock, or a quarter to six, I heard a tapping at the window. Now I am not an early riser, but I went to the window and opened it, and in walked a raven. I have a bust of Pallas, which I always carry with me in my movings and out goings. The raven climbed up and perched on the top of it. I don't know what came over me, or why I said it—but I said, "What do you want?" At which the raven gathered itself up (here Gill imitated with his two hands how the raven spread his wings and screeched).

I am a believer in the occult, and I remembered an old superstition that the dead could not rest while their bones were above the ground, so I wrote at once to Mr. [John Prentiss] Poe in Baltimore, and received a reply immediately inviting me down to visit. I went down [in 1885], and now Virginia's bones lie buried beside the body of Poe.

I had a small bronze box made for them. At that time there was only a little yellow mound marking the grave of Poe. But through the generosity of [philanthropist] George W. Childs, there is a beautiful stone, etc.

K—What became of the raven?

G—I kept it about a year and it showed no disposition to leave me. I then gave it to a friend.

*While on vacation with his parents at a summer resort near Quaker Hill, New York, James E. Kelly met another boyhood hero—Admiral John Worden, commander of the* U. S. S. Monitor, *the first ironclad warship in the U. S. Navy. This chance meeting gave Kelly the opportunity to portray the Admiral in bronze.*

## Admiral John Worden and the Monitor

On August 1, 1891, my mother, father and myself started on a vacation to Quaker Hill, and heard that Admiral John L. Worden, who commanded the *Monitor* in its' fight with the *Merrimac*, was visiting with his sister-in-law, on the road a little below us. It was a cottage which stood on a terrace about four feet high. The next day I saw the Admiral for the first time, as he stood in the doorway of the house. It was about six o'clock, so I merely got a glance of a tall old man with a white beard.

On Sunday, August 7th, I was taking a walk with a party of ladies, including Mrs. Busby and Mrs. Brady, when one of the younger girls called out to the Admiral, who was walking along the terrace at the edge of the house. He said, "Good morning!" adding, "I can't see you very well." Then he recognized her, and Mrs. Busby said, "Mr. Kelly, this is my father." I removed my hat and said, "How do you do, Admiral?" He leaned down from the terrace and shook hands; then there was some slight chat among us all.

Then one of the ladies said, "Are you going to church, Admiral?" "No, thank you," he replied. Mrs. Brady laughed, saying, "He thanks you." And they all began to laugh. He said, "I leave all spiritual affairs in the hands of my wife, as I know she will get to Heaven—and if she gets there, I'll get to her, if I have to fight for it."

He is very tall—fully six feet; his hair is of uncertain color, originally blond, now neither gray nor brown. The Admiral's beard was very long and white; his features very regular; straight forehead and a straight nose; lower lip full and sensitive. Eyes blue, but the left one showing the effects of the powder and splinters of shell received in the great fight—all bleared. The white and the pupil were peppered with powder marks, as well as a good part of his face about the eye. The general effect was that of a man with a black eye.

There was much more strength in his face than I expected from his pictures; I have never seen one that did him justice. Mrs. Busby told me, "When he sits for a photograph, he squints his eyes."

I told her that I had never met one of our distinguished naval officers before. She spoke of Gen. Grant, whom she had seen during his sickness, and it was of great interest to see how he had overcome his suffering. I said, "It is a lesson in resignation." "Yes," she replied, "He would talk to you awhile, and you would see him struggle with his sufferings, and then he would seem to conquer it." I asked her to arrange with the Admiral to sit for me as soon as possible.

On the 10th it was arranged that Mrs. Busby should take me to see her father. It was a beautiful summer evening as we walked down to the house. On our arrival we found the Admiral sitting on the piazza with a lady. Mrs. Busby introduced me to her, then turning to him she said, "This is Mr. Kelly." Then he said, "I met Mr. Kelly, Sunday." to which I said, "Yes." We shook hands, and he offered me his chair and took another to my right. Mrs. Busby turned to the lady, saying, "We will go inside; Mr. Kelly wants to talk with father."

I began, "Admiral, I am happy to have met you. You were my father's favorite among the heroes of the War. No matter who was brought up, he would say, 'But the *Monitor* is the thing.' So you see I have been brought up to appreciate you, and in coming, I am only following out family tradition." "I thank you," he said bowing. "I will call on your father," then stopped and asked, "How old is he?" "Sixty-six," I said. The Admiral hesitated on finding him so much younger than himself, then said, "I shall be pleased to have your father call on me."

The Admiral then detailed his taking command of the *Monitor* and the fight with the *Merrimac* in which he was wounded:

W—When I was struck with the shell, it knocked me senseless, and I was as blind as a bat. Dr. [Daniel C.] Logue, a friend of mine who saw the fight, took me to Washington, and put me in the hotel. My head was all bandaged up, and I was perfectly blind; afterward erysipelas set in. The doctor went to the President, who was in a cabinet council, and reported the fight. Mr. Lincoln seemed to think a great deal of the *Monitor*, and said to the members of his cabinet, "I don't know what you are going to do, but I am going down to see that fellow."—That's what he called me.

The President came down with Dr. Logue. I was lying on the bed with my face done up in bandages when he arrived. I said, "Mr. President, this is a great honor." His eyes filled up as he took my hand, so I'm told. "No," he replied, "It is an honor to me; you are an honor to your country, and I shall promote you." That was the last thing I thought of—promotion.

K—Now that would make a good picture; Lincoln coming to see you. It was a stirring incident. I expect to be here four or five weeks, and will make a little sketch of it for you. It will be of interest to your family; don't you think so?

He hesitated and then said, "Yes, I have no doubt that it would."

K—I think the most desperate part of the whole business was your going down in that iron coffin, not knowing the result.

W—Yes, several officers bade me goodbye, never expecting to see me again.

Lincoln was a splendid character—he was cautious and persevering. When his own party was against him for not pushing emancipation, he would not move until he was sure.

K—Now Admiral, can you arrange some day for me to get a sketch of your head?  I would like very much to have it.

W—Yes, any time in the morning would be fine.

Talking of his health he said, "I am a physical and mental wreck."  Mrs. Busby then came up, and after some unimportant chaff, said, "I don't want to be personal, but do you remember what we were talking about the other night?" (Referring to a conversation in which she said that Farragut's statue by Saint-Gaudens was not like him, and that it did not stand like a sailor, etc.)  "Look at father's legs."  "What do you mean?" he said sharply.

I said, "Mrs. Busby and I were talking about the statue of Farragut by Saint-Gaudens.  Have you seen it?"  "No," answered the Admiral.  "Well, it stands this way," said I, standing like it.  Mrs. Busby said that a sailor would not stand that way with braced legs.  "I had to stand this way at sea," he said, as he took the position with his legs apart and his knees slack.  "Well," I said, "Saint-Gaudens has Farragut standing with his legs bracing like a trooper."

We went inside and placing him in position, I started to work.  The old Admiral made a perfect picture resting in his large chair just back of the broad glare of the open door, with a mass of trees for the background, and the dark gray clouds sweeping across the sky.  I was too busy to catch much of the conversation, and in fact, very little of importance was said, the principal story being told me that he was a Son of the American Revolution.

The drawing being finished, I asked him to show it to the family, so that I could get their criticisms.  Some one criticized the nose, so I got him to sit at the end of the sofa, and kneeling down, made the correction.  I made up my mind that if I could get additional sittings, I would make a model of his head.

I got out my measuring tape and told him to stand up, and began to measure his head.  "What is this for?" he asked abruptly.  "Oh, I am going to model you."  "What, model?"  "Yes, I am going to enlarge this to life size and make a model."  He seemed bewildered, but before he had time to object, I had all the figures down.

One of the young ladies was going down to New York, and I asked her to order some clay for me.  The next morning, I took a long walk for about twelve miles, and on returning, found the clay had arrived.  I pounded it up, tempered it, had the clay box made, filled it and commenced the relief before night.  I was in fine trim and was sitting under some apple trees when his two little grandchildren came up.  Looking very seriously, one said, "That's grandpa; that's his big beard."

The next day the Admiral gave me an additional sitting when Mrs. Busby came in.  "The Admiral told me that he had been blind, I believe for six weeks," I said to her, "and the doctor had taken a great deal of the powder stain out of his eye and cheek." "There is a piece of steel in it still," said Mrs. Busby, and pointed to it with her fingers. He made a playful snap at the end of it with his mouth, as though she were a child. She then placed her finger in the mound on the left side of the bridge of the nose. "Feel it!" she said. I did so, and a little hard lump could be felt under the skin, which could be shifted with the finger. She then had me feel a peculiar bump under his hair, and said, "Father used to make me feel this when we were children, and would say that his brains were coming out."

In the intervals between the sittings, I would see little bits of character in the Admiral, which made me very fond of him. His great affection for Mrs. Busby and her four children was always evident. I used to see him stop in the road and kiss them. His great anxiety to save money for them and their future, made him very penurious. I also noticed his playful and affectionate allusions to his wife. My father and he became quite friendly. He told my father that he had become disgusted with the ways of society, where before it had been simple and natural, now it was so affected that when he did go out—which was seldom—he would pass through the parlors and go home. Many times he had gone to bed and cried in sorrow for the changes. He seemed very sensitive, and his nerves were much shattered. I think he told me that after the *Monitor* fight, he was seized with a fit of crying—a reaction from the intense strain and loss of sleep on the trip down from New York.

I completed his panel which he signed with his approval and I had it cast in bronze.

*Kelly's next commissions were bronze panels marking the locations of the August 27, 1776, Battle of Long Island fought in Brooklyn, and the September 16, 1776, Battle of Harlem Heights fought in Manhattan.*

## The Battles of Long Island and Harlem Heights

At the unveiling of my bas relief panel marking the line of defense at the Battle of Long Island near Fulton and Nevins Streets on June 11, 1895, I was called on for a speech. I asked Colonel Asa B. Gardiner to respond for me. He rose and said, "A friendship of more than twenty years makes me feel fully capable of responding to the name of my friend Kelly..." etc.

As he closed his remarks and sat down I forgot all my natural shyness, and stepping forward I said, "I wish to express my thanks to Colonel Gardiner for his kind reference to my work, and at the same time to testify that what historical accuracy my work is credited with possessing, I owe in a great measure to his extensive knowledge and generous advice."

As I made this statement I caught the eye of a gentleman in the crowd and directed my remarks to him individually.

Shortly after this occasion I received a letter signed by T. E. Smith, of the Tablet Committee, Sons of the Revolution, which said he would like to consult with me in regard to having me model a panel commemorating the Battle of Harlem Heights, to be placed on one of the new buildings of Columbia University at 116th Street.

Harlem Heights, the field of Washington's first victory, as well as that of the Colonies has not received the recognition it deserves. Lexington was little more than a tragic row. The British arrived where they started for, achieved what they started to do, and marched back where they started from, while the "embattled farmers" took pot shots at them from behind stone walls. At Bunker Hill, the British troops again attained their object. At Long Island, the Colonials were once more on the run.

Though at Harlem Heights the Colonials were at first forced to recoil before the weight of superior numbers, at which the British bugles in jubilant triumph blared forth the "Fox Chase," but the blaze of Washington's anger and the blows of his sword-arm from the stampede at Kipp's Bay tempered their malleable discipline. Washington took things in hand—ordered General Clinton, the New Yorker, to take command of the field.

Clinton charged the advancing Hessians near the junction of the present Broadway, forcing them to fall back on their supporting Light Infantry. While Colonel Thomas Knowlton with his Massachusetts troops and Major Andrew Leitch with his Virginia troops scaled the rocky ridge and struck the British flanks, in the neighborhood of Columbia University; in the melee Knowlton was killed and Leitch mortally wounded.

I called on Mr. Smith at Fraunces Tavern, where I met the other member of the Committee, Mr. Charles Isham. After a short talk they gave me the commission, and suggested I consult Henry P. Johnston, Professor of History at the City College, to whom Smith gave me a letter of introduction.

Professor Johnston had written a history of the Battle of Harlem Heights and was considered its greatest authority which made me naturally anxious to meet him.

Professor Johnston was tall, erect, showing the effect of his early training in the army from 1862-65. He was full-browed; long, lean swarthy face; dark, keen eyes, straight nose, black hair, moustache and short side whiskers, and a sharp, clear, crisp delivery.

As we stood by his table he gave me a hurried account of the battle and among other things told me that the flag used that day had no Union in the upper corner, but just thirteen red and white stripes.

As I was familiar with the lay of the land, I grasped the idea at once, and taking his pad lying on the desk, I sketched the composition in about five minutes; Professor Johnston meanwhile looking intently over my shoulder. When I had finished he said, "That is correct with the exception you represent Leitch in a hunting shirt, which is wrong."

I replied, "If I can show my authority for it, is the rest correct?" "Yes," he answered. I later showed him a copy of Washington's order to the Army early in '76, recommending that the recruits wear linen hunting shirts or overalls with leggings of the same, buttoned up the sides, to be dyed brown or green.

I then started to realize what I had merely indicated in my sketch of the Harlem Heights Memorial. Knowlton's portrait is founded on Trumbull's sketch in his painting "The Battle of Bunker Hill."

There was no portrait of Leitch available, so I made a study of my ideal of an American head, and to identify him I engraved his name "Andrew Leitch, Fredericksburg, Va.," on his powder horn, as it was quite common custom at the time. The sword by his side is a copy of the one given me by a friend, whose father had the grading Harlem Lane and St. Nicholas Avenue. My friend told me that he was present when his men dug it up, with some pistols under about twenty feet of earth, at about 120th Street. My friend Cashman told me when they were grading opposite the gate of the college grounds, he saw them dig up four skeletons, which lay in a space of about fifteen feet under three feet of earth. They were large boned men, and though there was nothing to indicate their uniform, they were probably Continentals, from the fact that the Americans held the field.

After the bronze panel had been erected on the Engineering building at Columbia College, Professor Johnston asked me to give him the original sketch which I had made on his desk at our first meeting.

*Kelly's next sculpture project proved to be his most ambitious—a bronze equestrian statue of Major General Fitz John Porter.*

## General Fitz John Porter Statue

In the early 1880's, Robert Henry Eddy of Boston, a cousin and steadfast admirer of Gen. Fitz John Porter, conceived the idea of erecting a statue to the General in Portsmouth, New Hampshire—the General's birthplace. Many old soldiers were opposed to this, being prejudiced against Gen. Porter by charges of treason after the Battle of Second Bull Run. A Wartime Court Martial found him guilty and he was dismissed from the service and although decades later he was exonerated, he never could shed the brand of traitor.

Gen. David S. Stanley told me that Gen. Porter was innocent and one of the worst abused men in the country, and that I should include him in my series of bronzes. I promised to do so.

I met Gen. Porter in 1895, and he agreed to sit for me. I visited the General and his family many times in Morristown, New Jersey, and we became close friends.

In 1899, Mrs. Fitz John Porter called and in a mysterious voice said, "Thirty thousand dollars has been left [by R. H. Eddy] for a statue of the General, I would like you to make it. How will we go about getting him to give it to you?" I said, "Do nothing. I do not want to place him in a position where he will be forced to give it to me through friendship. If I did not know him I could ask him." She went away and in the mail which came shortly after, was a letter from the General asking me to make the statue. Next day I received one from Mrs. Porter saying, "Think of it. When I was putting up a plan on the General, he got the best of me by giving it to you without my knowing it."

I went out to see him, and after a pleasant visit decided on the action. On my way to the station, I saw a beautiful horse pawing the grass and giving me the very action I desired. Returning to my studio, I began a study of "General Porter Saluting the Colors," representing the General holding his cap over his heart. The natural dignity of Gen. Porter made it imperative that he should be shown in repose.

Placing the model beside him on the table while he examined it carefully, Mrs. Porter stood beside him and placing her hand on his shoulder said, "There Fitz, isn't it fine to see yourself young and handsome like you used to be."

Gen. Porter died two months later, on May 21, 1901.

Col. John Pender was Mayor of Portsmouth at the time, and although there was a strong pressure brought to bear to give the model to a local sculptor, he stuck to me loyally. With the help of Gen. Joshua Chamberlain of Maine, the tide was turned in my favor and the contracts signed. Col. Pender was of Scotch stock and I never had a Scotchman fail me yet.

The monument was dedicated on July 1, 1904—the 42nd anniversary of the Battle of Malvern Hill, where Gen. Porter commanded the Army of the Potomac in McClellan's absence, and defeated the Confederate legions under Gen. Robert E. Lee.

# My Street—57th Street

I say "My Street" on account of having seen it grow from a country road, and in many cases an embankment over flats, swamps and streams, to its present condition; its primitive state in my youth I have already described.

One rainy day in 1899, I was looking for a studio and passing the newly constructed Young Men's Christian Association building, I saw a sign advertising one. Entering, I engaged it and remained there many eventful years—until February, 1922. The building had been the realization of the dream of Robert Ross McBurney, who wished to make it a headquarters for students of art and medicine who attended the Art Student's League and the College of Physicians and Surgeons. It was artistic, cozy and compact; an apartment of two rooms with an open fireplace was reserved for McBurney, but alas! When all was finished, he died—like Moses on the borders of the Promised Land, and as fate would have it, the apartment became my studio for the next twenty-three years.

The building had every convenience for the development of the mental and spiritual intellect. The library consisted of two floors with a vast number of rare books and manuscripts. The restaurant was on the top floor—a long sunny room—and almost every day, prominent men and women were to be seen there. Distinguished clergymen and military commanders along with students of art, literature and medicine, and who in many cases distinguished themselves in after years, used to call and visit my studio or sit at my table and dine with me.

After I had been there several years, one of the House Committee came to my room and asked me how long I had been in the building. I told him, and he said, "In consideration of that, the Committee says that, whatever we do to others, we will never raise your rent." This agreement was carried out for several years.

To describe all the characters and events that took place around my studio during the more than twenty years I remained in the building would take a volume, but while in danger of running into a catalogue, I would like to mention only a few of the names which occur to me. They were the heroes of my childhood—the defenders of our glorious Union—who came to my studio to sit for me and tell of their actions at Bull Run, Antietam, Gettysburg, Spotsylvania and Franklin.

## General Oliver O. Howard

General Oliver O. Howard was the first visitor to my new studio, and used to call on me quite often. The General had lost his right arm at the Battle of Seven Pines on June 1, 1862, where he was awarded the Congressional Medal of Honor for heroism. I had met and sketched Gen. Howard many years earlier while he was Superintendent at West Point and we became close friends. During the many years of our friendship, he learned to open his heart and express his feelings on many subjects; a few such as follows: "I like religion, but not religionists. When I in public receive any applause or attention, I always try to forget it, and think, 'How does God see me?'"

I asked him, while he was posing for his bust, to tell me the story of how he had ridden out alone in the Indian country to have a conference with the Indians. He said, "A Captain insisted on riding out with me. I ordered him back. He protested. I told him he had a wife and children and I did not want to be responsible for him. He said, 'Well, how is it you go?' I said, 'He who saveth his life shall lose it. He who loseth his life for my sake shall find it.' And I rode into the Indian country with no weapon but a small penknife."

Speaking of Gen. Grant, he said, "On his return from his trip around the world, as the vessel approached San Francisco, the wharves and the windows and roofs of the buildings were crowded with people. He turned to his wife and said, 'Look, Julia, see all the people turned out to look at you.' She protested saying they were looking at him. 'No,' he insisted, 'It must be you; for the last time I came here many years ago, there was not a single one turned out to look at me.'"

While working on his bust, a friend stopped by, Gen. Howard said, "Kelly always makes a man talk up to a picture." This was after I had cross questioned him in regards to his several interviews with Lincoln. The bust, when finished, was cast in bronze and presented by his family to Howard University.

## General Alexander S. Webb

During our long and intimate friendship, General Alexander S. Webb told me many stirring incidents in his historic career—in particular, how he defeated Confederate General Lewis Armistead's brigade at the High Water Mark on July 3, 1863, at Gettysburg for which he was awarded the Medal of Honor. While he was dictating his memories to me, he said, "They talk of Pickett's Charge, but they don't talk how we defeated them." Under his direction I made a sketch of the scene, and while the General posed for his own figure, he said, "I often sit and think of the past, and strange though I seem not to pay much attention at the time, being engaged in my work, the memories of things come back to me—the rolling smoke, its shadows and reflections—why the colors are beautiful, as they float through them; like colors on a soap-bubble—no artist has ever depicted it."

Gen. Webb was very interested in my equestrian statue of Gen. Porter and visited me frequently while I was working on it; one day he wrote to me:

> Dear Kelly,
> I have been four times to your statue and I have studied it—it is rather audacious in you to put in bronze an actual horse. The ordinary observer wants a Charger—a charger who is represented as anxious to enter a battle, but Generals in the field looked for horses with endurance. That horse of yours would carry anyone a long distance and he is of good blood and in working condition. As for Gen. Porter I prefer him without the full beard, but since you studied his head so often and you have in your studio the best profile portrait of him I ever saw so I will not discuss the likeness, but it is a grand picture of the man.

The last thing Gen. Webb said to me was, "Kelly, when I die I want you to make my monument," but feeling uneasy, I quickly changed the subject. His wish, unfortunately, was ignored by the New York State Monument Commission and his statue at Gettysburg was given to another sculptor.

## General Joshua L. Chamberlain

Another Medal of Honor hero of Gettysburg was General Joshua L. Chamberlain, who was awarded the decoration for his charge on Little Round

Top on July 2, 1863. I first met Gen. Chamberlain at Gen. Porter's funeral in which I served as a pall-bearer.

While working on his panel, Gen. Chamberlain described to me his being severely wounded at Petersburg—shot through the body—and while I was cross-questioning him about the incident, he said, "I don't see how you can show this in a picture." "Oh, yes I can," I replied, "you tell me the facts and I'll attend to the picture." He also told me that after Lee's surrender, he was personally selected by Gen. Griffin to receive the arms and colors of the Confederates at Appomattox.

Gen. Chamberlain was always a very kind friend to me. He later wrote me a short note in regards to my Gen. Porter statue:

> My Dear Mr. Kelly,
>
> I am very glad of the opportunity I had when passing through New York last Saturday of seeing your model of the figure of General F. J. Porter for the equestrian statue to be set up in Portsmouth, N. H. Your conception is perfect and your work is noble.
>
> Permit me to express this feeling and judgment. It may be in a line to confirm and comfort your own mind about your work.
>
> Joshua L. Chamberlain,
> Brevet Major General U. S. V.

# General John M. Schofield

General John M. Schofield was awarded his Medal of Honor for leading a charge against the enemy at Wilson's Creek in 1861.

As a pall-bearer at Gen. Fitz John Porter's funeral at Trinity Church, I went up to Gen. Schofield and introduced myself. I asked Gen. Schofield if Gen. Porter had written about me, as he promised to do.

After some conversation, he agreed to pose for his bas relief. Coming to my studio a week later, he took his seat in the big chair, I asked him to get up again, until I placed a cushion for him, saying: "These springs are not as comfortable as with the cushions."

"Your chair bears evidence of service," said the General.

"Yes, I have been advised to have it fixed up, but as it has been worn out by the great men that have sat in it, I prefer to leave it as it is."

Our talk eventually drifted to character and prayer, and he said: "Here is a subject one hardly cares to talk about, but as we were talking of character, I thought I would tell you. I am a very religious man, but I never prayed for my own safety. I always prayed, but I always prayed for courage and wisdom to direct my troops so that I may preserve their lives and serve my country." He then added: "I felt justified in praying for wisdom and spiritual help, and not in praying that Providence would alter the course of a bullet."

After the General was finished posing, he left and I walked with him up toward Columbus circle and took the Sixth Ave. cars down to 44th St., where he was stopping at the Iroquois Hotel. I then left him at the hotel steps, declining politely to go in to meet Mrs. Schofield as my hands were too dirty from modeling. On my return to the studio I passed my old home and looked up at the window where I used to sit with my mother while she read to me. Suddenly my childhood prophesy came to mind—*When I get to be a man, I am going to know all the Generals, and they are coming to see me.*

My daydreams did come true, and I have been truly blessed.

## Colonel Theodore Roosevelt

When Col. Theodore Roosevelt was elected Governor of New York, Col. Jerome Wheeler wrote to him at Albany, and asked if he would give me a sitting for a bust, telling him that I would take only twenty minutes to complete the study. That statement must have given Roosevelt a queer idea of me, and so far as I know, he paid no attention to the letter. Later, Gen. Francis V. Greene made a request that he pose for me, and I judge that the Governor gave a reluctant consent. On April 19, 1900 there was a knock at my studio door; opening it, there stood Roosevelt, with another gentleman who had been escorted up by Shackleford, one of the clerks at the Y. M. C. A.

Roosevelt at that time had a black slouch hat pulled down over his eyes. He wore glittering eyeglasses, and had a fine, ruddy complexion; blond mustache and prominent, strong white teeth. Walking in briskly, he said in a crisp, clear voice with a rather precise delivery, "Mr. Kelly, how soon can I leave?"

"As soon as you wish," I replied. He checked up at this, and said with a slight hesitation, "Well, can I go at 11:30?" "If you wish," I replied; "you know the value of your time better than I do." At this he smiled, to take the edge off. It was then fifteen minutes past eleven. "Well, Captain," he said, turning to his friend, "I will meet you at 11:30, downstairs." The aide remarked, "I think I had better come up." "Very well, come back at 11:30," Roosevelt answered. The Captain started toward the door, and I went out with him; he wanted me to go back at once, but I waited for the elevator.

Returning to the studio, I found Roosevelt rubbing off with his finger the dust that had covered my name on the base of *Sheridan's Ride*, and peering earnestly at it through his thick glasses, close to the bronze. Looking up, he said with a cheery smile. "Mr. Kelly, I beg your pardon—I did not realize who you were! This statuette I have in my possession. I bought it when a student at Harvard, with the last fifty dollars I had at the time. This, with Saint-Gaudens' *Puritan*, and Remington's *Bronco Buster*, I consider the finest type of American bronzes. I am entirely at your service."

I spoke to him of Col. Wheeler, told him of the bust the colonel had ordered, and commissioned me to make a statuette of Roosevelt at San Juan Hill, which he wanted to present to him. "I cannot take it as a gift," he replied, "but would like to do my part. I will talk it over with Mrs. Roosevelt, and see if I can afford it. You know I am not a rich man."

He came in several times after this. In posing he was always patient and considerate—never assertive. When I had the model of horse and man completed, he came and stood beside me, and we counseled over the action which he approved before I had it cast in enduring bronze.

## General Joseph Hayes

General Joseph Hayes was another close friend and frequent visitor to my studio. One evening while I was at work, a friend came in and announced that he had just been married to a young girl who was a friend of General Hayes. He said they had just had supper in a nearby restaurant, and would like to finish the festivities by bringing the party to my studio. I told him to come and shortly after they arrived. The rest of the party consisted of the bride, the groom, some of their young friends, and an aged veteran soldier, father of the lady who was the chaperone of the party, including also General Hayes' nephew, Whitney Blake. General Hayes sat down in the big chair that I used for modeling my subjects.

Finding chairs, the others formed a half circle in front of the General, who said, "Kelly, show the ladies my bust." "General," I replied, "the model is packed away among the others, and I don't see how I can find it in the black shadow caused by the electric light." The General's brows contracted as he growled out, "Kelly doesn't care a damn for me!" Then a look of blank horror came over his face, and he exclaimed with an appealing gesture, "Ladies, ladies, I beg your pardon! I beg your pardon, for never such an expression as that, I assure you, has ever crossed my lips before."

"Hold on! Hold on, General!" I said, springing up and diving for a pile of books. "What are you going to do, Sir?" growled the General. "Never mind," I answered, still rummaging. "What are you doing, Sir?" he again demanded. "Keep quiet," I replied, and opening a volume, read aloud the following statement:

"When our Nation was imperiled, and when the mothers of New England blessed their sons, and sent them forth to save our imperiled Republic, it was their comfort to feel that they had entrusted them under the command of that valiant soldier and noble Gen. Joseph Hayes. And I can recall, at the Battle of the Wilderness, when our lines reeled and wavered before the onward rush of the enemy, Gen. Hayes, riding down our lines, and waving his sword, <u>damned</u> us into position."

The General looked aghast. There was a hush—a ripple of enthusiasm, then the chaperone jumped to her feet, stepped forward and exclaimed, "General, I must kiss you for that!" Drawing himself up with a repelling gesture, he boomed out, "No, no, madam! No married woman shall kiss me!" She shrank back abashed, as the General turned and addressed himself to the rest of the party. At this I leaned over and whispered to her, "Tell him you will kiss his scar." "What scar?" she asked.

I pointed to the white scar near the crown of his head, from the wound which he had received while leading a charge in The Battle of the Wilderness. She then stood up, and stepping forward, said, "General, if you will not let me kiss you, will you permit me to kiss your scar?" And then, stooping reverently, she did so. At this, the little bride arose, stepped forward and said, "Dear General, I feel that I, too, must kiss your scar on this happy occasion." Taking his head fondly in her hands, she bent forward reverently and kissed the white scar, emblem of his heroism in The Wilderness.

As she stepped back, the General sat for a period with bowed head over his clasped hands. For awhile there was a hush, then he arose slowly, and in a wavering voice, choked with emotion, muttered, "I am going home." Then, with a faltering step, leaning heavily on his cane, Gen. Hayes departed.

## Admiral George Dewey

May 1, 1898, the news of Dewey's Victory over the Spanish Fleet [at Manila Bay] set our land aglow with rejoicing, and our lurking enemies throughout the world slunk under cover or sidled forth to hail us as "brother."

Dewey's portraits were on every side, and in the most unexpected places. One of the papers said young Dewey did not dare to go into a saloon to get a drink because he would see his father staring at him over the bar. Even a life-size wooden statue of the Admiral showing him in cocked hat and full uniform was set up as a tobacco sign in front of a cigar store on Third Avenue and 64th Street.

I was asked by the publisher Joseph Stoddard to model a small relief of the Admiral to be cast in bronze, that it might meet the demands of another class.

While working from his photograph it dawned on me that I had seen him before. I recalled I had met an officer in the Army and Navy Club, Washington, whom General David Stanley had introduced to me as Captain—Blank—the name I promptly forgot. With a shake of the hands and a few remarks we separated, but his eagle face made a lasting impression. He was deeply bronzed, black hair streaked with gray, as was his long moustache; a broad smooth brow; very brilliant dark brown eyes; a large assertive beaked nose; broad firm jaws, and a resolute chin; a compact head surmounting square shoulders. I carefully watched him standing in front of several friends who were sitting on a sofa. He was evidently telling them some thrilling incident, and I carefully studied his every movement. His rare personality attracted me so much that I stood studying him until I was called away.

My model being completed, I forwarded a copy in bronze to him on his flagship, and in due time I received the following letter dated Oct. 12, 1898:

My Dear Sir,
I am just in receipt of your letter of Aug. 17th and also the bronze panel of my head. For both accept my best thanks.

The panel is, I consider, very like me and the modeling is very fine. It would give me pleasure to give you a sitting or two upon my return.

Again thanking you, I remain,

Very sincerely,
George Dewey

On Dewey's return to New York, it was arranged before he received the honors of the city that his fleet should pass in review up the Hudson. My first sight of it was the *Olympia* booming responses to the salvos of batteries stationed on the bluffs of Grant's Tomb. She started to turn opposite where I sat with a friend on a block of granite mounted on a freight car at the foot of 131st Street. As the flagship neared the shore I distinctly saw Dewey standing on the bridge, silhouetted against the bright sky. At the sight of that unforgettable figure, I said, "That's the man I met in Washington."

After he had received the stupendous honors of our city and the nation, I wrote reminding him of his promise. He invited me to call on him in Washington.

On my arrival, he came into the room saying, "How do you do, Sir?" then looked searchingly and said, "I know you." "And I know you," I said. He shook hands genially. Behind him hung a copy of the picture by [William H.] Overend, *An August Morning with Farragut*, showing the fight between the *Hartford* and the ram *Tennessee*, in the Battle of Mobile Bay in which Dewey had fought as a young Lieutenant.

I asked him some questions about the picture in which I quoted Admiral Watson. Then he said, "Come, I want to introduce you to Mrs. Dewey," leading the way to the front room, saying "Dear, this is Mr. Kelly, sculptor from New York, who is going to make my bust." She greeted me graciously with a kind friendly manner.

One glance showed me the reason why she had won the Hero. Fine eyes; fine features; and a fine cultured bearing.

Then she said, "I want to show you what I think is the best portrait of the Admiral. "I don't like it," he said. "I do," I answered. "I don't like it," he said decisively, "I destroyed the negative." "There you were dead wrong," I replied, "Mrs. Dewey is right. It is the best portrait you have." He stopped, eyed me, and then said, gamely with a smile, "If you think so you must have a copy."

He then called his Chinese boy and asked him if he had a copy. "There is one left, Admiral." "Bring it here," he ordered. Inscribing it, "To J. E. Kelly, from George Dewey," he handed it to me.

We then went into his office, and I made a careful life study of his profile and front view with careful measurements. He promised to visit my studio and give sittings for the bust.

Some weeks later, at 10 A. M. a sharp knock at my studio door and there stood the Admiral and Mrs. Dewey. As I already had blocked out the bust in wax. I started to work at once, while Mrs. Dewey sat beside me and encouraged me with little suggestions, and helped entertain us. As I pointed him up with my calipers, he said, "You don't drink or smoke, do you?" "No," I said. "I thought so.

I noticed your hand does not quiver. I wouldn't let many people work around my eyes with those things as you have been doing."

I led him to talk of his experiences in the Philippines. He spoke of his feelings that night as he headed his fleet up the channel to Manila, expecting every moment to strike a torpedo; at the same time thinking of the loved ones at home. As he said this he turned round and touched Mrs. Dewey's hand with a slight caress.

Later during the sitting I said to him, "Admiral, it is pretty nearly time they begin to knife you." "What do you mean?" he asked. I said, "The American people have given you every honor, and placed you on the highest pinnacle. And now certain types seeing you there will feel that they should be in your place." He turned to Mrs. Dewey and said quite seriously, "I shouldn't wonder if they would." He then said, "I have given you an advertisement. The reporters asked me where I was going this morning. I told them I was going up to Kelly's to sit for my bust."

After the sitting was finished, I saw them out. Several of the artists' wives came in and asked me about Mrs. Dewey. I said, "She sat beside me looking over my shoulder for two hours and made suggestions about my work, but she did not distract me. It was a pleasure to have her there." "I'm glad to hear that," said one lady, "you could not give her a higher compliment."

The afternoon edition of one of the papers came out in red letters saying, "Admiral Dewey Gives Sitting to Sculptor Kelly." Next morning, a pretty looking girl with her hair in curls and a dainty little frock, with a note in her hand, came to my door and shyly asked to see Admiral Dewey. This was the starter, and for two weeks after I could do no work, with men, women and children coming in asking to see my bust and to sit in the chair sat in by Admiral Dewey.

## General James H. Wilson

Gen. James Wilson was only 27 years old when he took command of the Cavalry Corps, Military Division of the Mississippi, consisting of more than 20,000 men, the largest cavalry force up to that time in the history of the World. While posing for his relief, in answer to my questions, the General described his experiences with the Army of the Potomac, his campaigns with Thomas at Nashville, his pursuit of the defeated Hood, his Charge at Selma, and finally the capture of Jefferson Davis. I wrote down these statements word for word, as nearly as possible with his approval, as I remember him saying, "Kelly, put this down in your 'forgettery.'"

When the relief was about half finished, the Battleship *Maine* was blown up; war was declared with Spain, and Gen. Wilson volunteered for the front. His troops captured Puerto Rico, and after peace was declared, he served as commander of the Department of Matanzas, Cuba. He then volunteered for service in the Boxer Rebellion, in China, and commanded American and British troops at the Eight Temples. Returning to the United States, he declined further command or routine service, and in March 1901, was placed on the Retired List in accordance with Special Act of Congress, at the request of the President, March 2, 1901. He was then selected by President Roosevelt to represent the United States Army at the Coronation of Edward VII.

On his return from England after the Coronation, Gen. Wilson called at my studio and gave me the necessary sittings for the relief, which had been put aside when he started for the war. When finished, he approved and signed the work; some time after, he gave me sittings for a life-sized bust, and was untiring in helping me to carry it out to my satisfaction.

One day, there was a knock at the door; opening it, there stood a clergyman who smiled, saying, "I blew the bugle at Selma!" Then I knew it was the man who was known as "Chaplain Brown," who then told me that he had come to see the bust of Gen. James Harrison Wilson, on which I was working. I asked him to tell me the story of Wilson's Charge, which I took down:

B—Wilson, though only 27 years old, was a Major General, with a command of 20,000 cavalry. After Thomas's victory at Nashville, Wilson followed the retreating enemy, defeating them at every stand they made, until Forrest sought shelter behind the fortifications of Selma, Alabama. Then Wilson, so as to be conspicuous, mounted his gray war-horse, which he called Sheridan, took his position at the head of the column, ordered young Brown, a bugler, to sound the charge! and dashed full speed down the pike to the City Gate, which was defended by three batteries.

Just as he reached it, Wilson's gray fell, shot through the breast. Wilson was hit by a glancing shot in the left shoulder and the knee cap of his left leg, glancing off. Waving his men on, he jerked his bleeding horse to its feet, sprang into the saddle, and swept amid the cross-fire of shot, shell and bullets on through the gates of Selma, while Forrest fled from the captured city.

Rev. Mr. Brown told me how he had seen Wilson on his gray, as he cheered and waved his men on through the gates of Selma. After Mr. Brown had gone I could not get the story out of my mind, and as I went to bed that night, the refrain kept ringing in my ears—"I blew the bugle at Selma!"

Before the bust was finished the Chaplain called again. General Wilson happened to be posing. The joyful meeting of the two soldiers was delightful to see. Mr. Brown said his wife was down stairs. "I will go down to see her," said the General. "I would rather bring her up, so that she can see you and the bust together," replied the Chaplain.

As Mrs. Brown entered, it was then that cavalier and courtly gentleman could be seen at his best, as he greeted and entertained the lady and her gallant husband.

At last the bust was finished, and the General, having signed it, turned to me and said, "Kelly, you and I have not talked any business. Now I want to order three copies in bronze; one for each of my daughters and one for Springfield, the capital of my native State.

When the bust was cast in bronze he called to see it. Looking it over carefully, he said, "Kelly—that bronze will last for all time."

"Yes," I answered.

He nodded, repeating, "For all time."

Then taking a chair, with his back to the bronze, his hands on his knees and head bowed, absorbed in a line of thought too serious for me to question.

# Mark Twain

I saw Mark Twain but once. He was Chairman of the Lincoln Memorial Meeting at Carnegie Hall, on Feb. 11, 1901. General Howard's son Harry had organized it for the benefit of Lincoln University, at Cumberland Gap, Tenn. It was remarkable that the two principal speakers had been disunionists—Col. Henry Watterson and Mark Twain.

On the platform were General Nelson Miles, General John Brooke, General Joe Wheeler, General James R. O'Beirne, General F. V. Greene, General O. O. Howard, Colonel Findlay Andrews, and Assistant-Secretary of the Navy Frank W. Hackett.

Col. Henry Watterson spoke first. He was tall, with strong bold features, straight snow-white hair; moustache and imperial. His address was delivered with reserve, dignity and fervor as though appreciating the great subject and occasion. The following quotation gives the tenor of his eulogy on Abraham Lincoln: "The Man Bore a Commission from God on High."

Mark Twain followed. He was short, slight, and his disheveled shock of white hair made him appear top heavy, like a dandelion gone to seed. His cold, bright, insolent eyes glinted from under his bushy brows.

His manner of delivery with his far-away, very unconscious look, and drawl of the old time professional funny man seemed studied and mechanical. The following quotation from the *New York Herald* the day following is a specimen of Mark Twain:

"Colonel Watterson and myself were two former Rebels, and both are reconstructed, but he saved the Union. I proposed to drive General Grant into the Pacific—if I could get the transportation. I told Colonel Watterson to attend to the Eastern Army and wait till I came, but he refused to take orders; Colonel Watterson thus saved the Union." Then pointing dramatically to Col. Watterson added: "There sits the man."

After Miss Tracy, the soprano had sung and started to leave the stage, a flower-piece was handed up. Mark Twain received it and ambled after her. He delivered it with a bow and a smirk in such a manner that it raised a snicker from those in the audience who seemed to forget with him that the occasion of the meeting was to honor the memory the dead Abraham Lincoln.

# Washington at Prayer

Dining one day with Dr. George Hope Ryder, I told him how a Real Estate man—John J. Clancy, a veteran of Duryea's Zouaves—commissioned me to make a bust of Washington for the lobby of the Y. M. C. A., but I did not want to make it, as busts of Washington attracted no attention—they were often looked upon as simply furniture. I suggested a bas relief depicting a scene that could show Washington's spiritual character.

"I am sure that you will make something that is characteristic of Washington," he replied. "Yes," I answered and we talked it over. I then reversed the menu and made a design of Washington at prayer at Valley Forge. Handing it to Dr. Ryder, I said, "After seeing that, no boy will be ashamed at being caught at his prayers." He liked the idea and encouraged me to go on with it.

I then started to hunt all the authorities on the subject and persuaded Clancy to carry out the idea, which he had never heard of.

Having satisfied myself as to the historical accuracy of the incident as described by Isaac Potts and of other testimony when Washington gave expression to his spiritual character I started to realize the personal characteristics of Washington.

I dismissed the worsted work portrait of Gilbert Stuart and the theatrical ones of John Trumbull and settled on the keen, firm characteristic one by Charles Wilson Peale which he painted from Washington at Valley Forge. I also took the [Jean-Antoine] Houdon head which was cast from life.

I also studied his original uniform at the National Museum. The sword was copied from Washington's Campaign sword in the War Department. It was at the St. Louis Exhibition at the time, but they gave me special permission to have the case opened and measurements taken.

That bitter winter I made careful studies of bleak trees in the park. Then with all my fervid love for Washington, I put my whole heart in the work. I can recall perfectly when on the finishing touches, Clara Barton came in to sit for me and the relief was her background.

When the bronze was finished, I asked my friend, Father Francis M. Craft to Bless it as he was the first one to have the honor of wearing the badge of the Sons of the Revolution in battle (Battle of Wounded Knee) it seemed very appropriate he should do so. The bronze was placed in the Auditorium under the auspices of the Lafayette Grand Army Post; General Hayes made the address. The bronze was unveiled by Miss Helen Gould.

Clancy's head was completely turned by the notoriety of this event. Without my knowledge he then wrote to the [Assistant] Secretary of the Treasury John H. Edwards offering a bronze copy of this relief to be placed on the Eastern buttress of the Sub-Treasury in Wall Street. It was accepted subject to the approval of Sub-Treasurer Hamilton Fish.

When announced in the newspapers, the idea of Washington at prayer seemed to give a great shock to a certain type of Wall Streeters.

Protests against it appeared in the papers, most of them assailing the historic accuracy of the incident.  I have noticed when any story is told to Washington's discredit, it makes some people's eyes sparkle and their lips smack, but anything to his credit they demand the most exhaustive proofs.

I was astonished how the newspapers gave so much room to the assaults of the little 3 x 4 panel.  A thing the size of the Statue of Liberty couldn't have excited more.

The principle criticisms were much against the seams on his gloves and his sword; when a glance at either of my authorities would have settled both points.

One paper wrote an editorial to the President appealing to him as a historian and a soldier to stop this bad work.  Fish had accepted, but was overruled by Secretary Edwards and one of my friends, the next day with a broad smile handed me a clipping with a large heading which said, "The President Rejects the Tablet."  Clancy came in panic stricken and asked me to accompany him to Washington, but I refused to go, so he went alone.  I was sitting that evening with a friend who started to condole with me.  I told him I didn't care to be condoled with as my Mother had always taught me, "That all is not lost that is in danger."  Shortly after this a telegram arrived, "The President Accepts the Tablet."

Clancy told me on his return that when he went to Washington, Congressmen [J. V.] Olcott took him to see Secretary Edwards.  Clancy asked him why he had rejected the Tablet.  He said, "Because everybody said it was so bad."

"It is very strange the President bought two of Kelly's bronzes then suddenly finding out that they were bad," said Clancy.

"Did Kelly make that bronze?"

"Yes."

"Wait a while, I will see the President."

In a half hour he came back smiling, "The President accepts the panel."

I then saw Clancy had been so anxious to advertise himself that he had not mentioned my name in connection with the panel, so it was very natural for Roosevelt to reject it, having no Artist's name connected with it, and whose donor was in the Real Estate business.

Roosevelt made public that his initial reason for rejecting the bronze was that the panel was a copy; he felt that the United States should have the original, so I arranged with the Committee of the Y. M. C. A. to exchange.

The original was taken down and the copy put in its place.

Roosevelt also telephoned as there had been so much delay that possibly I could not get it inserted in the stone by Washington's Birthday and suggested that I lay it against the stone and insert it later.  But I took no chances; I got my friend Keller to set his men to work all night before the unveiling was to take place, so they could insert it in the stone.

Roosevelt sent out an order that all the troops, both Army and Navy, in the neighborhood be present at the dedication.  They numbered five thousand under command of General James Franklin Wade and General Fred Grant.

I did not go to the unveiling but sent the office boy John Thaler to report. At 12:25 the telephone rang: "John on the wire, Mr. Kelly, the Flag has been pulled off the bronze and the people are cheering." Later in the day, Keller's foreman came up, saying, "Mr. Kelly, we worked all night. We placed the bronze in position, knocked the heads off the rivets, then I threw a flag over it, put a couple of bricks on top to hold it in place, just as the Procession came round the corner. We had worked so hard and it was so cold, that our hands, from the sharp edge of the bronze cutting them, were covered with blood."

On September 16, 1920, a murderous explosion occurred in Wall Street. A horse-drawn wagon packed with 100 pounds of dynamite and 500 pounds of iron slugs was driven down through the crowded street, coming to a halt in front of the panel of *Washington at Prayer*, with only the width of the street between it and the J. P. Morgan building. The driver jumped out and disappeared, and shortly afterward a deafening explosion took place. Nearly 40 passersby were instantly killed and 400 maimed or injured, and the neighboring buildings badly shattered. Huge iron bars on the windows of the Morgan building were driven in, and several of its clerks inside were killed or wounded, and the Assay Office was badly defaced. The building on the northwest corner of Nassau Street was struck at the third floor, knocking out a large piece of granite from the window sill.

Only a few fragments were left of the horse and cart, and there was a deep scoop in the paved street where it had stood. The Washington panel nearest to it was uninjured; a slight mark, as from a piece of chalk, was on the arm, the edge of its granite socket still shows evidence of being slightly nicked. It was evidently the work of some Ellis Island invader, but he was never caught; the culprit seemed to have his eye on the bankers when he committed this Hell-inspired crime.

# The Defenders Monument, New Haven, Connecticut

In 1779, the citizens of New Haven and Yale College students had planned a patriotic celebration for July 5th (the 4th being a Sunday). Early that morning, signal guns announced a British fleet in the harbor, preparing to make a descent upon the town. After hastily removing the women and children to the North, the men returned to defend New Haven, which they did successfully, with some help from nearby hamlets, and the invaders retired during the night.

I received the commission for a monument to be placed in that city and while designing "The Defenders," I represented the group under the command of a gentleman, and by his side, a college student, and the muscular man at the trail of the gun I typified a yeoman. When asked why I put the gentleman in the fore and the yeoman in the rear, I answered:

"It was the gentlemen of the country who by their risks and sacrifices gave us our independence. Washington himself refused to receive anything until victory was achieved, and when requested by Congress for an account of personal expenses, they found that his outlay had been some $30,000."

I then quoted the lines of Oliver Wendell Holmes, "There is always more sympathy for the callous on the hand than the furrow on the brow; and people should remember that the heart could beat as loyal and true under the silk as under the fustian."

I had used the head of Henry T. Blake for the directing character on the group; he was a member of the Monument Committee, and from his age, activities and influence was known in New Haven as the "City Father." He proved a loyal friend through all the great strain of constructing the work. When Lincoln came east in 1860 to speak at Cooper Union Institute in New York, Mr. Blake was one of the Committee to receive him when he stopped at New Haven on his way to visit his son, Robert, who was studying at Exeter College, New Hampshire.

Mr. Blake strongly criticized the recently [1917] unveiled statue of Lincoln by George Grey Barnard—calling it "grotesque." He also criticized the characteristics brought out in many other statues of Lincoln, such as depression and melancholy; and from his close personal observations, he found Lincoln vigorous and alert, and at time jocose.

*In 1917, a controversial bronze statue of Abraham Lincoln, by George Gray Barnard, was unveiled in Cincinnati, Ohio. It depicted a beardless Lincoln, long-necked and knock-kneed, with huge veined hands crossed over a shrunken stomach, and dressed in a badly wrinkled, ill-fitting suit. The statue might have gone unnoticed by the public until a copy was offered to be placed in Trafalgar Square in London. Suddenly, Barnard's Lincoln became the center of a raging controversy in the newspapers, with editors, politicians, art critics and aging Civil War veterans all voicing an opinion on whether this statue should be sent overseas as a remembrance of Abraham Lincoln.*

## My talk with Henry T. Blake

Henry T. Blake's head was of the lofty Roman type, found in its perfection in the old-time American gentleman; a powerful brow; sparkling eye; bold nose; mouth refined and beautifully chiseled; shapely, sensitive hands, and a tall, well-knit figure. He had keen perceptions, great force of character, whimsical humor and a kindly heart.

While inspecting my Defenders model, during one of his visits to my studio, Mr. Blake turned abruptly to me and said, "Did you ever make a Lincoln?"

"I never thought of it," I answered, "He has already been made over and over again."

"But *you* should make a Lincoln," mildly persisted my visitor.

My interest being aroused, I asked, "Did you ever hear him speak?"

B—Oh yes, I have heard him. I was one of the Committee to receive him when he visited Bridgeport [on March 10, 1860]. He was tired after his ride in the cars, so I took him to the Sterling House, and said, "There, no one will disturb you." We then gave him a dinner at the home of Mr. Frederick Wood at Bridgeport, a wealthy citizen of the place. I remember that he took up one of those large Bridgeport oysters on his fork, looked at it quizzically, and asked, "Do I understand you to say this is a single oyster?"

I wish that you would make a Lincoln with the wide-open manner. He is generally represented with his head bowed down meditating, or depicted grasping his coat as if he were sick at the stomach, while he was really full of animation, and intensity jocose—very often out of time, but that was a relief to him; he was melancholy, and said he had to do it to be able to stand things. It is said that he often talked in a manner that showed his early environment, but his soul was refined—refined when he was elevated. His soul was bigger than himself—a common figure with the soul of a prophet. When he spoke he seemed to rise, and became transfigured with fire and vigor.

I wish you would make him at the Gettysburg Speech. Nothing better has ever been written. He could rouse the people by his power; he could stand like this (here Mr. Blake acted it out), and appeal for peace and kindness to all; no hanging of his head as the artists show him, but he stood up as a man—he was an athlete and a leader.

President Lincoln, sometime after visiting Bridgeport, met Mr. Amos S. Treat and said, "Do you come from Bridgeport, where they have the big oysters?" They are appreciating his qualities now, in fact, they are inclined to overdo it and give him qualities he did not possess.

Mr. Blake then stood up and gave me the action as he remembered Lincoln speaking.

B—I notice in the other statues of Lincoln in which the large size of his hands and feet are made the most conspicuous features, thus impairing the real purpose of a statue, which is to show the ideal man, such as posterity will want to know him in remembering his character as a statesman, rather than as a blundering product of nature—such as an audience who might be seeing him on the platform for the first time might be led naturally to notice his personal defects. Therefore, while his hands and feet should be represented as somewhat larger than the perfect symmetry would require, that should not be so much as to attract attention at first sight.

Mr. Blake then repeated, "I have often wondered if *you* could make him."

After Mr. Blake had gone I went over to the librarian at the Y. M. C. A., and read her my notes. She said, "Why don't you write a Life of Lincoln?" I replied, "How can I write a Life of Lincoln?" She answered, "If you write down what you have told me—what the Generals and other friends of Lincoln have told you, it would make a Life of Lincoln." I took her advice. I then started to gather materials confirming my conception of Lincoln. To have achieved what he did, could not have been carried through by a slack, downcast-looking man generally represented as a southern clay-eater, with a bad case of hookworm, and at the same time link him with New York City, when he struck the keynote of his career in the Cooper Institute speech, when he proclaimed the words:

"RIGHT SHALL BE MIGHT!"

From that very moment, I became desirous of gathering material—if possible—to justify me in making Abraham Lincoln an active, vigorous leader so much as inspired the poem by Walt Whitman, "O Captain! My Captain!"

My ambition was to model Lincoln in bronze—not isolated on a plinth 2 ft. by 2 ft.—but the embodiment of the spirit of the time, as well as the men whom he led to triumph. With my normal enthusiasm, I began to actively seek out any living witness who could tell me of Lincoln.

*After his meeting with Henry Blake in 1919, Kelly spent the next several years interviewing and corresponding with nearly sixty eyewitnesses who could provide details of Abraham Lincoln's physical appearance and personality.*

*Kelly realized the historical importance of these collected notes, and carefully preserved them for future study and reference, wishing that, "they be placed somewhere, where they will do the most good."*

# Chapter Four
# Tell Me of Lincoln

*Some of these notes on "Our Abraham" may seem unimportant and trivial, but as even a glimpse of one you love may give pleasure, I include them all.*

James Edward Kelly

## Lincoln's Speech at the Cooper Union Institute
## Interview with Major George Haven Putnam

With an introduction from Charles Scribner, I called on Major George H. Putnam, 24 West 45th Street. Shaking hands he said, "Mr. Kelly, I am happy to meet you and to greet you." He had a fine head, grizzled, wavy hair and a full beard; he had a fine brow, strong eyes and a well braced nose, inclined to be high in the bridge; he was short, but sturdy in build, with fine, well-bred hands. Explaining that I wanted to get details about Lincoln's [February 27, 1860] Cooper Institute speech, he replied in rather an assertive voice:

P—I was there. I saw him.

K—He is generally represented by artists as forlorn and depressed; to me he seemed the embodiment of strength. I want to show him assertive and vigorous.

P—His manner that night was not assertive and vigorous; it was, I should say, an impressive, solemn manner, as though he felt he were a prophet with a message to deliver, which affected his manner to the point of solemnity. One felt that when he first got up from his seat. He arose very slowly, and with his great height (I was sitting behind him and to his right), it seemed as though he would never get through getting up. He rose slowly; his head was bowed; he was thinking but of the WORD, HE, LINCOLN had to deliver.

He was speaking for the first time to an eastern audience, and his experience before had been with western farmers and western village folk. He possibly over-estimated the intelligence of that audience, although the men on that platform were the best in New York: William Cullen Bryant, who presided; Alexander Stewart, the dry goods man; Horace Greeley—"

K—Putnam?

P—Yes, my father [George Palmer Putnam]; I hesitated at first to say it.


Here he branched off into the causes which led to the formation of the Republican party, saying, "Slavery was a sectional accident, not a National institution." I asked, "Is that expression yours?" "Yes," he replied. He then detailed from what his father had told him how William Cullen Bryant had called a meeting of his friends in his office, and how he proposed they should send for Lincoln.

P—People now judge Bryant and think of him as a poet, but at that time he was an editor of the *New York Evening Post*, and a great power in politics. Bryant gave the whole tone to the meeting. His address was in substance that [William] Seward was the man who was the logical candidate for the Republican party for the coming election, but in case they could not agree on Seward, and to prevent a stampede for some dark horse made by some irresponsible man—an incident he desired to avoid—he preferred the delegates be inspired as to a second choice. He suggested that they send for Abraham Lincoln, "That young lawyer from Illinois, ask him to speak," and by that means they could judge whether he was to be the chosen man.

The proposal was agreed to by those present. I think it was Stewart who suggested that, as lawyers were not apt to have too much money, they had better send him a check for expenses. So they sent him a check for $500 to pay his expenses to and from New York. Bob Lincoln told me he was at Exeter Academy at the time. His father wanted to visit him, but could not afford it, but at last Bob received a letter from Mr. Lincoln, saying, "Dear Bob, I just won a case. When I get the fee I will go and see you." Later he received another letter: "Dear Bob, The fellow will not be able to pay me for six months. So I can't go." A week later he received another note: "Dear Bob, Some fellows in New York want to hear me talk, and have sent me some money to pay my expenses. I can manage the rest of the way."

That "talk" was the most important speech ever delivered in the United States.

K—Considering its influence, it probably was.


Then I showed Maj. Putnam a couple of prints given to me by Frederick H. Meserve, which he had printed for me from the original negative in his possession, taken by Brady on the day of the Cooper Institute speech, February 1860. One was the exact size of the negative; the other an enlargement of the head and shoulders. The Major looked earnestly at them, and said with great decision, "That fits in perfectly with my memory of the man—the sadness, the beauty of the eyes; dignity of the forehead; the homeliness and set purpose of the mouth; the clear-cut lines of the whole face!" This was said in a voice full of pathos and admiration.

While still holding them, Maj. Putnam said:

P—When he first got up he did not look awkward. He had on a new black frock coat that had been made for the eastern trip, but no tailor could make a fit for Lincoln. According to my memory, the coat hung behind him like a meal sack (I was behind him). The sleeves were not long enough, as his arms went out in the gestures, and there was a similar difference with the trousers—they went up. When he began, old-time speaker as he already was, he was beginning to adjust his voice to the hall, trying to get what speakers call, "the tone of the hall," to make his voice carry distinctly to the man on the last bench.

At first, while he was experimenting, his voice was harsh; during the same period he was shuffling his feet, and his big hands seemed to get in his way. But after a few minutes he got the tone of the hall, and became so absorbed in his thought and its utterance that he forgot all about his voice, his hands and his feet. And then his voice took on a solemnity, with a musicalness [sic] of appeal that won the hearts of the whole audience. At first the audience was inclined to be disappointed; they had heard about Lincoln's humor, and were expecting something more or less "wild and woolly." They thought there would be some stories or anecdotes to lighten up, but there was not one anecdote or quip in the whole address.

Lincoln had a full sense of harmony and dignity, and he was incapable of marring a well-rounded arrangement and a solemn invocation with bandiage [sic] or trivialities. Other people, who had heard Henry Clay, were expecting something in the way of what might be called "architectural" eloquence, or elaborate construction—the auto rotundo [sic] style of oratory. But this man gave them the simplest language in straightforward statements. He was talking to his friends and neighbors—trying to make clear what their forefathers had done in founding the Republic, and the nature of the obligations entered into by their sons and grandsons.

Only at the close of the speech did Lincoln permit himself to utter an invocation, a solemn appeal. "Let us have faith that right makes might, and in that faith let us dare to do our duty as we understand it." He had made clear to his fellow citizens what were their rights and their duties under the Constitution, and he now made an appeal to see that their duties were fulfilled, and that their responsibilities should be handed down to the next generation committed—not to slavery, but to Freedom.

I was sitting there as a youngster trying to understand, and looked for help into the faces of the men on the platform whom I knew. Whatever disappointment, or at least preliminary disappointment, may have been felt by the audience, I resolved that the leaders of opinion in New York—Bryant, Cooper, Greeley, Stewart and others, found themselves in full accord with the speaker.

They accepted his conclusions as their own, and were prepared to follow Lincoln's leadership. My father's face, of course I knew well, and his expression made clear to me his admiration and satisfaction with the speaker and the words that had been spoken.

My father introduced me to Mr. Lincoln after the speech, but I never spoke to him again, although I had the pleasure of lifting my hat to him three or four times in Washington. The memory of those eyes as I saw them as he turned his head during the speech, remained with me through the years of the Civil War. I was always thinking in the trenches of "The Man Behind the Guns."

## Lincoln at the Athenaeum Club

On the night of February 27, 1860, during a snow storm, Abraham Lincoln, after his great Cooper Institute speech, was brought to the building, then the Athenaeum Club, on the southwest corner of 16th Street and Fifth Avenue, by two members of the Young Men's Central Republican Union. These men were Hiram Barney, afterward collector of the Port of New York, and Mr. Charles Nott, afterwards one of the editors of the Cooper Institute Address.

Upon their arrival, five or six members of the club joined them, and they had a "simple supper," as Mr. Nott describes it. After this entertainment they started to walk downtown, but Mr. Lincoln's had on new boots which hurt his feet so they took a Sixth Avenue car. Mr. Nott got off to go to his home at No. 53 Laight Street, having instructed Mr. Lincoln to continue down to where the cars stopped at Vesey Street and Broadway, which was directly opposite the side door of the Astor House, in which Mr. Lincoln had a room at the time.

What a contrast—that sad, solitary, storm-beaten man, that night alone in New York. He had made his supreme effort. On February 20, 1861 he rode past that same Athenaeum Club on a brilliant sunny day, in a carriage drawn by six noble black horses, escorted by great men, and greeted at the front entrance portals of the Astor House by cheering crowds as President Elect of the United States.

## Abe Lincoln and His Folks
## Interview with Col. Harland Page Christie, 58th Ohio Infantry

Colonel Harland Page Christie was of medium size, trim, sinewy and energetic. His features were sharp and shrewd, humorous and well balanced; altogether pleasing. A tawny gray mustache did not conceal his kind, winning smile. His clear delivery with a slight western intonation gave it piquancy.

Mrs. Christie was fairly tall, most ample in outline, and reposeful in manner, with a sweet, gentle voice. She suggested the ideal Southern lady, sincere and deliberate, yet with a latent drollery.

C—The first time I saw Lincoln was in Dayton, Ohio in [September 17] 1859. He made a speech there, and was introduced by Robert Schenck, afterwards General, who had been with him for two months during the Douglas Debate, and had simply won by him. It was there [at Dayton] Schenck in his introduction, suggested that he be nominated for President. This was the first time it had been mentioned.

He said, in introducing this candidate for Congress: "He is the man who will be named before the Committee of the Republicans for President of the United States, at the Election two [one] years from now."

Lincoln was staid, solemn as a Methodist preacher. You could not see that this statement interested him at all. He was perfectly stoical.

As he stood up and began his address, he was terribly awkward and his long arms swung through the air. His gestures were emphatic and vigorous. He never went to a dancing school—you could know that, but his words moved the crowd. His language was clean-cut and clear as any that could be taken from the best of authors, and he simply held his neighbors spellbound by surprise. His words warmed up the crowd.

He wore a black frock coat like all professional men of the time. He was not an eccentric, but just plain. He was tall and angular, and it took an artistic tailor to fit him. He had to depend on home tailors, but they got to know him; in disposition he was old fashioned.

When the war came on I joined the 2nd Ohio, Company H. I was the first man to enlist in the State. I was in the First Battle of Bull Run.

And here the Colonel gave a most laughable description of the battle, and the humor of it lost nothing in the telling, and he spared himself least of all.

C—Later on, I was detailed on some official business in Washington, and I called at the White House and told the Secretary that I wanted to see President Lincoln.

I went in and Lincoln was sitting back in a chair. He was like as I had seen him before, ministerial and solemn. He had his feet crossed on a chair in front of him. When he saw me he put his feet on the floor and started to rise; it seemed to me his head would go through the ceiling. He extended his long arm and gave me a grip of his long hand that I remembered.

He immediately began to refer to the citizens of Decatur, and asked after them, never forgetting any of the older ones. Then speaking of the Cantrell Family, after I had told him what I had remembered, he said after speaking of the older children, "There was another little girl—a younger one." "Yes," I replied, "I married her two months ago."

Here Colonel Christie laughed and said, "My wife has a funny story about meeting him."

C—At the time [1856], she was about twelve years old, and was visiting Lincoln's cousin Susanna Hanks. They went over to visit [Stephen] Douglas. After seeing Douglas, she said to her friends, "Let's go over and see Cousin Abe." And she went trailing along. He shook hands with the party and held out his hand to her.

She said, "No, I am a Democrat!" and she stuck her hand behind her, "I've just shaken hands with Mr. Douglas."

Lincoln laughed and said, "I guess she is a strong Democrat like her father." Her father was the leader of the Democrats, but he and Lincoln were close friends; they did not let politics interfere.

Although she never met him again, it was she he asked for. He remembered her.

I knew the Hanks family very well—a plain Illinois family. There was old John Hanks; he was the one that brought the rails to the Convention.

Dennis Hanks was a genteeler man in dress and appearance, just like an ordinary country lawyer. He taught school and could read and write fluently, and was considered a pretty smart man for his day and generation; he was quite a man.

Old Johnny always remained a farmer, and every Saturday attended the village market.

No, Lincoln was not coarse, as many tried to make him out. You put him in a crowd of a thousand, and you'd pick him out as being a grade above them. He wasn't low at all, nothing low about him. He was solemn and when he told a story, original or quoted, he never laughed. He let others attend to that.

Mrs. Christie then joined us and told me of Lincoln.

Mrs. C—In making Lincoln you must be careful to bring out his good nature. He used to have a smile.

C—Yes, a smile without a grin.

Mrs. C—Yes, his clothes used to hang on him. They were not tailor-made; no one wore tailor-made clothes in those days. They had no tailors in those little towns. They were mostly made by women.

Turning to her husband, she said, "I made a vest for him."

Mrs. C—My name was Sarah Cantrell. My father was William Cantrell. There is a street in Decatur named after him. They called him the "wheel horse of Democracy." I felt very proud when I danced with Douglas at a reception given him, and with him led the March. He was the personification of neatness. He was small of stature. His manners were perfect, very polite, very polished. His wife was a great beauty. While (here she laughed) Mrs. Lincoln was a sort of a tyrant, and very high strung.

Sarah Ford used to tell how when she was a young girl, Lincoln used to visit her, but she was disgusted because he used to come to town barefooted.

He used to come from the Hanks farm with a load of wood, with his shoes hung on the coupling of his wagon. And when he reached town he would put them on.

She afterwards married William Wheeler, who never got higher than Sheriff. She used to say after, "If Abe Lincoln had not come barefoot, I might have been the wife of the President of the United States."


C—It was not unusual; Senator Dick Oglesby used to go barefooted. I lived a block from him. They all did in the summer time. You can see the characteristic. You can see what the times were. After Lincoln became President, all these things came up.

K—Did you ever see Oglesby barefoot?

Mrs. C—I don't remember.

C—It was so common she wouldn't notice it if she did.

Mrs. C—The women used to card and spin on a wheel and weave cotton and wool into lindsey-woolsey or blue-jean. It was closely woven and dyed with indigo, which was easy to get. When I knew Lincoln, he had got beyond that—into broadcloth.

I saw him when he was debating with Douglas. He talked in a conversational way, not demonstrative. He would interest you—like a story, not carry you off with great things.

C—Yes, he was himself—no one else.

K—My friend, Oliver Poole, told me it was fortunate that Lincoln met Douglas in those debates—it was equal to a college education. (Reading from my notes) Poole said, "Douglas was just the man to whet Lincoln's powers to the finest point. It seems providential that Douglas was on the ground with Lincoln; it was such steel that he wielded that brought such brilliant flashes from Lincoln's steel, and keyed his intellect for the great contest in which he was to meet the greatest minds of the age. After Douglas, they all came easy."

## Lincoln Voting for Winfield Scott in 1852
## Letter from Mr. Robert O. Mills
Mill Valley, California, November 6, 1922

My dear Kelly:

Yours of late date received and I now proceed to give you the information asked for—depending on Memory.

My personal acquaintance with Abraham Lincoln dates from the early summer of 1844, when he visited the office of the *Coles County Reporter*, Illinois, but I had seen him twice a year for the two previous years, when he came to Charleston, Ill., to attend the spring and fall term of the Circuit Court, in the early spring of 1850.

His [brother-in-law] law partner was Ninian W. Edwards, both of them having terms in Congress.

Mr. Lincoln was elected in 1846—the Mexican War period.

I also knew Stephen A. Douglas personally, and was present at one of his largely attended meetings at Centralia, Illinois during the campaign in 1858, when he and Mr. Lincoln were candidates for U. S. Senator.

Mr. Douglas had a stenographer with him who sat at his feet at the left on an elevated platform; it was the first time I had ever seen a stenographer in action. This young man was a page in the Senate; I believe Mr. Douglas had caused him to be appointed. His name was [Arthur Pue] Gorman and afterwards he was made U. S. Senator from Maryland.

I saw Mr. Lincoln many times a day when he was at home, and when Henry Clay died in 1852, I was present in the crowded Court House in Springfield when Mr. Lincoln delivered his most pathetic eulogy on the life and services of Mr. Clay.

I witnessed men voting on Election Day in 1838, 1840 and 1842, by the "viva voice" system, and which would, I think, if in use now, eliminate the distracting system of the printed ballot, especially at Primaries.

When Mr. Lincoln and I voted at the November Elections in 1852 [Democrat Franklin Pierce vs. Whig Winfield Scott], it was near the noon hour, and we were attired in our everyday togs, which I am glad to say was of a far superior texture than today.

Mr. Lincoln and I voted at the North front of the Court House at Springfield—I was just ahead of him, and voted first; he came next. There was no secret booths to mark tickets, for the Democratic and Whig Parties had supplied their own tickets and the ballot boxes, in which every voter deposited his own Ballot, dropping it into a slot about 3 inches long by a half inch wide—the boxes being eighteen inches long by twelve with locks on same.

On our return from the Election Polls, Lincoln said to me: "Young man, I think I have killed your vote."

I replied that it looked more like a "Stand-off" to me.

That night Lincoln and I were the only passengers in the Fink & Walker Stage Coach—about 9 P.M.—going east. And at every relay, where the horses were changed, we both made a run to the telegraph office for the latest returns. And at Shelbyville, Mr. Lincoln stopped off to attend the fall term of Circuit Court there—my destination being Charleston, about twenty miles east.

When we shook hands, Lincoln remarked: "Young man, from the latest returns I think your candidate has been elected."

# Lawyer Lincoln and Mrs. Cracker
# Interview with Mrs. Sarah K. Hart

Mrs. Sarah K. Hart, of Hastings-on-Hudson, was born in Illinois and saw Lincoln frequently when she was a little girl. She was a bright little lady and had grown old quite gracefully—for she told me she was 80 years old. Her mind is as good if not better than mine is now, and I shouldn't mind growing old if I could do it as well as she has. She certainly thinks Lincoln was the most wonderful man ever created.

Mrs. H—The world has never seen another man like Lincoln. I never saw him after he was president, but quite a few of us younger people who were very much interested in him followed him when we could in his debates with Douglas.

He was never well dressed, partly because he didn't have money enough. He wore homespun pantaloons made of half cotton and half wool and they never seemed long enough. He had blue stockings and homemade shoes with laces of buckskin. I remember his shoes particularly because when we were children our father was very particular about our keeping our shoe laces neatly tied and Lincoln's laces were untied. He always wore a battered rusty hat.

His eyes were bluish gray but they seemed to change with his moods. When he was talking his eyes were dark and seemed to light up within, but often he had a sad, far-away look for there was quite a strain of melancholy in Lincoln. At times he was very quiet and would not talk and apparently didn't hear when any one spoke to him, but at these times his friends and those who knew him left him alone. His mouth was large and not prepossessing and his jaw impressed strangers as bull-doggish, but when he smiled his face was transfigured—I can't—and no one can—describe the beautiful light that would come into his eyes and his sweet wonderful smile. He was so kind, and loved children and old people.

I first knew Lincoln when I was a little girl and he stopped at my father's cabin. We lived between Springfield and Peoria in the 8th judicial district. They had circuit court then and they traveled from one place to another. The stage stopped at our house for water as there was not much good water in the country then.

Now I'll tell you my pet story of Lincoln. I was playing one June day with my rag dolls. Then the country was sparsely settled and we had to depend upon ourselves for amusement. I had quite a few rag dolls but my favorite was Mrs. Cracker, who was larger than the rest. The house stood back from the main road on a little knoll and the grass sloped down in front. Close to the house was a picket fence which went all around the house. I had lined up Mrs. Cracker and the other dolls against the gate when I heard the stage horn which was a long brass horn. I forgot my dolls and climbed up on the fence for the stage then was quite an event. The stage stopped and several people got down but I only remember two clearly. One was a tall lanky fellow with a linen duster which hadn't seen the wash tub in some time and a dirty felt hat. He was not at all well dressed. The other was a short very well dressed man with a gold headed cane. I had never seen a gold headed cane before and I was quite impressed. I had forgotten Mrs. Cracker while looking at the tall man and when they came to the gate, Mrs. Cracker blocked the way. The shorter man shoved the gate open and struck Mrs. Cracker with his cane knocking her aside into the dust. You can imagine how I felt. He might as well have struck me as my doll and I was very angry as well as hurt. But before I could rescue Mrs. Cracker, Lincoln picked her up, brushed her off with his red bandana handkerchief, laid her carefully in my arms and with the most wonderful smile said, "Never mind, Black Eyes, your baby isn't hurt."

Ten years after Lincoln's death I went to a memorial service at his grave. A Mr. William Affleck spoke and it was one of the most impressive services I have ever seen. I afterwards met Mr. Affleck who was an Englishman. When Lincoln was made president he had come from England in a very critical state of mind to see what this rail splitter was going to do. But he came to criticize and staid to love. He rented a room near the White House so that he could watch Lincoln closely. Every morning very early he could see Lincoln walking up and down, up and down outside wrestling with the problems of the day before him. After he had watched him for some time he said his heart just ached for him and he wished that he could help him. One morning he could stand it no longer and he went out and stole between the guards and followed Lincoln up and down. Lincoln did not see him but he walked and prayed and wept, and finally walked beside him and slipped his arm through Lincoln's and tried to tell him without words all that he felt. Lincoln looked down into his face and laid his hand over Mr. Affleck's. Neither spoke, and together they walked up and down. Every morning they walked together, and they never spoke. Mr. Affleck said that now America was his home for "where he lived I live and where he died I die." He said he only wished that he might be buried near Lincoln. Robert Lincoln heard this and gave him a deed for a plot near theirs.

## Recollections of Abraham Lincoln and Horace Greeley in 1861
## Interview with Andrew J. Provost

Calling on Mr. Andrew Jackson Provost of 403 Washington Avenue, Brooklyn, he greeted me very friendly, and in regard to introducing Horace Greeley to Mr. Lincoln, he said, "It is a short story," and dictated the following:

P—I was a member of the legislature of 1860-61; the last year I was unanimously elected for Kings County. Another member of the legislature was Benjamin Camp, one of the assistant editors of the *Tribune*. I was appointed one of the committee to receive the newly elected President Lincoln when he arrived at Albany.

The night before we were to meet Mr. Lincoln, Ben Camp came into my room and said, "Provost, I want you to do me a great favor. You know that the 'Powers that be' here now is the Seward group of the Republican party; they intend to take Mr. Lincoln in charge, and prevent Greeley from having anything to do with him. Now I want you to manage it in some way to get Mr. Greeley a chance to have an interview with Mr. Lincoln."

"Well," I said, "Ben, I'd like to do anything I could for you, but why come to me, a Democrat, and not one of your Republican friends?" He replied, "You know I can't trust them—and I can trust you." I said, "Ben, I like to help the under dog, and I will do what I can for you. You have Mr. Greeley on the depot platform at Utica at 8 o'clock sharp, and if I can, I'll get him on the train, and seek an interview with Mr. Lincoln."

Well, the first man I saw on the platform at Utica was Mr. Greeley, whom I knew by sight, but never had any acquaintance with him. As the Presidential train came in, I got Mr. Greeley's arm, and told him I would try and get him on the train, which I succeeded in doing. I was taken up to Mr. Lincoln and introduced. I lay back until the other members of the Committee were away; then I said, "Mr. President, perhaps I have been very indiscreet, and if I have, I want to be reprimanded for what I have done." At this time he had gotten himself up, and it looked as though he would never stop. He looked down on me with a smile, such as I had never seen before—it lighted up his whole countenance, and said:

"Well, my son, what have you been doing?"

"Well, I said, "Mr. President, Mr. Greeley was anxious to have an interview, which the Republican gang in this State intend to frustrate, and I, feeling that Mr. Greeley ought to have an interview with you, if he wants it, I have smuggled him on this train." He said, "Do you mean to tell me that Mr. Greeley is on this train?" I said, "Yes, may I bring him to you?" He replied, "No, Sir, you take me to Mr. Greeley." I took him over. When we approached Mr. Greeley, he got up and they shook hands cordially; then I left them together—they had a half-hour's talk.

After Mr. Lincoln had gone back to his seat, I went over to him again and said, "Mr. President, our Committee is in trouble. We have arranged to entertain you at the best hotel in Albany, the Delavan House, where all the people can see you. And the Republican Powers that be have arranged to take you to the house of the Governor, where they will be the exclusive members of the party, to benefit by your stay. Now, I am a Democrat. You are President of the United States, and we Democrats want to show you that we realize that fact—"

Just then the man [Benjamin Welsh] in charge of the train came hurriedly up and said, "Mr. President, the Governor has completed all arrangements to entertain you while in Albany." Mr. Lincoln turned sharply around and said, "Gen. Welsh, you telegraph to Gov. Morgan that I am going with the Committee to the Delavan House, and if I hear any more about this matter, I'll go through Albany and not stop at all." And as he turned around, smiling, and with a most pleasant smile on his face, he wrinkled his nose, and said, "I guess that will settle Welsh."

Mrs. Lincoln sat in the seat just opposite the President, and she said, "Young man, come here (I was about 25 or 26 at that time); I want to have a talk with you. Sit down here by me." She said, "You are a Democrat?" I answered, "Yes—perhaps that's unfortunate." "No," she replied, "I am a Democrat too; the only trouble between Mr. Lincoln and I, is my Democracy."

We had a very pleasant conversation all the remaining way to Albany. That night at the Delavan House, Mr. Lincoln was nicely dressed, very polite and gentle, and well received. He was entirely transformed—neatly dressed and well dressed.

He was in good shape, and made a good impression on everyone, while Mrs. Lincoln, who was about 45 years of age, dressed like a young girl of 18—shoulder straps, bare arms, with white gloves to the elbows. She had on every ring she owned, on the outside of her gloves. After Mr. Lincoln had his dinner, he went to his room.

## Lincoln and the Telegraph Operator
## Interview with Alonzo J. Burton, March 22, 1923

I met Mr. Alonzo Burton, a former telegraph operator, at his home at 139 South Oxford Street in Brooklyn. He met me on the stoop of his home and taking me into the parlor, we then started our talk on Lincoln. He told me he saw Lincoln on his way to Washington to be inaugurated. He said:

B—I first saw him February 19, 1861, on his way to Washington at Fishkill Landing. The train he was on stopped there. He appeared on the rear platform. It had not been reported that he was coming, and, as I remember, there was a very small number to greet him.

At that time, on account of the disturbed condition of the country there was great fear of his enemies obstructing the tracks, and that was the reason the train was watched so closely.

He had a black Prince Albert coat and pants and every thing to correspond. It was a fairly cold day, a pleasant day.

The train only stopped for a couple of minutes. We were on the qui vive. In those times people were very uneasy; there was great unrest. You did not know who was your friend—I tell young men—you do not know what life is till you go through those periods.

The train went on and I did not see him again until I saw him on his way from Washington to West Point on June 23rd, 1862.

I had left Fishkill and was the operator at the 30th Street Depot [New York City]. At about 3 o'clock on June 23rd, we received from the War Department at Washington a request to have a car ready at midnight to go to West Point, but no names were given to whom the train was for. So the last train went out at 9 o'clock, and the Depot was locked for the night. So there was no one left but the watchman, whose name I forgot, and Mr. J. M. Toucey. We were waiting so that the people would get into the Depot when they came.

Just about 11 o'clock we heard a carriage coming down to 30th Street and we went to the door to see if it were the people coming to the train. The carriage stopped, out stepped Mr. Lincoln and one army officer in uniform; I never asked his name. Mr. Lincoln was about three quarters of an hour ahead of time. The engine was not quite ready, so he took a seat. Mr. Toucey sat at Mr. Lincoln's right and I sat at Mr. Toucey's right. The announcement was made that the train was ready, and he got aboard. It is positive that no soul in New York other than us three knew that Mr. Lincoln was in New York. He was very polite. He did not act arrogant—he was mild and affable. I do not remember if he shook hands.

As soon as the train arrived at West Point, they telegraphed down to New York that the President had arrived.

And when he returned next day about noon, 30th Street was a mass of people to see the President. But we had a nice little "picnic" the night before. When he arrived at the Depot, as near as I can remember, he got into his carriage and rode right off. The published accounts that he got in at Chambers Street and came up to the Depot at 30th Street in a car drawn by horses, as they used to do at that time, is not true; he came in a carriage as I tell you which was a quicker way.

In December '59 while I was the telegraph operator at Fishkill, a cousin of mine—David Young, was a conductor on the Morning Express. The train reached Fishkill about 10 o'clock. Young rushed into the office—the train only stopped at Fishkill about a minute—and says, "Go quick to the baggage car to see the box that John Brown's body is in." It was in a very plain pine box—not even painted, and as crude as a box could be. I took a good look at it and the train was off.

## Lincoln's Reception at City Hall, New York, February 20, 1861
## Interview with Laurus Loomis

Laurus Loomis, the author, cotton man and philanthropist, had written an article for the *New York Herald* describing the reception at which he had been present. I wrote to him about it, and he invited me to call at his office. I asked him for further details about his article, and he said:

L—I was about seventeen-years-old, and lived with my widowed mother in East Broadway near Pike Street. I was one of those who formed in the line from Broadway and Chambers Street, through the Park and up the rear stairs of the City Hall, through the rotunda to the Governor's Room, where President Lincoln was receiving the citizens during his passage through New York on his way to Washington, February 20, 1861. Mr. Lincoln was standing in the Governor's Room, Mayor Fernando Wood was on his left, and asked the name of each visitor, then would repeat it to Mr. Lincoln, who would shake hands with each one.

I remember there was a very tall man in front of me, and Mayor Wood got our names mixed, introducing him by the name of Loomis, and me by the name of—we'll say, Johnstone—that was not it, but will do; I blushed and said, "Mr. Lincoln, my name is Loomis." Then he shook hands and repeated it. I thought him the greatest man. He was tall, with a kindly expression; looked the very personification of heart; he was an all right, upright man.

I showed Mr. Loomis my sketch of the scene; he said, "That's about it."

L—Mayor Wood stood on President Lincoln's left. I was dressed in a short jacket and knickerbockers, and wore a cap. I did not notice anything else, and the line filed out on the east side of the Governor's Room to Park Row.

I was a worshiper of Lincoln. I worked for George W. Powers Co., Dry Goods, at 11 Dey Street, for two dollars a week. I was very much shocked to hear Mr. Powers say that Lincoln was a backwoodsman, a rail-splitter, and not fit to be President. I went home and told my mother how badly I felt; she said, "My son, when Mr. Powers is dead, forgotten, and buried in some lonely cemetery, Mr. Lincoln's name will stand out through the ages!" My mother said, "I had a dream about President Lincoln. I dreamed that he was carrying a pole, and that he came to a place in the ground; he sat the pole down in the ground, and it stood upright without support at its base, and he dropped dead beside it. Now I fear he will meet with some tragic end."

When President Lincoln was assassinated, I was a member of the Norfolk Street Methodist Church—now a Jewish synagogue. On Saturday morning, there was no emblem of mourning on the church so I started with a man much older than myself and bought several dollars worth of crepe and with it we draped the church and balcony. The minister was a copperhead. Sunday morning when he came in, he saw it but made no allowance to President Lincoln's death.

That afternoon, the Clinton Fire Company went round to his house and told him if he did not make an address about the death of President Lincoln, he would be mobbed.

I remember Boston [Thomas P.] Corbett who shot John Wilkes Booth; he was a Sunday School teacher in the Norfolk Street Church. He used to part his hair in the middle; I never noticed he was [religiously] eccentric then.

The sexton of the Willett Street Methodist Church, Mr. Peter Relyea, was a friend of mine. He had the contract for the catafalque which was used when Lincoln's body lay in state at the City Hall. When he was working on it, he said, "Would you like a piece of this," and taking a pair of scissors, cut a piece of the black cloth and some of the silver fringe and gave it to me. I had a box with a brass binding in which I kept it for years, but it has become mislaid.

After President Lincoln was assassinated, boy as I was, I started on to Washington and saw Ford's Theatre where he was shot, and where Booth had run out when he jumped from the box. I remember there was an old colored woman who had a shanty in the alley at the rear of the theatre; while I stood there she came out and spoke of Booth, and in that colored vernacular she said, "Thar's whar he stood his lil black horse. Ah seed him dar. Ah seed him jump on."

## Lincoln Raising the Flag at Independence Hall, February 22, 1861 Interview with William H. Thomas

I saw Lincoln raise the flag on Independence Hall, February 22, 1861. He arrived in Philadelphia on Thursday afternoon the day before. He got in a carriage and the procession marched; I did not follow him further. He went to the Continental Hotel. I was a great admirer of Lincoln—my father took the *Tribune*. I saw him later when he made a short address from the Continental Hotel and I heard he was to raise the flag the following day at Independence Hall at 7 o'clock. I arrived early and Lincoln shortly after. He rode down in a carriage escorted by the Scott's Legion and two Battalions.

The people greeted him with cheers. He went into Independence Hall first—the room where the Declaration was signed. It was in there he made that famous speech. There had been a drizzling rain, but it had cleared off. A platform had been erected in front of the building; it was draped with a large flag. He came out and mounted the platform. He then made a short address, but he was so far off and the crowd was so dense and there was a row of trees between us—I could not hear it.

He had on an overcoat, but took it off before starting to raise the flag. He then said: "I will now carry out why I am here."

After the flag-raising, a salute was fired from the batteries which were in the rear of the Hall. The flag had a new star on it as Kansas just entered into the

Union.  He referred to the new star in the speech—I could not hear it, but I read it in the newspapers. It was reported as follows:
(Here Mr. Thomas read me Lincoln's speech.)

"Mr. Cuyler:

"I am filled with deep emotion at finding myself standing here, in this place, where were collected together the wisdom, the patriotism, the devotion to principle, from which sprang the institutions under which we live.  You have kindly suggested to me that in my hands is the task of restoring peace to the present distracted condition of the country.  I can say in return, Sir, that all the political sentiments I entertain have been drawn, so far as I have been able to draw them, from the sentiments which originated and were given to the world from this hall.  I have never had a feeling politically that did not spring from the sentiments embodied in the Declaration of Independence.  I have often pondered over the dangers which were incurred by the men who assembled here, and framed and adopted that Declaration of Independence.  I have pondered over the toils that were endured by the officers and soldiers of the army who achieved that Independence.  I have often inquired of myself, what great principle or idea it was that kept this Confederacy so long together.  It was not the mere matter of the separation of the Colonies from the motherland; but that sentiment in the Declaration of Independence which gave liberty, not alone to the people of this country, but, I hope, to the world, for all future time.  It was that which gave promise, that in due time the weight would be lifted from the shoulders of all men.  This is a sentiment embodied in the Declaration of Independence.  Now, my friends, can this country be saved upon that basis? If it can, I will consider myself one of the happiest men in the world, if I can help to save it.  If it cannot be saved upon that principle, it will be truly awful. But if this country cannot be saved without giving up that principle, I was about to say I would rather be assassinated on this spot than surrender it.

"Now, in my view of the present aspect of affairs, there need be no bloodshed and war.  There is no necessity for it.  I am not in favor of such a course, and I may say, in advance, that there will be no bloodshed unless it be forced upon the Government, and then it will be compelled to act in self-defense.

"My friends, this is wholly an unexpected speech, and I did not expect to be called upon to say a word when I came here.  I supposed it was merely to do something toward raising the flag.  I may, therefore, have said something indiscreet. (Cries of "No, no")  I have said nothing but what I am willing to live by and, if it be the pleasure of Almighty God, die by."

I cannot recall his appearance very well. What I first saw was that he wore a stove pipe hat. He did not look depressed or melancholy, but he was a somber-looking man. After the flag-raising, he started for Harrisburg. Then without any one knowing it, he went direct through [Philadelphia and Baltimore] to Washington to be inaugurated.

Later in the war I joined the army for a short time, and after the war I became a member of the Pennsylvania Grand Army Post No. 2.

One evening at a meeting, I think it was in 1902, I thought this is the anniversary of Lincoln's "Flag Raising," and it occurred to me that it should be commemorated.

I recalled when I was in Westminster Abbey, I saw the tomb of George Peabody—it consisted of a flat stone inserted in the pavement and I thought that would be a good honor of marking the spot where Lincoln had stood during the flag raising—on account of Washington's statue standing near and never could an upright memorial be placed on that spot. I mentioned this idea to a comrade who sat next to me. My comrade stood up and suggested that I should be invited by the chairman to make a few remarks; I then explained my idea. A committee was appointed with me as chairman. I sent out circulars and the panel was procured; my daughter unveiled it.

K—Then you are responsible for the tablet being there?

T—Yes, I am responsible for the tablet being placed there.

## Interview with Captain W. W. Burroughs on Lincoln Raising the Flag at Independence Hall, February 22, 1861

On June 6, 1924, I met Capt. W. W. Burroughs at the New York Custom House and speaking of Lincoln, he said:

B—I saw him raise the flag at Independence Hall. It was at sunrise, February 22, 1861. Although the papers had announced it the evening before, there was not a great rush. I was a boy at the time. I got there early; I was first in line. It was roped off to keep the crowd back; I was against the rope.

He came from the center door of Independence Hall, with three citizens, who were the committee, I suppose, on the occasion. He was dressed in the customary garb—tall hat, long frock coat, black trousers. He was perfectly neat; his clothes fitted him well.

Half way from the door to the flagstaff, which had been raised for the occasion, the committee stopped. Mr. Lincoln stepped over and advanced to the position of the staff, where the flag was, and commenced to raise it by the lanyards. The flag was in a ball. After he raised it from ten to twenty feet from the ground on the sixty foot staff, then he dropped the lanyard and the flag fell to the sidewalk.  Then he took off his coat, which incommoded him, handed it to one of the committee; then in his shirtsleeves, he took the lanyard and raised the flag to the peak, and broke it out.  He did that himself.  The ceremony was entirely simple.  No guns were fired; no ceremony.  It is possible there was cheering; I recall none.  My eyes were busy; my ears were not.

The flag was folded man-of-war fashion, in a sort of a ball—kept in that shape by a loop in the lanyard.  As it was drawn to the peak, he jerked the loose, or running line, which detached the loop, and the flag flashed to the crisp breeze.

## Interview with Artist George Henry Story, Painter of Lincoln

George H. Story was born in New Haven, Connecticut, January 22, 1835, and in 1859, went to Washington D. C., as an associate of photographer Mathew Brady.  While at Washington, Story painted portraits of Lincoln and other distinguished men.  From 1889 to 1906, he was curator, Department of Paintings, Metropolitan Museum of Art, New York City, and curator emeritus from 1906 until his death on November 24, 1922.

I first met Mr. Story at the gallery of the Art Students League which was formerly the studio of J. Gurney & Son, photographers, and the building itself was on the southwest corner of Fifth Avenue and 16th Street.  In 1860, that was the Athenaeum, where Abraham Lincoln was entertained by the Young Men's Central Republican Union on the evening of the Cooper Institute speech.

When I first met Mr. Story, he was blue-eyed, rosy-cheeked and golden haired—a perfect type of blond.  He wore a long mustache and goatee, southern fashion.  His whole manner radiated the sunshine of his face.  I will never forget the encouragement that he gave me in those early days.

I called on Mr. Story a few years before his death, and received from him the following interesting and valuable information.

I showed him the picture of Lincoln that Brady gave me.

S—That's good, but it looks relaxed.  The portrait that I painted of him was the best contour, although Robert Lincoln liked this one—this is the homey, fireside Lincoln; not the vital or one in action; it was taken by Brady in 1863.

K—I think "Bull Run" [Sir William H.] Russell's description of Lincoln caricatures him; he spoke of his enormous hands, long arms, long legs and knocked knees.

S—He had long arms; he had long legs, and he had a long head, but he did not have large hands.

K—You can see in my photograph, his hand was like mine, very like. His were thin and shapely, so were his feet. He was not knocked kneed.

S—The purport of his inmost thoughts were enforced by gentle gestures. He had a very fatherly tone in speaking to his Cabinet. He did not drive them.

He once had a Bill he decided must be put through. He called his Cabinet together and they voted against it unanimously. Instead of scolding and talking about it and telling them they must do it, as he had the power to do, he merely turned to the Secretary and said, "The vote seems to be unanimous, please record it in favor of my motion," at which the Cabinet all laughed.

Lincoln did not assert himself. One time Grant made some demand. Lincoln wrote out an order to [Edwin] Stanton; Stanton sent word back he would not carry it out. Lincoln put on his hat and went over to the War Office, sat down and talked to Stanton, but did not refer to the order. At last Lincoln got up and started to go, and then said, "Stanton, what about that order?"

Stanton said, "No, I won't obey it."

Lincoln went over to Stanton's desk, sat down, and said with a smile, "Stanton, I guess you will have to do it."

And he did it. As he knew if he did not he might as well hand in his portfolio. Now that is the way he did things. He knew he had the power. He chose to do it that way instead of storing, and saying, "You must do it; I am President of the United States!"

K—How did he speak in public?

S—He began low and his voice would rise in proportion to his inmost thought. It was round and smooth, it seemed to come from within, not bellow. He never threw up his arms. He might bring them down to enforce his idea with gentle gesture.

I have heard him speak over and over again. I did not hear his Gettysburg speech.

K—I had heard in that speech, Lincoln held his hands clasped in front of him.

S—I shouldn't wonder, it only took a few minutes. As a contrast, I have heard General [Congressman Roger A.] Pryor speak to Congress before the War—I have never mentioned this before. His speech was bitter and sarcastic. He became greatly excited. He called out, "I hope the South will decide as quickly as lightning follows the thunder!" In his excitement, he got it mixed. He got the cart before the horse at which the congressmen began to laugh, at which it broke him all up.

He [Lincoln] got to like me. I have heard him speak over and over again. He had a habit when he was speaking of placing his hands on his hips and rising on the tips of his toes which made him look ten feet high.

K—Did Lincoln close his fists on his hips or place them with his hands open with his fingers to the front?

S—I think open with his fingers to the front. Fists on the hips would look like a scolding woman.

I stood up and took the action I proposed to carry out.

S—That looks like him and that appeals to me!

I showed him a photograph of Barnard's statue.

S—Barnard is theatrical and wanted to represent him as a rail-splitter; he split rails, but that did not make him a rail-splitter. Lincoln was above his surroundings—a leader of the other boys; he had fine beautiful hands. His feet were not knotted like Barnard's statue; Barnard makes him look as though he had rheumatism. Even his clothes are wrong—he did not wear that kind of clothes. There was nothing grotesque about his hat or his clothes.

In regards to Barnard, he then referred to a story that Lincoln told:

S—When Lincoln told a story it was to illustrate a point. In a law case he said of the opposing counsel, "My learned friend reminds me of a fellow who had a steamboat on the Mississippi River, with a twenty pound boiler and a forty pound whistle; and when he started to blow the whistle, the boat stopped. That is the way with our friend—when he begins to talk, his brain ceases to work."

Here Mr. Story made a lot of bristling adjectives in depreciation of Barnard's statue. He then got up and showed me a letter from Robert T. Lincoln, thanking him for and praising a photograph of that painting, which is in the National Portrait Gallery, Washington. He said that Robert Lincoln felt very badly at the way his father had been abused and vilified—the Barnard statue seemed to be the crowning insult, the way it misrepresented him. I asked Mr. Story how Robert Lincoln liked Saint-Gaudens' statue. "He seemed to like it, but I do not," he answered.

S—I painted Lincoln's portrait. In June 1861, I was asked by [Alexander] Gardner to fill an order for a portrait of Lincoln from a photograph. I replied that I must have sittings, and was told that the President could not give the time for them; but that the artist might sit in his office while Lincoln transacted business, and get what he could.

[Secretary John G.] Nicolay said, "You come whenever you like and sit in my room and sketch the President." I went to his office for three days; he did not give me regular sittings, but I watched him as he was dealing with men. I have seen him sit for nearly half-an-hour in deep thought while probably twenty men sat around waiting. He would then look up and beckon to a man and go on talking; I watched Lincoln at work.

K—Did Lincoln know?

S—Yes. He said, "Don't you bother me and I won't bother you. Go right ahead. I have no time to sit for you." I had a good chance to study his character and expression when off his guard. Of course when sitting at his desk, he would sometimes droop when tired, but not when speaking. I made a dozen sketches.

K—What did he think of them?

S—Oh, he said, "All right." He didn't care anymore about pictures than a street gamin.

Mr. Story then referred to his painting of Lincoln.

S—Some people think it is not serious enough.

K—From what I understand from his character, it is very characteristic.

S—Yes, there was always about his mouth a suppressed play of humor. I never saw him in shabby clothes. He was one of the best dressed men in Washington. He always wore fine broadcloth. I never saw him wear that shawl; he may have. Most men wore them in the 60's. I wore one myself. It was gray Scotch plaid.

K—How was Nicolay?

S—He was lovely. He was very delicate. I would go over there and he would receive me and say, "Come right in," and he would bring me into Mr. Lincoln's office. Mr. Lincoln would be at work. He would look around, never would stand up; he would smile and nod towards a chair which Nicolay had placed for me. I would watch and sketch Mr. Lincoln until it was time for him to go to dinner.

[Secretary John] Hay was very small; he was a little fellow. He sat in the same room. Nicolay was really Secretary, and had a room to himself. Hay was his assistant. He used to belong to the same club I did. He was very opinionated, and if it were not for his literary ability and his power of expressing himself in writing, he would never have reached the political position he did.


Referring again to his painting of Lincoln, which was very fine in drawing and detail as well as in the entire spirit, though the complexion struck me as very pure or fresh, not swarthy or weather-beaten as I imagined Lincoln to have been. Mr. Story said, "Now that was not Lincoln's complexion. I believe in idealizing the complexion of a man, and not painting in sunburn and blemishes. Washington did not have the complexion which Gilbert Stuart painted in his portraits, as shown by the paintings of Peale and Trumbull. Stuart made the best of him.

So far as I know, I am the last [surviving] artist who saw Lincoln, for which I deserve no credit, as I merely happened to be around. [Leonard W.] Volk's Lincoln is merely a copy of the mask, with all the features drawn and sunken, and that is not the way Lincoln looked—his face was not sunken."


Mathew Brady's memory is so intimately associated with Lincoln that I asked Mr. Story about Brady's method of running his gallery in Washington.

S—In the 1850's, I used to carve figureheads for the ships in Maine—got sick and in 1859, I came to New York and called on Brady's Gallery. Brady told me not to be discouraged, and gave me a note to Alexander Gardner, the manager of his gallery in Washington. Gardner proposed I should paint portraits in the studio, and he would give me $1,000 a year, but we settled on $20 a week. Gardner was a good business man, as well as a practical photographer, and [Timothy] O'Sullivan was his operator. Brady would run in once in a while, but was generally in New York. Brady had a manner with people—that brought out their best qualities—that was his value. I had a room there; he would get me commissions, and I would give him half. If I got anything independently, I kept it all myself.


Hearing that Mr. Story had looked after Mathew Brady during his last hours, after Father Thomas J. Ducey had attended the photographer in his spiritual way, I asked about Brady's passing.


S—When Brady became ill here in New York late in 1895, I went to Dr. C. Irving Fisher, Superintendent of the Presbyterian Hospital, then at 41 East 70th Street. I also knew Henry S. Marquand, then on the Board of Managers. There was one room costing $50 a week, which I told them to give to me until it was called for. They did so, and Brady went there on December 16. On my way downtown, I stopped in to see him every day.

About 4 o'clock in the afternoon of January 15, 1896, I found Brady in bed talking about the gallery he proposed to start on Broadway, and describing the different rooms. As I was leaving, the doctor said it would be all over that day. Brady died an hour or so after I left. S. P. Avery, the art dealer, and I collected $50 to get a coffin and sent the body to his people in Washington.

Though he did not state it to me, it may be inferred that the hospital bill was paid by Mr. Story.

K—Tell me of Lincoln.

S—There was never a man more abused and belied than Lincoln. He was called uncouth and coarse, and all sorts of stories were told of him which were not true. He was not at all coarse or rough in build.

His soul seemed to rise above his personality. He was full of fire. He would awake and become translated and exalted and forget himself. He indulged in no flourishes of oratory or studied oratorical gestures. He was himself—nerved to gesture by the force of his own mind and the action of his soul; without giving it a thought, which gave him a Lordly quality. It is wrong to represent him drooping; he was alert.

The picture [of Lincoln] that I posed for Alexander Gardner was made on February 23, 1861. Lincoln was exhausted. He had ridden all night in the cars and had expected to be assassinated as he went through Baltimore. Allan Pinkerton, the detective, had warned him.

Gardner was manager for Brady, and I had my studio in the same building. Gardner knew nothing about art, and used to pose his patrons all one way. If there were a Senator, he would have him standing erect with his hand in the breast of his frock-coat, and the other hand resting on a pillar, or a table. It was laughable. I used to say, "Gardner, why don't you change your pose?" But he would say, "Oh, it's good enough. They don't know the difference."

But sometimes, when important men came in he would come to my studio and say, "Old Seward is coming, or, old [Salmon] Chase,"—that's the way he used to refer to them—"and I wish you'd come down and pose them for me." So I would go down and arrange the pose for him.

One day [February 23, 1861] he came in and said, "Lincoln's here. Come in and pose him." I was very much pleased with the prospect of meeting him, and immediately hurried in. When I went in he was carelessly seated at a table waiting to be posed. He did not utter a word and seemed absolutely unconscious of all that was going on about him.

His appearance showed that he was overwhelmed with fatigue, care and anxiety. They wanted me to pose him. "Pose him!" I exclaimed, "No, bring the camera at once." I did not pose him. It was so characteristic of him, I said, "Take him as he is." I saw that in that unconscious pose or attitude a great picture might be taken—and it is at least one of the finest photographs of Lincoln, showing him seated at the little walnut table in Brady's studio, with his tall hat placed upside down upon it.

It was the first time I had seen him, and he had just taken his night trip through Baltimore to his inauguration. He was very much depressed after the night ride, and looked as though he had the cares of the world upon him. After this when I saw him he was entirely different.

As soon as I saw the man, I trusted him. I had received private information that undoubtedly war would come, but knew instinctively that he was the man to handle the situation. There was a solemnity, dignity and a general air that bespoke weight of character that was convincing at our first meeting. Honesty was written in every line of that face. In dress his appearance was elegant, his clothes being of the finest broadcloth. Nor was he awkward, in spite of his great height, and his hands, considering his size, were small and shapely.

I heard him make his inaugural address. Mrs. Hannibal Hamlin was a schoolmate of Mrs. Story, and it was through her that we became intimate with the Lincolns. We attended all his functions.

K—You knew Hannibal Hamlin?

S—Yes. His second wife [Ellen V.] was an Emery and a schoolmate of my wife. They always kept up their friendship, and when we went to Washington, of course that brought us right into the Lincoln circle. He and President Lincoln were in perfect accord. They were very friendly. Not like some of our later Presidents and Vice-Presidents. Hamlin always wore an old fashioned swallow-tail coat—never an overcoat, but of course heavy underwear in winter.

K—Why did he not serve a second term?

S—Oh, I don't know; maybe he was too old. He did not care for society and was very quiet. So was Lincoln. He did not care for society, but endured it, while Mrs. Lincoln liked it, and was severely criticized. For instance, she would drive down Pennsylvania Avenue in a barouche drawn by a pair of high-metalled horses, and would draw up to the curb and buy a half a dozen oranges from a peddler. People would criticize this, but it doesn't do to judge. It may have been just naturalness. She was herself. It was Springfield all over again.

K—When did you see him [Lincoln] for the last time?

S—It was in 1862. Just after [Second] Bull Run. My health was bad, and I left Washington and went to Cuba. I had a studio in Brady's building, and knew a great many Southerners. I used to hear them talk. They talked treason. And when they did, I used to report them to the Government, till at last I became sort of a spy, and had to report some of my best friends. It was hard to do it, but it had to be done. At the boarding house one of them said, "All men above the Mason and Dixon's line were cowards!" I said he was a liar. He drew his pistol across the table. I drew mine. The guests separated us. He sent me a challenge. I sent him word that I accepted it, and that he had better make his will, as I would kill him. I was a dead shot, and he knew it. I could hit a bull's eye, nine times out of ten. I knew if I got him scared by sending him this message, he could not shoot as he otherwise could. He sent back an apology that he was sorry; he was drunk when he said it.

## My Last Meeting with Mr. Story—March 17, 1922

Mr. Story called at my studio, and as usual I led him up to talk of Lincoln by asking him if Lincoln knew when they were trying to put things over on him, as I heard it was hard for him to say, "No."

S—He was a keen one. I have heard him say, "No." And he would say it in a manner that they would never come back.

Some men would come to him with an application for Consulship, who probably was interested in many other businesses.

Lincoln would say: "You come here recommended by your Congressman. Now what are your qualifications? Are you a lawyer?" Etc.

And after putting half a dozen questions, the man would incriminate himself.

Then Lincoln would say: "You have stated so and so, which proves your disqualification for the place which you are soliciting. No!"

K—They say Douglas held Lincoln's hat during his first inauguration.

S—He did. I saw him. Douglas held his hat.

Lincoln stood on the rough platform. He took off his hat—in his right hand—So (Story imitated him). He held a paper in the other. He looked round hesitating.

Douglas who was sitting near, leaned forward and took it and held it during the ceremony.

K—How did Lincoln act when he did it?

S—Oh, as a matter of course. He handed it to him as he would to anybody.

Mr. Story then started to leave and turning, said with a smile, "It all comes back to me by your questioning." This was the last time I met my friend, George H. Story.

## Lincoln's Third Secretary—William O. Stoddard
December 20, 1919

I had written to William O. Stoddard, who served as Lincoln's secretary along with John Nicolay and John Hay. Mr. Stoddard responded to me from his home in Madison, New Jersey.

My Dear Sir:
I am indeed interested in your proposed Lincoln sculpture. Perhaps I could criticize a sketch with proposed conditions. I will not say anything unpleasant concerning other attempts to present Lincoln in stone or otherwise. Some have succeeded pretty well. One idea seems to have been generally forgotten: DO NOT represent him as if he were half asleep, or in mourning. Make him living! For he was one of the most "all alive" of men; such a man sitting for a photograph is sure to look as tired and sleepy as he knows how.

Remember that he was exceptionally vigorous physically, and notably outspoken in all his utterances—NEVER WEAK. I have seen his face light up as if God had kindled a bonfire behind it. He was always plain and simple in dress, but never seedy or odd. Try and make his face living. Make it as if he were leaning half-way across the table in his room and reading an important paper he was preparing to send. As he said, "I can form a better opinion of it after I have heard it read aloud." But in reading, his face was all alive.

What I hope for is that you will not attempt another picture of the dead Lincoln. His photograph is before me while I write. Study the firmness of the mouth, and the uprightness of the head. His neck was NOT limp or stooping. I do not now think of any other suggestions.

Yours truly,
William O. Stoddard

On November 29, 1921, William Stoddard's daughter, Mrs. Harold S. Buttenheim, personally typed and sent me the following notes on Lincoln:

S—If there was any one thing more than another concerning which the people of the United States knew nothing of any consequence in the year 1861, it was war. They had read about it, and that was about all, except for a few regular army men, and a few who could boast of having served in the war with Mexico. In the city of Washington, as in other cities, there were Militia organizations, but none of those were worth much to the country just then. The "crack" corps was a company of eminent young men who regarded themselves as the pink of chivalry. Almost all of them were either from slaveholding States or natives of the District of Columbia.

As the prospect of hostilities grew darker, the secessionist captain of the Rifles resigned and went to offer his services to the Sunny South, and more than half of his comrades in the militia business followed his example. This had a remarkable consequence for me. Hardly was it known that I was appointed Secretary to President Lincoln before a fine young fellow came and told me that he was trying to get recruits for his company, but that all the men he had tried were averse to taking commissions as private soldiers. The current notion seemed to be that what the country needed was an army of finely uniformed and highly paid officers. If, he told me, the President's Secretary would set a patriotic example, he felt sure that the high pride of certain heroes would yield, and they would enlist in the Rifles. Of course I accepted the proposition and went in.

Things were getting thicker, and the day came when we were informed that we were to be sworn into the services of the United States, although no call for troops had yet been sent out by the general Government. It put into my head a very natural question of personal duty, and I decided that I must see Mr. Lincoln about it. That was by no means an easy thing to do in those crowded days. Early in the morning of April 12, 1861, I went upstairs and looked into the official rooms, but they were empty, as I expected to find them.

A bit of topography will help just here. Along the full length of the second story of the White House runs a broad hall with rooms of various sizes and uses on either side of it. Beginning at the eastern end, on the right is a somewhat narrow room which was soon to become my own. On the left is the Private Secretary's room—of the same size. Next to that was a large room, the President's [Office] Room; opposite to that is the large chamber then used by Nicolay and Hay as a sleeping room. Just beyond the grand stairway, the hall over the western wing of the house. On the left is the library, and I had ventured in that far when the folding doors slowly opened. It had been a sunny morning outside, if it were not that every soul in the land was waiting for news from the Rebel siege of Fort Sumter. Not a shot had yet been fired, except at the steamer *Star of the West*, but a sort of pall hung over Washington, and it seemed to me as if there was the gloomiest kind of shadow in the White House.

The doors slowly opened, and Mr. Lincoln very slowly came forward, leaving them open behind him. All beyond was the family part of the house. He was bent until he almost appeared to stoop, and was looking straight before him, as if gazing at something in the distance, or like a man who is listening intently. Just in front of the Library door, I stopped before him, and dared to say, "Good morning, Mr. Lincoln!" He stood stock still for a moment, looking down at my face, but the expression of his own did not change—he may have been listening for the sound of guns in Charleston harbor.

I was astonished—almost alarmed, for there were deep, dark circles under his eyes, and they were vacant. "Why, Mr. Lincoln," I exclaimed, "You don't seem to know me!" "Oh, yes, I do," he responded wearily, "You are Stoddard. What is it?" "I'm here to ask a favor," I said. His lips contracted, for that was about what everybody he met was saying to him then, and he asked in almost petulant manner, "Well, what is it?"

"It's just this, Mr. Lincoln," I said, "I believe there is going to be fighting pretty soon, right here, and I don't feel like sitting at a desk in the Patent Office, or here either, while any fight is going on. I've been serving with a company already, and if it's ordered to duty, I want to go with it." "Very well," he interrupted, with a very different expression on his face, "Why don't you go?" "Why, Mr. Lincoln," I said, "Only a few days ago, I took a pretty big oath to obey your orders, and now I'm likely to be asked to take another to obey somebody else. I don't see how I can manage them both without your permission. I may be ordered to service outside of the District of Columbia.

He half smiled as he cut me short right there. "Go ahead!" he exclaimed, "Swear in! Go wherever you are ordered to go." "That's all I want, Mr. Lincoln," I said, and was turning away when he called back to add with some emphasis, "Young man, go just where you are ordered! Do your duty!" Something else I have forgotten and ended with this, "You won't lose anything by this." Off I went, and he continued on into his office, having granted really the first favor I ever asked of him.

As nearly as I can count it, that was just four hours after the firing of the first Sumter gun; he may have heard the report of it as he was coming out to meet me, but it was many hours before any regular news of it reached Washington. Then came Sunday, but the President's proclamation which went out to the country that night was dated Monday, the 15th. While the people of the North were reading it in the morning papers, the National Rifles, myself among them, were being sworn in in front of the War Office, the first company of volunteers sworn in at the beginning of the Civil War.

Another bad feature of the case for me was a strong idea in my mind that the President's Secretary must set a good example. Therefore, whenever Maj. Smead or Gen. Stone came into the armory and called for volunteers from among our over-wearied fellows for any special duty, it was my place to be on my feet and call out, "Here!" before any other fellow. It speedily obtained for me a laughing sobriquet, for the sergeant on duty would immediately respond, "Stoddard Number One!" Well, it was no disgrace to be known as "Stoddard Number One."

# Lincoln's Orderly
## Interview with William H. Tisdale, Co. D, 11th New York Cavalry

The first time I saw Major William Tisdale was in the Court House. He was standing at attention beside the desk of the presiding Judge. He had the peculiar lofty bearing of an Indian Chief. He afterwards told me he had Indian blood. He had a head of iron grey hair, strong, vigorous, sharp-cut features; bold fronted, full-chested, with powerful, youthful hands. He was one of the finest types of soldier and cavalryman. He enlisted as a bugler in the 11th New York

Cavalry—the unit that served as Lincoln's Body Guard in 1862-1863, and after the war he served with Gen. Custer out west.

I sent Maj. Tisdale the introduction of Mrs. J. R. O'Beirne which assured me a warm reception.

I asked him about Lincoln, and complained that painters and sculptors generally made him slack, like a poor-white with a bad stomach. I told him that I considered Lincoln vigorous and powerful.

K—How did Lincoln strike you?

T—He was not slack. He was one of Nature's noblemen.

K—How did you meet him first?

T—It was when I captured that spy. I was sent over from Georgetown to the War Department with some dispatches. When I got near 19th Street or 20th Street, a fellow came up to me and said, "If you let me look at those dispatches, I will give you $100. We can go right in here (pointing to a saloon) and nobody will know."

I said, "That's not enough for taking such a risk."

"What will you do it for?" he said.

I said, "I will not do it for less than $200. He handed it to me. I put my hand out as though I was going to give the dispatches to him. I had my revolver with me and drawing it I covered him and walked him to the Provost Guard and handed him over. He was from Richmond and worked on a newspaper. He was a Southern spy.

Why things were run so loosely at that time that when a movement was to take place, it was published in the papers before the Commander knew it.

Lincoln heard of what I had done and sent for me. He asked me where I was stationed. He said, "I'll appoint you my personal orderly and all dispatches from me shall go through you. Then we can have one responsible head."

That made me very close to him, and I became like one of the family. I only worked about two hours a day. The rest of the time I amused myself with Willie and Tad, breaking the pony and goats.

I was always with him. I went with him everywhere.

K—Did you go to Gettysburg with him?

T—Yes.

K—Did you hear the speech?

T—Yes.

K—Tell me about it.

T—He says to me, "They expect me to make a speech. I am afraid it will be very short. I am a poor hand at making a speech." I suppose he said, "impromptu"—I may have heard that from another source. Then he said, "I will write a little something. I suppose they will have a good laugh over it."

K—How did he write it?

T—He wrote it in the cars on a little slip of paper—just as you are doing now. I thought he was merely taking down notes. When he finished he said, "That will be about it."

It was the greatest speech ever written. I was actually inspired when I heard it. Some of the Copperheads tried to make fun of it. They undertook it, but it wouldn't go.

K—How did he act when he delivered it?

T—He stood there like a steadfast—warhorse. He was so tall and upright. He had his hat in his hand and when he got through, he bowed and put it on. His right hand was in his vest. His hat was in his left hand. There was not very much applause. There was some not hearing.

I thought at the time—that's a pretty big speech. He thought it was a failure. He said, "I think they will have a good deal of sport over that speech of mine."

I said, "Mr. President, you have said a big speech in a few words."

He said, "Do you think so?" I said, "Yes." He said, "I thank you."

One day out on the grounds he came over to me and said, "You guessed right about that speech; see what the papers say about it."

K—How was he as an eater?

T—He was an average eater, and liked good things well-cooked. One day he visited camp, and sat down to eat with the soldiers. He took a piece of hardtack, broke it, and there were two white grubs. He said to another soldier, "Look at that."

The soldier said, "That's nothing. We often have that happen."

"What do you do about it?" said Lincoln.

"Eat the grubs and all, without looking at them."

Lincoln raised a row over that. He ordered the hardtack destroyed and sent them flour. We had more flour sent to them after that. They made stone ovens and baked their own bread. Of course when they were on the march they had to eat hardtack. This was toward Lee's Ferry, near Harper's Ferry, called Point of Rocks. They were two companies of my own regiment.

K—Did he wear boots or shoes?

T—He wore boots, like a farmer's boots. Sometimes around the grounds, he wore slippers. He generally wore a high hat, sometimes a broad slouch.

K—I saw an article in which he was said to have worn an old, torn, office coat going to [the July 12, 1864 Battle of] Fort Stevens.

T—I don't believe it. If he tried it, Mrs. Lincoln would not have stood it. She would not let him. "Abe," she always called him, "Abe, get a good coat."

He would sometimes go round like a regular old farmer—a backwoods brand. Lincoln had a remarkable gawky way of putting his clothes on, yet, he always looked neat and clean.

Mrs. Lincoln was a stickler for society. He always yielded to her. She was a good woman.

I knew Tad very well. Willie died, and Tad—Tad had a lisp. I did not see much of Rob. He was in college. He was very quiet. He was very studious. I don't think he could tell you as much of his father as I could; he did not see him. He might tell you about his character.

Willie was a little fellow; the second [third] son of Lincoln. He told me how he bought him a pair of goats, and the saddler made part of their harness, and I made another part. When Willie died [on February 20, 1862], President Lincoln was never the same man after that.

He was very fond of children. Any snotty runt in the streets that struck his fancy, he would talk to. That was out of his good nature. In the street, one little fellow took his hat off to him; I suppose he knew him. [Lincoln] stopped and said, "Whose boy are you?" The boy told him where his father was working; I believe it was in one of the Departments. He would stoop to any little child and shake hands with him.

As I think over those days, things come back, but I think they are too trifling to mention. There was a fellow in our regiment who kept a diary. I used to wonder what he found to write about. I understand now.

K—Did you ever see him keyed up?

T—Oh, yes! (Here he laughed heartedly at the recollection) Senator [George H.] Pendleton, father of Judge [Francis Key] Pendleton (nodding his head in the direction of the court room), he was a bit of a Copperhead. I watched [Congressman Pendleton] as he came in, and he said, "Mr. President, wouldn't it be well to make some compromise with the South and settle it."

Lincoln then showed the soldier in him. He straightened right up, as he could when he liked—he generally stooped a little, but I think that was acquired. I noticed he stooped more toward the end of the war. I suppose he felt the growing seriousness of things. But he liked to see people stand straight. He used to give me credit. He used to say to me, "My boy, I'm glad to see you stand with that soldierly straightness."

He stood up spider-like, as he didn't at other times, and said, "Mr. Pendleton, we will compromise with those people when they lay down their arms. We can then talk of compromise." Here Pendleton sneaked off.

I have heard him say about the Southerners: "It is not their fault, but they have not been properly directed by their leaders." He said he did not want to punish them more than he was actually obliged to, as their leaders had not shown judgment.

I asked him what he thought of Nicolay and Hay.

He said guardedly: "They were nice men."

"Is that so," I said, giving him a look that seemed to make him lower his guard.

T—If they had been away from their surroundings, they would have been very up-startish. They were not like the old fellow—Our Abraham.

Nicolay wrote his own ideas instead of truth, aching to make history. Hay I did not know well. He may have been a prince for all I know. He was just like he looked: pug-nosed and pig-headed.

Referring to Nicolay and Hay in their ideas that there was nobody quite as good as the Western soldiers, he said, "The boys (11th New York Cavalry) kinda went against them for that; both of them. We didn't have any use for any of those fellows."

K—Did you know [Secretary of the Navy Gideon] Welles?

T—Yes, I used to take messages to him in the Navy Department. It was on one end of the building; the War Department on the other. Welles would unbend a little. He was not like Stanton, who would never unbend.

K—Nicolay says Lincoln did not write the Gettysburg speech on the [railway] cars.

T—I can say he did, for I saw him write it. If I remember right he had a newspaper in his hand. He folded it and pulled out of his pocket a note book and put down little notes. He did not write it out, but noted it down. I did not know he was going [to Gettysburg] till the very last minute. I had on my citizen's clothes. I used to wear them a great deal in the White House. He said, "Put on your uniform and come along." I sat a little back of him. I, of course, sat back of him just as an orderly would act. He did not expect me to stand fifteen paces behind him. I cannot remember who was there.

K—I have a picture of the [David Wills] house where he stopped.

T—I remember the house right on a corner; I did not stop there. There were some tents pitched there. Three or four of us slept in one. It was an Officer's wall tent.

Lincoln went over the ground on horseback. I went with him. I kept behind, in uniform. The horses were from a cavalry regiment. He had a big bay, 16 hands high, with a regulation saddle. An officer furnished him with his horse; one of the men furnished mine. He went over the grounds to Pickett's Charge, and different places. Debris of the fight were all around, guns, dead horses. Why, dead men were found six or seven months after, among the rocks and brush—rebels and our men.

K—Did Lincoln wear gauntlets?

T—I think he did. He wore the old plug hat and an old overcoat. Mrs. Lincoln wanted him to get a new hat, but he stuck to the old plug. It was very tall. Not bell-crowned like they are now, but straight, like a stove-pipe.

K—Did he read the speech?

T—He did not read it off that piece of paper. He did not have it written out. He just had it noted, and glanced at it sideways. It was the fly leaf of a note book; four by six.

K—Nicolay and Hay seem to eclipse Stoddard. He should not have been eclipsed.

T—Stoddard was a man, when he said a thing, you could depend on it.

K—Do you remember the Emancipation?

T—Yes; it was when he went down to Maryland, to Port Tobacco. The Body Guard went with him. He went to look over the country. It was there the Underground Railroad was run over the river.

Underground railroad crossing a river may seem like a bull, but it was a popular name for a system adopted by an organization of Abolitionists to pass slaves from one to another who sheltered them and provided them with food and money till they got through the Free States into Canada. There were 5,000 niggers that followed us back.

He could be seen talking to the niggers—some of the old gray-headed fellows—they were characters, interesting characters.

Some of the officers wanted to send them back. He [Lincoln] said, "No, they shant go back; they can help us build our Forts. They were Contrabands. They brought small-pox into Washington. They had a camp; I did not know where it was. I was sent as a messenger. I rode right through [the camp] as a cross cut. When I got where I started for, they asked me how I came. I told them. They were quite uneasy about it, but I never caught it. I guess I was immune.

K—I have heard that Mrs. Lincoln was in favor of the South.

T—That's not so at all. It would be against her husband's interests and the country's. It was the rough element in the war that said that. I do not believe that. I never saw anything that would make me believe that. The class of people that seemed to take to her, showed her to be all right.

I served for a while on [Gen. Henry] Halleck's staff. He had no push in him, but he was a nice man to serve under. McClellan should have rolled up the Rebels like a ball of yarn, but he was taken up with too many little things.

Lincoln had no Body Guard till we came. There were all sorts of rumors about killing and kidnapping him. Officers told him he was taking a great many chances. We used to ride out to the Soldiers' Home with him and stay all night, till two companies of infantry came. Then we used to go out for him in the morning and bring him back to Washington. He used to ride in a carriage.

K—Was he a good horseman?

T—Well, (here he hesitated) he needed a very large horse to look well. He sat on his saddle good. He would drop his toes as I do. He went back a bit. He wore boots, and Army spurs, and when he rode his trousers worked up and showed their legs. When I went with him on horseback I carried a sabre—not in my belt, but strapped to my saddle according to orders. I carried two revolvers, one on my right hip and one on my left.

Lots of times he used to get tired of sitting round the White House. He would go out alone. Somebody would follow him. One night he started out and two detectives followed him. He walked toward the Capitol, they told me, and looked at it. The dome was not yet finished. Then he walked off towards the Navy Yard; then he came back. He must have walked five miles. He supposed he was alone, but all the time he had been followed by those two men. If he had known it, he would have been as mad as hops. He wore a slouch hat, and most people would not have known him. Nobody guessed.

Before we came he had no body guard. When it was suggested, he thought it was putting on too many airs, but Stanton insisted on it. Officers told him, as President, somebody was always ready to take his life. In the fall of 1864, we left him and took steam for Alexandria. Then [Major James R.] O'Beirne came [as Provost Marshal]. He stood well; he came highly recommended.

K—You said something about a picnic, where Lincoln was under fire.

T—Yes, he was under fire that day—in 1862. That was at Cabin John's Bridge, where the reservoir crosses the Potomac—it takes the reservoir over there. I never knew where it got its name. Lincoln was under fire there. A man I knew, who saw him at Fort Stevens, said he did not seem to fear anything, and I believe it.

We started on a picnic. He went up there with Mrs. Lincoln and Mrs. [Elizabeth] Halleck and the children. The Body Guard went ahead of us. There was Company K of our Body Guard on Provost Duty. As we started to get down [to the Potomac River], some of Mosby's Cavalry waded right over the river from the Virginia side, and made an attack. The river was quite low at that part; a man could wade over. Mosby did not command them; they were commanded, I believe, by a Major White. Troop K held them back and with the Body Guard, we all pitched in. We had four companies: the Body Guard, and three other Companies.

The entire regiment was ordered out, and Mr. Lincoln went along with the Body Guard. He was on horseback, and they had to ride hard to keep ahead of him. We finally drove them back across the river. The regiment followed them up as far as Leesburg. The Rebels seemed to melt away. They scattered in all directions and went back to their homes, where all of them said they were law-abiding farmers, until they were called upon to make another raid. Our command killed a few Rebels who lived on a farm within ten to twenty miles of Leesburg.

I do not think the President carried any weapons, as I did not see any when he came back. The troop captured seven or eight prisoners. When we were attacked, Lincoln who was on horseback, was perfectly cool, and called out, "Get the ladies back!" They were on horseback. That was the reason I was not in the fight, on account of getting the ladies and children back. Lincoln stayed there and did not leave until the Body Guard had driven them across the river. The officers told him he had better go on with the women and children—but he was no coward.

Mrs. Lincoln was nervous and flighty, but I quieted her by telling her there was no danger. Mrs. Halleck was cool as a cucumber. She was a Hamilton; one of Alexander Hamilton's descendents. She was much younger than Gen. Halleck.

When we came back [to Washington] some gentlemen who were close to Mr. Lincoln inquired where he had been, and he laughingly told them he had been on a little picnic at Cabin John's Bridge. They said: "Mr. Lincoln, the grounds around there are pretty dangerous for picnickers." "Well," he said, "I enjoyed it while it lasted!"

We captured the Rebel commander some time afterwards. He had earlier captured some of our men whom he outnumbered two to one, and took off their uniforms and made them put on their own gray lousy ones, and robbed our men of their watches and everything. Some of our men not knowing of this, started to reinforce the advance, and meeting the Rebels, we now being two to one, captured them, among them their Major. We found some of them with several watches in their pockets. The Major had several. The boys took his uniform off, and he had only his underclothes. They gave him a blanket to cover himself when they arrived in Washington. I took a ring from him which I have yet. It got so thin, I do not wear it. He said he did not want to part with it, as it was a family relic. I said, "You should have thought of that when you were stealing our boys' watches and things. They might have thought as much of them as you do of that. Now if you don't give it to me, I'll cut your finger off!" He gave it to me. I understand after the war, he became a Baptist Minister.

Another rebel we captured was a man who used to visit Washington. We always thought he was friendly, but he was a spy. He was taken to prison, the Old Capitol. I never heard what became of him.

Another time, he was investigating things at Tennallytown, this side of Harper's Ferry. The troops were stationed there. He went in a tent and asked the boys how their food was. The sergeant asked him to sit down and have some. He had pork and beans, homemade bread and honey. Some of them did not know him at first. I guess he wondered when they, "got it."

I told Major Tisdale of my plan to make my statue of Lincoln, when the major said, "Right shall be might."

K—Would he be apt to show vigor from what you know about him?

T—In a case like that, Lincoln showed great vigor—spoke loud—gesture and speech strong. He did not bring it out in a nabby-tabby way. But it was a vigorous and decided way. Right out, and coming!

K—Did you ever see him trim Stanton?

T—No. He would probably do that in private. I used to hear them talking when I was called to the office; on going in they shut-up.

K—Did he ever speak to you about the Emancipation Proclamation?

T—No, but I heard him speak to his own individual family, and to officers near him. I remember overhearing some one make a remark that the colored people should be taken away from the rebels or they would arm them and make them fight against us. Otherwise they would take the colored population over and offer inducements that would make them fight the North. The rebels claimed a nigger could be trained to do anything.

K—Did you know Francis Carpenter who painted the Emancipation picture?

Here his face lit up.  "Carpenter?  Yes.  Is he alive?"

K—No.

T—I knew him well.  There was another Artist who had the run of the White House—Davis.  He went afterwards with us on the plains.  There was another Artist, Waud.

K—Yes.

T—And a man [Edwin Forbes] from Leslies [*Illustrated Weekly*], with a withered arm.  I knew them all.  Davis was a queer little fellow.  He did do things.  He was a braggart; a little impudent cuss.  Yet people did not give him credit for what he could do.

K—Did you know Brady?

T—Brady?  I knew Brady.  He had a little covered wagon for a dark room which he took to the field with him to fix his pictures.  Some of his men took great chances right out in the front.  He was there and went with them.  After [the battle of Bull Run near] Fairfax it was one of his men who said:  "Brady was too much of a fighter; I wanted to get away from him."  His men stood there, when our men were driven back.  They [the soldiers] rallied, and drove the Rebels back.  He was devilish near being captured.  The bullets were flying around.  Brady took some photographs there in the White House; one of the President and Mrs. Lincoln and children all together in the same room at the same time.

Looking at my statuette of Sheridan, he said: "You've got him to a dot."

# Lincoln Visiting West Point, June 24, 1862
# Letter from Gen. Thomas Ward

I was much interested in learning details about President Lincoln's private meeting with Gen. Winfield Scott at West Point on June 24, 1862, as very little information had been published about it.  In response to my inquiry, I received the following letter from Gen. Thomas Ward:

Dear Mr. Kelly,
     In reply to your inquiry as to President Lincoln's visit to Gen. Scott at West Point, June 24, 1862, I have to say that I was a Cadet at the time at the Military Academy, graduating the following year, June 11, 1863.  The tax on one's memory of details which occurred 58 years ago is rather strenuous, and more or less uncertain.  So before replying, I have taken

time to consult my records, which accounts in a measure for this delay in replying to your letter; and I am now cheerfully giving you all the information I have on the subject.     To begin with, my records show that President Lincoln visited West Point on June 24, 1862 (Tuesday), coming from Washington, D. C. to West Point, N. Y. by Express train, arriving at 3 A. M., whither he had come to consult Lt. Gen. Scott, it was supposed on matters of great moment.  After a conference of some hours' duration, the President returned to Washington in 8 hours and 20 minutes from West Point, the fastest train on record up to that time.  Our greatest President, as it is well known, was no hand for show; I have no recollection of a review, etc., in his honor.  After his talk with Gen. Scott, he was off again without delay.

Col. A. M. Bowman was Superintendent of the Military Academy at that time.  His surviving daughter, Mrs. Elwell S. Otis, widow of Gen. Otis, I believe was at her home (then a young lady) at West Point, at the time.  It may be that she can give some details of the visit of the President not generally known, as to entertainment, etc.

                                                    Yours truly,
                                                    Gen. T. Ward


After receiving the letter from Gen. Ward, I then called on Mrs. Otis at the home of her brother-in-law, Gen. Abram A. Harbach.  She was a beautiful, stately lady of the old school American type.  Talking of Lincoln, she said in reference to his visit to West Point:

O—He called on my father, Col. Alexander H. Bowman, who was in command at West Point.  He was in company with Gen. Scott.  They drove up in the old-fashioned coupe which Gen. Scott always used when driving around West Point.

I have never seen a picture that seemed to do justice to a portrait of President Lincoln.  He had a fine, noble, splendid face—with no personal beauty. He was very tall and loosely made, but no croucher.  He did not slump down.  He was erect, animated and very sweet to children.  He stayed for a long time in our house, but his visit was unofficial—my father did not give him the usual review.

The President was dressed, as he is usually described, in a frock coat with a plain bow tie.  My father wore the regulation uniform of the Engineer Corps of that day.  We were dressed, I fear, in the hideous mid-Victorian costumes prevailing at that time.  The President was seated in an arm chair which we have in our living room today, with the rest of the party grouped about him.  The impression I have of the President's face is that it was most kindly, lighting up and showing a genuine interest when talking with the younger persons—a pleasing, noble face, and not at all homely, as is so often depicted in his various pictures and statues.

There was no reception for him that I recall.  There may have been an impromptu reception at the hotel, but I was too young to go there—my father may have gone. The visit must have been secret. My father may have known why he came. When I was a girl, Gen. Scott stood for all that was known in war; there was no one who could be compared with him at West Point to consult with him. He [Lincoln] only stayed a day.

K—In that case, why did not Gen. Scott go to him?

O—Gen. Scott had retired from the Army, and was an invalid; he was enormous, a man about 6 feet 4 _, and very unwieldy. He used to be helped into his coupe, and was so large that when he got in, there was little room left for anyone else.

K—So that was the reason, I suppose, the President called on him to consult him. And the importance of the visit may be judged by the acts of some of Lincoln's so-called friends, who never mentioned it. I suppose they were afraid it would take away from the wonderful military genius he showed in his letters to the officers in the field, forgetting that the great man is one who can take advantage of the special knowledge of others, and that Lincoln showed his greatness and patriotism by seeking advice from the great military genius, Gen. Winfield Scott.

That reminds me of a story told by Gen. Ulysses Doubleday of an Englishman, a Frenchman and a German who were asked to make a painting of a camel. The Englishman went to Africa to study the animal, the Frenchman to the Jarden des Plantes, while the German retired to an upper chamber of his house and evolved a camel out of his inner consciousness. Nicolay was a German, so that was the way he tried to show how Lincoln conducted the war.

## Lincoln's Telegrapher at the War Department
## Meeting with David Homer Bates

David Homer Bates, author of *Lincoln in the Telegraph Office*, was associated with the Wilcox and Gibbs Sewing Machine Company, which is on the southeast corner of Bond Street and Broadway.
I had written to him:

> From your close personal relations with the president, can you furnish me with details that will support my position, as to his personal appearance, his structure, his manner, and his costume. An author is not apt to put in details that an artist sometimes finds necessary to realize his picture. If you can furnish me with those you will put me under great obligation to you, and I hope the result of my work will be satisfactory to you.

I met Mr. Bates for a short interview. Calling at his office, with a copy of his book, he greeted me saying: "I received a very fine letter about you from General Carty, and I wrote to him that I would gladly do anything for you I could. I will give you all the time now until I find it necessary to cut off the circuit."

Mr. Bates was a very handsome man; I should judge about six feet big; a fine figure, and a very compact, symmetrical head. Short iron-gray hair and mustache; very regular and well-proportioned features, strongly modeled about perceptives.

He told me he was 76, the time I met him, September 26, 1919. I told him I had read his book which he had presented to General O'Beirne.

B—Oh, yes, Gen. O'Beirne was one of the men who helped capture Booth by rounding him up. I tried to get more material from him for the book, but he kept putting it off till it was too late. If he had spent half the time writing me the material I wanted, that he did in sending me apologies for not doing so, I would have had a fine article.

K—I lost a great opportunity in not knowing General [Thomas T.] Eckert, as I could have done, but I did not know his services till I read your book.

B—General Eckert was a fine man.

K—Yes, and your book is his monument.

B—As to Lincoln, he was a masterful man, and had a very suave, gentle, patient way of expressing it, but the grip of his hand was always there.

I was only seventeen when I went to the War. That made me at the end about twenty or twenty-one, so I was not old enough to notice things as I should.

In the old War Department (here he got out a print of it and marked it 1861), to the left of the entrance was the room. Later, we had an office above marked by that star. And originally we had one at the head of the stairs. But at that time, after the Battle of Bull Run we had it here.

Mr. Lincoln used to sit in here with his left shoulder towards the window. Out here towards the left was an old fashioned lounge, on which he used to lie while waiting for a telegram, or for people whom he expected to meet.

Here Mr. Bates laughed saying: "I never told this before."

B—One day he found a little brown insect on his coat. He stood up and said, "I will have to give up using that. I was fond of it as a lounge, but it has turned out a little buggy."

## A Drummer Boy Whose Hand was Clasped by Lincoln in 1861
## Interview with William Vallete, 20th New York Volunteers

At Kingston, New York, May 30, 1920, the day my bronze memorial to the Soldiers and Sailors of the World War was unveiled there, Joseph Drake introduced me to William Vallete, an unusually small, dainty little gentleman who wore a broad-brimmed hat and had a long, bristling mustache. The rest of his face, including his eyes and voice, was both mild and gentle. Drake introduced him as "The Major," which was a title of courtesy, as he told me he had been a drummer boy in the 20th New York Volunteers.

K—Did you ever see Lincoln?

V—Yes, I have not only seen President Lincoln, but I have met him. He was one of the sweetest men of the age. When I am reading my bible, in the book of Matthew where it describes Christ—I think of Lincoln, with that loving sweet expression. I think that Abraham Lincoln's eyes must have been like HIS.

Our meeting came about in this way: I was a drummer boy in the company of George H. Sharpe, when he was a Captain in the 20th N. Y., Company B; he afterwards was promoted and became a General on Grant's Staff. He had been a great friend of Lincoln before the War.

I was eleven years and five months old when I enlisted. I was so small that I could not carry the regulation drum the government gave me, so my brother bought me a smaller one and I sent my first one home.

One time while I was away from the regiment, they elected me corporal. I suppose it was because although the youngest, I was the best drummer in the regiment. I had been drumming since I was eight years old. I could play scientifically, while the others just drummed. I had been taught by a member of C. S. Grafulas band of the Seventh Regiment.

In July, 1861, we had been in camp at Annapolis, Maryland, then marched to Baltimore and went into camp. Captain Sharpe happened to be invited to a reception at the White House and he came into my tent and asked me if I would like to attend the reception. Of course, I was only too glad to go. He got me a leave of absence to go to Washington. We had to go the night before, so we stopped at the National Hotel and slept in the same room used by Henry Clay and the same bedstead.

Next day we visited the Capitol and Congressman Steel showed us round and placed me beside him in a chair at his desk. In the evening when the reception took place, I went with Captain Sharpe to the White House. Of course I had on my uniform with corporal chevrons. My uniform was a dark blue coat with a light blue shield on my breast with buttons all round; light blue trousers. I was eleven years and eight months at the time. There was a large line of ladies and gentlemen. I fell in behind Captain Sharpe. When Lincoln saw Captain Sharpe, he shook hands with him and the Captain went on, and when I reached the President, I extended my hand.  He looked down on me and I looked up and fell in love with him right away.  I never saw such a lonely, kind expression on a human face—so loving and kind and so affectionate—most wonderful.  He took my hand in both of his and shook it and drew me out of the line and stood me at his right and detained me there until the last person had passed through.  Then he was at liberty and he took me into an adjoining room, I forget which it was, where the members of his cabinet were, and personally introduced me to every one of them.  So you can just imagine what I thought—this man was...he had the sweetest and loveliest expression and the handsomest man I ever laid my eyes upon.

They say he had lines in his face—my eyes would not see it.  I never saw anything to equal his face—never since.  He looked so like my mother that I fell in love with him at once.  He wrote a letter to my mother and told her I was with him and that I was all right.

You see I had a very eventful evening—wasn't it great!  I only wish you could see his eye—those eyes of his.  I think of our Savior having eyes like that.  It showed his kindly disposition.  They say he was homely and awkward; he did not appear so to me.  No one who ever saw Abraham Lincoln can say anything like that.

During the reception with these crowds of people passing, the smile never left his face.  He never showed signs of weariness.  Sometimes he would put his hand on my shoulder; when I think of it sometimes, I can hardly control myself.


Then bowing his head and looking at his fine small weather-beaten brown hand—tears came to his eyes and he musingly said: "Think of that hand having been clasped by the hands of Abraham Lincoln."


## Lincoln Visiting the Wounded
## Newport News Hospital, May 1862
## Letter from Robert P. Black, Co. E, 103rd Pennsylvania Volunteers

For J. E. Kelly—
I was a country lad raised on a farm with a very limited country school education, and enlisted on Nov. 25, 1861, in Company E, 103rd Pennsylvania Volunteers, and we had got as far as Newport News when I was taken sick with cholera morbus, which ran into Typhoid fever.  I was taken to No. 1 fever ward—an old horse stable, where a lot of Cavalry horses had been wintered and after partly being cleaned out was used as a ward for typhoid fever patients.  The sandy soil was saturated with stable juices, and was dug over and lime mixed in enough to kill the rank smell which some of us country boys, who were used to being in horse barns, could stand the rank smells.  We were laid on wet, musty, moldy hay to

fight it out with fever, being assisted by a few irregularly given medicines, mostly given by doctors who knew a little more about treating us than we knew ourselves.

I got well enough over the fever to walk with a cane, when I was detailed as nurse, and had charge of all medicine given in that ward.

Soon after I was promoted to Surgical Ward No. 4 (walls built of pine poles, 100 feet long and 20 feet wide containing 60 patients), where in short order I had all the patients cleaned up and improving. The head Surgeon, on inspecting, gave me praise, and I got quite intimate with him, and mine was the model ward to which all visitors were taken—a good cleaned up cow stable would have been much better in looks and smell. Many other wards were terribly filthy, and patients neglected. This is why President Lincoln and wife, on a visit to the Post were taken to my ward to see it.

The morning of his visit, Dr. [Edward] Shippen's orderlies came and told us of it, and we cleaned up some extra.

Dr. Shippen met the Dispatch Boat at the wharf. They came up on that boat from Fortress Monroe, and the Doctor did the honors by escorting the visitors around. They were saluted by firing cannon: a President's salute. I had on my best bib and tuckers, viz: clean pants and shirt, perhaps my shoes blacked, too, and met the party at the main front door, and the President asked me to conduct him to each patient, tell him the name and regiment of each, and nature of his wound, how bad, etc.

Mr. Lincoln shook hands with each of them. Spoke a few cheering words to each as he left the cots. I showed Mr. Lincoln how the Rebel doctors cut off arms and legs; often by cutting square off instead of leaving a flap cover to heal over the end bone, and form a callous to protect limb from injury. The Rebel doctors often did this and we got the stumps as healthy as we could, then cut round end of bone pushing flesh back, sawed off 4 to 6 inches of end of bone, when healed could not hurt so readily.

The words I recollect of Lincoln's were: "What A Pity." Referring both to job and intent, as I understand it, and I think Dr. Shippen understood it the same way. Lincoln's eyes and whole face expression indicated, "What A Pity," too.

Mrs. Lincoln came after, with a clothes basket carried by two negro boys, and handed each one an orange out of the basket, or laid one beside him. She wore a light colored, large figured dress with medium sized hoop-skirt, and a light hat with a plume or feathers. Mr. Lincoln was dressed in black, with a high, "greased" hat, and gloveless hands, which when they grasped mine, seemed awful big, and had a grip to them like an iron vise. He again shook hands with us at the door as he left, slight bowing and charged me to take good care of my patients, and get them out again as soon as possible, saying, "We need them, every one."

## Lincoln at Fredericktown, Maryland in 1862
## Interview with Lawrence B. Kemp

In 1906, I received a commission, from Lawrence B. Kemp, for a bronze bas relief portrait of Barbara Fritchie to be placed over her grave at Mount Olivet, Cemetery in Frederick, Maryland. Mr. Kemp told me an interesting story of President Lincoln's visit to Frederick:

Mr. K—My Grandfather was a [Maryland] borderman and was loyal. His name was Lawrence John Bringle. I was named after him, Lawrence Bringle Kemp. He was a banker and farmer as well as President of the Canal that ran from Frederick to Washington. He used to buy corn, hay and oats for the Government to supply the armies. He would call to see the President on his visits to Washington. I think it was after the battle of Antietam, he invited President Lincoln to Frederick so that people could see him and express their loyalty. Our home was a sweet old place in Market Street—that's where the reception was held.

I remember when Jule—Julius, our negro coachman, drove up with our carriage in which were President Lincoln and a couple of our leading citizens. He came in the house through the hall and parlor to the rear room which was a smoking room; he was there for about three hours. Before they allowed people to pass through they took a little refreshment which had been prepared. Old Aunt Maria, our servant, had made her famous molasses beaten biscuits and sandwiches.

Mr. Lincoln, with a sandwich in his right hand and a cup of coffee in the other, sat enjoying the stories. He had quite long, straight hair, and he pushed it back with his wrist. He talked a great deal with his right hand with a sandwich in it. One story told was how grandfather had told our Preacher, he could not preach from the pulpit any more because he had allowed his four sons to join the Rebels. Grandfather was one of the pillars of the Church and told him he had better get out [of Frederick] and go to Pennsylvania till he learned better and send for his sons to come out of the Rebel Army.

Barbara Fritchie went to his Church. Stonewall Jackson worshiped there twice. I saw him as he sat behind Grandfather's pew which belonged to the Minister. My attention was attracted by the clanking of a sword. I looked round and saw a tall man with a dark beard. Grandfather said [Gen. Jackson] was a worshipful man. The lines were very sharply drawn in those days. My father would not speak to his own brother because he was a Rebel, or did we children speak to his.

At the reception Mr. Lincoln took his position between the two rooms, and when he stood to receive the people, Grandfather stood at his left to introduce the people.

K—How was he dressed?

Kemp—His coat wasn't buttoned, and hung not in a draggled or shriveled look, but not in such nice shape as my grandfather's. He was pretty tall; pretty long. He was what the negroes call, "long-coupled." He was very easy mannered.

K—Did Barbara Fritchie go to the reception?

Kemp—No, she was not famous then. We always looked on her as an old leather-faced woman, who would not let the children sit on her cellar door. She would let me on account of my Grandfather, and would go in and bring me out a large piece of molasses cake, which I would divide with the other boys.

K—And to think it was through you, her "old leather face" should be modeled by me for the bronze memorial over her grave. It would make a fine subject if Barbara met Lincoln.
What were Lincoln's hands like?

Kemp—He had a long hand; a white shirt without a hand cuff, a soft cuff. What impressed me was the distance from his coat-sleeve to the end of his hand. He wore an old-fashioned Prince Albert coat. He was the apex of gentleness, with all that one wishes. He took great notice of us children, brushing back our hair from our brows. My brother Charlie, a black-haired, blue-eyed, clinging little fellow, stood on his right, cuddled into him, stroking Lincoln's left leg which was crossed over his right, while Lincoln, with a sandwich in his right hand would "eat around" Charlie.
Meanwhile, Grandfather was urging him to take more nourishment. Grandfather believed in people eating a great deal. Jule, and the other servants assisted Aunt Maria in passing things around, but really came up to look round.
He had comfortable, large boots. Aunt Maria said, "Marse Lawrence did not have feet like Mr. Lincoln." Jule said, "Look how tall he is. He needs more feet than Marse Lawrence."
As the people passed through I can recall old Lyandel, who was almost a hermit. He seemed to live away off to himself. He was a wonderfully loyal man. He came in his old long-tailed coat; was supported by a cane. In his right hand a bunch of flowers, largely blue. He said, "Mr. Lincoln, you see, Sir, almost everyone of these flowers are blue, and every one of them would have been blue if my garden would have produced them. (He had some other straggling flowers mixed with them) They are hardly the 'true-blue', he said, "but I've tried to be just as true-blue as the flowers I bring you, as the Colonel and Mayor will tell you. And I thank the Lord for having spared You that I can shake your hand!"
The people in the crowd began to smile at the old fellow giving the President such flowers as these.
Mr. Lincoln bowed to old Lyandel, and taking the flowers the people had smiled at, shook his hand and said, "Mr. Lyandel, it is the loyal people like yourself that believed in our Country and in me that have made our Nation."

The old man had come dressed for the occasion, and his old long-tailed coat shone like a tin-pan. I could see Mr. Lincoln's eyes follow him as he passed out the door.

At the reception, grandfather had invited all the farmers who had provided all the hay and corn which was so hard to get for the Army. Billy W---- was one of them. On seeing him, grandfather calls out, "Mr. President, here's Billy, foreman on the Gettysburg Pike! Even the women on his farm helped bale the hay for the Government." The President said, "Where are they? Where is the family? I want to see them and shake hands with them."

They were brought over and stood and talked with him.

After the reception, when the doors were closed, my Aunt Jane who was head of the Sanitary Committee, and all the women workers were brought up to shake hands with the President.

My experience was his taking me by the hand and patting me on the head. Grandfather was telling him, "I borrowed these two boys from their Mother to make me happy."

Mr. Lincoln said, "Well, you mustn't overindulge or spoil them, but make them useful citizens like yourself." Grandfather replied, "We always keep them employed and busy, and that makes them useful and happy."

Lincoln then shook hands with us, and shook hands with all the servants. Aunt Maria said, "Jule, did you see me wipe my hand twice before I let him take my black paw? And he squeezed it!" Aunt Maria talked about how he had the same kind of bow as Marse Lawrence. She said to me: "He did not smove your hair once; he smoved it two or three times; you must never forget that!"

Old Jule kept the whisk that brushed off Mr. Lincoln and the handkerchief he dusted Mr. Lincoln's shoes with. When he was dying he gave the whisk to his son, and the handkerchief to me.

Julius always used to point out just where he stood. He would say, stooping and pointing: "Marse Lincoln stood right there! You can almost see his feet."

## Shaking hands with Lincoln
## Interview with Major Henry Swords, August 25, 1920

My friend, Lawrence B. Kemp, introduced me to Major Henry Swords, keeper of the records of the New York Customs House.

He was a very handsome man; shapely, regular features; clear, ruddy complexion; kindly, sparkling blue eyes; silver white wavy hair and short mustache.

Starting on the subject of Lincoln, he said:

S—The first time I saw President Lincoln was after the Battle of Antietam, when he came to review the Army, I think it was at Pleasant Valley.

I was a member of Company B, 26th Massachusetts Infantry—an enlisted man. I was in the front rank, and General McClellan who was handsomely mounted and had a very brilliant staff, a part of which were foreign officers, came down the lines to review, and as they passed the President who was mounted on a small horse and in contrast to the brilliancy of the staff, was a prominent figure because of his citizens garb—that high hat, long frock-coat, low shoes. He did not wear boots, but shoes as I remember. Shirt and trousers showed strained relations and he looked very odd to say the least. He rode a dark horse with military equipments.

McClellan was leading the column and was quite considerably ahead of the President. Which, as McClellan was giving the complimentary review to the President, he should have been [riding] at least even [with the President]; the horses' heads should be on an even line.

I cannot remember seeing Lincoln at the review at Falmouth [in April 1863].

Later as an officer in the 59th Massachusetts, we had marched from Annapolis to Washington after being refitted at Annapolis preparatory to the Spring [1864] campaign.

Arriving at the outskirts of Washington a day or two after we were informed that President Lincoln was to hold a levee and the officers were invited to attend and a few of us, myself among the number, cleaned up, washed up, put on clean paper collars, and blacked our boots and put on our regalia, hired an old carriage, what in Washington they call an old fashioned charge, with an old darkey driver who drove us to Washington.

We all of us went out to attend the levee as they called it, then arriving at the White House we entered. He stood there in the receiving room, Mrs. Lincoln with him, with the members of his cabinet. We fell into line. We shook hands. I forget whether he had on a swallow tail or a frock coat, in any case he was in proper apparel.

He was exceedingly pleasant. His smile was a very genial one, and he seemed in a good mood. He did not impress me as ugly. He had a very kindly, sweet amiable face, and greeted everybody in a most cordial manner. His eyes had a very kind, gentle, sweet expression. He impressed me as a kindly gentle soul, and greeted us as friends most cordially. He did not impress me as a homely man at all. There was nothing about him that made me think of a coarse and ill-gained man.

After passing the receiving line, we returned and stood opposite where he was standing and observed him and his greeting to everybody; he was cordial, smiling pleasantly and making remarks to those he knew. I remember when he shook hands, his grip was cordial, on both our hands.

The next time I saw him was when we passed down Pennsylvania Avenue on our way to Virginia. He was on the balcony at Willard's Hotel reviewing us; I think Stanton was with him. Gen. Ambrose Burnside was in command [of the Ninth Corps] and rode ahead. I was on the staff of Gen. [Orlando] Willcox. I never saw Lincoln again.

I came very near being present at his assassination. I arrived at Washington that fatal morning from Annapolis as a paroled prisoner, and after attending some official business, I called on an old Washington family by the name of Todd whose acquaintance I had made in the early part of the War and was invited to accompany them that evening to Ford's Theatre where Laura Keene was playing, and as an inducement for me to attend told me that President Lincoln and General Grant would be there. I declined with thanks and my excuse was that I had received a three days' leave of absence and decided to go home and see my Mother and Father whom I had not seen for nearly two years.

I took the last train out of Washington that night and on nearing Philadelphia, the conductor awakened us with the terrible information that President Lincoln had been assassinated at the theatre. Many distinguished officers, both Army and Navy were in that car, but somehow I cannot recall their names.

Excitement was most intense. No sleep the rest of the journey, but everybody muttering imprecations on the assassin, and on the future hard luck that had befallen our Southern Brethren, for it was indeed a misfortune for them.

On reaching New York, I went directly to the Astor House for breakfast. Never had I witnessed such excitement. Crowds called for vengeance, and imprecations loud and deep—the crowds just clamoring for somebody's blood, and it seemed less than an hour and Broadway was a mass of black and white mourning.

K—You said you had met Robert Lincoln at Petersburg?

S—Yes. We lay before Petersburg in 1864-65. Our headquarters were so near the enemy that we could see the city, and on Sundays could hear the church bells; with a glass we could see the people on the sidewalks going to church. On the picket line I remember that we could hear the chirp of the birds and above them the whispered communications of the Rebels. Our men used to fraternize with them; they would say, "Hello, Johnny, how's the tobacco?" "All right, how's the coffee?" they would ask. They would go over the earthworks and make the exchange. It was while there I first met Bob Lincoln.

Bob Lincoln was a tidy looking lad. I first saw him when he had first come out of college and the President had him appointed an aide on Gen. Grant's staff. It was an afternoon in (?), a right pleasant day. I was an officer on Gen. Willcox's staff. The General had gone to the front with all the rest of his staff; why he left me behind I forget—I may have been sick. At any rate I was at the Headquarters of the First Division, Ninth Army Corps, when I might say like James, "I saw a solitary horseman approaching," only he had an orderly with him.

He was a gay, handsome officer; he rode up to my tent and asked if Gen. Willcox was at Headquarters. I replied that the General with a number of his staff had just ridden to the front, but would return shortly. I asked the officer to dismount, and he introduced himself as Capt. Robert Lincoln, of Gen. Grant's staff. I introduced myself as Major Swords. I called an orderly to take care of his orderly and his horses, and invited him to sit down. We had a pleasant conversation.

I can remember him as a tall, well informed, rather pleasing personality. He was fairly dark, wore a cavalry jacket, and uniform of a Captain and Aide de Camp. The General returning, introductions followed; and he remained to supper with the General and his aides. He asked if there was a station near on the railway which ran to City Point, as he would like the station master to flag the train, so that his horse could be taken aboard with him, to save the long ride to City Point. The General and a number of us rode with him to the station, and [Capt. Lincoln] asked the station master, who was a soldier, to flag the train to City Point, as he wanted to get on board with his horse and orderly.

The station master refused. When Lincoln told him who he was, the soldier replied that the train could not be flagged even for Gen. Grant himself. He thought it was rough, but the soldier had to obey orders. We therefore rode some distance with Capt. Lincoln on his way to City Point, and said goodbye.

K—Did Lincoln see much service during the war.

S—He saw the same service as did the officers on Grant's staff. They were continuously between Headquarters and the firing line.

## Lincoln at the Navy Yard
## Interview with Lieutenant George D. E. Barton, June 24, 1920

With an introduction from Col. Henry L. Swords, I called on Mr. George Barton at 150 Broadway. He is an erect, handsome man with a full straight brow, a very straight nose, bright and impressive blue gray eyes, gray hair and mustache and beautiful shapely hands—a thoroughbred. I told him I wanted to find a man who had seen Lincoln in New York. He replied, "I cannot recall having seen Lincoln in New York, but I saw him often afterwards."

B—Where were you born?

K—On 30th Street, near Eighth Avenue.

B—That ought to make us friends. I was born on Washington Place. I was an officer in the Navy for four years. I am a sailor and like to talk—I live in the past.

Lincoln was a big man, loose jointed, but his eyes—his face and manner—no one looking at him could say he was ugly or homely. He had such a nice voice. He did not dress in the Broadway style; he wore a black frock coat and a black satin vest; black trousers, long; black necktie and white shirt; old fashioned turned down collar. His clothes fitted like all the men, like the general run of public characters in the United States.

As a recreation he used to enjoy coming down to the Washington Navy Yard; he used to ride down on horseback. At first he used to come without any body-guard, and would say, "Nobody wants to kill me!" Later, members of his Cabinet insisted that he have a body-guard; he used to have a squad of cavalry from Cincinnati, all mounted on black horses. The Washington Navy Yard was then commanded by Capt. [Commander John] Dahlgren, an ordnance expert. There was a proving battery for trying out experimental guns; targets were set up opposite. The President was accustomed to visit the yard, and took great interest in the experimental guns.

At one occasion just as Capt. Dahlgren was about to commence firing, he looked around to see if the President was in a safe place. The President shouted, "Go ahead, Captain (Dahlgren was Captain then), I'm all right—I am behind a sapling," and was laughing. That was a characteristic thing of him.

The *Monticello* was at the Navy Yard for repairs, having been in a fight with the battery at Sewell's Point, Va., opposite Fortress Monroe. When she lay alongside the dock, the President walked down, and picking up some splinters from a shot hole, looking up at the officer of the deck with a twinkling eye, he said, "Well, I guess they meant to hit you."

I never met him except to shake hands with him while he wished us God Speed.


## Mrs. Lincoln's Carriage Accident
## As witnessed by O. H. Burlingame

Mrs. Lincoln's accident in July, 1863, when she jumped from her carriage as the horses ran away, may possibly account for her alleged eccentricities during the latter part of her life. Mr. O. H. Burlingame who saw the accident, writes, giving the following account:

I was standing on the west side of the road one day [July 3, 1863], near the Mount Pleasant Hospital, Washington, D. C., with other comrades, nearby and looking towards the White House. We saw the President's equipage coming our way, with the driver's seat off and the horses running away frantically. When the horses reached the place where I was standing, and during the horses' intense motion, the lone occupant, Mrs. Lincoln, jumped from the carriage, fell on the side of her head and shoulder. We picked her up from the ground, stood her on her feet, and she bled considerable from quite a wound on the head. Her mind was substantially a blank at the time, as she paid no attention to the answers we gave to her constantly repeated question, to wit: "Am I in the city or am I in the country?" Two of the comrades carried her in to Mount

Pleasant Hospital, and a while afterwards she was taken to the White House.

No doubt she grieved very much for her dead boy, and afterwards for her martyred husband. Since that time I have entertained the belief that her physical and mental condition resulted largely from the accident.

In response for my request for further details, Mr. Burlingame wrote:

My Dear Sir,

Your valued letter was received last week. Will try and furnish information asked for that the Mrs. Lincoln article in the *National Tribune* does not supply.

Question: As to the time the accident occurred; please permit a little personal "Speal", in which I will try to explain the approximate date of the episode, as recorded in my 146th N. Y. S. Vol. Infantry Regimental History. Our command marched on Saturday, June 14, 1863, through rain and mud until late in the night, then bivouacked until sunrise the next morning.

After a short respite from packing up, we commenced a 25 or 30 mile march, Sunday the 15th inst., under a very hot sun with our outfit drenched with water.

Within two miles of our destination that day I became prostrate and unconscious. The next morning, June 16, I boarded the train at Manassas Junction and was taken to the Fairfax Seminary Hospital, located near Alexandria, Virginia.

I must now depend entirely on memory:

I remained in this hospital two weeks, when through the efforts of my brother-in-law, George Wheelock, Secretary Stanton's clerk at the time, I was transferred to Mount Pleasant Hospital, Washington, D. C., about July the 1st, and to the best of my recollection I had been in that institution about a week when the accident occurred.

Therefore would it not be safe to place the runaway and accident within the week of July 7, 1863.

Your question as to what part of the head she received the wound or her condition at the time?

Since that time I have often had a mental picture of the occurrence but I find it a great stretch of memory in regard to detail, and to gratify my desire to be accurate.

The horses were running on this west road toward the city, with the driver's seat off; and Mrs. Lincoln jumped from the west side of the carriage where I stood and fell mostly on her left side and head.

I observed she was dressed in spotless attire; her dress was dark.

After lifting her from the ground my position was on the right center in front. She bled quite freely from a wound on the left side of her head. Her physical condition seemed good. There was no diagnosis at the time, as she was taken to the hospital by two soldiers, directly following the accident, but not before we had discovered and realized that she had gone daft. She evidently repeated the last thoughts in her mind, before jumping from the carriage.

To wit: "Am I in the city or am I in the country?" paying no attention to the repeated answers: "You are in the country."

However, the conditions existing in that locality at that time are entirely obliterated at present, as it contains some of the most beautiful residences in Washington, D. C.

Question: You ask if I was in uniform at the time.

Yes, I was, and looking very much like a soldier of Mahomet. A new uniform our regiment drew not long before we started on the Gettysburg march, and I cannot refrain from giving you a description of it:

Measuring six feet in height I must have been somewhat conspicuous, wearing what seemed to be combination French-Turkish uniform, consisting of baggy trousers, light blue in color, fastened at the knees; a bright red cap with red tassel; a long white turban around the cap only worn on dress parade; a red sash ten feet long, wound about the body at the waist; white cloth leggings extending to near the knees, the trousers covering them; a strap under the instep; a light blue jacket trimmed with light orange braid scrolled on the breast.

I didn't learn anything about what caused the runaway.

Question: Did I ever see President Lincoln?

I never saw him on his feet. The west road mentioned seemed to be their favorite route in going to and from the city. I saw the carriage passing several times when I was near the road. And one day when Mr. Lincoln was in the carriage alone, evidently destined for the White House I took a position of attention facing the equipage, and gave the President the army salute. It has certainly always been a very pleasant recollection that he politely raised his proverbial silk hat in recognition. While Abe was tall and stalwart and called homely, I revered him so much he did not look that way to me.

Cordially,
Orrin H. Burlingame

# Lincoln and the Furlough
## Letter from Henry W. Berthrong
Co. E, 140th New York Volunteer Infantry

I was enjoying the only furlough granted me during the Civil War and on my way home to Rochester, N. Y., arrived early one morning in Washington. As my train north was not to leave until evening, I decided to visit the various Government departments and public buildings. Having seen the Capitol, Department of the Interior, Post Office and Treasury, I started for the War Department. On the way I had to pass the White House; so I sat on an iron bench, took out a pad and began making a pencil sketch of the White House.

I had about completed my sketch when I became conscious of a tall form standing in front of me; looking upward, I saw President Abraham Lincoln. I became greatly agitated, but he put me immediately at my ease and addressed me in a very kindly manner. "Young man," said he, "What are you doing here?" I told him what I was endeavoring to do. He asked to see the sketch, and I handed it to him. For a few moments he compared it with the original, and then said, "It is excellent drawing. Have you ever taken any lessons?"

I told him that before the war I had studied to be an engraver on wood. He then asked, "Why are you here?" I told him that I was on my way home on furlough. He asked me where I lived, how long a furlough I had been granted, and then about my home and family. Then he said, "Two weeks is a short time to visit your home and return to your regiment. You come with me." So we walked to the War Department on the way he asked the name of my regiment, when I enlisted, in what battles I had fought, etc.

At the War Department, we entered the office of Adj. Gen. Samuel Breck. President Lincoln said, "This young soldier has but two weeks' leave; extend his furlough two weeks more." While the papers were being attended to, the President plied me with many questions relating to my company, regiment and Colonel, as well as to my home. The document authorizing the extension of my furlough was handed to him, and by him to me. During this entire time he held in his hand my little sketch. I felt highly honored when he said, "I like this sketch. Do you mind giving it to me?" I told him I would be delighted to have him accept it. He then asked me to write my name, company and regiment on the back of the sketch, and he would then take it. I did so—H. W. Berthrong, Co. E, 140th N. Y. Vols. President Lincoln then extended his hand, wished me a pleasant journey home and a safe return to my regiment.

At my home I have a crayon portrait of Lincoln, said by everybody to be the best likeness ever made of him. It has been photographed, etched and engraved for various purposes. I might add that I have one of Grant, said by the entire family to be the best likeness of the General they ever saw. Nearly every Grand Army Post in the United States has an etching made from the original which was made at Mount McGregor, New York, where Grant died.

## Lincoln in Church
## Letter from George Rowland

Dear Mr. Kelly,

My uncle, Governor Edwin D. Morgan of New York, attended Dr. Phineas D. Gurley's Presbyterian Church in New York Avenue, Washington, D. C.

I always sat with him about one pew behind President Lincoln; I could almost touch him. He was very churchly—very quiet, not a restless man. I never saw him kneel, but he was serious and very attentive, and when the sermon was finished he used to come out with the others and come against our pew, and my Uncle and he would have a chat.

There was nothing about him that attracted me but the wonderful expression of his face and wonderful eyes. He was the most modest of men.

His kindly eyes were so deep, so serious and so soft. You often see serious eyes—these had something in them that gave perfect confidence and trust, not only in his kindness of heart, but in his nobleness of heart and great ability. They show him to be one of the highest types of perfect gentlemen.

I looked at that man very carefully, and I have seen him surrounded by great statesmen and Generals and public men of that period, and I would pick him out as a man in whom you could feel every confidence and trust.

After the Surrender of Richmond, there was a grand meeting held in the Capitol on the Sunday night following, composed of Senators, Members of Congress, important Generals and Naval officers, together with the Diplomatic Corps, and the people who had come to Washington to inquire about the great victory.

There were many speakers, as well as patriotic music, and the House of Representatives was crowded.

The enthusiasm of the people was almost beyond limit. After probably two hours had elapsed, along about nine o'clock, President Lincoln accompanied by one or two friends came to join the celebration. His appearance was greeted with such enthusiasm that he could hardly get a chance to speak. The cry was: "Lincoln! Lincoln! Lincoln!"

The President modestly raised his hand for silence, and the people responded. He simply asked that the band play:
"The Battle Hymn of the Republic."

The people joined in that wonderful hymn, until the very walls shook with the wondrous response. Then he returned to his seat and listened to the proceedings, which were of wonderful rejoicing. His subdued and one might say devotional manner, convinced me of his impressive religious character.

## Lincoln and Baseball
## Interview with Cornelius Savage

I met Mr. Cornelius Savage when he was connected with the silver department of the Gorham Company at the time they were casting my equestrian bronze of Caesar Rodney for Wilmington, Delaware. He was a fine, courteous gentleman, verging on the 80's. Hearing that he had known Lincoln, I questioned him, and he gave me the following:

S—I was too young to enter the army—my father would not let me go, so I got a position in the Ordnance Department.

I had to go every day to the Adjutant General's Office, and used to see Secretary Stanton when I passed his office. I used to meet President Lincoln every day and walk with him. Sometimes in passing Stanton's office, I could see through the open door, and see him standing in conversation with President Lincoln; it was always, "Mr. Lincoln," or "Mr. President."

Once, I took a short-cut from one building to another; the President frequently made a trip from the White House to the War Department Building, and in that way I passed him several times. The President finally came to recognize me, and nodded or gave me a cheery greeting; he always had a greeting for every one. Then I commenced to fall in next to him and walk with him. Yes, he would sometimes tell me some of his famous humorous stories.

But he had slightly more important things on his mind than entertaining a casual friend. He would talk of things of the day, of the progress of the war and the condition of the army, making such remarks as, "The Army of the Shenandoah is doing well," or "Sherman is making great strides toward the Sea." I wish my memory was better, then I could tell more of his conversations.

I never saw Mr. Lincoln appearing bowed down or crushed by the responsibilities of the war; he seemed always cheerful and hopeful—perhaps it was because it was early in the morning, and he was not yet tired with the toils of the day. I may be wrong, but I never noticed a gray hair in his head; his complexion was very pale, and he was thin, but you know Mr. Lincoln was a tremendously strong man; his hands gave the impression of vigor—they were large and muscular.

We boys formed a baseball team in Washington, and the field where we played was right back of the White House, not more than 100 yards away, I should judge. While out there playing, we would often see the figure of the President standing in the back of the White House, dressed in his black coat and with his tall stovepipe hat on. Many times he seemed to be watching the game with great interest; one day he actually walked down from the White House to the field, and standing back of the catcher, threw the ball into the field. We counted this quite an event. Sometimes he would sit on the rear piazza and look at our game.

One day a new Commissioner of the Public Buildings was appointed, and discovering the crowd of boys playing ball back of the President's home, he came to us in a flurry and said we must find some other place to play. A few days later I met the President on his walk and told him that the Commissioner had ordered our ball games away from his house. He said, "Consider me a member of your club, and when I want you to go, I'll let you know." That was the last I heard of having to go.

Many times I have seen President Lincoln when he was walking alone without protection nearby. One night I was returning from town at 2 A. M., and met him on his way to the War Department. He was alone, and it was only in the distance I saw his bodyguard following. He did not want any bodyguard at all, but it was insisted upon. I used to see Stanton every day, but we never spoke to him; I used to go to his office and see his head clerk. We lived three or four doors from Stanton; four or five times I saw Mr. Lincoln going to see him at 2 or 3 in the morning.

One time I spoke to him and asked him if he was not afraid, "No," he said, "No one wants to hurt me." I noticed afterward that a guard was following him, but he did not know it. The last time I saw the President was a few weeks before his assassination; he seemed as cheerful as ever. The night of his death, I was in a bar room on Ohio Avenue, where the Brooklyn boys used to gather sometimes to chat and play cards. Suddenly we heard cavalry go thundering down the street, and then a man burst in shouting, "YOUR PRESIDENT HAS BEEN SHOT."

We would not have believed it if we had not heard the cavalry go by. I ran as fast as I could to the theater, and saw a large crowd at the house on 10th Street, where they had carried the President. A guard was thrown around the house, and no one was permitted to go in or out. I knew most of the Provost Guard, and could have got by, but I couldn't go in there. The President was in the room that Safford had asked me to take with him.

Many southern refugees used to come to the place on Ohio Avenue. I have often seen John Wilkes Booth there eating crackers and cheese and playing cards. He was a good looking fellow. Oil had recently been discovered in western Pennsylvania and I understand that he was in Washington selling stock.


Mr. Savage said that after the battle of the Wilderness, he used to visit the hospital wards in Washington to see if any of his friends were hurt. He also told me that he was born at 44 Fifth Ave., between 10th and 11th Streets. On returning to New York, he became connected with Ball, Black & Co., on Pearl Street, but had been with Gorham, Co., for over 37 years. The last time I had a talk with Mr. Savage, he told me that the Company had made some changes, among them to make it more comfortable for him by providing a chair for him, surrounded with cases of drawers from which he could display the silver, but he said it was a mistaken kindness, as he stood at the counters for so many years that it was uncomfortable for him to sit and do business.

## Lincoln Delivering the Gettysburg Address
## Interview with Mr. Arthur Briggs Farquhar

Mr. Arthur Briggs Farquhar, President of A. B. Farquhar Company of York, Pennsylvania, was an eye-witness to Lincoln's Gettysburg Address and had written of the scene for the *Saturday Evening Post*. I wrote to Mr. Farquhar for an appointment to interview him on his next visit to New York City. I have long wanted to meet someone who had seen Lincoln on that historic day and who heard those immortal words.

I called at his office in the Cotton Exchange Building. Mr. Farquhar greeted me in the most hospitable manner. His personality was very attractive. He was short, sturdy and active; well-balanced, strong features; a close-cropped full white beard; showing no signs of age although over 84.

Our talk drifted to Lincoln:

F— Mr. Lincoln had most wonderful eyes, but they were kinder. He had the Divine afflatus. All men have something of the Divine in them, but he had Divinity to an exalted extent. No artist can make Lincoln without idealizing him.

When the Rebels took York and threatened to burn the city, I was the man who called and arranged to pay them that they might spare it. No one else could do it, as my father knew General Lee. The Rebels made an agreement and kept it faithfully. Not a horse or thing was stolen. They made a requisition for what they needed and paid for it. I then asked General [John B.] Gordon for a pass to go in our line which he gave me. It was a funny thing to ask the enemy to give me a pass to go in our lines.

After the enemy had gone, lots of people would not speak to me. They used to take off their hats to me while the enemy was there, but they said I must be a rebel, to be enabled to arrange it. I shall never forget those days, being pointed out as "the man who had sold York to the Rebels."

So I went to Washington. I saw John Hay, and explained that I wished to see President Lincoln. Hay declared that I had done right and deserved public commendation, but tried to persuade me not to insist on seeing Lincoln, as he was overworked and very much worried. But on second thoughts, he pointed to a door where I could stand and see him when he came out. President Lincoln received me very kindly, and we walked together to the War Department and when I explained what I had done, he said, "You saw an opportunity and embraced it. Opportunities do not knock at a man's door every day, and those who do not open the door, fail. You opened the door and succeeded in doing something that you will always take pride to remember—I like that. Your trouble is what people may say about it. Go through life satisfying your own conscience and you will do well and be happy. I would be dead if I worried myself about what people say."

We walked up the steps to the War Department and through to Secretary Stanton's office. Stanton was personally known to me, my cousin, James

Hallowell, being his private secretary. When Lincoln told my story to Stanton—Stanton replied, "Well, I judge by that act he has saved the country some thousands of dollars."

Now here is a story that I know to be true: Lincoln gave an order which Stanton on reading said, "Lincoln is a Damn Fool!" When this was reported to Lincoln—Lincoln laughed and said, "I have a great respect for Stanton. If Stanton said that, it must be true." And after that remark was reported to Stanton, it started a friendly feeling between them; it took Seward longer to get over his jealousy.

Mr. Farquhar expressed great interest in what I was doing, and standing up, took a piece of paper from his desk and holding it in his left hand said, "I will show you how President Lincoln delivered the speech, as I remember every word and action."

And rising he stood square—on both feet, slightly apart, with chest full, and head erect. Taking an envelope from his desk and holding it in his left hand, in a clear voice he repeated the entire address slowly and deliberately, calling my attention in every change in action, while I sat back and took notes and made sketches of the telling points in the phrases and actions; although the difference in their personalities was so extreme. His earnestness, reserve and quality of delivery seemed to bring Lincoln before me, like a reincarnation of the past. When with his right hand he gave a few deliberate, calm gestures, he would occasionally glance down at his left hand which hung easily at his side.

When Mr. Farquhar had finished, he said, "Mr. Lincoln had a couple of small pieces of paper in his left hand, at which he would occasionally glance during his speech. There was very little applause. People do not applaud a great sermon. But I think the people were disappointed; they thought it was too short. They did not realize it was finished. Someone asked Seward who wrote it, and Seward said, 'No one could have written it but Abraham Lincoln.' [Edward] Everett stepped over to him after it was finished and congratulated him saying, 'My address will only be remembered because it was made on the same day.'"

The Lincoln he realized for me that day is my hope to put in bronze some day. We exchanged several letters after that in regard to Lincoln, and in signing his book, *The First Million is the Hardest*, he inscribed the following verse:

> "The thing that we call living is
> not gold nor fame at all;
> It is laughter and contentment and
> the struggle for a goal;
> It's everything that's needed for the
> shaping of a soul."

# Letter from A. B. Farquhar

February 18, 1921
My dear Mr. Kelly,

I have received your letter of Feb. 16th, in regards to Mr. Lincoln's appearance at Gettysburg—answering your questions in the order given, would say:

1) President Lincoln was simply dressed, in a business suit, but with a frock coat and high hat, such as he is usually depicted in.

2) He stood, as usual, in an easy unconventional attitude, as though he were alone.

3) He stood erect, but as usual with tall men, had something of the appearance of stooping.

4) President Lincoln was always full of vigor. He had an attractive personality, one you would love to talk with but never feel safe in attacking.

5) It is utterly ridiculous to depict Lincoln as incapable. He had a wonderful personality. I regard him as a superman—made such an impression upon me that I sometimes wake up at night seeing him stand before me, and this I can say of no other man.

6) There was no rail in front. It was a rustic platform.

The statue in Cincinnati by Barnard does not do him justice at all. The feet and hands are too prominent. You never thought of his feet and hands. It is true, I remember his fingers were long (which was perhaps natural in a man of his stature). I could not help noticing this as he took hold of my hand; his feet I never noticed. We walked together in Washington. He walked in an easy manner, but I had to take about two steps to keep up with one of his. It might have occurred to a stranger seeing him for the first time that he was a little rustic in appearance, but with a second glance that would vanish, and ever afterward you would look upon him with admiration. To me he was a very attractive and powerful personality. You must remember, my shaking hands with him at Gettysburg and being close to him there, was not an unfamiliar incident. I had met him in Washington, walked and talked with him, heard both his inaugurals.

Sometime when I am in New York will be glad to have a chat with you about Lincoln.

## Speaking of Lincoln with General Fred Grant
August 19, 1907

One time while visiting Gen. Fred Grant when he was in command at Governors Island, among other things we got to talking of President Lincoln. He said, "Through being shot, Lincoln became the American patron saint; he was not a popular man before his death, and people gathered very little [history] about him. Nicolay and Hay were fine literary men, had everything about Lincoln, and wrote it up well. Others who had written up the country side of him, people won't pay any attention to.

"Lincoln is said to have liberated the slaves. He wrote the Emancipation Proclamation emancipating the slaves of the South, but said nothing of the slaves in Delaware and Maryland. He did not free them, and by not doing that he prolonged the war, as it gave the South something to fight for. The South said we were fighting to free the negroes; we were not, but to save the Union. By that Proclamation, he put men in position of fighting to free the negroes, who were not. It prolonged the war, as the South might have come in otherwise, but it could not after that—men will fight harder to save their property than for anything else.

"How Bob Lincoln resents the fact that people treat him as though he was his father's son, and wants to be treated as a personality himself. Now I'm different; I am very proud to be considered my father's son."

To my question about the first meeting of Grant and Lincoln:

"Yes, I was there with my father, but not that I ever heard my father say anything about it, but from what I had heard others say—I had not much of an opinion of the officials in Washington. I felt that all they did was to interfere with the work of its officers in the field, so it did not make much impression on me."

## Grant's Message to Lincoln
## An Interview with Rev. Henry E. Wing

On May 4, 1864, Grant and his army headed South and disappeared into the Wilderness, leaving no sign as to their destination. Then came a heart-breaking silence, and the whole North was filled with bewilderment and apprehension.

How the news from Grant and his army reached Lincoln and lifted the burden from his heart is told by the Rev. Henry E. Wing in a small book written by him, entitled, *How Lincoln Kissed Me*.

I read it with great interest, and was filled with a strong desire to see the hero. Rev. Wing was one of the four correspondents at the front for the *New*

*York Tribune*; he was detailed to the Second Corps with my old friend Alfred R. Waud, the artist for *Harper's Weekly*. After the close of the first days' fighting in the Wilderness, the reporters met, and it was decided that one should start for the North with the report of the battle, and Wing as the youngest of the group, volunteered for the dangerous adventure through territory controlled by rebel guerrillas. He went to Gen. Grant's headquarters and told of his plans, and asked him if he had any message for the people, to insert in his dispatches for the Tribune.

"Well," Gen. Grant replied, "you might tell the people that things are going swimmingly down here."

Wing took it down in his note book and turned away. He had only gone a few steps, when Grant came up and laying his hand on his shoulder, said, "You expect to get through to Washington?" "Yes," said Wing, "I will start at daybreak." Then Grant in a low voice said, "Well, if you see the President, tell him from me that, whatever happens, there will be no turning back."

Next morning, Wing with his saddle bags filled with notes and dispatches, and a peck of oats strapped behind, mounted his horse, "Jenny," and headed for the enemies territory. Waud took him to a loyal man named Wykoff, who advised him as to his trip. He was to disguise himself in a butternut suit, coarse brogans, and a disreputable, quilted cotton hat.

Mr. Wykoff also gave him general directions as to blind trails, and the story was arranged that if he was apprehended and questioned, he was to say he was going to Washington, that there had been a great battle in which the Yankee army had been overwhelmingly defeated and that he was hurrying with the news to the Southern sympathizers in Washington. Mr. Wykoff also gave him the names of half a dozen Southern sympathizers in Washington.

Wing destroyed his bundle of memoranda, and then made a harrowing ride through enemy held territory, to reach Washington and personally deliver Gen. Grant's message to Lincoln.

The following brief passage from Rev. Wing's book, tells of the moment when Lincoln realized that Grant wasn't going to retreat as previous commanders had done:

> The vision that opened through those wonderful eyes from a great soul glowing with a newly kindled hope is the likeness of Mr. Lincoln that I still hold in my memory, and ever shall. And that hope was never to be extinguished. Others had turned back. Every other one had. But there had come an end to that fatal folly.
>
> Mr. Lincoln put his great strong arms about me, and, carried away in the exuberance of his gladness, imprinted a kiss upon my forehead. We sat down again, and I disclosed to him, as I could not do except in the light of that pledge of the great commander, all the disheartening details of that dreadful day in the Wilderness. But I could assure him that the Army of the Potomac, in all its history was never in such a hopeful spirit as when they discovered at the close of a day of disappointment, that they were not to "turn back."

This story prompted me to call on the Rev. Mr. Wing at the home of his daughter, in Glendale, Connecticut, and I was very much interested in hearing more of Rev. Wing's description of Lincoln.

Mr. Wing received me in a glowing hospitable manner. He was a handsome, bold featured gentleman of medium size, and still retained a graceful, boyish figure. A sweep of strong gray hair drooped over the right side of his brow, and bushy brows shaded his handsome bright eyes, with deep comedy lines in their corners; a fine high-bred nose, and a long gray mustache, and swart complexion. His left hand showed a wound at the end of his thumb, and the second and third fingers had been cut away.

In response to my remark about his book he said: "He kissed me on the forehead," pointing to the spot on the left of the brow; at the same time his eyes filled with tears.

W—I can feel the kiss now. It was like the kiss of a Prophet in olden times, which conveyed a blessing.

K—Mr. Wing, I am going to make a sketch of that scene, showing President Lincoln kissing your brow.

W—Oh, I don't want to be in it.

K—Never mind.

I started at once making a sketch of the composition. As I did so he looked on smiling all the time. "Stand up," I said, which he did. I then took the pose of Lincoln saying, "I put this hand on your shoulder, the other on your arm, Lincoln stooping over you." Here I took the pose, and said, "Is that right?" "Yes," was his answer.

And as he sat down he gazed reflectively, as he lowly murmured:

"AND HE KISSED ME!"

Then he continued:

W—After I met the President, I went over to the National Hotel and went to bed. Next morning I went downstairs and there was a man (another correspondent) addressing the crowd, saying that my news dispatch just published in the *Tribune* was not true—that no message had come through the lines. Then some one caught sight of me and yelled, "There he is!" They all pulled me up and made me stand on the billiard table and tell all about it. Then the man stood up and threw me a fifty dollar check, saying, "That's for beating

Stanton!"  And others began to throw me money; thus they expressed their feelings against Stanton [for withholding news from the front].

K—Some say Lincoln was ugly; is that so?

W—It is hard to describe him.  I never saw the great Lincoln.  I never heard him make one of his great speeches.  He had a way of slouching and letting himself settle on his joints—slouching as though he was tired—carrying burdens.  But when his face lit up, then he was beautiful.  You would not have thought of anything ugly in that face.

Here Mr. Wing stood up and acted out his statements by standing with his shoulders formed.  His head thrown back and his knees inclined to bend.

W—Like in the story I wrote.  Lincoln walked to the window and looked out for two or three minutes, but seemed to see nothing.  Then he drew his giant figure up to his full height.  His face became transfigured.  His face looked too beautiful.  Oh, oh, that was fine—the most wonderful face—it showed triumph—spiritual ecstasy—it was transfigured—spiritual power had triumphed over fear.

The other occasion that I distinctly recall was early in August [1864].  These might be remembered as the very most dismal days in the whole political campaign, following the fiasco of the mine explosion at Petersburg, and before the successes at Atlanta and Mobile.

I had never seen the President so utterly disheartened.  I tried encouraging him as I thought I had detected a slight turning of the tide in his favor.  But his response was only a slight shake of the head.

Then after sitting a moment in silence, he rose and walked to the window.  He stood in his weary posture for two or three minutes, and then I saw his gaunt frame straighten to his full height as he turned about, his face was transfigured.

Some miracle of grace had been wrought in him while he stood before the window.  As he advanced toward me, I got on my feet.  "Henry," he said, "do you believe in prayer?"  I was too surprised to make an articulate answer, but my face must have given him encouragement, for he continued:  "If the Lord did not answer prayer, I could not stand it; and if I did not believe in God who works his will with nations, I should dispose of the republic."

In the election, Mr. Lincoln received nearly 78 per cent of the soldiers' ballot count; in the tense formula of the period—the veterans voted as they shot.

On another occasion—a humorous one—I was taking down notes at a table and President Lincoln was talking to a tall man at the door.  It appeared he had called on the President to see if he was as tall as he was.  Now Lincoln seemed to have the ability to stretch up and make himself as tall as he liked; so Lincoln proved himself the tallest.  The fellow went away and Lincoln came over to me.

Now I have never known Lincoln to laugh. He had a way of gurgling away down in his stomach. But he came over and said to me with a chuckle, "The fellow when he found I out-measured him said, 'Mr. President, you may beat me, but I have a brother eleven feet high.' 'Is that so,' said I, 'I never heard of such a thing. I'd like to see him.' 'You'll never see him,' he replied, 'He's down in Tennessee. You see I have two half brothers five feet seven inches tall, and two halves make a whole—and that makes him just eleven feet.'"

## Lincoln under Fire at the Battle of Fort Stevens, July 12, 1864
## A visit to the Battlefield with Gen. Horatio Wright

While I was in Washington, D. C. working on a bas relief portrait for Gen. Horatio Wright, the general told me of his first meeting with President Lincoln:

W—My brother-in-law was a Southerner, and was arrested and without any trial, simply because he was a Southerner, Secretary Stanton had him locked up in Fort Lafayette.

I called on President Lincoln and asked him if he could be released. The President said, "I suppose after I have done that, you will be coming after something else."

I said, "Mr. President, that is the first favor I have ever asked of you and I hope it will be the last. But it seems hard that I who am fighting in the field for the Country that should have my brother-in-law put in prison simply because he is a Southern man, without any trial, while I am willing to be responsible for his loyalty. At this the President said: "Sit down."

I said, "Mr. President, I prefer to stand."

At this President Lincoln wrote a note and holding it out to me, said, "Take that to Secretary Stanton."

I said, "Mr. President, I am not your servant to deliver notes."

At this, President Lincoln stood up, smiling and bowing and said, "General Wright will you kindly oblige me by giving this note to Secretary Stanton."

I said, "Certainly, Mr. President." I took the note to Secretary Stanton. It was ordering the release of my brother-in-law.

K—How did Stanton take it?

W—He did not seem to like it. The next time I saw President Lincoln was at Fort Stevens [where 14,000 Confederates under Gen. Jubal Early threatened Washington, D. C.].

Gen. Wright then gave me details of President Lincoln being under fire at Fort Stevens on July 12, 1864, and we drove out to the battlefield in his carriage and he showed me the very spot where Lincoln stood. I made a quick sketch of the scene which he approved.

Later the next day I visited my friend, William V. Cox of the National Museum, and told him the story. He wanted to see the spot, so we went over to the fort and I pointed out President Lincoln's position.

Mr. Cox, unknown to me, drove a stake to mark it.

The following summer, I returned to Washington and arranged a meeting between Gen. Wright and Mr. Cox, to meet at Fort Stevens; Gen. David Stanley was also present.

I brought with me the General's nearly finished Relief and after the General approved and signed it, Mrs. Wright said: "It is perfect; I am delighted with it." So I wrapped it up and she added, "I would love to see it in bronze, but I suppose I never shall." "Yes, I will try to bring it on so that you can see it," I answered.

We had lunch, and then made arrangements to start for the Soldiers' Home and meet Gen. Stanley and visit Fort Stevens, where I had arranged that Dr. Marcus Benjamin and Cox should meet us.

We got into the carriage, I riding on the box with Jackson the Driver; the General and [his daughter] Mrs. Smith riding in the carriage. I carried the relief of the General along with the reliefs of Generals Stanley and Pleasonton, between my feet to keep them from jarring.

Arriving at the Soldiers' Home, General Stanley came down, and after some disjointed conversation, I got the reliefs out.

Gen. Wright looking at the relief of Pleasonton, said, "I recognize the forehead, eyes, and nose of Pleasonton, but I do not recollect the back of the head, how it was."

I said, "He wore long hair at that time," and got the photograph of Pleasonton to show him. They also approved of Gen. Stanley's head. Mrs. Smith saying, "You have not only got the character of the men, but their very atmosphere. As to Gen. Pleasonton, I do not know him, but as it is so different to the rest I think you must have gotten his. You have got the individuality of each one without losing your own."

Then it was proposed that we start for Fort Stevens. Gen. Stanley's carriage was brought around, and Gen. Wright said, "Kelly, being Master of Ceremonies, it is for him to decide when we are to start." And with lots of jolly remarks from the jolly soldiers and bright ones from Mrs. Smith, we pared off. I drew back to give Gen. Wright the first place in the carriage, but he drew up and bowing with an old-time courtesy and a kindly smile that was inimitable, said, "You are the Master of Ceremonies, and I am to have the honor of following you."

There was nothing to say, but to give in and take my place. The old General riding on my left leaning on his gold-headed cane and his round-brimmed soft hat pulled way down; Gen. Stanley and Mrs. Smith following in their carriage. It was a beautiful day, splendid sunshine, keeping with the red of the road and the green of the trees.

I asked him if he had ridden up with the troops.

W—I think not.  I went up another road; I forget which.

K—Were you mounted?

W—Yes.


As we drew near Fort Stevens I saw Dr. Marcus Benjamin and Mr. Cox of the Smithsonian.  On alighting from the carriage, I introduced the party and we adjourned to the earthworks.  Cox asked Gen. Wright where Lincoln stood.  The General took his bearings and said, "Here."  Cox looked at me and smiled, and as the General moved off Cox came over and brushed away the earth where the General's heel had rested which disclosed the head of a stake.  That reminded me when I visited him the year before and told him of Gen. Wright's locating the spot where Lincoln had stood under fire.

Cox then said, "After you had gone I came out and drove the stake in the spot where your heel had marked.  And now Gen. Wright has placed his heel on the same stake—which is strong testimony of your memories."

This coincidence and Gen. Wright's story so impressed Mr. Cox that he later bought the Fort to preserve it, and the Sixth Corps Association had my sketch modeled in bronze and inserted it in a boulder which was placed on the spot where Lincoln stood.

On leaving we shook hands, and as we drove off, Gen. Wright had not yet entered his carriage.  He saluted us.  It was a fine memory.  The old General standing there in the sunshine, his blue army overcoat, with the reddish earthworks, the plains and the distant hills—the scene of his victory as a background.  That was the last time I saw him.

A copy of his Relief is now over his grave at Arlington.


## Lincoln at the Battle of Fort Stevens
## Interview with Dr. George T. Stevens
350 West 85th Street, July 29, 1919


Dr. George T. Stevens was a surgeon in the Sixth Army Corps during the war and met with President Lincoln shortly before the Battle of Fort Stevens.  I met with the Doctor at his home and he provided me the following details:


S—Behind Fort Stevens was a temporary Hospital, made of logs, I think.  I was standing in front of it alone.  A carriage drove up in which was President and Mrs. Lincoln.  He addressed me and I went over and stood beside him while he asked me questions.

K—Did he go to the Hospital?

S—No.  There was no one there.  I was merely waiting round for business to begin—the battle had not begun.

President Lincoln said, "Hadn't you better get in so we can talk better?"  It was an old fashioned barouche, the seats faced each other.  President and Mrs. Lincoln sat in the back seat, I sat in the front.  President Lincoln questioned me about the arrival of the Sixth Corps, but he seemed to know all about it himself.  Then Gen. Wright rode up at the head of his Staff, and after some remarks with President Lincoln, he rode off.  President Lincoln said, "Don't you think we ought to go with them?"  I was young then, and of course was agreeable to anything the President suggested, and President and Mrs. Lincoln descended from the carriage.  A lieutenant came up and escorted us to the Fort.  There was a set of wooden steps leading to the parapet.  We went up.  Gen. Wright, who was a little distance off, came over and advised us to get down.  The President stayed there; I beside him.  Then the troops deployed in advance, shots began to fly around.  An officer who had sat on the top was hit in the leg; he limped off.  Gen. Wright came over again and said, "Mr. President, I shall have to insist on your getting down."  At which President Lincoln, raising his long hat, said, "General Wright, I obey my superior officer."  And then he got down.

K—Then Mrs. Lincoln was not up there when the firing was going on?

S—No.

K—But the picture in your book shows her on the parapet.

S—That was only to indicate that she was there.  She was not there during the firing.  I drew the picture years after the War.  I did not know anything about perspective.  It was engraved by a man in Troy who used to engrave stoves and other mechanical work.

I was in the uniform of a Major.  I think I wore a cap; no sword.

K—Was the wounded man near enough to appear in the group?

S—No.  I attended to his wound later.

K—Please describe Mrs. Lincoln.

S—She was very agreeable.  She was a plain, good looking woman; but very agreeable.  She was not stout; not fat, but rounded.

Mrs. Stevens said, "No, she was not fat, like the women in these days.  I have seen her at receptions where she was very agreeable."

K—Did she say much in the carriage?

S—No. He took the lead in the conversation.


Dr. Stevens then told me he attended John Brown's funeral.

S—I was one of four men who lowered him into the grave. It was toward the end of the year; there was snow in patches on the ground.


## Lincoln Playing with Children
## Letter from Alfred Denton Cridge, Portland, Oregon, May 9, 1920

Dear Mr. Kelly,
 Yours of the 5th received. My recollections of the great Lincoln are rather dim, and would not have been kept in my memory but for my mother and aunt telling me about some of the events as I grew up. However, I remember sitting on his lap, looking into his face and the outlines of some of the stories he told us; his second inauguration; the excitement attending the fall of Richmond; the terror of alarm the night of his assassination, and many other little matters.
 My father, Alfred Cridge, was chief clerk of the inspection division, Quarter-master General's office, for a number of years, beginning with the outbreak of the Civil War, he was, in fact, chief expert accountant, and also was assigned the duties of condensing reports of different officials for review by Lincoln. He frequently reported to him in person, and my mother was on speaking terms with him sufficiently to be recognized by him whenever he saw her, and to make appeals to him for pardon for young soldiers, and on behalf of Quaker boys willing to serve but not to bear arms, and have them assigned to hospital duties, field work, etc. She was reared a Quaker in part and wore the costume a great deal.
 At the time we were caught stealing flowers in the White House grounds, the Cridge family resided on Seventeenth Street about half a block from the White House, and my brother, Afton, was about seven years of age. He wore a white ruffled shirt, imitation blue soldier's cap, brown velvet pants to the knees, embroidered with a zig-zag pattern down the sides, and what we called the George Washington shoes, because they had silver buckles on them and were what we now call Oxford. He had long curls and golden hair, and people often stopped him on the street to ask his name and get him to talk to them.

He died a few months after the event of flowers and Lincoln of which you write.

I was younger and was wearing my first pants with red shoes and short bobbed hair. I was not four years of age at the time. My brother was slender and I was a stout little fellow. Nobody ever complimented me on my looks and very few outside the family ever gave me any pennies to smile at them, as they did Afton.

We tore the fuchsia branches off along the side of the graveled walk leading directly from the graveled walk at the Seventeenth street entrance. I had the bushes pointed out to me some years after, and the marks of the vandalism were evident even then. One of the branches was quite a little drag for me, and my brother had a larger branch and several smaller ones, loaded down with the beautiful bell-shaped flowers.

When Lincoln first appeared we were receiving quite a threatening lecture by the gardener, a white-haired and stooped over old man, I remember, and we were not more than 20 feet from the iron picketed gateway. Lincoln seemed to me to be very tall, and my first impression of him was that he was an ugly man. The gardener went away and Lincoln took us to a bench on the grass and cut the branches slowly off the main stalk with a large knife which he opened up to let me look at the blades. I think it had three blades. Meanwhile he explained how it hurt the fuchsia plants, or other plants, to tear them off, and the right way was to cut them off. He illustrated it by pulling a single hair from each of our heads, and then by cutting several hairs, quite a little ringlet, I remember, off my brother's head, which he put in his pocket very slowly, winding it around his fingers.

I sat on his lap during part of this interview, and my brother was pressed close to his knees. Lincoln did the fuchsias up in a neat bouquet, throwing the refuse on the ground and then carefully picking each piece up because, he said, the gardener didn't like the litter. As Lincoln talked to us he occasionally smiled, and I came to the conclusion that while he was not much for looks he was a good man. Lincoln escorted us to the gate and waved his hand to us when we were safely across Pennsylvania Avenue. He told us to give the flowers to my mother with his compliments.

A few days afterwards, we were with my mother when Lincoln accosted her on Pennsylvania Avenue near where we last parted from him, and shook hands all around. He again invited us when we wanted flowers to ask the gardener for them, and invited my mother to let us come over to the White House at 4 P. M., where, he said, a number of children friends came to play with him three times a week, and sometimes oftener. We went a number of times that summer into the fall. One afternoon he came out to a bunch of little folks rather late, and somewhat hurriedly. There had been a great battle, and my mother said he left a cabinet meeting to meet with us. He always met us at a little grove sheltered from the sight of the street and in the rear of the White House.

There several benches were drawn up and the tall, grave, sad-eyed man would tell us stories, and laugh himself, as we laughed. I often stood on the bench beside him, and sometimes sat in his lap. He would have first one child and then another in his arms, or pressed against his knees. The girls would drop their dolls in their interest in the stories, and I remember one little girl who resided next door to us whose doll he used as an illustration on his arm to show how an Indian rode, and his motions, words, grimaces and smiles made us laugh so loudly that a lady came out of the White House and told Lincoln that he must come in because he had a large number of people to see him who had been waiting an hour or more. That was Mrs. Lincoln, as I afterwards recognized her at some function where I was taken. Mrs. Lincoln told my mother that Lincoln would leave his cabinet meeting any time to romp with a bunch of children. On this occasion I can remember how he stopped smiling, his face became sad, and he sighed, bowed his head and went away apparently in deep thought. My brother told me that Mr. Lincoln owed people so much money that they made him miserable asking for it, and I can remember an Uncle of mine roaring with laughter when my brother evolved the same theory to him that evening.

# Lincoln's Body Guard
# Letter from George Coates Ashmun
# Late 2^nd Lieut. Lincoln's Body Guard
# 7^th Independent Company Ohio Vol. Cavalry

March 18^th, 1920
My Dear Sir,

In response to your note of the 15^th, I have to confess that my impressions of Mr. Lincoln's appearance, as I saw him, have probably been somewhat dimmed by time.

The cavalry company of which I was a member, was recruited in this state, one man from each county, in Nov. & Dec. 1863. It served as body guard and escort to Mr. Lincoln, from Jany. 1^st 1864, to the time of his death.

From the various pictures of Mr. Lincoln, which have appeared before and after his death, I have readily appreciated that he was a difficult subject for artists. To those of us who saw him frequently, it was a common remark that his facial expression and general bearing varied greatly from time to time, both in sitting and walking, and the change to his features during the last year of his life was very marked—the lines which give expression were deeper, and the whole face was very different from that of his pictures of earlier date.

I can give you three instances when I had a good opportunity under favorable circumstances:

1) During the summer of 1864, the Lincoln family was located in a cottage in the grounds of the "Old Soldiers Home," four miles north of the White House. The routine, daily duty of our company, at that time, was to escort and protect the President, in the trip back and forth, between those points. In several of those trips, Mr. Lincoln rode a horse with the company. He was a good rider, and sat on his horse as firmly and erect as other men of the company.

2) When making short speeches to people from the balcony of the White House, he often became much stimulated by his audiences, and at such times, standing erect and with more or less of gesturing with head and arms, he certainly had none of the "slouchy" about him.

3) Our company served as escort and guard for Mr. Lincoln, at his second inauguration, March 4, 1865. While he was delivering his inaugural address, he stood on the granite platform, which forms a part of the steps at the Senate end of the Eastern front of the Capitol. With his height, strength of limbs and earnestness of manner, while speaking, so clearly outlined at midday, he presented, to me, a typical figure of heroic leadership.

The truth appears to me, to be that Mr. Lincoln was so intense in feeling regarding the condition of the nation, and his relation to it, that after the stimulation of his efforts to express himself passed away, a period of physical exhaustion followed, and he had learned to accept it and regain his poise. His attitude in the open carriage, riding from the Capitol back to the White House, after his inaugural address did give a very different impression from that of the man on the Capitol steps. Some of the photographs of scenes of that day will be better guides to his appearance than I can convey in this way.

The small cottage near the Old Soldiers Home was occupied by the Lincoln family during the summer of 1864, and was the one that had been used by officers and their families connected with the Home. It stood north and a little east of the Main Home building, four or five hundred feet from it. In regard to the domestic affairs in that cottage at the time, I have no knowledge.

In the service of the body guard (escort rather) during that summer, it was the ordinary duty for the company to be at the White House front, with some variation as to hours, on notice received from someone at the White House, but usually at about 5 P. M., seldom as early as 4 o'clock, or as late as 8 o'clock. Usually not more than forty men were on duty for each trip, and when going out to the Home before sunset, the company rode 40 or 50 feet behind the carriage. At times when the trip was made after dark, the company rode nearer the carriage and in times of special anxiety, men and horses were paired front, sides and rear for protection of the occupants.

The driver of the president's carriage was not an enlisted man or definitely under control of the Escort officers, but he was instructed to maintain an even rate of speed in order to permit the guard to be placed properly. This was usually formed "by fours," sometimes changed to "platoons" or "by twos." The streets and roads were uneven in width and surface. Arriving at the Soldiers Home, Mr. Lincoln passed to the care of the regular infantry guard on duty about the buildings and grounds. The escort guard then returned to its tents for the night, which were several hundred yards from the cottage, but within the Home grounds.

For the return to the White House in the morning, on ordinary days, the escort was at the cottage at 8 o'clock and rode behind the carriage. Frequently on the morning return trip, a stop would be made at the residence of Secretary Seward, who came out to the carriage on the street for a few moments, and then to the War Department building, where Secretary Stanton came out to the carriage. These conferences with the secretaries varied in length from a few minutes to considerably more.

After Mr. Lincoln entered the White House, the escort went to quarters to await the next call. Several times during that summer, trips between White House and cottage had to be taken late at night. Mr. Lincoln alone or with some member of the family usually occupied the carriage which was guarded as mentioned before. In regard to a reason for Mr. Lincoln's choice of the cottage instead of the specially prepared room in the Main House building, I can only infer that he wished to be with his family.

The Old Soldiers Home buildings of that date were not attractive. It was during the summer of 1864, while the President and his family were making that cottage their domicile, that Confederate troops under Gen. Early, came within two miles of that spot!

## Another Letter from George C. Ashmun

Cleveland Heights, Ohio
January 6, 1921

In response to yours of the First, I will endeavor to outline some events which took place in Washington, on March 4, 1865, the day of Mr. Lincoln's second inauguration, of which I have memory. Our company was directed to be at the White House front, at 9 o'clock A. M. It was raining steadily, but the company in best form took its position as directed, promptly.

At about 11 o'clock the company was moved to just inside the gate of the west exit to the driveway from the White House front. Shortly afterward the supposed president's carriage came to that point, the company taking position behind it.

Pennsylvania Avenue at that hour was filled with a mixture of military and civic bodies moving to take positions for the parade to the capitol. After a delay of fifteen or twenty minutes, Mrs. Lincoln's face appeared at a window of the closed carriage and she inquired if a way could not be cleared in the street for the carriage to pass? We then learned that Mr. Lincoln was not in the carriage, but was already at the capitol attending to the business of a closing session of congress and his first term.

On Mrs. Lincoln being assured that a passage for the carriage could be made, she directed it to be done, and with the escort placed in front, a rapid ride was made to the East entrance to the Capitol.

The condition of Pennsylvania Avenue, owing to rain and traffic, was such that men, horses and carriage were so badly spattered, it was necessary for escort to get cleaned up before the return trip was to be made. The company retired to the ground near or where the congressional library building now stands, and another carriage was obtained for Mr. Lincoln's return to the White House—an open carriage, for the rain had ceased and the sun was shining.

As soon as the escort and carriage were ready, we moved through the mass of people to a position in the road way directly in front of where Mr. Lincoln was speaking, at an estimated distance of from 3 to 4 hundred feet. The escort was so occupied with its own duties of the occasion—horses excited by the close contact of so many people, we could give little attention to the speaker or his speech. We saw him and heard his voice, but (speaking for myself) could not follow his words. As the picture of that scene rests in my memory, Mr. Lincoln, in the closing part of his speech, did not read from, or in any way refer to any manuscript or notes. His attitude, manner and voice indicated an intense earnestness and determination. Whether or not his closing words impressed any or many in that mass of people, as something ages would quote, I can give no opinion.

The escort wore the uniform of ordinary cavalrymen with no distinctive markings. Pardon so much to tell so little.

## Lincoln's Expressions—Letter from Ervin S. Chapman

My Dear Sir,

Since the appearance of my article in *Colliers* of Feb. 12th, 1921, I have been so besieged by letters that none of the number has received the attention it has been in my heart to give, since yours of April 6th, has until now been unanswered, as your picture of Washington at Valley Forge has remained unacknowledged. For the latter I thank you very sincerely. It is a great picture of a very great relief work. The subject is one to which I have given much thought. I could write you at length about it, but other matters of present interest to you should receive my attention.

When Lincoln was about to read his Second Inaugural, one of the audience called out: "Put on your specs!" "Yes my friend," said Mr. Lincoln, "I am no longer a young man." He read his Second Inaugural Address without glasses.

In my opinion the scene could not be as well represented in relief as otherwise.

Yes, Washington and Lincoln are the companion characters in American History. Neither is comparable with any other in American History. Washington might be compared with some world character, but Lincoln could not be. He is in a class by himself. Washington being the only one who approaches him, and yet the differences are so many and so prominent as to make comparison difficult.

There were five distinct and pronounced expressions of Mr. Lincoln's face.

1) When listening to routine proceedings in court, at church, in company, and when in meditation. At such times he had a far away solemn look. That was his appearance when seated, before delivering the Second Inaugural Address. Sometimes that look took on a pathetic look of melancholy that was indescribable.

2) When listening to music or an address that pleased him. I have one such picture—only one and I cannot part with it, and I will endeavor to have one sent to you, and if I fail I will loan you mine.

3) When listening to something that pleased him or interested him so deeply that he intended to make approving comment or to pursue the same subject further. Number 2 above, is the nearest approach to his expression at such a time.

4) His face was animated and winsome in social conversation, and simply luminous, almost transfigured when speaking in soulful discussion—*It is not in art.*

5) During the devotional part of public worship, he was impressively solemn and devout.

Mr. Lincoln sometimes attended the mid-week prayer meeting at the New York Ave. Presbyterian Church (Dr. P. D. Gurley's) at which times he occupied a side room with the door sufficiently ajar to enable him to hear the singing and Dr. Gurley's lecture. At such times he seldom lifted his eyes, and was always exceedingly devout in looks and manner. At preaching services, he usually looked at the preacher, sometimes with a far away dreamy look, and at other times with the look of "taking it all in."

## Lincoln's Second Inaugural, March 4, 1865
## Timothy H. Roberts, 24th Regiment Veterans Reserve Corps

I had read in a newspaper that Col. Timothy H. Roberts was to give an illustrated talk on Lincoln, to the men of the Bowery Mission. I attended and it was very interesting, and as he came out, I introduced myself. He was a tall, impressive, erect and vigorous looking man, with a military bearing.

During our short talk he said:

R—Lincoln was one of the handsomest men because he was one of the most natural. He was polite and considerate to everybody—was natural with everybody, and everybody loved him. George Washington will never be the same to the people as Lincoln is. Lincoln was like what everybody needs; he is one of the people, and he knew the people. He was a literary genius, wrote from the heart, and is understood by the people. I stood on guard by his body in the Rotunda of the Capitol at Washington, and as the people went by, men, women and children were crying. Did anyone cry when a President died, except for President Lincoln?

The first time I ever saw him was on March 18, 1864, the closing night of the Ladies Sanitary Fair at the Patent Office, Washington. He came from behind the scenes and said, "I came here to say a few words." And he read a short speech.

I was at his last New Year's reception at the White House. At President Lincoln's second inauguration, I was within forty feet of him, and one incident I particularly remember. The day had been stormy and clouded up, but as President Lincoln came out, I saw in the sky a bright, brilliant star. I remember it—a bright, brilliant star; I saw it myself! Afterward I read somewhere a mention of it. During the Second Inaugural Address, everyone was as still as death.

K—Did you hear him say, "With Charity toward all, and Malice toward none?

R—Yes.

Then at my request he stood up, went over the lines and gave me the action as he recalled it. I sketched it as he stood there; the Colonel looked at my sketch, and said: "That's it—exactly; you have every gesture!"

R—I remember Mrs. Lincoln. Four men went up on each side of her the day she went up the steps to the inauguration. Lincoln was always manly; he stood just like a man. Whatever he said carried weight. He was straight, and firm; his voice was clear—a good clear voice. I can see him now—the whole world could not phase him.

I carried dispatches to him time and time again when I was on Gen. Halleck's staff. I have gone in; he would be sitting in the telegraph office about 2 o'clock in the morning, with an old shawl over his shoulders. I would hand him a dispatch; he would read it, then go over to one of the telegraphers and listen to some message, and I have seen him come back with his eyes full of tears.

I was sergeant of the Guard all night, April 19, 1865, when the body lay in the Rotunda of the Capitol at Washington, with a guard at each corner of the catafalque. There were four doors leading to it—North, South, East and West, and two guards at each door with gun and bayonet. I had merely a belt and bayonet. 30,000 people went by that night. Fathers would lift up their children to look at his face. I remember that as the embodiment of real grief.

During the Assassination Conspiracy trial, I was in charge of Mrs. Mary Surratt; she was a very nice woman, a pleasant, nice woman. I did not go to her execution; I could have gone, but knowing her, I did not care to see her hung.

## Lincoln visiting the wounded at City Point, Virginia
## Interview with Dr. Jerome Walker

Calling at the home of Dr. Jerome Walker at 142 St. Mark's Avenue, Brooklyn, the Doctor received me in his office. He was a fine type of old time American, suggesting Gen. Fitz John Porter in his later years.

He said:

W—I was not a surgeon in the Civil War, only a relief agent of the United States Sanitary Commission from July '64 to the end of the war and a while after—I was 19 to 20 years old.

We will start at the beginning so you will understand. In 1851, Florence Nightingale started in the Crimea to nurse the soldiers—the first woman to do so. In 1859, after [the Battle of] Solferino, it was suggested by a man [J. Henry Dunant] in Geneva that an International Association should be formed to attend to the wounded soldiers. In 1861, the U. S. Sanitary Commission was organized, and wore this "badge."

Handing me a small oval badge composed of a narrow silver band, encircling a cross of the same metal.

W—This is the one worn by me, and since the war I have never seen another. In 1864, the Red Cross Society was formed, and our badges were called in; originally it had the Latin Cross, but it was altered to the Geneva Cross by cutting the red off (the Swiss flag). I was only eighteen when I became an auxiliary Relief Agent in the Auxiliary Relief Corps.

My first sight of Lincoln was in 1861, on his way to be inaugurated at Washington. He stood on the platform of the car as he was passing through. The boys crowded round and after he passed, one of the boys proudly said, "I touched his rubbers!" This gave the boy great importance in our eyes after that. I never thought I would be brought near him myself.

At the Base Hospital at City Point, April 8, 1865, President Lincoln visited the hospital. Three tents, 14 by 14 feet were lashed together and formed what was called a ward. I was selected to show President Lincoln through our Wards, so I only know what happened while he was with me. He may have gone through other wards and been conducted by others—I cannot say. How he came that day, and where he went after that, I do not know; and how I met him, I do not remember. I do know I started to show the President the wards; I did not appreciate it at the time. I only felt he was President, and it was my business to show him around.

We came to one ward and I, boy-like, said, "Mr. President, you won't want to go in these—they are only rebels."

He put his large right hand on my left shoulder, and I almost feel that hand now, and looking down on me he said, "You mean, Confederates. We will go in now."

Now look at that rebuke, yet it was said in such a kind way. It has been Confederates ever since for me. We went through the hospital; some were lying down in their hospital garments, some were sitting up as convalescents; he went through and talked with them, and I noticed that no matter what sort of man he met, tall or short, stout or thin, he made some telling remark or told some appropriate story. I wish I could remember some of them, but I cannot.

As he was leaving, he said, "Boys, now if you don't get all you ought to get, see that my young friend here gives it to you." Then we went into the next ward. We could hear them talking through the canvas—

"Who's that," said one.

"That's Abe Lincoln."

"Lord, you don't mean to say that's Abe Lincoln. Ah, you give us taffy."

"That's not so," said another.

Lincoln heard what they said, he could not help it; there was only canvas between us. He did not say anything, but a little smile went over his face. Next day a tall soldier said to me, "You uns have a better man for President than we uns have."

President Lincoln wore a high hat, a long frock coat, of course cow hide boots; trousers so tight, they were wrinkled, and did not go all the way down. He was a tremendously big man—tall; big feet, big hands; rolling collar, big black necktie hanging down, but not a long neck, as they insist on making it; he had a normal neck. He was not ungainly. He walked as a man would, who has long legs. I kept pace with him, which I could not have done if his walk had been ungainly. His face was heavily furrowed, deep furrows each side of his mouth. He looked tired. His face looked careworn. Every once in a while it would light up with a smile and that smile would take away all the furrows.

The doctor then showed me a paper published at City Point by the soldiers, dated April 9, 1865. There was a description of the President's visit. It said he looked "careworn and weary." The article was signed, "Frank." The doctor added, "That just about explains it."

W—On April 15th, a courier in Army uniform rode into camp, threw up his head and cried, "The President is assassinated!!!"

There was great commotion and excitement. I saw men cry—not all, but some. The tears ran down their cheeks. It had only been a week before when he had been with them. Gloom settled down in the hospital. Next day I was walking past the wards. I saw a man shot out of one as though thrown by a catapult. I went up and found he was a rebel convalescent who said about Lincoln's death, "I'm damn glad of it." A soldier who had lost his leg two or three hours before, jumped up on his one leg and with a blow between the eyes that sent the rebel through the doorway; [and by] the force of the blow—knocking himself down. We ran over and picked him up and put him on the bed. The fall had torn open his stitches and the bed was full of blood.

## Serenading Lincoln at City Point and Richmond
## Letter from Dr. William J. Critchley, July 30, 1922

Dear Mr. Kelly,
It was my privilege to be selected to serenade President Lincoln near the last of March, 1865, at Grant's Headquarters, City Point, Va. Our division commander, Gen. Charles Devins, of Massachusetts, ordered me to take my band to City Point, three miles away, and serenade Mr. Lincoln. There were three or four brigade bands nearer than mine, but I received the honor of being selected.

We pitched our tents in front of Grant's Headquarters, and at sunset serenaded the President. I played the best stuff we had for the President of the United States. After playing a half hour he came and placed his hand on my shoulder, saying, "Mr. Leader, will you please play 'Dixie Land?'" (He called for it every night—it was his favorite tune.) The Confederates had used 'Dixie' as their National march, and we had not played it for more than a year. I said, "Mr. President, that's a Confederate tune." He smiled and replied, "But we've captured it, making 'Dixie' a National tune."

After finishing our serenade, Mr. Lincoln said, "That reminds me of a little story." And he told the story of himself, and told stories for half an hour. He was the best story teller I ever heard. There was a great crowd of officers getting as near as possible to hear him, but he seemed to be talking to the Band.

The following little incident occurred: A battle was going on at our left; we could hear the big guns, but not the rifles. A Captain Fitzgerald rode up to Grant's headquarters, Lincoln sitting on a camp stool nearby. The Captain got off his horse, threw the reins over the horse's head and said to Mr. Lincoln, "Here, old man, hold my horse!" Lincoln got up and took the reins. The Captain went inside Grant's tent with his dispatch, and in a few minutes came out, Grant following him.

He took the reins, threw them over his horse's head and was going to mount when Grant said, "Captain Fitzgerald, Let me introduce Abraham Lincoln, President of the United States." The dumbfounded captain jumped on his horse and disappeared. The President and Grant both laughed at the joke. Lincoln asked, "How much does a hostler get in the Army?" Grant laughed and replied, "It depends on how he performs his services." Lincoln replied, "I do not think I'll get much, for this Captain did not think enough of it to even thank me." Grant said he would next time: "We will tie his horse to the rail put up for the purpose."

Lincoln was full of jokes, and very democratic. He was the only general officer who came and asked me to play. The others sent a note, or an orderly requesting such and such a tune. Lincoln came himself.

My Brigade Band was the first to enter Richmond, Va., on April 3, 1865. After playing National Airs while the "Stars and Stripes" were being raised on all the public buildings, I dismissed the Band for an hour or more in front of Libby Prison, and John Harrison and myself went to find Jeff Davis' house.

Few white men were on the streets. I met an old "darkey" and said, "Boss, can you tell me where Jeff Davis lives?"

He said, "Yea, Massa, I'll show you." And he did. At the gate I asked the darkey to come in and he said, "No, Sar, if ah goes in dar deyd trash me ter death."

I said, "Don't worry. Thrashing days are over."

He would not enter. The door was not locked, and the table was set for breakfast and the tea warm. I and John took a cup of tea, and then went to Jeff's office. On the desk were two orders directed to Quartermaster, C. S. A., for two ambulances to report at 6:30. Evidently, they did not wait for them. I took them and his pen and pen wiper and put them in my pocket.

On [April 4th] at the corner of Second Street, I saw President Lincoln and little Tad along with eight or ten sailors marching behind the President; their side arms in scabbard.

Lincoln looked at me and smiled. He recognized me, as we had serenaded him at City Point several times the week before. Lincoln was walking slow; little Tad trolling as fast as his legs could travel. I reached out my hand, and Lincoln shook his head slowly and said, "Not now, not now." He could not shake hands with me, but with cane in right hand and Tad's in the other, he could not do it. I shall never forget that look. He was anxious to reach Jeff's house.

He was on his way to Jeff Davis' mansion to tell the Washingtonians that we had captured Richmond. Little Tad was dressed like "Little Lord Fauntleroy"—nothing military about him. The President was in black broadcloth and that tall hat.

Shortly after that they returned to City Point. We of course thought we were to follow the Johnnies. But we never left Richmond until discharged.

I stood close to Abraham Lincoln when the first 100 prisoners were exchanged from Belle Isle and they were so emaciated it took two men to lead them across the gang plank. Mr. Lincoln on the shore took them by the hand, tears running down his cheek—too full to speak. They were exchanged for a hundred Johnnies from our prisons in Baltimore—ready for immediate service.

I don't blame General Grant for stopping the [Prisoner] exchange. Many did, but we were recruiting Lee's army with able bodied men, while it took two to care for each of our returned boys.

## Lincoln's Visit to Richmond—April 4, 1865
## Interview with Lieut. William A. Scott, 115th U.S. Colored Troops

Mr. Scott was tall, broad bowed, firm-jawed, with a clear, cool, deliberate eye; grayish hair, short mustache, resolute nose, serious in expression, with "Verity" written all over his face; a strong, firm, manly figure, with a soldierly bearing. He detailed Lincoln in a manner that showed him for the lawyer he was.

S—I do not think any Sculptor in the world could depict Lincoln as he was standing up. Lincoln had no bend in his back.

He then started in abusing the Barnard Statue.

S—On his feet he was massive looking—you could not but be impressed by his strength. Another quality was his neck. It was strong and muscular. He did not have a scraggy neck! I do not think that statue by Saint-Gaudens does him justice. John Hay's article has a picture which depicts him well; it's in his *Century* History."

S—I first saw Lincoln in 1864. Gen. [Charles H.] Collis took me to the White House. I was a boy, only seventeen. I was frightened to death.

He was sitting down when we entered. He stood up and shook hands and said, "My boy, you are very young." I was in uniform. He asked what regiment I was in. He had the most appalling appearance of melancholy in the face you can imagine. Then it lighted up with a peculiar little smile which came easily. When he smiled it impressed me with its deliberateness. It developed easily and gradually as though it belonged there. His eye lit up attractively. When he raised himself up, you wondered when he was going to stop. He was the embodiment of strength. When I saw him first, he was in a chair; he seemed to be sitting in the middle of his back, with his legs stretched out full-length. He seemed awful long. He was a strong man in the kindliness of his nature, but too tender hearted. I said nothing to him after being introduced, but watched him while he talked to the General.

Stanton was the strong man of the War. I was sent to Washington to pass my Examination for Lieutenant before the Board. I had no money and wanted transportation. I called on Stanton and took my place in the line. My father had been Pastor of his church, before the War. I said, "My name is Scott. I am the son of—." His memory went back twenty years. "Granted," he said, and an orderly took me away. He was a great man, but domineering and absolutely aggressive in every way. He had abused Lincoln like a dog at the beginning of the War and yet Lincoln made him Secretary of War.

K—Can you describe Lincoln when he visited Richmond?

S—I saw Lincoln when he visited Richmond. I did not see him when he entered the City; it was later in the day. He was coming down hill, I was going up.

K—You said Lincoln was expected in Richmond.

S—The papers, I think it was the *Richmond Whig*, said he was expected, but did not say when.

K—Can you describe his appearance and dress?

S—I cannot. I don't think that he dressed anytime so as to be distinguished; he was always the same appearing man. My recollection is that he was holding the hand of a boy, whom I assumed to be Tad. I have heard it stated so often that Tad was there, I almost begin to believe it myself.

There were lots of negroes around. They were jabbering around, saying, "Marse-Lincoln—Marse-Lincoln." A few women with hands out saluted as he walked along. They seemed to stand round him awestruck; as though God had appeared to them.

K—Were they kissing his hands? One report says that.

S—I did not see any kissing his hands. There were very few whites around. The City was on fire at that time. I came into the City that morning at 4 o'clock.

Now here is how it was. Let me tell this story and you can remember it better than I can dictate it.

I was taken prisoner near Petersburg. It was the custom of the pickets to talk with each other and to trade coffee for tobacco and also to trade newspapers.

My Captain came to me and said, "Take this bundle of papers and exchange them for me for some Richmond papers." I took them, and made the usual signals [of parley], then went over to the Rebel lines. They advanced and took me prisoner, and took the papers from me. My bundle consisted of about 28 copies of the *Philadelphia Inquirer*; the last pages only—they were seditious. They described how the enemy were getting discouraged and deserting into our lines, and how the President offered amnesty to them and found them good employment, and there were large meetings of loyal people who were raising money to help them.

I was taken before [Gen. G. W.] Custis Lee.

Lieut. Randolph told me that if I gave the word of a gentleman, that I would make no attempt to escape, that he would let me sleep in his tent that night. In the morning I was sent over to the Provo Marshal, at Castle Thunder. They took me up where all the officers were cut off from the stairway. As the prisoners who preceded me entered the room they were grabbed by the other prisoners, and their coats were taken off, and their shirts, and in fact they were left almost naked.

K—Were they our own men?

S—Yes. They were robbed by the other prisoners. I said to myself: "Have I got to go through that!" I was tempted to give a false name, then the thought my parents would not know what became of me.

The fact that I was an officer in a colored Regiment added to my troubles. The officer ordered me to be taken to the dungeon. To my great satisfaction I found it occupied by a man named Lanman, who was a Union spy; also an Englishman by the name of Roberts.

Roberts was a wealthy Englishman who came over to this country to see the sights. Our authorities gave him a pass to visit our front. While doing so he was overtaken by Mosby's men. He had a lot of jewelry on him, watch, gold-sleeve buttons, and money. The only excuse they had for taking them was to accuse him of being a spy. So he was captured, robbed, and sent to Castle Thunder. He wrote several letters to the British Consul, but they were burned by the officer in command.

On Sunday morning [April 2] a brother of Lanman who was in the Rebel Army although a Union man, called, and told us Grant [Maj. Gen. Godfrey Weitzel] was about to enter the City. The news reached us before Jeff Davis heard it. So we began packing up. Some of the prisoners asked us what we were packing up for, but we did not tell.

At midnight, they started with us to Danville. While in the streets, in front of Castle Thunder, were papers piled up five feet high on fire. As we marched along (I forgot the name of the street—I think it was Broad) we reached 8th Street, and a six-mule team was run across and blocked it. Roberts grabbed the mules' heads and swung it aside, and ran up 8th Street. We followed. A guard with a gun and bayonet tried to stop us, but Roberts knocked him down with a bottle of molasses which we had for rations.

We ran on till we reached Elizabeth Van Lew's home. But the gate was locked and they were too weak to climb over the fence, so I got over the fence and opened the gate for them.

We went into the house, and found something to eat and got an Arkansas toothpick—a big knife about so-long (about 18 inches), then we started for the Fredericksburg railroad. We found a hand-car. It was not run by a crank as they do now, but we poled it along, like a raft.

We met a fellow who said Grant was entering the City, which was being fired up. We started back and hid in Van Lew's cellar.

About 5:30 we could hear Grant's guns. I said, "That sounds safe." So I went out and found Jo Chandler, where the Headquarters had been established. I reported to my regiment. I was then sent out with my regiment to put out the fire. It was in the business district. It was a big tobacco factory where they made what was called, "Kinnikinnick." It was a famous tobacco at that time put up in small canvas bales perfectly square or oblong.

K—Yes, I remember them. My father used to smoke it. And some of the boys used to call me: "Kinnikinnick."

S—While we were at work in the City, I said, "I did not enlist to put out Rebel fires." So I marched my boys back—for which I came pretty near being dismissed from the service.

Later, I saw President Lincoln coming down. He was not attracting great attention except from the negroes. The street was fairly clear.

K—Had he a guard with him? I understand he had a guard of sailors.

S—Not sure if they were sailors. If "Tad" was with him, he was holding him with his left hand. There was somebody on his right.

It was in the forenoon; the fires were going on—the whole heavens were full of clouds and smoke. There was fully a mile square burning. The fire was on the left of Lincoln. It was bright weather, in April. Lincoln was walking on the right side of the middle of the street, furthest away from the fire. There was no parade, no display. He seemed to be walking around just aimlessly. No attention was being paid to him. That is the way it appeared to me. I don't remember any sailors—don't remember any uniforms.

I showed Mr. Scott the painting of Lincoln entering Richmond by Nast.

S—Nast evidently composed it from description. The portrait of Mr. Lincoln is pretty good, but his whiskers are too long. He was not a luxuriant whisker grower. My impression is that to the right of him there was a hill, four or five feet high, with a shanty on top, but elaborate buildings near him. He was on a hill. The fire was in a hollow. I was on the other side of the street about twenty-five or thirty feet away. I was dressed in uniform. I passed right on.

## Lincoln's Last Gift to His Soldiers
## Interview with Colonel John Yapp Culyer

My friend, Col. John Y. Culyer, was an assistant to Frederick Law Olmstead in the designing of Central Park and had also served in the U. S. Sanitary Commission during the War.

K—Did you ever speak to Lincoln?

C—I spoke to him only once—toward the end of the war. I found the Sanitary Commission had a stack of supplies on hand, much needed by the soldiers—underclothing, socks, etc., the government did not have these things and I thought it would be well for the soldiers to have them.

I went to the Quartermaster General's office and spoke to him—I think it was [Montgomery] Meigs—to my surprise he did not show the enthusiasm I expected. I told him we had the goods but had no trains to deliver the goods to the soldiers. He said he could not aid us because he had no authority to order trains for anything but for military purposes. He was pleasant about it, but I suppose his duties were barred by official routine. I then went to Nicolay; I knew Nicolay. He listened to what I had to say and seemed interested. He got up and went into the next room. When he came back, he said, "Go in and speak to the President." I did so.

When I entered he sat there behind a big table, with his long legs stretched out. I told him I had called to see about getting trains for the Sanitary Commission from the Quarter Master General to bring supplies to the troops and explained that we had underclothing, socks, etc., for the soldiers and the Government did not have them, but we were willing to supply them if we had trains, but without them we were all at sea.

He did not need any argument after that. He sat there with his legs stretched out. He listened to me; he knew what he had to say, but waited until I had finished. There were no questions, but a practical response; he took up a small card and wrote upon it:

> To the Quartermaster General,
> Please supply Mr. Culyer for the use of the Sanitary Commission
> what trains he may require.
> Yours Truly,
> A. Lincoln

And with that card, I secured the authority to get the number of trains necessary to carry supplies to the front to clothe the soldiers. These clothes were worn by them for the expected Grand Review [on May 23-24, 1865]. This was Lincoln's last gift, as tribute to the soldiers.

K—How did you come to Ford's that night?

C—I read in the papers that Laura Keene was to play the American Cousin on Good Friday night. I was quite anxious to see it. I went to the theatre that afternoon and asked for seats. The clerk said, "I have saved these seats for a party till one o'clock—you can now have them." The seats could not have been arranged better for an opportunity to see what happened that night. They were back from the stage in the middle of the house. I do not remember whether they were in the middle aisle or on the side aisle, but in any case our seats were in the middle of the house.

It was expected that Lincoln and his cabinet would be present. The President's party came in at last—I think the audience rose at their entrance and cheered him; not wild cheering, but cheered him.

When he entered the box, he came forward and arranged his rocking chair and sat down with an air, like—well, I am here—I might as well make myself comfortable and have a good time as I can.

As he rocked back we could not see his face, as the box was twelve feet above the stage and the line of vision cut us off from seeing him. No one could see him unless his vision ricocheted.

Mrs. Lincoln sat on his right and Major Henry Rathbone and Miss Clara Harris on the opposite side of the box. They were two boxes made into one [by removing a dividing wall].

As the play proceeded, he would accordingly lean forward and then lean back in his chair, so we could not see his face. Of all great tragedies in history, I think this one was the most undamnable for no one [eyewitness] could see him when he was shot.

As Booth entered from behind, it was dark. He put the pistol a few inches from his head and fired. Lincoln was below the line of sight of the audience. All they could hear was the crack of a small pistol. The audience naturally looked toward where the sound came from, but suspected nothing.

Then Major Rathbone made a belated effort to catch Booth. He broke away and vaulted over the side of the box. They say he fell—that's not so. His spur caught in the flag that was draped in front of the box and he stumbled as he fell and landing on one foot, he broke his femur bone. He ran across the stage and disappeared. I believe he had the help of someone and got out of the stage door, where his horse was waiting and got away.

The people at first did not know what had happened, till someone called out from the Gallery: "The President's shot!"

The next minute all was excitement. Many people rushed the door, women fainted, and people began to climb on the stage—I got on the stage myself. I remember there was one of the popular actresses in New York that I used to admire, and I found myself standing beside her. Her face was covered in powder and makeup which may have been all right from the front—she must have known her business, but I was disillusioned.

Then I saw the people crowding toward the aisle and going over I saw them carrying President Lincoln out. As I remember it was an improvised stretcher—something they got off the stage.

I was quite near, but I was quite young and knew my place, so I stood aside when they carried him past.

I remember he was partly disrobed and I remember they had thrown his coat across his chest and shoulders.

When he was shot, he did not bleed as his hair was very coarse, short and black—and the blood did not stain the floor.

As he was borne by, I think Mrs. Lincoln followed behind, but I cannot recollect distinctly—she may have been supported by Major Rathbone; I did not know the others. As they bore him out, a cordon of soldiers were formed and it did not take over a minute to take him to the house across the street.

In these days such a thing never could have happened. Booth never could have got near him.

Here the Colonel showed me a photograph of Booth.

C—You see, he had all the qualities of an actor and his vanity made him do it, thinking his name would live for eternity. If he had not broken his bone, he might have got further south than he did. But in any case, in time they would have had to give him up. You see how well he planned it. He knew the theatre and he knew the play. He knew when the Yankee character, who sat whittling a stick, left the stage—as he did so there was [going to be] an immediate change of scene. And that was the time—the other actors had all gone to their rooms. It was then—he knew it was the time to do the deed.

I have after thought of the flag [that decorated the box] and the connection with the event. It was through that flag, Booth tripped and injured himself and through that injury caused by that flag, it led to Booth's final capture and death, and through that flag, Lincoln was Avenged.

On another occasion, I visited Col. Culyer at his home in Mount Kisco, New York. We had lunch and I asked him if he saw Lincoln when he came to New York in 1861. He said, "No," that he was out of town at the time. Mrs. Culyer then spoke up and said, "I saw Lincoln after he had landed at the 30th Street station, and was on his way to Washington to be inaugurated." I asked her to describe what she witnessed:

Mrs. C—The parade had come down Ninth Avenue from 30th Street, through 23rd Street to Fifth Avenue, down Fifth Avenue to 14th Street, and then down Broadway. We were living at 23rd Street on the north side, No. 171. We sat at a big window full of friends. Mr. Culyer was away. The procession halted, and the carriage stopped right in front of us. We all cheered him. He looked around and bowed; his face had a dear, kindly smile. I called out to him, "Ah, how nice it is to see you!" He stood right up in the carriage, took off his hat and spoke to me.

I cannot recollect now what he said—he was a dear, anyhow.  He wore a high hat, and I noticed a black coat buttoned up.  He looked quite ministerial; he did not wear a shawl—may have taken it off, as it was a pleasant day.  Ah! he had such a sweet smile.

As the old lady told this story, her large beautiful brown eyes lit up as though they reflected the golden memories of her youth.  And her smile suggested what must have been his—the smile she saw that day on the face of Abraham Lincoln!

## Further Details of the Assassination
## Letter from John Y. Culyer
November 15, 1920

Regarding these several stories of the Lincoln tragedy, no two agreeing in the even simple essential details, I feel like the twelfth juror who remarked so complacently, that he had disagreed with the other eleven.

I do not believe that Booth spoke those words as some claim—"Sic semper tyrannus."  If he did, no one could have heard him.  And as to [waving] the dagger!  Imagine a man climbing over a balcony 12 ft. above the landing place with a pistol in one hand, a dagger in the other after that fearful explosion—Sic semper etc.—finding an opening; simultaneously—etc.

Speed, free movement and a definite outcry, was all too clearly in his mind, so it seems to me.  The tendency is, I think, in the personal recollections of such incidents—is to add to details and in a way, to vindicate what one has seen and to unconsciously absorb what has been stated by others.

Take parts of [James P.] Ferguson's case for example: his statement [claiming that he saw Booth shoot Lincoln], as I have said no one but Booth saw Lincoln shot—nor could I have done so, from the point he said he occupied.

No great event in History involving such tragedy, in all recorded time, is so strangely devoid of spectators as the death of Lincoln.  The sound of the discharge of a small pistol, almost instantly followed by the blurred vision of a man of insignificant form, climbing over the balcony of the flag draped box, 12 ft. above the stage, his dropping to the floor below and despite a slight halting owing to the spur incident, passing across the stage occupied at the time only by stage hands, some of them were in collusion with the Assassin, and so out by way of the alley in the rear.

## The Assassination of President Lincoln—April 14, 1865
## Interview with Judge Wesley Rogers Batchelder
Cranford, New Jersey, October 5, 1919

Judge Wesley R. Batchelder was of medium height; a large head, very high in benevolence and veneration; eyes keen, very keen; large, round spectacles; a large, bold, hooked nose; tight clamped straight lips; a crisp, sharp, precise voice and manner, and yet with a cheerful hearty laugh, and a humorous, hospitable manner.

B—As Secretary to General Benjamin Butler I have seen President Lincoln many times. I have seen him at receptions, at Reviews, and in the street. I have seen him serious after a defeat by the enemy. He must have been depressed, but did not show it. The first time I saw Lincoln was when I was sent with a message by General Butler. I had two letters; one an introduction, and the other a private letter to President Lincoln. I sent in the introduction and a messenger came out and said the President wanted to see me. He was sitting at his desk. He did not rise. He never rose to anyone, except General Grant; I suppose another reason [he did not rise] was that he was so very tall. My first impression of him was I had heard people say he was the homeliest man in the country, and I thought they were about right.

Referring to Lincoln's personality, Judge Batchelder said, "Lincoln had lots of 'go.' He would step right out. He would walk through the streets of Washington. He had no guard with him; it was not like it is now. Everybody knew him and saluted as he passed, and he would take off his hat and bow. He never carried a cane.

"I was born in 1843; that made me twenty-two at the time [of the Assassination]. I joined Gen. Butler in 1863, and stayed at Fortress Monroe before I went to Washington. I was not so fortunate as to be with him in New Orleans."

Handing me a picture of Barnard's statue published in the *Times*, showing the unveiling at Manchester, he said: "It is a horrible, grotesque thing. Lincoln never looked like that in the world! I never saw him droop. He always had a slight stoop, but I never saw him bowed with sorrow. He was not that kind of a man."

Settling down he said:

B—He had a kindly face, but nervy. I have seen many a business man have a more care-worn face than Lincoln, when they were under extremely heavy business worry. On one occasion, a woman came to him in great trouble. After listening to her, he said, "You go down to Secretary Stanton. Tell him what you have told me, and tell him I said to attend to it, and let me know what he says." She came back. Lincoln asked her if Stanton had helped her. "No," she said. "What did he say?" asked Lincoln. She hesitated. He insisted on her telling him. She answered, "He said you were a G. D. fool."

"He did?" said Lincoln, "Let's go down and have a talk with him."

They went back, and Lincoln took Stanton aside and had a talk with him, but could not seem to bring Stanton around. He was full of sympathy, but Stanton was a different kind of oyster.

So, they came back, and Lincoln sat down and wrote a note to the man which was a direct order to the officer in charge to do what he wanted—going right over Stanton's head.

Lincoln was remarkable for not bearing resentments. He was a most forgiving man. Take the case of Stanton—the way he did abuse Lincoln, both before and after he was elected. Stanton was an old lying Democrat, but was a Union man. It was terrible the way he abused Lincoln and yet Lincoln sent for him and offered him the position as Secretary of War; he seemed staggered by it and Lincoln gave him three days to decide it.


Judge Batchelder told me that the night [April 10, 1865] after the surrender of Lee, the people made a demonstration at the White House.

B—They were crazy with excitement; knocking off each other's hats, elbowing each other, waving umbrellas, and cheering.

Lincoln appeared at that large window over the entrance. I never hear that window referred to now. We used to hear a great deal of it at the time. It was a window that opened almost to the floor; you could see him at full length as he stood there. Of course you could not see his feet.

The band had been playing the patriotic airs, and the people were wild with cheering and excitement.

Lincoln at last held up his hand and quieted them, saying, "The Band will now play 'Dixie.' We've captured it, and we want it."

It was announced that Lincoln would make a speech on the following night. The whole grounds and the circular drive were crowded with thousands of people; they extended out into Pennsylvania Avenue. It was in that speech he outlined his policy of conciliation. This was his last speech.


Judge Batchelder then said, "I got a letter for you." Going in the other room, he brought out an old letter and handed it to me. "There's a letter I wrote to my Mother the Sunday after the assassination. General Butler had gone to Fortress Monroe the day [Friday, April 14] before, and I was to go after him, but missed the boat; and having nothing else to do, went to the Theatre, and there the assassination took place, and I was present. I started the next day for Baltimore to take the boat for Fortress Monroe. The trains were stopped at least a dozen times by the Cavalry and every man had to show his credentials and tell where he had been and where he was going."

K—Did you have your uniform on?

B—I did not wear a uniform. I had my credentials with me.

K—Am I right in saying that the last thing you saw of Lincoln he was smiling?

B—Yes.

K—That he went to his death with a smile?

B—Yes. It was his hour of triumph. All was over. The whole house was on their feet cheering as he went with a smile into the box, bowing right and left; principally to the left—the audience was on that side. The Presidential party came in a little late—he came in the theatre last. The Presidential party walked right behind me—about six rows from where I sat. Dear old man; he never knew what killed him. He died with a smile. I did not see the Presidential party after they went into the box; no one could, as they sat back, except a few on the front seat on the opposite balcony.

I did not see Booth go in, but would not have noticed as Booth was always strolling around the theatre. We heard a shot, but paid no attention to it. There was no one on the stage. I saw Booth as he jumped out of the box. He put his left hand on the rail and vaulted over. His right spur caught the festoons. The box was festooned with flags. He left foot came down first. He shattered one of the bones of his leg near the ankle. He got up, waved his dagger over his head and called out something; I did not catch what it was, but found out it was: "Sic semper tyrannis."

K—I had a friend who was there who said he did not say it.

B—He did say it, as sure as you're a foot high.

Booth then ran across the stage down through the flies and disappeared. There was a dead silence. The people did not know what had happened. Only one man had the presence of mind. He sat in the pit near the front. He jumped up, climbed the stage, and ran after Booth, but Booth had got away. The people did not know what had happened; we thought it was the theatre that was on fire. Laura Keene ran out and called to the people, "Be quiet; there is no fire." Then Mrs. Lincoln screamed. It was then pandemonium broke loose.

The people called out, "Who did it? Hang him! Murder!"

I did not see anyone but that one man get on the stage. Then the people made a rush to get in the President's box, struggling and pushing each other aside, some people calling out, "I am a Surgeon!" But they could not get in, as Booth had locked the door with a wooden bar he had prepared that afternoon.

It seemed like a half-an-hour, it may have been three minutes, before they got in. Afterwards I went down and saw them carry him out.

Lincoln was shot back of the ear. He never knew what hit him.

It was sad what happened to their guests. Major Henry Rathbone married Miss Clara Harris some time later, and was made Minister to Germany. He went mad and killed his wife [on Dec. 23, 1883]. He was put in the asylum, and lived many years [until 1911]. And you know in after years Mrs. Lincoln seemed to have lost her mind.

I again visited the Judge a few weeks later and asked him to read the letter that he had written to his mother the day after the assassination, and while I was hesitating to ask him if he could trust it with me long enough to make a copy, he said: "I have no son, or anyone I care to leave this to; I want you to have it." He then inscribed it, and handed it to me:

Sunday, Oct. 26, 1919

This letter is presented this day to my good friend, J. E. Kelly as a memento of the scene I witnessed Friday evening, April 14, 1865.

Baltimore, April 16, 1865

My dear Mother and all:

I left Washington yesterday forenoon on my way to Fort Monroe and Norfolk, but there being no boat I am obliged to stay here until there is one allowed to go.

How can I describe to you the scene I witnessed last Friday evening? I was at Ford's Theatre at Washington and saw the murder of President Lincoln. It was a fearful sight. Words cannot express the scene.

You have undoubtedly read the newspaper accounts which are minutely true. The first I heard was the crack of a pistol. I thought it was a part of the play and looked at the part of the stage from whence the sound come, and saw a man in black clothes (in the President's Box) waving a large knife over his head and saying something, I could only distinguish the words, "The South", and then he jumped to the stage about twelve feet below. But as he jumped, his foot, or spur, caught in the festooning or flags about the Box and he fell to the stage, but as quick as a flash he was up, and like lightning ran behind the scenes on the stage.

In an instant he was gone. One of the spectators jumped up on the stage after him, but when he reached the door he saw the assassin mount a horse and gallop away. If he had a pistol he could have shot him or his horse. It was all done in a minutes' time, and cannot be told as quick as the deed was done.

Of course the audience was spellbound.  And for a moment no one could move.  I realized it all, but for a moment could move neither hand nor foot but sat staring at the President's Box.

In a moment after I collected my thoughts and screamed, "The President is murdered!" and ran towards the Box.  At the same time Mrs. Lincoln screamed and fainted.  Perhaps you can judge the scene that followed, but I doubt it.  Ladies fainted; strong men wept; soldiers rushed in and cleared the house with their bayonets.  (But I was at the President's Box and was overlooked by the soldiers and saw him stripped and carried away in an insensible state.)

The cries of Mrs. Lincoln were frightful to hear.  Such a scene I never want to be witness to again.  I cannot at this time realize that it is real.  It seems like a dream.  To think that he who came in but a few moments before so full of happiness smiling and bowing at the audience who cheered, stamped their feet and waved their handkerchiefs, was so brutally murdered.

I cannot realize it.

The streets are decorated in mourning here, and gloom pervades everywhere.

The General [Butler] had left for New York at 7:30 the same evening.

B—I later met Sergeant Corbett.  He called at General Butler's quarters shortly after his return to Washington and detailed the capture and death of Booth.  He was a religious fanatic, and used to hold religious meetings on Boston Common.

## The Death of President Lincoln
## Interview with Corporal James Tanner

Corporal James Tanner contacted me through Col. Swords' introduction to meet him at the St. George Hotel in Brooklyn.  He was universally called "Corporal" having earned the rank in the battles of Yorktown, Williamsburg, Fair Oaks, Seven Days and Malvern Hill.  At the Second Battle of Bull Run, his legs were both taken off above the knee by a cannonball.  Equipped with artificial ones, he came to Washington as a clerk in the Ordnance Bureau of the War Department.  He walked with difficulty, even with the aid of a cane.  While recovering, Corporal Tanner was taught stenography and happened to be staying in the rooming house next door to [the Petersen House] where Lincoln was taken when he was shot.

Corporal Tanner is a large stout man.  He had an unnaturally large head (7. 7/8) a lean well developed full brow; a pair of soft, kind eyes, bushy eyebrows, and a heavy full mustache under a plump nose; the whole face denoted benevolence and strong emotion, but did not suggest anything aggressive.  He sat in an arm chair and greeted me and told me of his wounding at Second Bull Run, and then about the night of Lincoln's Assassination.

T—At about 12 AM, I was standing on the piazza of the Hotel on the right as you looked at the building where Lincoln lay dying. It ran across the front—on top of a saloon. Some one came to the door and asked if there was any stenographer in the crowd. I called out, I was. I went down and was taken in the room where Lincoln lay. Stanton dictated what I was to put down. Towards morning, about 7 o'clock, it was seen that he was dying. President Lincoln was breathing his life away and Mrs. Lincoln sobbing in the next room.

At Corporal Tanner's suggestions, I made a diagram representing the bed on which Lincoln lay diagonally with his head to the left of the headboard and his feet to the right of the footboard.

T—I stood at the head of the bed near the left corner. Robert Lincoln at my immediate right with his arm on Charles Sumner's shoulder and his head bowed weeping. To my rear were two other men, on my left Rev. Dr. Phineas Gurley was standing on the left of the bed. Surgeon General Joseph Barnes was sitting on the left side of the bed—once I saw him kneel down and put his ear to Mr. Lincoln's heart. He had his finger on Mr. Lincoln's pulse when he breathed his last.

Mr. Lincoln had been breathing stertorously, and as we stood at the head of the bed, we could see his chest heaving up and down; at seven [A. M.] it ceased motion and at 7:20 he died. Dr. Barnes then crossed Mr. Lincoln's hands, and Dr. Gurley stepped forward, raising his hands said, "Our Father and our God..." here my pencil broke, otherwise we would have had the prayer and the name of all persons as I would have recorded. There were a great many looking in and I would have asked them for their names.

Then, the steel-mettle-tempered Stanton broke; buried his head in the bedclothes, and shook with his sorrow. As he looked up, his eyes streaming—I never saw more agony in a human creature—and then said the words: "He belongs to the ages now." And when I heard Stanton's words—it overcame me.

K—Had you seen Lincoln before?

T—I never met President Lincoln to talk with him, but there is one story he told I would like to have heard.

I was going up stairs in the old War Department. I had just put my foot on the bottom step, when I saw two men at the top of the stairs about to come down. I stepped down and they descended. One [seemed] lame and the other very tall. As they descended, I recognized Lincoln and other was Gen. Sheridan. Lincoln was telling a story after which they both laughed heartedly. As they passed me, I did not understand it, but I would have given a good deal to have heard that story.

Lincoln was a man who was compelled by his high ideals and was surcharged with absolute deliberation to liberty for all. He was an impressive figure to those who studied him carefully with an intelligent eye. I never saw him to study [before the night of the Assassination], but I was impressed with the idea that I was contemplating who, it seemed to me, through his tender loving sympathetic heart, carried a weightier burden of the care of humanity than was ever carried by any man in human form since the Savior of mankind spent the night in the Garden of Gethsemane.

Corporal Tanner then turned toward me with a half smile and said:

T—Can you imagine anything humorous that could be connected with the death of Lincoln?

K—No.

T—Well I'll tell you. There was a Grand Army man—a Hebrew by the name of Abraham Hurst. He had quite an idea of his elegance and liked to air it. One day he called at the Pension Office with three or four Grand Army men. They had their medals on and I knew what that meant. I said, "Be seated Comrades." They sat down, but he said, "I prefer to stand." He started off by saying, "We called on behalf of the referendum of the man [William Petersen] who opened his hospitable door to our dying President, and hope you will come to their aid for consideration under a grateful Government."
I said, "I suppose you refer to Petersen. If so, I want to tell you that when President Lincoln lay dying—and we could hear him breathing his life away, and Mrs. Lincoln suffering and moaning. Petersen—that tailor—was in the basement drunk and saying, 'That Damn Abolitionist—what is he doing here? If they don't take him out, I'll call the police!' Next day he sold the pillow slip stained by the blood of President Lincoln for five dollars. Gentlemen, they'll see no consideration in this Department!"

# The Lincoln Home in Springfield, Illinois
## A Letter from Carlton Greenleaf, 24th Michigan Infantry

For Friend Kelly:
   The time arrived when I determined to become a soldier in the Union Army that was striving to preserve the Union under the leadership of President Lincoln.
   I faced a stern old Recruiting Officer. "How old are you?" he asked.
   I was less than sixteen, but I knew better than to give this age.
   "Eighteen years old," I responded promptly.

He looked me over with keen, cold eyes. "You are not eighteen," he said coldly, "You must enlist as a musician."

"Oh! I cannot," I cried, "I do not know one note from another. I cannot tell Dan Tucker from the Rock of Ages."

For the first time there was a glint of a smile. "That makes no difference," he said. And it didn't for I never touched an instrument while in the Army. In how many different ways do we all beat the devil about the bush; had that Sergeant said to me: "You will be a member of the 24th Michigan. That regiment will be one of the five forming the Iron Brigade. Your regiment will lose more men at Gettysburg than any other Union regiment. In fact every man will be either killed or wounded. The Iron Brigade will earn that title but they must do terrible work to hold it. Sign here."

Would have I signed? I know.

Well, in the Spring of '65 the regiment had been recruited to full strength, but it was never the old 24th again. Some one higher up may have thought that we deserved a rest, and, be that as it may, we were ordered to report at Camp Butler, some six miles from Springfield, Ill.

We found our duty there was to guard a lot of Southern prisoners, bounty jumpers, deserters and the tough elements of both armies. And there were some tough cases, too. We had to form a close chain guard in order to hold them in check.

One morning in April, the Sergeant came in and called two names, mine and another soldier. Of course we came to attention and saluted.

"You two men are to go into the city and report. Here are passes and directions."

"Take our guns?" I asked.

"No. Brush up the old uniforms. They will do."

At the office in the city we were told that we were to guard the residence of Mr. Lincoln till relieved. "You will have but little to do," the officer said. "Do not let people into the house. Answer all civil questions."

Many persons came to look at the house. I saw many of them shed tears. Some cursed with bitter emphasis. While waiting, a photographer came along and asked if he could make a picture of the house. I told him that I had no orders concerning it.

"Then can I go ahead?" he said. And he did.

I gave him a dollar and asked him to send me a print to my army address. And he did.

This was sixty-four years ago last April. The photo of the house has just been copied from the original, which is still bright and sharp.

If wise I should stop right here, but I am not wise. I left my comrade in charge and went to the door in the rear of the house; I tried it gently. It yielded and I went in, holding my breath. It was the kitchen part and looked neat and clean.

I went on into the front part of the house and entered what I feel certain was Mr. Lincoln's library; books on three sides, many of them well worn. Rather an old desk, open; with pens and pencils and small articles. I think there was a quill pen.

I was no saint at that date and I have not gained in that direction in all of the years. Property belonging to other people does not attract me as a rule. But, really, I had to fight the devil and all his hosts for they were all right there and urging me to help myself. *But I did not do it!*—believe it or not.

I believed at that time and still do, that Mr. Lincoln intended to come to the old home for a rest as soon as he could leave Washington and get some relief from the terrible burdens that had oppressed him. And I believe that some one had put the house in order and were keeping it so, against the home coming.

Ah, Me! It was a long time ago and nearly all of his soldiers have followed their great Commander-in-Chief to their eternal rest. And the last ones will soon follow. And I remember as I stood there on that April day, I thought, "here I am, a tough little soldier, with the great Civil War only a memory and a history, guarding the empty house of our great Commander who will never need again an earthly habitation, all this—and I—not yet—nineteen years of age."

## Dan Butterfield and Boston Corbett
## Interview with John R. Johnston, 12th New York Militia
June 9, 1920, Custom House, N. Y.

An interesting little story was told to me by John R. Johnston, veteran of the 12th Militia. Mr. Johnston is inclined to be tall with a fine highbred American type of countenance—like an eagle. Bold browed, beaked nose, flowing mustache; well clamped jaws and chin; a brilliant gray eye—a typical cavalryman, as he became after his three months service in the 12th Regiment New York Militia under Col. Dan Butterfield. Corp. Johnston also served in the 12th Militia with Boston Corbett, the man who shot John Wilkes Booth [inside the Garrett barn near Port Royal, Virginia].

J—I saw President Lincoln but once, except at Reviews. I was in Company F, 12th Regiment Militia. We arrived at Washington on April 21, 1861 and I think it was at a May Day festival—they always had that at the White House on May 1st.

Lincoln was straight, genial, and smiling—no slackness there. He was going round accompanied by high functionaries whom I did not recognize. The children were playing round, the Marine Band was there, and all were having a good time.

We were sent as a guard; there were a great many Rebels in Washington and it was thought necessary. Some of our men were posted round, but I was in the relief which consisted of about twenty men all told. Gen. Scott was there; he was in command of Washington at that time, so I served under Scott—there's not many men alive today who can say they served under Scott—there he stood looking so great and gigantic; full uniform and cocked hat.

Boston Corbett was in the 12th Regiment, he was a religious enthusiast. He was sincere I believe. He was put in the Guard House for some breach of discipline; he sang hymns all night and kept the camp awake. He objected to work on Sunday, so they made it light [duty] for him. It was too much trouble to force him. He'd call down a non-commissioned officer for swearing as quick as any one else. The men used to tease him, but he did not care, he would laugh. He was a short, stocky fellow for a soldier; with light hair, parted in the middle; flushed face.

Dan Butterfield was the Colonel of the Regiment; he was a great disciplinarian. He drilled us every day except when it rained. If things did not go right, he would swear. The boys used to call him Damn Butterfield, which they paraphrased Damn, Damn, Damn Butterfield.

One day we were marching company front, and as we marched by—now I saw this myself—one of the companies showed a waver in the alignment; then Butterfield "Damned." At which Corbett stepped out of the line and said shaking his finger at Butterfield, "I rebuke you for blasphemous language!" The Colonel ordered him back to the line. I suppose Butterfield had it out with him later, but he could not punish him and Corbett knew it. You know those kind of people are very cunning and have a great deal of method in their madness.

It was at Point of Rocks, Maryland, when Corbett's time of enlistment was up, the very day, without waiting to be mustered out, he lay down his gun and would not do another thing. They had him up before a Drum Head Court Martial, dismissed from the service. Butterfield ordered him cropped, cut his buttons off and drummed him out of the Regiment. Corbett afterward went into the [16th New York] cavalry.

*Early in the morning of April 26, 1865, John Wilkes Booth was discovered hiding in a barn by a detail of the 16th New York Cavalry. Refusing to surrender, he was shot by Sgt. Boston Corbett and died a few hours later at daybreak. Booth's body was then brought to Washington and placed on board the monitor* Montauk, *where an autopsy was performed. Determined to keep the burial place of Booth a secret, Secretary of War Edwin Stanton had the corpse taken from the ship and brought to the site of a former federal prison—the Old Penitentiary—which was located at the Washington Arsenal. The body was buried in a shallow grave beneath the brick flooring of a basement cell. The disposing of John Wilkes Booth's remains was the most surreptitious government operation of the war, and James Edward Kelly met an eyewitness.*

## The Body of John Wilkes Booth
## Interview with Mrs. Ella Morrison

The ceremonies of unveiling the small bronze panel on the parapet of Fort Stevens, marking the spot where President Lincoln stood with General Wright under fire from Jubal Early's troops took place July 12, 1920. It was a copy from the sketch I had made of the scene as described to me by General Wright as we stood on the same spot some years before.

In the evening I called with Marcus Baldwin, the engraver, on Colonel Morrison and his wife. Colonel and Mrs. Ella Morrison had great experiences during the war. Mrs. Morrison described to me how she had seen the body of John Wilkes Booth when it was brought to Washington on April 27, 1865.

She said:

Mrs. M—I was fishing with the children of General Alexander Webb, on the private dock of the Washington Arsenal, when a boat came from the Navy Yard, under the command of Captain [Lafayette C. Baker] Brown. It was a ship's yawl, rowed by four men, with a body wrapped in a dark blue blanket with a red border.

The Captain said: "What are you doing here?"

I was angered by the remark—as though he could not see what I was doing. So I answered: "I think I am fishing."

Then he said: "Haul in—I think you have caught the fish."

Then they took the body and put it on one of the seats of the private dock, and I turned and saw the foot—it was terribly swollen. Then the wind blew the blanket from the face, and I turned to the Captain and said: "Oh! That's Booth!"

Then he said with a smile: "Oh, did you know him?"

I said: "No, I did not. I never saw him before."

He said: "How do you know that it is him?"

I said: "I know him from his pictures."

I then left and was going off the dock when I met Major James Benton and he asked: "Ella, what is that on the dock?"

And I said: "It's Booth's body."

He put his finger up and said: "Don't you speak of it."

Then they put the body in a plain pine box, and then put it in the north storehouse till twelve that night. Sergeant Thomas Vickers, an old English Sergeant, told me they buried him that night in the old penitentiary in the Arsenal grounds. That night there were three men besides Stanton present, and after he was buried, Stanton locked the door and put the key in his pocket. Afterwards [in 1869], the body was given to some member of the Booth family.

The reason they came over to the Arsenal dock was that people heard that Booth's body was in the Navy Yard, and they were clamoring at the gate. So they brought it over to the Arsenal.

K—You were at City Point [during Lincoln's visit in March, 1865]?

Mrs. M—Yes.

K—Who was in the party?

Mrs. M—In the party with Lincoln was Mrs. Lincoln and Mrs. Webb with the General. I think Mrs. Custer was there.

I went down to City Point and stayed there about a week; I remember during the last of the week, Fort Number Two was captured—the forts were numbered. One night we were in bed, and the cannons were going dreadful; in the morning our men recaptured it.

About ten o'clock I went over to the hill, and was looking at the boats in the James River. President Lincoln came out of the log cabin, and came over and shook hands with me and said, "Were you frightened last night?"

"Yes, Mr. Lincoln, I was."

He said, "We are all safe. Don't fear," in that kind fatherly way.

Then he went back.

When he came out, he was gentle and kind as could be. He made me feel at home.

He was plainly dressed, but his manner and dress were alike—kind and good.

K—Was he stooped?

Mrs. M—Oh, him! Don't let them say that! He was a tall, straight man! He was straight! He had a pleasant smile, but not too much of it. It was a gentleman's smile.

He seemed to have something on his mind on account of the fighting, but he seemed anxious to quiet me. He said, "It's all over now. You needn't fear."

I can just close my eyes and see him now—not a handsome man, but a pleasant looking man. His voice was not a loud voice, but mild. He would look down upon you in such a quieting way.

As Mrs. Morrison described him I stood up and imitated President Lincoln's action, as her description had impressed me. Her face lit up with surprise, and she said in a startled way: "That's it! You're him!"

*On April 21, 1865, President Lincoln's body left Washington, D. C., in a nine-car funeral train on a 1,700 mile trip—returning by the same route of his 1861 inauguration journey—to Springfield, Illinois for burial.*

## Lincoln's Funeral in Philadelphia—April 21, 1865
## Letter from Rev. Everard P. Miller of Perth Amboy, N. J.

Dear Mr. Kelly,

I saw President Lincoln alive only once; I was eight years old. He was to raise the flag on Independence Hall, February 22, 1861. My grandfather thought it would be well for me to see President Lincoln, so I could remember—he took me down. It was very early in the morning, seven o'clock. I was some distance away, and there was a dense crowd. I can only remember a long figure in black, waving his arms. I have a faint impression of seeing the flag as it was drawn up.

After his assassination his body was brought to Philadelphia and lay in state in Independence Hall, in the room where the signing took place. My uncle took me to see it. We started at Broad Street, at about 14th Street, at about nine o'clock, and joined the line which walked very slowly. By half past one we had reached 9th Street, and we began to get faint with hunger.

So we went home, had something to eat and rested ourselves.

In the evening, my uncle said, "I think we had better try it again." The authorities had stretched ropes from Independence Hall, extending up a couple of blocks; the people marched between them two abreast, which acted as a sort of sieve, otherwise there was such a crowd of people they would have been unmanageable.

We walked down to 6th Street, where the rope had been broken or something had happened. My uncle pushed his way right into line, and then called out, "Some one is breaking through the line!" Then the police came, but as the people who had broken into the lines made the most noise about it, they were not suspected, and the police did not know who to arrest. Through these questionable means we got into the lines. We entered Independence Hall through a window. A scaffold had been built to enable us to do it.

Mr. Lincoln's body lay at the head of the Hall, with his feet toward Chestnut Street and his head toward the Park. They would not allow you to stop, but kept you moving steadily. I had a good chance to see his face through the glass, though it was quite dusty. The tramping of the crowd raised a good deal of dust, but the soldiers would occasionally rub it off. After passing we went up another scaffolding through the opposite window and down into Independence Square.

## Lincoln's Funeral in New York City—April 24, 1865
## Interview with William M. Morgan

William M. Morgan enlisted in the Seventh Regiment on October 10, 1864, when he was eighteen years old, and served continuously for fifty years in that regiment.

Desiring to get some first-hand information about Lincoln's funeral in New York City, which I unfortunately missed seeing when I was a small child, I spoke to my old schoolmate, Horace E. Fox, who had served many years in the Seventh Regiment, asking if he could suggest any member who had been in the guard of honor. He sent me the following introduction:

21 West 4th St.
N. Y. Jan. 6, 1920

My Dear Kelly:
        The address of my friend Wm. M. Morgan, is 267 W. 79th Street. He served in the Seventh from 1864 to 1915, the only one living who served in that wonderful organization 50 years. If any one can give you the information you desire, he should.
                                            Yours sincerely,
                                            Horace E. Fox

Calling on Mr. Morgan, and presenting my introduction, he told me the following:

M—I was one of the Seventh Regiment who escorted the body of President Lincoln when it was brought to New York on April 24, 1865.

The body arrived at the Desbrosses Street Ferry, up Desbrosses Street to Hudson, through Hudson to Canal, through Canal to Broadway, down Broadway to the [City Hall] park.

I was one of the guard from the time the body arrived, until placed in the Rotunda of the City Hall. I stood guard through the night directing the [estimated half a million] people coming in from Park Row and Broadway—a living stream all night long, till the body was removed, and escorted by the entire 7th Regiment, up Broadway, and through 34th Street, down, to the Hudson River Railroad at 29th Street near 10th Avenue.

I think our watch was two hours on and two hours off. It was exhausting, as it was hot, extremely hot weather. Lines of people extended as far up as Canal Street all night.

Colored people were largely in evidence, and gave way to their feelings on account of their recently having received their freedom from the hands of their martyred President.

I did not get inside the Governor's Room. You know the stairs came up on each side to the small platform at the entrance of the Governor's Room—it was originally intended to have the body in the Governor's Room, but fearing the floor would not stand the weight of the people, the body was placed at the entrance of the room, so that the line of people could ascend by the north stairway, view the body, at the head of the platform, descend by the south stairway, then out.

We were stationed there to direct the people.

K—Did you see the face.

M—Did I see it! I saw it till it upset my nervous system! I stood there for hours at the head and foot, watching the pale face.

His hair was black, and his coat was black. I don't recall whether he was on view full length, but I could see his coat down to his hands.

The marching of the people started up so much dust that his hair and coat became the color of mine (pointing to his gray coat).

The undertaker came several times and begged of us to stop the crowd long enough to dust off the coffin and his coat, which he did with a brush, and wiped off his beard.

I stood guard over him about eight hours, not continually, but two hours on and two hours off; it would vary. Some of the men could not stand it—to march by and look at the face; it became a memory—but to stare one or two hours at it, affected some of the men so, they asked to be excused.

Speaking of the officers at the "Watch," I remember General Tom Sweeny with his one arm, and General Butterfield. There were all sorts of Organizations represented. I did not see the 1812 Veterans; it may have been another Watch.

Our company was Company H, or what was called the "8th Company." Technically, it was the 8th Company, the 8th letter of the alphabet.

We were the company that marched on each side of the body. I marched on the right side of the body, as we were joined by the rest of the regiment. The weather was hot. I had been up all night, except I caught an occasional nap.

When we reached the station, the body was taken in the door. General Scott drove up in his carriage, and passed into the Waiting Room of the station.

# Guarding Lincoln's Body
## Interview with John Neild, Veterans Reserve Corps

One day, my friend Dudley introduced me to Mr. John Neild, who was just starting from his house to a meeting at the Masonic Temple, Brooklyn.

Mr. Neild was tall and spare, with all the characteristics of a fine-bred American. He asked me to accompany him, and described his relations with Lincoln, as follows:

N—I was born in Maine, but we moved to Paterson, New Jersey. I was not quite seventeen when I joined the 13th Regiment, New Jersey Volunteers, Co. K, and left Newark for the front on August 30, 1862, and fought in the Battle of Antietam eighteen days later; we had no training before entering into the fight.

After the battle, our regiment spent considerable time in training. We were stationed near Harper's Ferry. A short time after the battle, I was on picket duty, along the Baltimore [Chesapeake] and Ohio canal. I saw what I thought a crowd of prisoners approaching, but I soon saw that the pickets down the line were presenting arms. A soldier passed me, and said, "Abe Lincoln is paying us a visit."

It appeared that he had reviewed the troops and then came out on the picket line. He then came up to me and I saluted. He stopped and said to me, "How old are you?" I said I turned seventeen on Sept. 29th. "That's pretty young," he said, "What State are you from?" I told him New Jersey. "Don't forget the State you come from," he said, and walked on.

I thought Lincoln was one of the homeliest men I had ever seen, but when he smiled his whole face lit up; it was such a sweet smile. To see Lincoln you would never forget him; you would know him anywhere. He appeared to be a kindly, fatherly sort of a man. I don't believe he could utter a cross word.

I was afterwards one of the guard over the martyred President's body, as it lay in state at Albany; I believe I am the only one left living.

I had been seriously wounded in the right side at the Battle of Chancellorsville, and I was attached to the Invalid Corps, the 18th Veteran Reserves, stationed on recruiting duty at Albany. When President Lincoln's body was brought on, as I was rather tall, I was selected as one of the Guard of Honor when it lay in state at the Capitol.

When the body arrived, it was placed on a large flower-laden truck drawn by eight steel-gray horses. I led the forward horse on the right side, through the streets which were packed by the surging crowd.

A photographer took a print of the guards and hearse. Later a print was sent to me, but I feared it would be injured, so I gave it to a woman and asked her to keep it till later, but to my regret I could never locate it.

The guards stood round the coffin; we were armed with guns. We had great difficulty in keeping people from taking flowers for mementos. Thousands viewed Lincoln's body. There were not many negroes in the crowd as there were but few in Albany, but people came from every direction. We could relieve one another whenever one wished to rest. The guards stood round the coffin when the undertaker closed it. I was on the left side. The officials were there but took no part—Governor Morgan, the Mayor and others.

We did not carry his body. I believe that was attended to by local military. When the lid of the coffin was closed, the face was beginning to get black. It was then sent on its way to Illinois.

*The cross-country funeral of Abraham Lincoln continued westward to the cities of Buffalo, Cleveland, Columbus, Indianapolis, Chicago, and finally home to Springfield where his remains were buried at Oak Ridge Cemetery on May 4, 1865.*

## My Visit to Lincoln's Death Room
Petersen House, Tenth Street, Washington, D. C.

From the many pictures of Lincoln's death room, which I had been familiar with, I figured it out as a large, lofty, bleak room capable of holding a large crowd of people. On July 13, 1920, I arrived at a four story brick house, with steps running across the front to the second floor, from left to right as I faced it, as was the style of many old houses in Washington, the landing was directly over the doorway leading to the basement.

As I ascended, the door was opened by an attendant, who collected thirty cents. He had the bearing of an old soldier, which he proved to be, for as he told me later, he was one of the guards at the execution of Mrs. Mary Surratt. To the right was a hat-rack, and back of it a stairway leading to the floor above. To our left, a door led to the front parlor; a little further down, a door opened on the rear parlor. Passing these, a door led to what struck me as a passageway.

I was brought suddenly to a halt and a slight check by the attendant saying, "It was here President Lincoln died." I felt a slight compression, as from a confined space, and at first could not contract my former conception to the reality before me, and the shabby sordidness with what I had pictured of a vaster bleakness. After going over the pictures, prints, framed and unframed, with which the walls were closely covered, Mr. Osborn H. Oldroyd entered, and the attendant introduced me. After explaining who I was, he greeted me with a very friendly interest.

He was of a fine English type of gentleman, a slight-eagle cast of features, modified by a mildness of expression, and low sympathetic voice, indicating the spirit which prompted him to devote his life as administrator at the shrine of Lincoln. The bronze button of the G. A. R. showed the mettle which sustained him in his ideals, in spite of long neglect of the Government officials. Taking my position at the end of the room facing the door we had entered, I tried to visualize the scene of the tragedy as shown in *Harper's* and *Leslie's* weeklies of that time.

I asked Mr. Oldroyd if we could measure the room. He got a three foot rule, and he gave me the points and I took them down. The room is of peculiar construction. From where I stood, the wall on my right, as I faced the entrance, contained two windows looking out on a courtyard, and was 7 feet 10 inches high. The door we entered was 17 inches from the wall, and 32 inches wide, and 7 feet 3 inches high. The side wall on the left was 8 feet 8 inches high, which caused the ceiling to slant down from the left to right, making the drawing in Harper's to look out of perspective, though it was correct in that respect.

The room is about 10 feet wide and 18 feet long; it had a short passageway leading to a rear room, and a jamb from the corner was taken out of the death room for the stairs to descend to the basement, which could not be seen. The original flooring still remains. The wall still has the original figured paper, with broad perpendicular stripes and a narrow frieze of ornamental figures running around the walls where it joins the ceiling, which is also papered, and is now beginning to sag, which adds to the effect of the room being askew. The original engraving which hung on the side wall, hangs there still. It is 40 inches by 32; the subject is: *The Village Blacksmith*, by [John F.] Herring. The other pictures, Mr. Oldroyd said he has been able to trace; they are the stables and farm yards, by the same artist, and one of: *The Horse Fair*, by Rosa Bonheur.

Mr. Oldroyd told me that at the time of Lincoln's death, the room had been hired by William T. Clark, a soldier of Company D, 13th Massachusetts Infantry, but he was out of town that night. "On the floor above there were also a couple of brothers named [Henry and Julius] Ulke," he added.

I told Mr. Oldroyd that I had once met Mr. Thomas Proctor of Brooklyn who was living in the house the night of the assassination. "Yes," he said, "Proctor had a room upstairs in the front. His roommate was Henry Safford. There is a copy of his letter," pointing to one in the frame, "he called here often and I had an interview with him and he gave me all the names of the boarders here, and he gave me all the details correct."

Mr. Oldroyd said that when one artist started to make the picture of the death scene, he interviewed everyone he could find who was there, and had made the picture without putting in Vice President Johnson. Later he felt satisfied that Johnson was there, so he had a photograph made and pasted it on the original (here Mr. Oldroyd showed me where the photograph had been applied.)

I said, "Now you have talked with the different survivors, and as there has been considerable discussion affirming and denying the presence of Johnson at the death bed, from what you have learned do you feel justified in saying he was there?"

Mr. Oldroyd replied, "From what I have learned I feel justified in saying he was there."

He then pointed to the picture showing Dr. Charles Taft holding Lincoln's head. He said he had written to Dr. Taft who replied that he had gotten some men to carry Lincoln across the street, and he supported Lincoln's head in his hands. And yet Oldroyd told me that he had people claim that Lincoln's head hung down.

Mr. Oldroyd said, "I wrote to Dr. Charles Leale and asked him to write out a statement to preserve. He wrote back that there had been so much written about it, that he did not care to write, though he may do it some time. But I never heard from him."

We went through the other three rooms and examined the relics of Lincoln, and the various manifestations of Oldroyd's energy and patriotism in making his collection.

I found Mr. Oldroyd a charming, sociable man, and he told me he would gladly write a reply to any inquiry I sent him. He also suggested that I might try to locate Thomas Proctor for further details.

# My Search for Thomas Proctor

Some twenty-five years earlier, in 1896, my friend Timothy Daley, 286 Adelphi Street, Brooklyn introduced me to an associate of his named Thomas Proctor who had a law practice in the Garfield Building, 26 Court Street, Brooklyn. Mr. Daley told me that Proctor had an interesting story connected with Lincoln which very few people knew of, for Proctor did not spread the story widely.

After shaking hands, Proctor told me that he worked in the War Department as a clerk and roomed in the Petersen house and was an eyewitness to the death of President Lincoln. He provided proof by showing me an old woodcut that appeared in *Frank Leslie's Illustrated Weekly* depicting himself standing alongside the deathbed.

I urged Proctor to record his memories for history, and it was some time after this, an article was published in the *New York Times*, February 12, 1899:

### STORY OF LINCOLN'S DEATH
#### The Last Scenes Vividly Described by Thomas Proctor
#### Brooklyn Lawyer Lived at the Time in the House
#### Where the President Breathed His Last

"I recall that night and everything that happened with perfect distinctness. I was a young man living in Washington and connected with the War Department, and when I found that a great tragedy had been brought right to my door I knew that I was in the centre of a big historical event. If I should get out my notebook of that time I could tell you everything that occurred in detail, and almost to the minute.

"I was attending a meeting of an organization known as the 'Mosaic' that evening. It was literary in its nature, and was started by a number of Southern women, most of whom had members of their families in the Southern army. Such men as belonged to the families who were in Washington attended, and there were a few outsiders who were invited. I was one of the two or three Northern men.

"The meeting of the Mosaic that Good Friday night in 1865 was at the house of Philip Y. Fendall in Judiciary Square. At the close of the evening usually a Virginia reel was danced. There was always some discussion about this. The women with interests in the South were not in a mood for festivities in those days; they did not give entertainments, they dressed chiefly in black, and they did not like even the mild festivity of a Virginia reel. But the dancers usually carried the day, as they had that evening.

"I was talking with Miss Mary Fendall, the eldest daughter of the house. Her father was an invalid, and she devoted herself to him, and that was the first time I had met her. It was reported among her friends that

Thackeray had said to her, when he was in this country, that she was the wittiest woman he had met in America; so I was delighted to have the opportunity of talking to her. We were standing near the door of the parlor leading into the front hall when her brother, Reginald Fendall, entered the house, and said to me, as the first person he met, in a low, excited tone: 'The President is shot."

"'How much shot?' I asked. I remembered the quick, awkward expression I used.

"'Killed probably,' he answered.

"He did not intend to be overheard, but those near caught his words, there was much excitement, and the company broke up immediately, and I started for home. The streets were filled with people, some talking in loud tones and others whispering together.

"When I came to my street at the corner of the block below the house where I lived I found a cordon of soldiers, and it was with some difficulty that I obtained permission to pass. When I came to the house, which was just opposite Ford's Theatre, I found the stoop in possession of an officer and a guard of soldiers, who refused to allow me to pass. I was endeavoring to make them understand that I lived there when Henry S. Safford, who occupied a suite of rooms told me to be quiet, as the President was inside. That was the first I knew of it. That also established my identity, and I was allowed to enter.

"The President was on the bed in a small room on the first floor at the end of the hall. I went down through the basement and through a back door into the yard and up a pair of rear stairs and through a small room in the back of the house over the extension, and entered by the rear door the room in which the President was lying.

"It was a small bed, too short for so tall a man, and he was lying crosswise, with his head at the front toward the door. He was lying on his right side, with the wound in his head in full view, and the surgeon was probing it with his finger when I entered. The room was almost, if not entirely, filled with prominent men of the Nation. Charles Sumner stood at the head of the bed with Robert Lincoln leaning on his shoulder weeping. Mr. Welles, the Secretary of the Navy, sat in a rocking chair, and when I came in he was asleep. He was an old man, there had been a great deal of excitement, and I suppose he was worn out. There were Safford, the Ulke brothers, and other inmates of the house standing in the doorway.

"Mr. Stanton, who came into the room at intervals during the night, was busy in the back parlor receiving dispatches and dictating answers to a stenographer. That stenographer was the man since so well known [to the American public] as Corporal Tanner. He then lived next door, and Safford, who knew every one, had recommended him as a stenographer.

"Mrs. Lincoln, laboring under great stress of emotion, was brought in two or three times after I came in by two ladies who were with her. She remained only a short time, calling to her husband to speak to her, and then was taken away up stairs again.  The ladies spent the night in the suite of rooms belonging to Safford and myself.

"There was a large front parlor or library with sleeping rooms at the rear.  I have heard a great many different versions of the story, but it was due to Safford that the President was brought into the house.  He was sitting at the window of the parlor when he saw the excitement outside.  They were taking the President to the nearest place that seemed open, a lager beer saloon next door, when he called to them to bring him into the house.

"With the exception of a short time when I went into a rear room and lay down for a half an hour, I was in the room with the President all night.  I was there when the breathing which had been so labored that it could be heard through the house gradually modulated, and in the morning when the physician, who had his finger on the pulse, said, 'The pulse has ceased to beat.'

"An interesting but untrue story about the gold pieces that were placed on the President's eyes and afterwards stolen has been written by a prominent man.  I know the story of those 'gold pieces.'  After the President had ceased to breathe the doctor put his hand in his pocket and brought out four new, shiny two-cent pieces.  Two of these he put on each of the eyes to close them.  Every one had left the room then except two attendants, and after a time the coins were removed and placed carelessly on a table near the hair which had been cut from the President's head around the wound.

"After the body had been taken away I took the four coins, which were blood stained from the fingers of the physician; the hair, which gathered together made a good-sized lock, and one of the blood-stained pillow slips from the bed.  One of the coins I gave to Safford, another to William T. Clark, another occupant of the house, in whose room and on whose bed the President died.  He had chanced to be absent that night.  The other two coins, the most stained, I kept myself.

"That disposes of the question of the stolen gold pieces.  The story was non-sensical on its face, for every one who knew the times knows that the doctor would not be likely to carry gold pieces around in his pockets; that they were only to be seen as curiosities in a brokers' window.  My two coins were eventually lost, I don't know how.  The stains wore off, and they may have been spent or I may have thrown them at something.  I did use coins that way frequently.  We didn't think much of fractional copper currency in those days.  You could almost pick it up on the streets.

"It was a prominent official in Washington who, writing of Lincoln's death, said, 'He died in the house of a sordid rebel, who stole the gold pieces from his eyes.'  I must have been that sordid rebel who took the two-cent pieces.

"The politics of poor old Mr. Petersen, who owned the house, consisted in an intense admiration for Andrew Johnson.  Petersen was a merchant tailor, and Johnson used to drop into his place to see the men work and tell about his own experiences as a tailor. Because he had been a tailor and had risen to a high position, Petersen considered him a great man. That was about all the politics he had.

"There have been various stories told also to the effect that the room in which Mr. Lincoln died had been occupied by his slayer, John Wilkes Booth, for some time prior to the act. The room had been occupied by Mr. Clark for many months. I know him well, and he was a friend of Mr. Safford's. Before that the room had been occupied by an actor named [John] Matthews, and it is possible that Booth might have visited him, though I think I should have heard of it if it had been so.

"The pillow slip, which was very much stained, I have now a great portion of it. The lock of hair I thought I had until at one time I visited Peoria, Ill., where I met a bright woman. Mrs. Brotherson, the wife of an ex-Mayor of the city and a poet who wrote the poems for the city celebrations. Peoria was the seat of the great Lincoln and Douglas debates, and she was an ardent admirer of Lincoln. I promised to send her the hair. But when I went to get it I found that all but a few hairs had been destroyed by insects, and nothing but the blue ribbon with which I had tied it was left.

"There was only one reliable picture of the scene of Lincoln's death made. That was made by Mr. [Alfred] Berghaus of New York for an illustrated weekly of this city. He went to the room and made a very accurate sketch of it, even to Clark's pictures on the wall, and we gave him a careful description of everything that took place and the people present. I know that was the only picture, for though Safford and Clark left the house and city not very long after, I remained for more than a year, and no one else came to see the room or to ask particulars. We gave Berghaus a certificate as to the correctness of his picture."

By 1920, Mr. Oldroyd thought that there were only three surviving eyewitnesses to the death of President Lincoln: Robert Lincoln, Dr. Charles Leale, and James Tanner; with a possibility of a fourth, if Thomas Proctor was still among the living. In order to gather further facts, I made an effort to find Thomas Proctor. At first my search was unsuccessful; letters written to his Brooklyn address received no response and our mutual friend, Mr. Daley was unable to locate him. None of his old associates knew his whereabouts; the thought being that Proctor had probably died.

My search went over two or three years and quite by accident I heard that he had a relative in New York. I called and was received rather passively; he told me that Proctor suffered financial and mental hardships and he had since lost track of him. After cross-questioning, I was told it was possible that he was in some public charitable institution, which he was placed many years earlier in 1910. I believe I searched every one in Brooklyn, but with no success. Later, I learned that he might be in the asylum on Blackwell Island, and I started on that trail.

I asked Mr. Daley if he would want to go over with me, as he had known him. We started over on September 25, 1921. After some considerable trouble I was told I might find him in one of the detainee buildings. After going through two or three buildings filled with the destitute, the insane, and a mix of criminals, we caught sight of a man in a group resembling Proctor, dressed in paupers' garb. At the sight of us he lit up. He rushed over to meet us, giving my friend his right hand and me his left. He beamed on us delighted, and said, "This is a joyful surprise. I am glad to see you."

Taking chairs we talked on various subjects—then Lincoln—and finally the assassination. He was a little vague at first, saying musingly, "It is a long time since then, and I have not thought much of it lately." Then Proctor said feelingly, "I knew him well. I used to have nice times with him (smiling reflectively)—he used to tell me jokes and make puns. Oh, he was nice! I was a clerk in the Property Revenue Department."

And suddenly he began to recall his past experiences the night of the assassination:

P—I stopped in a hall room. I think it was a middle one. It was small. I had never witnessed anybody die, and I was particular to notice everything. As soon as he died, I left. The Doctor sat beside him and held his pulse. Then the Doctor said, "He has ceased to breathe. His pulse has ceased."

The wound at the back of President Lincoln's head was not large, and they cut off his hair around the wound to get at it. I picked up all the hair I could. I gave some to the Doctor, and afterwards gave mine away to a friend who collected those things.

At this my companion broke in and said, "I saw the other day in the paper that a lot was sold for $600.00." "Think of it now," Proctor said with a smile, "I also had the two copper cents they put on his eyes."

Proctor quickly grew fatigued. At first, I did not realize his mental torture. The excitement of seeing old friends was joyful, but must have been exhausting to him. It was pitiful to see the once brilliant man struggling with the memories of the past. At the beginning of a sentence, his memory seemed to be clear and detailed, and then suddenly he would fade into a mysterious fog. We bid him good bye and promised to return after he had rested.

Returning to my studio thinking how I could help Proctor, I intended to call on his relatives, explain the condition in which I had found him, so that they could have the opportunity of helping him.

About one o'clock that night I was awakened by a telephone call from the Editor of the *New York Times*, saying a man (Daley) had presented an article on Proctor, and asked me if I would vouch for it. I said I did not know what he had written, but from what I knew of him, what he would say was apt to be truthful.

They rang off, and the following morning on the first page of the *New York Times* was a big display announcing that "Proctor, in whose room Lincoln died was an inmate of Blackwell's Island." This was only a slight error with the facts, as Proctor's bedroom was on the floor above where Lincoln died.

This article brought Proctor's case to the surface, and for quite a time furnished material for writers and photographers and collectors of "Lincolnia." And although it might have proved profitable to the original enterprising news gatherer, it prevented me from inducing the family to help Proctor out of his immediate trouble.

### Man in Whose Bed Lincoln Died is Now in Almshouse Here
*New York Times*, October 1, 1921

The present plight of Thomas Proctor and the historical incident in which he apparently played a part was made public yesterday by his friend of many years, Mr. Timothy Daly, who visited the former lawyer on Sunday in company with Mr. James E. Kelly the sculptor.

"Mr. Kelly asked me where to find him," said Mr. Daly. "I had heard that he had gone down hill and was in the almshouse. We had a long search of it, but we finally found him on the island. Mr. Kelly was interested as a sculptor in the scene at Lincoln's deathbed. He had studied the pictures purporting to be the deathbed scene and wanted Mr. Proctor's recollection of who were present and how they were arranged around the bed."

"Recently I became interested in the subject of Lincoln, and sought especially to get information about the scene when he breathed his last," said Mr. Kelly. "On that account I visited O. H. Oldroyd, who now has the house where Lincoln died. He said that Proctor had visited the house some years ago and had told him of his connection with the death of Lincoln. I understood from Mr. Oldroyd that Proctor's story had been established to be true. In addition, I have seen the woodcut, I think in Leslie's, showing Proctor and giving his name."

"Mr. Kelly knew Proctor years ago, when he was a prosperous and able lawyer. "He did not tell me the story until I knew him well," said Mr. Daly, "he was very reticent about it and few persons knew of it."

*Dr. Charles A. Leale was in the audience that night at Ford's Theatre and was the first surgeon to reach the dying President and remained by his side until the end. Dr. Leale had seen the front page story in the* New York Times *and wanted to meet Proctor and verify his story. The doctor's visit to Blackwell's Island the following day was also reported by the newspaper.*

## Two Who Saw Lincoln Die Talk Over Scene
*New York Times*, October 3, 1921

A curious interview took place on Blackwell's Island yesterday afternoon between two men who were last in each other's presence on the morning of April 15, 1865, when they were together in the room in Petersen's house in Tenth Street, Washington, where Abraham Lincoln died, after having been shot the night before by Booth in Ford's Theatre.

One of the two men was Dr. Charles A. Leale of 500 Madison Avenue, a distinguished physician, who fifty-six years ago was the young army doctor who first ministered to Lincoln in the box in Ford's Theatre, and later caused him to be moved across the street to Petersen's, where he remained in charge of the dying man until the arrival of Surgeon General Joseph K. Barnes.

The other was Thomas Proctor, a pauper in the City Home. It was in Proctor's bed that Lincoln died, according to some of his friends and the evidence of the woodcut in *Leslie's Illustrated Newspaper* of April 29, 1865, which pictures Proctor at Lincoln's bedside and names him. With the exception of Robert T. Lincoln, these two are probably the only men living who saw Lincoln die.

Dr. Leale, though nearly 80 years old, is a man of great vigor and mental energy, still practicing his profession. Proctor, formerly a fairly well-known lawyer, is still in fair bodily health, but his mind has weakened. At first Proctor's memory seemed nearly blank on everything. For a while he responded mechanically. Then, apparently falling under the magnetic influence of Dr. Leale, Proctor replied more brightly and had more success in searching obscure corners of his memory for the events connected with the death of Lincoln. After some preliminary questions, Dr. Leale asked:

"Were you in Washington when President Lincoln was killed?"

"Indeed, I was at his deathbed," said Proctor quickly. "He died on my bed."

The old man could not remember where the house was. He said he thought it was an institution. He seemed to take hold firmly when the name of Petersen was mentioned and was quite sure that he remembered the Petersens.

"Where did you live in Washington?"

"Right there. Right there in the—" he paused in search of a word and completed the sentence by saying "right there in the ward." He has lived in a ward for six years and the ward evidently had dispossessed his mind of all other ideas of habitations.

"Was that near Ford's Theatre?"

"Of course. Ford's Theatre was right there."

Coming down to the scene in which the two men had participated, Dr. Leale asked:

"Did you see President Lincoln?

"Of course.  He died on my bed.  He was carried in there by those who carried him and put him diagonally across the bed because he was a tall man."

This was true, to the knowledge of Dr. Leale, who had himself tried to break out the panel at the foot of the bed to make room for Lincoln's six feet four inches.

"Did you stay there all the time?"

"Yes, pretty nearly," said Proctor.  The aged pauper became lost again, when he was asked on which floor the room was.  He thought a while, frowning and distorting his face, which reflected sympathetically the torture he inflicted upon himself in goading his fading memory.  He said he thought it was not the attic, and then added that he was positive it was not the attic.  He would not commit himself further.  The imprint of a long career of a conservative lawyer was plain, as the old man guarded and limited his statements, withdrew statements which appeared over-strong and refused to have himself on record unless he had the strongest possible support from his memory.

Proctor thought that Lincoln was shot in the right temple, but Dr. Leale told him it was on the left side of the head, and indicated the place on Proctor's skull.

In answers to questions, Proctor was saying that he continued to live in the room for some time, when a nurse came up to the benches where the conversation was going on, and said:

"Oh, there you are, daddy.  They told me some men had taken you away."  Then the nurse said it was all right, but that she was a little worried, because Proctor was in the habit of getting lost.

The old man remembered distinctly that he had been a friend of John Burroughs, as he had been told by Timothy Daly and James E. Kelly, the sculptor, who were friends of Proctor many yeas ago when he was doing well as a legal practitioner and devoting all his spare time to natural history.

"But you were a student of entomology?" Dr. Leale asked.

"Oh, yes, indeed, and of ornithology and botany, and of mammalogy, too."

Proctor could not remember whether he had a roommate.  At the mention of Clark he thought he did have a roommate of that name for a short time.  He was trying to recall where Stanton, Welles and others were sitting, when three women visitors approached the bench, and one of them crammed into Proctor's hands a tin of small cigars, a box of tobacco and two handkerchiefs.

"The cigars are for you to smoke between the acts when you go to the movies," she said.  "The white handkerchief is for Sunday and the blue one with the polka dots for every day."

Proctor said that while he was employed in the War Department he had seen and talked to Lincoln, but that he could not remember anything Lincoln had said to him.

"When we were crossing the street, carrying Mr. Lincoln from the theatre, a man ran out from Petersen's and told us to carry him in there. We had found two other houses dark and closed, so we carried him where the man told us. Were you that man?" Dr. Leale resumed.

Proctor could not remember. His story, as he told it years ago, was that he met the bearers of the wounded man on the first floor up, when they were undecided which room to enter, and directed them to enter his room.

"If you had your choice," asked Dr. Leale; "if some man came and said, 'I'll give you anything you ask for,' would you ask to leave this place?"

"By Jove," he replied, "I don't know what I would ask for. I would be afraid of making a big mistake."

"You mean you might be making a mistake in leaving this place?"

"Yes."

"Are you satisfied with your place here?"

"Yes, I'm satisfied with it as long as it lasts."

Proctor said he had "an intuition" that he had seen Petersen, candle in hand, ushering the party from the street into the house, and that Mrs. Lincoln had arrived later.

"But confound it all," he added, "the particulars of the thing, they whirl away from me."

## My Last Interview with Thomas Proctor
October 16, 1921

For a while Mr. Proctor seemed to enjoy the attention from reporters and admiring visitors who presented him with small gifts—or just wanting to shake the hand of an eye-witness to the death of Lincoln—but these experiences exhausted him.

I had promised to visit him again, but waited some weeks until the initial clamor died down. Although at first animated in conversation, Proctor quickly grew fatigued:

K—Did you know Stanton?

P—Yes.

K—Did you admire him?

P—Well, I took him. My best friend was not Stanton, but in spite of that he was good to me.

K—Did you ever see him and Lincoln together? How did they get along?

P—(laughs)

K—Your laugh explains how they got along.

P—How in the world could you pick out a thing like that and not be in it? (meaning Stanton-Lincoln) I knew Stanton and I viewed it. He had his good qualities too. Mr. Stanton and I got along very well together. Ordinarily he was fiery. But he wasn't fiery with me. I had a temper and he kept away from me.

K—Keep off a hot stove. (All laugh). Were you in the street outside of Ford's Theater?

P—It seems to me I helped carry him in.

K—Then you were in the street.

P—Yes.

K—They say you were in the street and they wanted to take him in the next house.

P—They were taking him to a saloon—that liquor store.

K—The crowd was rattled.

P—I wasn't rattled. They wanted to take him into the liquor store. I tried to be practical and do something. I tried to do all I could think of. The idea of taking the President of the United States to a saloon...

K—General O'Beirne?

P—He was provost general.

K—You remember Johnson?—that night? Some people said Johnson wasn't there.

P—I couldn't tell.

K—He came in there for a while? Just think—of that.

P—I hardly can, but it is too difficult.

K—Think it over.  They say he was due there.


General conversation followed.  I showed Mr. Proctor the *Sunday Times*, October 2, [1921] there was published a picture of Lincoln's death showing among those about the bed, Mr. Proctor.

K—The picture shows the doctor with his fingers on the pulse.


Mr. Proctor enacts pose: places his left fingers on the pulse of his right hand.

P—I was there all the time; the breathing of him—(signifying a rattling sound in throat).

K—They put a penny on the eyes.

P—Yes.  I put the pennies on his eyes.  They gave them to me and I put them on.

K—And you had some of his hair.

P—I got quite a portion of it.  It was distributed, but I did keep some of it. I gave some to my mother.

K—Did you have the pillow case?  It was stained with blood.

P—It was brought to me.

K—He did not bleed much at first?

P—I don't remember, much if any.  His head was turned so that it was exposed (sideways).
That curious noise lasted until he was dead.  It was a snoring noise between a snore and a death rattle.  He did not move.
I stayed up all the night.
I wanted to see the first and the last of Abraham Lincoln.  Like he was then.
Lincoln was a good man.  My father was a sailor.

K—Your family is from England?

P—Yes.

K—Was it from Fountains Abbey?

P—I wonder.

K—What was the name of that friend of yours—that friend of Booth?

Proctor shook his head—he could not recall.

K—In *Leslie's*—not a bad picture of you standing there, by his bedside.

P—Mr. Lincoln was a good honest man. He was a friend of mine. The place where he was shot the hair was cut away. I was pretty fond of him. I was a friend of his.

K—Can you describe him?

P—Of course, he looked like he could—when you got him in conversation, he could hold his own. He wasn't an ignoramus. He was tall and erect. Lincoln was a friend and companion—as father and son.

K—I am going to make a study of him. I want to make him erect like that.

P—Good! Make him erect. Mr. Lincoln was a good man. He was not ordinary. He had big hands.

K—I think they exaggerate him a bit.

P—As I think they did. I didn't get any thing of that kind but of course we weren't together a great deal. Many men make a splurge and peter out.

K—It must have been a horrible sensation when you heard he was shot.

P—I was so rattled with the idea of Lincoln being shot, I was furious. If I could have done it, I would have captured every one who did it myself.
The bullet went in through the back of the head and out over the eye.

K—Then you laid him in the house.

P—Why of course I did.

K—Did you live in the house?

P—I was alone as far as my job was concerned.

Break in questioning to permit Mr. Proctor a rest. I was afraid that his struggle with memory might exhaust him, so we shook hands and I promised to return and visit soon.

In the days following my meeting with Proctor, newspapers throughout the country repeated the *Times* story of Proctor's pitiful circumstance, and as a result I received many letters from concerned people, principally veterans, offering assistance to Mr. Proctor:

Dear Mr. Kelly,
    I have seen in Boston papers the story of Thomas Proctor in whose bed President Lincoln is said to have died. Your name and address is given in connection with the article.
    If the story is true and Mr. Proctor is in want, I would like to take steps to relieve his wants if possible.
    I am prompted to this as a Veteran of the Civil War and my almost reverence for the Memory of our great Martyred President.
Very Sincerely,<br>Ira Mowery

*Kelly's efforts to help Thomas Proctor were finally realized a few weeks later when the old man was taken from the almshouse on Blackwell's Island to a religious retreat in Pennsylvania where it was reported, "he had every comfort and consideration."*

Thomas Proctor Gone.
*New York Times*, November 25, 1921

Thomas Proctor, who gave his bed to President Lincoln the night he was shot by Wilkes Booth, ate Thanksgiving dinner this year in St. Andrew's Brotherhood Home at Gibsonia, Penn., after having passed the last six [eleven] years as a ward in the City Home on Blackwell's Island, New York. Arrangements for the transfer of Mr. Proctor, who is over 80 years old, were made by Chaplain Sidney N. Usher, representing the Episcopal City Mission Society.
    In his new home the aged attorney will be permitted to enjoy many comforts of which he has been deprived for the last twenty years.

# Chapter Five
# The Final Years
# 1922-1933

"Kelly was a man of charm and dignified personality, with a retiring nature except among his intimate friends, among who were many distinguished Americans, but was militant, even combative, when his views of the principles of art and sculpture were challenged. He was the personification of nervous energy and in his prime worked long hours under pressure and strain."—Robert Bruce

*Shortly after his last meeting with the destitute Thomas Proctor, Kelly was faced with a similar circumstance. The sixty-five year old sculptor's health and finances had never been robust, and by late 1920 both began to fail him. Despite nearly fifty years of steady work, Kelly had saved very little money and was forced to give up his beloved 57th Street studio in early 1922.*

*It was during this time that Kelly married a long-time lady friend, Miss Helen McKay—a fifty-year-old spinster and a daughter of a Civil War veteran—whom he had known since she was a young girl. Not much is known about their romance, as Kelly left little written evidence about their lives together. In a short note written in 1910, James refers to Helen as his "betrothed," and in another letter written after they married on February 27, 1922, he refers to her as, "an uncanonized saint," and gratefully remarked, "she helps me save."*

*Friends and admirers did what they could to help the "K's," as they were now known, and Kelly's most loyal friend, Gen. James H. Wilson, rode to his rescue with a $30,000 commission to create an equestrian statue of Delaware Patriot Caesar Rodney, to be placed in Wilmington. Although Kelly's unbounded enthusiasm for his proposed Lincoln statue remained strong, it would have to wait until after the completion of Caesar Rodney.*

## Caesar Rodney

Gen. James Wilson called one day and told me that a delegation of Irishmen called and asked if he would be President of the Association formed to erect a statue of a most gallant officer, Gen. Thomas A. Smyth. He was a Delaware man, and had been Major, Lieutenant-Colonel and Colonel of the 1st

Delaware Infantry before attaining the rank of Brigadier General in 1864. Smyth was very popular, and the last general officer killed in the Civil War, having been mortally wounded at the battle of Farmville, Va., on April 7, 1865, and died two days later, on the exact date of Lee's surrender.

"Yes, I shall be glad to do so," replied the General, "if you will give the work to my friend Kelly." "No, General," they said, "We want to give it to Mr. Dunbar of Washington." "All right," answered Gen. Wilson, "I'll have nothing to do with it," and they departed.

"Now, Kelly," he said to me, "I have been thinking there ought to be a statue erected in honor of Caesar Rodney—a gentleman as then understood, and a member of the Continental Congress, as one of the three delegates from Delaware. While in Dover recruiting [on July 3, 1776], the bill for Independence was proposed and a vote called.

"Several members, though approving, still hesitated, thinking it untimely. Thomas McKean was much in favor of it; George Read, the other delegate on the ground, was against it as untimely, and [the Declaration] was proposed for a final reading on July 4th. McKean sent a messenger calling on Rodney to be in Philadelphia the next day, and the messenger started, leaving a relay of horses every ten miles. Rodney received him at Dover, mounted a horse and with one attendant, started out on his epoch-making ride of eighty miles.

"The roads at that time were so bad that he had to take to the fields, and then a violent thunderstorm came up, but on and on he rode through the night and into the morning—on through Wilmington, until at last, his blown horse almost dropping, was brought to a halt in front of Congress Hall in Philadelphia. Then dismounting, he was greeted by McKean, who had been anxiously watching for him, just as the bell in the tower tolled 10 o'clock. Booted and spurred, with hat and whip in hand, Rodney slipped into the hall; raising his hand, he declared:

> "'As I believe the voice of my constituents and of all sensible and honest men is in favor of Independence, my own judgment concurs with them. I vote for Independence.'"

Gen. Wilson succeeded in collecting $30,000, and I started putting the job through. One day, while I was visiting the General in Wilmington, we looked over several proposed sites for the statue. The General pointed to the old Court House opposite the du Pont Hotel, saying, "That would make a good site, Kelly!" "Yes," I replied, "if it wasn't already taken." "Pull it down, pull it down!" said Gen. Wilson, with the same spirit with which he led the charge at Selma. I laughed and we walked on. Later I heard that with the help of a judge, the building was removed, and my statue of Caesar Rodney stands on the spot. It was unveiled by a young Rodney girl, in the fourth generation from Caesar Rodney, in the presence of 15,000 people. Gen. Wilson made a stirring address, and sat on my right during the ceremonies.

*In his memoirs, Kelly wrote sparingly about the extreme hardships he faced in creating the Rodney statue; in fact, the job nearly killed him.*

*Some evidence of his disputes with members of the National Sculpture Society—who criticized his Buford and Defenders Monuments—can be found in Kelly's private letters, which were never intended to be published. Gen. Wilson teasingly wrote to Kelly saying certain members of the Society were privately discrediting his artwork. This fired up Kelly's combative nature, and although he never spelled out the name of his chief critic in his letter, it is most likely that the "Franco-American artists," Kelly refers to is Daniel Chester French.*

*Kelly responded to Gen. Wilson:*

> You say that people in the art world have given evasive answers about me. I am not surprised, and am surprised that they did not go further and attack me. I do not expect to succeed by the endorsements of men who know that my work has a grip that they in their conventionality cannot equal. It is only through men who have the courage of their convictions, such as you showed at Gettysburg [in 1895], and Mr. Blake at New Haven [in 1909], that I have any hope of success. How would Poe have stood if he depended on the verdict of the "Yankee Poets?" As you are on guard, I do not trouble myself as to the attacks of the Franco-American artists. "Damn the French!"

*More than any of his previous works, the Caesar Rodney statue took a great physical and mental toll on James Kelly. Always somewhat careless in regards to his personal finances, Kelly habitually trusted the so-called honorable gentlemen (who usually made up monument committees) with the business side of art. This enabled Kelly to concentrate fully on his sculpting, but this neglect of business eventually cost him dearly.*

*The death of Gen. James H. Wilson, on February 25, 1925, left Kelly without an ally to look after his financial interests, and he was sorely taken advantage of by the Rodney Monument Committee, who did their best to short-change the sculptor.*

*Kelly was due to be paid $27,000 upon completion of the statue, but payment was withheld for over a year, and as a result of questionable deductions ($8,000 for the cost of the pedestal—Kelly estimated a $3,000 pedestal—and $12,400 in foundry overcharges), the artist received only an additional $3,600 for several years of intense labor. His lawyer also tried, unsuccessfully, to collect the $11,000 in interest while the money was in escrow.*

*After Kelly was deceived by the monument committee, he was forced to borrow money from friends to survive, and the fight seemed to go out of the normally combative artist. In October 1926, with rent coming due and in desperation, Kelly wrote to his close friend, Dr. George H. Ryder for assistance:*

Dear Doctor,

I am in TERROR of three wolves, which are lined up with their teeth filed sharp—one is called Landlord, the other Butcher, and the other Grocer.

I find I have been the victim of misplaced confidence. I thought I was in the hands of gentlemen and friends. Any business man would know that the proportion of 8,000 for the pedestal is ridiculous.

I think General Wilson felt it as he kept repeating, "I hope the next job will bring you some money." But his health was failing and he could not put up a fight for me.

They did not even put my name in the program.

But I don't whimper, but will forget them in another job(s).

I will show them up in the future—gibbet them.

I have had a very hard time physically and mentally, since I saw you. I am quite done up from pain and loss of sleep. But I am improving. I pass the time by dictating the book.

I am still disabled, getting very little rest, day or night, but feeling a little better every day. I think my condition was caused by excessive worry—I could hardly sleep for two or three weeks.

Who could foresee that I should have been the victim of such persons?


*The Caesar Rodney statue was Kelly's last major work. He never fully regained his health or was able to recover financially, and perhaps the final insult was that in 1999, the U. S. Mint used Kelly's design (without credit) of the Caesar Rodney statue for the reverse of the Delaware State Quarter.*

*Kelly had only one hope to repair his failing finances. He concentrated on the publication of his memoirs—a rambling manuscript he had begun writing in the 1890s after the deaths of his mother and father. With the help of his wife Helen, a former school teacher, the couple transcribed thousands of pages of unedited handwritten memories until Helen fell ill with pneumonia the day after Christmas 1928, and died a week later on January 2, 1929.*

*The Great Depression doomed Kelly's vision of Lincoln in bronze, as well as any hope of publishing his memoirs or his Lincoln research. In those harsh economic times, few public sculpture projects were being commissioned and Kelly could find neither work nor a publisher interested in his past; as a result, he became nearly destitute. Dr. Ryder supported him in those final months, and in one of the last passages recorded in his memoirs, Kelly wrote: "Dr. Ryder is my invisible pillar and my main support—to him, I dedicate these memoirs." Kelly also bequeathed to Dr. Ryder his life's work—his bronzes, paintings, books, and a rare collection of Revolutionary and Civil War uniforms and accoutrements.*

*James Edward Kelly died of chronic urinary-prostate infection at Columbia University-Presbyterian Hospital in New York City on May 25, 1933. He was 77 years old. After a Mass at the Church of Our Lady of Lourdes, his body was brought to St. Raymond's Cemetery in the Bronx and buried in section 3, range 7, plot 33, grave 3. Whereas some artists achieve recognition and fame after death, Kelly quickly fell into obscurity. He had spent his entire life perpetuating the deeds of American heroes, but his bronze tributes to Washington, Lincoln, and Roosevelt were eventually dwarfed by carved mountains and towering national memorials. His grave went unmarked for 73 years, until on October 1, 2006, when a granite marker was dedicated by a few newfound admirers of James Edward Kelly—A Sculptor of American History.*

## Chief of Chiefs

As Lincoln plowed and swung his flashing axe
Could mind conceive that he was consecrate;
That he would bow beneath a Nation's woe,
That in his hand would rest a race's fate?


Alone he carved his pathway to the peak,
Inspired he stood against the Union sky,
And at his call the Volunteers respond,
He gave the word—they marshaled forth to die.


As Chief of Chiefs he foiled the Union's foe,
With potent pen he set the bondman free,
He raised his hand and ordered, "Peace, be still"—
Out rang a shot, that crowned his destiny.


His dying sigh blew out the flame of hate,
His life blood made deathless laurels bloom,
The North and South, as at a sacred shrine,
Both decked with bays their Father Abraham's tomb.


As Chief of Chiefs, he like a sunbeam soared,
His chosen chiefs all blazing left and right,
He brought the day at Freedom's darkest hour,
And she will march in triumph by his light.

James E. Kelly

# Index

**PICTURE CREDITS**: